Many Happy Returns on
this Happiest Birthday
in Years.

Love,
Edwin

May 25, 1926

THE INTIMATE PAPERS OF
COLONEL HOUSE

❋

Behind the Political Curtain
1912–1915

'*House longed to get good accomplished and was content that others should have the credit.*'

VISCOUNT GREY OF FALLODON

The President and Colonel House
New York 1915

THE INTIMATE PAPERS OF COLONEL HOUSE

Arranged as a Narrative

BY

CHARLES SEYMOUR

Sterling Professor of History, Yale University

BOSTON AND NEW YORK
HOUGHTON MIFFLIN COMPANY
The Riverside Press Cambridge
1926

The Riverside Press

CAMBRIDGE · MASSACHUSETTS

PRINTED IN THE U.S.A.

TO

SIDNEY EDWARD MEZES

PREFATORY NOTE

By COLONEL HOUSE

This book written around my papers is in no sense a conventional *apologia* such as, despite my best intentions, I should probably have written had I attempted to describe the stirring and controversial events in which it was my fortune to play a part. The reader must bear in mind that it treats only of such matters as came within the orbit of my own activities. The President and his Cabinet dealt with many questions which could not enter into this narrative. My chief desire has been to let the papers tell their own story, and for this reason I have preferred to leave their arrangement in the hands of an historian.

Dr. Seymour in arranging these papers has felt it his duty to assume a highly critical attitude toward some of the chief actors. Especially he has attempted to present the great central figure of the period, Woodrow Wilson, in a purely objective light. As for myself, I frankly admit that I was and am a partisan of Woodrow Wilson and of the measures he so ably and eloquently advocated. That we differed now and then as to the methods by which these measures might be realized, this book reveals as one follows the thread of the story, and never more sharply than in the question of military and naval preparedness.

The President, I believed, represented the opinion prevailing in the country at large, apart from the Atlantic seaboard; and I was not certain, had he advocated the training of a large army, Congress would have sustained him. But I was sure, given a large and efficient army and navy, the United States would have become the arbiter of peace and probably without the loss of a single life. When the President became convinced that it was necessary to have a large navy, Congress readily yielded to his wishes. But, even so, it is not certain that had he asked for such an army as I advocated he would have been successful. The two arms do not hang together on even terms, for the building of a great army touches every nerve centre of the nation, social and economic, and raises questions and antagonisms which could never come to the fore over a large navy programme.

In my opinion, it ill serves so great a man as Woodrow Wilson for his friends, in mistaken zeal, to claim for him impeccability. He had his shortcomings, even as other men, and having them but gives him the more character and virility. As I saw him at the time and as I see him in retrospect, his chief defect was temperamental. His prejudices were strong and oftentimes clouded his judgments. But, by and large, he was what the head of a state should be — intelligent, honest, and courageous. Happy the nation fortunate enough to have a Woodrow Wilson to lead it through dark and tempestuous days!

Much as he accomplished, much as he commended himself to the gratitude and admiration of mankind, by some strange turn of fate his bitterest enemies have done more than his best friends to assure his undying fame. Had the Versailles Treaty gone through the United States Senate as written and without question, Woodrow Wilson would have been but one of many to share in the imperishable glory of the League of Nations. But the fight which he was forced to make for it, and the world-wide proportions which this warfare assumed, gradually forced Woodrow Wilson to the forefront of the battle, and it was around his heroic figure that it raged. While he went down in defeat in his own country, an unprejudiced world begins to see and appreciate the magnitude of the conception and its service to mankind. The League of Nations and the name of Woodrow Wilson have become inseparable, and his enemies have helped to build to his memory the noblest monument ever erected to a son of man.

NOTE OF ACKNOWLEDGMENT

Some three and a half years ago Colonel House gave to Yale University, for deposit in the University Library, his entire collection of political papers. For permission to select and publish the most significant of these, I myself and all students of recent history are deeply in his debt. The responsibility for the choice and arrangement of these papers, as well as their interpretation, must rest upon me. Colonel House, whose sense of the scientific historical spirit is very lively, agreed that no essential document which might affect the historicity of the narrative should be omitted. Whatever deletions appear in the published papers have been dictated by the exigencies of space or by a regard for the feelings of persons still alive, and in no case do they alter the historical meaning of the papers.

The comment and advice of Colonel House have been invaluable. He has carefully avoided, however, any insistence upon his personal point of view, at the same time that he has offered priceless aid in throwing light upon innumerable aspects of the political story which would otherwise have remained obscure. For the time and interest and freedom which he has given me I am profoundly grateful. It is a rare privilege for the historian that his documentary material should be explained by the chief actor in the drama. I am indebted also, and beyond measure, to Colonel House's brother-in-law, President Sidney E. Mezes, and to his secretary, Miss Frances B. Denton, for constant assistance and criticism. They have read the manuscript and proof, and by reason of their intimate first-hand knowledge of the events concerned, they have corrected many misinterpretations.

My gratitude must also be expressed for the help given by many of those who themselves played an important political rôle during the past thirteen years; they have been willing to discuss freely the history of that period and to permit me to publish their letters. I would mention Ambassador James W. Gerard, Ambassador Brand Whitlock, Ambassador H. C. Wallace, Attorney-General T. W. Gregory, Postmaster-General A. S. Burleson, Mr. Frank L. Polk, Mr. Vance McCormick, Mr. John Hays Hammond, Mr. Gordon Auchincloss, Viscount Grey of Fallodon, the Earl of Balfour, Mr. Lloyd George, Sir Austen Chamberlain, Sir Horace Plunkett, Sir William Tyrrell, Mr. H. Wickham Steed, Mr. J. A. Spender, Sir William Wiseman, M. Georges Clemenceau, M. Ignace Paderewski. All of these came into close touch with Colonel House, and the personal and political sidelights which they have thrown upon him have been of inestimable value.

The volumes owe much to those who have cordially permitted the publication of letters now in the House Collection of the Yale University Library. I take pleasure in thanking Mrs. Walter Hines Page, Mrs. Thomas Lindsay, Mrs. Franklin K. Lane, Lady Spring-Rice, Mrs. William Jennings Bryan, Secretary of State Robert Lansing, Secretary of the Treasury William G. McAdoo, Secretary of Agriculture David F. Houston, Justice James C. McReynolds, President Charles W. Eliot, Mr. J. St. Loe Strachey, Mr. A. H. Frazier, Mr. E. S. Martin, Mr. George Foster Peabody, Mr. James Speyer.

In the arrangement of the papers and their interpretation I have made constant use of the numerous letters from President Wilson to Colonel House now deposited in the House Collection. It seemed wise to the literary legatee of the President not to grant permission to publish these letters textually; something of the personal attractiveness of Mr. Wilson has thus been lost. But the sense of the letters, setting forth his intimate feelings and policies, has been freely translated into the pages which follow. A list of the letters which I have thus utilized is appended.[1] None of them have been published; many of them were typed by the President himself without a copy being made, often in the private code used only by Colonel House and himself.

To the authorities of Yale University who have provided facilities for the care of the House Collection and to the staff of the University Library, especially the Librarian, Mr. Andrew Keogh, I would express warmest gratitude, as well as to those alumni of Yale who by financial assistance have made possible the filing and organization of documents given by Colonel House and others. I am indebted in particular to my assistant in the curatorship of the House Collection, Miss Helen M. Reynolds; every page of these volumes bears witness to the devoted effort she has expended upon the construction of the manuscript, the verification of references, and the correction of proof. Finally I must acknowledge the constant encouragement and practical assistance of my wife in the large task of selecting the most significant documents and arranging them so as to make a coherent narrative.

C. S.

YALE UNIVERSITY
January 1, 1926

[1] See page xv.

LETTERS FROM WILSON TO HOUSE

Utilized for the period, October 1911–March 1917

DATE		SUBJECT
1911		
October	18	Wilson's party regularity.
	24	Desirability of abolishing two-thirds rule in National Democratic Convention.
December	4	Engagement to dine with House and Dr. Houston.
	22	Pre-Convention campaign organization.
	26	Pre-Convention campaign organization.
1912		
January	4	Personal. Bryan's attitude.
	27	Personal.
February	6	Personal.
	14	Personal.
March	15	Pre-Convention outlook. Political strength of Champ Clark, Underwood, Harmon.
May	6	House's political organization in Texas.
	29	Personal. [Telegram.]
June	9	Plans for Baltimore Convention.
	24	Convention organization.
July	17	Plan of electoral campaign.
August	22	Plan of electoral campaign.
	31	Plan of electoral campaign.
September	11	McCombs' possible resignation as National Democratic Chairman.
November	7	Comment on result of election. Gratitude for House's services.
	30	Personal. House's Washington visit for study of Cabinet material.
December	3	Personal. House's Washington visit.
1913		
January	6	Discussion of Cabinet material.
	23	Discussion of Cabinet material.
February	5	Cabinet appointments.
	7	Cabinet appointments.
May	9	New York appointments.
	17	Federal Reserve Bill.
	20	Personal. [Telegram.]
July	17	Personal. [Telegram.]

DATE		SUBJECT
1913		
September	4	Personal.
	18	Massachusetts appointments.
	26	Request for House's help in personal matter.
	29	Personal.
October	17	One Hundredth Anniversary of peace among English-speaking peoples.
November	5	Mexico.
December	9	Message to Congress.
	27	Personal.
1914		
January	3	Trusts.
	6	Trust Message. [Telegram.]
	9	Federal Reserve Board appointments.
	28	Panama Canal Zone.
	30	Personal. [Telegram.]
February	16	Federal Reserve Board appointments.
	18	Federal Reserve Board appointments.
	25	Federal Reserve Board appointments. Mexican situation.
March	7	Federal Reserve Board appointments.
	30	Federal Reserve Board appointments.
April	2	Federal Reserve Board appointments.
May	2	Federal Reserve Board appointments.
	15	Departure of House for Europe.
June	16	House's mission in Europe.
	22	French proposal for revision of commercial treaty between France and the United States. Mediation between the United States and Mexico.
	26	House's mission in Europe.
July	9	Endorsement of House's mission.
August	3	Situation in Europe.
	4	Mediation in European War. [Telegram.]
	5	Mediation in European War.
	6	Mediation in European War. Shipping Bill.
	6	Mrs. Wilson's death. [Telegram.]
	17	Personal.
	18	Personal.
	25	Attitude toward European War.
	27	Personal. [Telegram.]
September	8	Approval of House's letters to Zimmermann and Ambassador W. H. Page.
	16	Approval of House's suggestion on taxes.
	17	Appointments.
	19	Approval of House's negotiations with Bernstorff. [Telegram.]

DATE		SUBJECT
1914		
October	10	Negotiations for purchase of cotton.
	16	Negotiations for purchase of cotton.
	19	Appointments.
	22	Personal.
	23	Attitude of Ambassador W. H. Page.
	29	Attitude of Ambassador W. H. Page.
November	2	Personal. [Telegram.]
December	1	Presidential Message. Belgian relief.
	2	Foreign relations.
	9	Presidential Message.
	14	Personal.
	16	Personal. [Telegram.]
	22	Personal. [Telegram.]
	25	Personal.
	26	Industrial relations. [Telegram.]
	26	Trade Commission.
	28	Personal.
	28	Personal. [Telegram.]
	31	Personal. [Telegram.]
1915		
January	5	Approval of House's letter to Zimmermann.
	6	Appointments.
	7	Federal employment bureau.
	11	Personal.
	16	Mediation in European War.
	17	Personal. [Telegram.]
	28	Situation in Germany.
	29	Personal. [Telegram.]
	29	Purpose of House's European mission.
February	13	House's negotiations in England. Note to the Allies. [Cablegram.]
	15	Gerard's information on situation in Germany. [Cablegram.]
	20	Relations with Great Britain. [Cablegram.]
	25	House's negotiations. [Cablegram.]
March	1	Conditions in Germany. [Cablegram.]
	8	House's negotiations. [Cablegram.]
	23	British Order in Council. [Cablegram.]
April	2	Approval of House's negotiations. [Cablegram.]
	15	Messages to President and Foreign Minister of France. [Cablegram.]
	22	Pan-American Pact. [Cablegram.]
May	—	British blockade. [Cablegram.]
	4	Sinking of *Gulflight*. [Cablegram.]
	5	British blockade. [Cablegram.]

DATE		SUBJECT
1915		
May	16	Possible compromise between British blockade and German submarine warfare. [Cablegram.]
	18	British blockade. [Cablegram.]
	20	Possible compromise between British blockade and German submarine warfare. [Cablegram.]
	23	British blockade. [Cablegram.]
	26	British blockade. [Cablegram.]
June	1	House's return. [Cablegram.]
	20	Personal. Wilson planning visit to House. [Telegram.]
	22	Wilson's visit to House. [Telegram.]
July	3	Mexico. [Telegram.]
	3	Mexico.
	7	Mexico.
	12	Counsellorship of State Department. Note to Germany.
	14	Strained relations with Germany.
	19	Contraband and cotton.
	20	British blockade.
	22	Contraband and cotton.
	27	Counsellorship of State Department. British blockade.
	29	British blockade. Bernstorff.
August	4	Appointments.
	4	Mexico.
	4	German plots.
	5	Contraband and cotton.
	7	Contraband and cotton.
	21	Asking for advice on *Arabic* case. Attitude of Ambassador W. H. Page.
	25	Bernstorff. German plots.
	31	Personal.
	31	*Arabic* crisis. Federal Reserve Board.
September	7	Austrian plots. Sinking of *Hesperian.*
	20	Bernstorff. *Arabic* crisis.
	27	Bernstorff. *Arabic* crisis.
	29	Personal.
October	4	Personal.
	4	Armed merchantmen controversy.
	18	Possible offer of help to Allies.
	18	Attitude of Ambassador W. H. Page.
	29	Personal.
November	10	Possibilities of peace. Domestic politics.
	11	House's messages to Grey. [Telegram.]
	12	Conditions in Germany. Sinking of *Ancona.*
	17	House's mission to Europe.
	24	British and German Ambassadors in Washington. House's mission to Europe.

DATE		SUBJECT
1916		
January	9	Assurance of American coöperation in policy seeking to bring about and maintain permanent peace. [Cablegram.]
	12	The Senate and British blockade. [Cablegram.]
	13	Approval of House's negotiations. [Cablegram.]
February	16	Armed merchantmen. [Cablegram.]
March	3	Personal. [Telegram.]
	20	Gerard's report from Germany.
April	15	Appointments. [Telegram.]
	21	*Sussex* crisis.
	22	*Sussex* crisis. Domestic politics.
	29	*Sussex* crisis. [Telegram.]
May	5	*Sussex* crisis. [Telegram.]
	8	Relations with Great Britain.
	9	Possibility of peace.
	16	Offer of help to Allies. British blockade.
	17	Attitude of Ambassador W. H. Page.
	17	Chairmanship of Democratic National Committee.
	18	Offer of help to Allies. Relations with Great Britain.
	18	Request for advice on speech before League to Enforce Peace.
	22	Relations with Allies. Request for material for speech. Chairmanship of Democratic National Committee.
	29	Chairmanship of Democratic National Committee.
June	6	Chairmanship of Democratic National Committee.
	10	Chairmanship of Democratic National Committee.
	11	Chairmanship of Democratic National Committee. [Telegram.]
	22	European situation. Mexico. Plan for electoral campaign.
July	2	Relations with England. Appointments. Electoral campaign.
	23	British Blacklist.
	27	Relations with Great Britain.
September	20	Personal.
	29	Electoral campaign.
October	10	Relations with Great Britain.
	24	Electoral campaign.
	30	Madison Square rally.
November	6	Personal.
	21	Drafting of note calling on belligerents to state terms of peace.
	24	Relations with Germany. Attitude of Ambassador W. H. Page.
	25	Peace note.
December	3	Peace note.

DATE		SUBJECT
1916		
December	4	Personal.
	8	House's information from England.
	19	Peace note.
	27	Attempt to secure confidential peace terms from Germany.
1917		
January	16	Drafting of speech on peace terms before the Senate.
	17	House's negotiations with Bernstorff.
	19	House's negotiations with Bernstorff. Speech before the Senate.
	24	House's negotiations with Bernstorff.
February	12	Refusal to consider coalition government.

CONTENTS

ILLUSTRATIONS

THE INTIMATE PAPERS OF

COLONEL HOUSE

THE INTIMATE PAPERS OF COLONEL HOUSE

∴

CHAPTER I

INTRODUCTION

I look forward now to your book. It is, I hope, books like yours and mine that will bring people to reflect soberly upon the war. If so we shall be helping to form a public opinion that will make for peace.

Viscount Grey of Fallodon to House, October 16, 1925

The practice of interring historical documents in securely locked archives, where they may lie forgotten until popular interest in the period evaporates, has much to be said for it. It prevents their use for partisan political purposes; it protects the sensibilities of those political leaders whose rôle, viewed at close range, may have been less heroic than the public imagined; it guarantees, through the lapse of time, the growth of that magical touchstone, 'historical perspective,' which supposedly eliminates bias and ensures the truth.

Unfortunately, if the materials of real history are absent those of legend replace them. 'History,' said Voltaire, 'is a fable which men have agreed upon.' And one may ask whether it is not the duty of the historian to establish the facts before the fable has crystallized, and the duty of whoever possesses the documents to make them available to the historian at the earliest possible moment. The argument is the stronger if we accept the view that mankind learns from its past. Granting that a lesson of value is to be secured from history, surely our own generation has a right to insist that its benefits ought not be reserved for the unborn of the future. If the inner history of the decade which saw Europe caught in the horror of war and its aftermath can help us to avoid another such disaster, the disadvantages of keeping that history in cold storage until the twenty-first century are apparent.

Such thoughts may have crossed the mind of Colonel House when he determined to have published sufficient of his papers to elucidate what he regarded as the true story of the decisive years in which he played a rôle of major political importance. A newspaper cartoon of 1916 represents the Muse of History (rather a frowsy Clio, to be sure, bespectacled and distraught) presenting a tightly corked bottle labelled *Foreign Policy* to a silent and impassive Colonel House, and in desperation demanding the opener. After the lapse of a decade, the Colonel has produced it.

The anxiety of the Historical Muse is comprehensible as the student pores over the pile of papers which indicate the extent and variety of the personal and political contacts that House established. Here are great sheaves of letters from the European statesmen of the war period — Grey, Balfour, Bryce, Lloyd George, Plunkett, Reading, Briand, Clemenceau, Zimmermann, Bernstorff, Spring-Rice — with the Colonel's replies; yet more extensive files of his correspondence with the American Ambassadors in the capitals of Europe — the Pages, Gerard, Sharp, Penfield, Whitlock, Willard; letters to and from the members of Mr. Wilson's Cabinet, covering the details of appointments and departmental policy; and finally the eight years' series of correspondence with the President himself, intimate and affectionate, which explains the origin and development of Wilsonian policies, domestic and foreign, from the beginning of Wilson's race for the Presidency in 1911 until the Peace Conference of Paris in 1919.

As he sorts the dusty files, the curious investigator finds himself introduced into the very *penetralia* of politics — the making of a Cabinet, the origins of currency reform, the American attempt to prevent the World War, American offers to help the Allies made and refused, the intimate

'COME ON, NOW! GIMME THE OPENER!'
From the Montgomery (Ala.) *Advertiser*, April 14, 1916

details of American coöperation in the war, in the Armistice and in the Peace Conference; he sees at close range, the President himself, Bernstorff and the Kaiser, the European Premiers and Foreign Ministers, American Ambassadors and Cabinet members.

If it had not been for an aid of exceptional character, the preservation of these papers would have been difficult or impossible. Fortunately House possessed in Miss Frances B. Denton, the daughter of an old friend, an assistant who was more collaborator than confidential secretary, and one whose rôle proved to be of increasing importance. In the midst of the negotiations which Colonel House carried on with Cabinets and potentates, she found time to gather and file the material without which the story could never have been told. She combined the discretion and tact demanded by House's diplomatic activities with an instinct for the preservation of documents that will always endear her to historians. 'She has not only kept the record,' wrote House in 1916, 'but has kept the faith and with an enduring loyalty and self-abnegation.'

Through Miss Denton was made possible the diary which forms the heart of the entire collection of papers. Every evening, with rare exceptions and during eight years, Colonel House dictated to her his résumé of the events of the day. Definitely and objectively he related his conversations with, often the very words of, his political associates, and he was associated with the men who made the history of the decade. The result is a journal of more than two thousand pages, a record drafted at the moment and with a frankness which suggests that it was not designed for publication. It has the Colonel's comments on men and events, opinions which he sometimes changed, prophecies which upon occasion were fulfilled and again remained unfulfilled, a personal document such as the biographer dreams of and seldom discovers.

Upon the basis of such papers and his recollections, Colonel House might have written the conventional 'Memoirs,' which too often confuse the after-impression with the event itself, but which, through the possession of hindsight, preserve the author from ever having committed an error. Instead, he chose to let the papers tell their own story and permit the reader to decide whether or not the Colonel was right in this incident and in that. If there is prejudice in the pages that follow — and what historical narrative is innocent of prejudice? — it is that of the man who, after many months of arranging the papers so as to let them make a story, came to see events through the eyes of Colonel House himself. But at no time was a chapter begun under the influence of a preconceived thesis, and nothing could have been more exciting than to watch the behavior of the chief figures as each chapter took form; in this they did well, in that they were disappointing.

An objective narrative, such as the documents themselves recount, was the more necessary in view of the paucity of published information touching the career and accomplishments of Colonel House. There are few, if any, instances of men exercising so much political influence about whom so little was known. The personal story of a man holding public office must needs become public property. A searchlight is immediately turned upon his past career. The press will have it so and, if skilfully utilized, political propaganda of value may conceivably be developed from it. Since we demand of our public personages a certain blameless rectitude of conduct, without which one is ill-advised to seek office, the subject of inquiry, even though he may never have accomplished anything of note, is generally well pleased with the conventions of political advertising designed to engage the interest of the voters.

With Colonel House it was bound to be otherwise. He sought no office for himself — in itself a peculiarity and one that would naturally puzzle opinion — nor did he seek office for his friends. His methods and purposes were quite different from those of the party boss, for he never worked through a 'machine'; he disliked the details of party politics, and in later years he generally managed to evade them. He aimed certainly at influencing political events, as the sequel will show, but he accomplished his aim through personal influence very different from that of the orthodox politician. The story of how he acquired such influence is the explanation of his success, and to understand it we must read his political papers. But it is easy to comprehend at first glance that to him conventional political advertisement could bring no profit and might bring much harm. He strove constantly to stifle the public adulation that zealous press agents sought to inspire, and he was careful to bring it about that credit for this or that measure in which he was interested should go to the political office-holders. House's papers are filled with references to the efforts he made to obliterate the intimate personal sketch, so familiar in American politics; and when finally a brief biography appeared which gave him full credit for his influence in the Wilson administration, at his special request the edition was withdrawn by the publisher.

The desire to escape publicity was largely a matter of common sense, for in this way only could he hope to avoid political enmities and jealousies: President, Cabinet members, Ambassadors, all knew that he stood ready to help them and yet would seek no public recognition. It was also instinctive, springing not from undue modesty, for Colonel House was as coldly objective in judging himself as another, but rather from a philosophic pleasure in accomplishment rather than reward, and perhaps in part from a sardonic sense of humor which was tickled by the thought that he, unseen and often unsuspected, without great wealth or office, merely through the power of personality and good sense, was actually deflecting the currents of history. Whether this supposition is borne out by the intimate papers of the Colonel, the reader must judge.

The path which House laid out for himself was entirely untrodden, and it is fruitless to seek an historical parallel. Monarchs had shared their secrets with father confessors and extracted wisdom from their advice; Presidents had created their kitchen-cabinets. But neither the one nor the other suggests the unofficial functions which House exercised. He was a combination of Richelieu's Father Joseph and Thurlow Weed, but he was very much more. At the same time that he played the part of adviser to the President, of buffer between office-seekers and Cabinet, of emissary to foreign courts, he indulged in a complex of activities which kept him in close touch with business men, local politicians, artists, and journalists, lawyers and college professors. His intimacy with European statesmen was as close and his friendship as warm as the personal associations he created at home. Long after the war, when their political relations had become ancient history, he visited Grey and Plunkett, Clemenceau and Paderewski. Long after the Democrats lost power in the United States, the officials of Great Britain, France, and Germany sought his advice. His range of contacts was so great that he became a sort of clearing-house for all who desired to accomplish something. He avoided high office, which comes to many men, but he reserved for himself a niche which is unique in history.

Inevitably, the public was mystified, especially during the early years of the Wilson administration. The circle widened that recognized in him a powerful factor in national and international politics, and yet few could answer the simplest questions about him. Who and what was he? Many replies were given, but, as Colonel House refused to say which were true and which false, no one was the wiser. He became the Man of Mystery and, since facts were lacking, fiction supplied their place. Myths of the most varied sort developed about this 'Texas Talleyrand,' this 'backwoods politician.' He was represented as a lover of devious methods, reticent as the Sphinx, emotionless as a red-skin. Such tales must be strung with the other mock-pearls of history. And the interesting point to note is that the public, deprived of facts, none the less refused to accept the legends fed to them which, had they been true, would have disqualified House utterly for the work that he undertook. Puzzled but untroubled, they accepted him finally as 'the President's adviser.' Here and there were to be heard grumbles at this strange departure in American politics; but in general, knowing little of his activities and nothing of his advice, the people came to look upon him as a wise institution.

Thus Colonel House disdained fame and achieved it. His fame, however, rested primarily upon the fact of his relations with Wilson and not upon what he was or what he did. Of that the Colonel and those close to him alone could tell, and they told nothing. It is, therefore, with the greater interest that the historian turns over the mass of papers from which the story of his dramatic career may be disengaged.

SH!
From the St. Louis *Post-Dispatch*

CHAPTER II

BACKGROUNDS

Your success has been without a parallel in Texas politics.
Governor-elect Sayers to House, May 17, 1898

I

'We originally came from Holland and the name was Huis, which finally fell into House. Father ran away from home and went to sea when a child, and did not return to his home until he had become a man of property and distinction. He came to Texas when it belonged to Mexico. He joined the revolution, fought under General Burleson, and helped make Texas a republic. For his services in this war he received a grant of land in Coryell County. He lived to see Texas come into the Union, secede, and return to the Union. He lived in Texas under four flags.'

Thus wrote Colonel House in the summer of 1916, when a brief lull in his political activities gave opportunity for him to reconstruct on paper something of the background that lay behind his rapid rise to national and international eminence. Although the family was in its origin Dutch, his forbears were for some three hundred years English, and it was from England that his father ran away. House himself, a seventh son, was born in 1858, at Houston, Texas, and this State he has always regarded as his home. Even more than those of Wilson or Walter Page, with whom he later was so closely associated, his first years were touched by the excitement and turmoil of the events of the time.

'Some of my earliest recollections are of the Civil War. I began to remember, I think, in '62 and '63, when our soldiers were coming and going to and from the front. I remember quite distinctly when Lincoln was assassinated. Father came home to luncheon, and I recall where Mother was standing when he told her that the President had been shot. I remember, too, that he said that it was the worst thing that had so far happened to the South. He saw farther than most men, and he knew from the beginning of the war that it must end disastrously for the South. He knew the Northern States possessed the resources which are potential in war, and that the Southern States, lacking them, would lose. The blockade which the Federal Government was able to throw around the Southern coast, while not absolute, was rigid enough to make it difficult to break through and obtain from the outside what was needed within.

'During the war he sent many ships out from Galveston with cotton, to run the blockade to the near-by ports, such as Havana and Belize Honduras. At that time we had a house in Galveston as well as in Houston. The Galveston home covered an entire block. The house was a large red brick Colonial one, with white pillars, and an orange grove took up most of the grounds, and oleanders encircled them.

'In determining when to send his ships out, Father was governed largely by the weather. Dark, stormy nights were the ones chosen. In the afternoon he would go up to the cupola of our house, and with his glasses he would scan the horizon to see how many Federal gunboats were patrolling the coast. Then his ship would go out in the early part of the night. In the morning, at daylight, he would be again on the lookout to count the Federal gunboats, to see if any were missing. If they were all there, he felt reasonably sure his ship with her cargo had gotten through the blockade.

'It would be months before he knew definitely whether his ships had come safely to port or whether they had been captured. When he lost one, the loss was complete; but when one got through, the gain was large. He had a working arrangement with the Confederate Government by which the return voyage brought them clothing, arms, and munitions of war of all kinds.

'The terrible days between Lee's surrender and the bringing of some sort of order out of the chaos in the South made a lasting impression on my mind. I cannot recall just now how long the interim was, but it must have been a full year or more.

'There was one regiment of Texas soldiers that came to Houston and disbanded there. They looted the town. They attempted to break into Father's storehouse, but he stood at the doors with a shotgun. . . . Murder was rife everywhere; there was no law, there was no order. It was unsafe to go at night to your next-door neighbor's. When Father had this to do, he always reached for his shotgun or six-shooter and held it ready to shoot while both going and coming.'

Those who later were to accuse Colonel House of ill-considered pacifism, would doubtless have been surprised to learn of the atmosphere in which he was reared. In later life he was often asked whether he considered himself a pacifist. 'Yes,' he replied, 'so far as international affairs are concerned. War is too costly and ineffective a method of settling disputes between nations. But as an individual I have not been able to escape the conviction that there are occasions in life when a man must be prepared to fight.'

As a boy and later in early manhood, he learned from personal experience the meaning of lawlessness and bloodshed. Because of this, perhaps, he was brought to perceive not merely the horror but the stupidity of war; and it was easier for him, when he attained an influential position, to utilize it to bring peace, in that his personal courage was beyond question. It may have been from these early experiences also that he learned the value of audacity. In the days of his great political influence, Colonel House was frequently pictured as a man dominated by the spirit of caution. Nothing could be further from the truth. He believed always in careful preparation and foresight whenever possible; as an English statesman once said, 'House always sees three months ahead.' But he believed more fervently yet that nothing worth while could be accomplished without a daring that might wisely be allowed to approach recklessness. Like Cavour, whom he admired, he knew how to wait for the supreme moment and then risk everything.

'Even the children of the town [he wrote] caught the spirit of recklessness and disorder, and there were constant feuds and broils amongst us. My brother James, six years older than I, was the leader of our "gang." We all had guns and pistols. We had "nigger shooters" (small catapults), and there were no childish games excepting those connected with war. We lived and breathed in the atmosphere of strife and destruction.

'In the evening, around the fireside, there were told tales of daring deeds, and it was the leader of such deeds that we strove to emulate. Often the firebells would ring as a signal that a riot was imminent, and the citizens would flock together at some given point, all armed to the teeth. These disturbances were, as a rule, between the old-time citizens and the negroes and carpetbaggers.

'I cannot remember the time when I began to ride and to shoot. Why I did not kill myself, one can never know, for accidents were common. My eldest brother had the side of his face shot off and has been disfigured by it all his life. He hung between life and death for weeks, but finally came through with one side of his face gone.

'I had many narrow escapes. Twice I came near killing one of my playmates in the reckless use of firearms. They were our toys and, as a matter of fact, death was our playmate.'

The young House was taken to England as a boy and went to school at Bath. His experiences with his schoolmates by no means presaged the cordial relations which he was later to establish with British diplomats:

'James attempted the same sort of rough play we had been accustomed to in Texas, and we were constantly in broils with the young English lads, who were not familiar with such lawlessness. My old darkey nurse used to tell me that if I had not been the seventh son of a seventh son, I would never have survived.'

At the age of fourteen, after the death of his mother, he was sent to school first in Virginia and then in Connecticut. House's recollections of the former are not pleasant: 'I shall never forget my depression when we arrived. . . . The nearest town to us was thirty miles away, and a more desolate, lonely spot no homesick boy ever saw.' Scholastic pursuits evidently made less impression on his mind than the cruelty of the older boys, which soon furnished an opportunity for House to display his mettle. He says little of the particular incident which evidently gave him a preferred place among the boys, but that little indicates something of the determined temper which was to appear on various occasions during his political career.

'I made up my mind at the second attempt to haze me that I would not permit it. I not only had a pistol but a large knife, and with these I held the larger, rougher boys at bay. There was no limit to the lengths they would go in hazing those who would allow it. One form I recall was that of going through the pretense of hanging. They would tie a boy's hands behind him and string him up by the neck over a limb until he grew purple in the face. . . . None of it, however, fell to me. What was done to those who permitted it, is almost

E. M. H. AND MAMMY ELIZA
Taken in Bath, England

beyond belief. . . . The only thing that reconciled me to my lot was the near-by mountains, where I could shoot and enjoy out-of-door life.'

Clearly a change, even to a Yankee atmosphere, was an improvement; and House hailed with relief, if not enthusiasm, the plan which at the age of seventeen sent him to New Haven, Connecticut.

'I had expected to be able to enter Yale, but I found myself wholly unprepared and reluctantly entered the Hopkins Grammar School of the Class of '77. . . . What I had been taught was of but little use, and I would have been better off as far as Latin and Greek were concerned if I had known nothing and had started from the beginning. I studied but little, and I soon found I would have difficulty in joining the Class of '81 in Yale. Meanwhile, Oliver T. Morton, a son of Senator Oliver P. Morton of Indiana, and I had become fast friends and we agreed to tutor together and go to Cornell instead of Yale. Both Morton and I were more bent on mischief than upon books and, while the mischief was innocent, it made us poor students.'

It was less mischief, however, than budding enthusiasm for his lifelong interest that kept House and Morton from their books. Already the young Southerner was intoxicated by a passion for politics and public affairs; he read politics, talked politics, and in his first year at the Grammar School, a boy of seventeen, he brought himself into close contact with the mechanism of politics. It was the year of the famous Hayes-Tilden campaign.

'Every near-by political meeting I attended, and there was no one more interested in the nomination and election of the presidential candidates of 1876 than I. At every opportunity

I would go to New York and hang about Democratic Headquarters which, I remember, were at the Everett House in Union Square. I used to see Mr. Tilden go in and out, and wondered then how so frail a looking man could make a campaign for President.

'Bayard, Blaine, and others I heard speak whenever the opportunity occurred, and I believe that I was as nearly engrossed in politics as I have ever been since.

'Before the nominations were made, I was, of course, hoping to see young Morton's father nominated for President, and it was a bitter disappointment to us both when the telegraph operator handed us out the first slip giving news that the Republicans had compromised upon Rutherford B. Hayes. The operator knew us, for we were continually hanging about the office instead of attending to our studies. Morton's father was such a power at that time that there was no difficulty in his having access to any information that was to be had.

'Ardent Democrat that I was, and ardent Republican that he was, young Morton and I had no unpleasant discussions. After the election and during the contest that followed, it was utterly impossible for me to bring myself to think of desk or books. I was constantly going to Washington with Morton, in order to be near the centre of things. I was usually the guest of the Mortons, who lived at that time at the Ebbitt House. I knew much of everything that was going on. Republican leaders would come in day and night to consult the distinguished invalid who was directing the fight for Hayes. In this way, directly and indirectly, I saw and met many well-known Republicans in public life at that time.'

No clearer proof is necessary that the child is father to the man, for, as his papers will show, the mature Colonel House displayed an invincible obstinacy in making personal friends of his political opponents. The characteristic proceeded, perhaps, from a natural inability to remain on anything but good terms with those whom he met, whether in conflict or coöperation; it resulted in giving him an insight into the motives that actuated his opponents which was of no small political value.

The election of 1876, we may remind ourselves, was disputed and was ultimately settled by an Electoral Commission which, despite the protests of Democrats at the moment and heedless of the criticism of later historians, awarded the Presidency to Hayes. Such a conflict formed an incomparable opportunity for the young House to study political operations, and one which he did not fail to utilize, regardless of the fact that school was in session.

'When the Electoral Commission was organized and began to hold its sittings in the Supreme Court Room at the Capitol, young Morton and I were permitted to slip in and out at will, although the demand for admission could only be met in a very small way. I heard Evarts speak, but the speech that impressed me most was that of Senator Carpenter who, although a Republican, pleaded for Tilden.

'In those days, too, I had the entrée to the White House. I remember General Grant and Mrs. Grant and several members of his Cabinet. All this was educational in its way, but not the education I was placed in the Hopkins Grammar School to get, and it is no wonder that I lagged at the end of my class. I had no interest in my desk tasks, but I read much and was learning in a larger and more interesting school.

'When I entered Cornell, it was the same story. . . . I was constantly reading, constantly absorbing, constantly in touch with, public affairs. I knew the name of every United States Senator, of practically every Representative, the Governors of all the important States, and had some knowledge of the chief measures before the people.

'I had found that I could neglect my studies up to the last

minute and then, by a few days of vigorous effort, pass my examinations by a scratch, nothing more. I cannot remember getting a condition, nor can I remember getting much more than a passing mark.

'My Washington experience perhaps changed my entire career. Fortunately or unfortunately for me, I saw that two or three men in the Senate and two or three in the House and the President himself, ran the Government. The others were merely figureheads. I saw Senators and Representatives speak to empty benches and for the purpose of getting their remarks in the *Congressional Record* sent to their admiring constituents. I saw, too, how few public men could really speak well. I can count on the fingers of one hand all the speakers that I thought worth while. In some the manner was good, in others the substance was good, but in nearly all there was lacking one or the other. Therefore I had no ambition to hold office, nor had I any ambition to speak, because I felt in both instances that I would fall short of the first place, and nothing less than that would satisfy me.

'Yet I have been thought without ambition. That, I think, is not quite true. My ambition has been so great that it has never seemed to me worth while to strive to satisfy it.'

Matters might have been different had it not been for the delicacy of House's health. 'Up to the time I was eleven or twelve years old,' he wrote, 'I was a robust youngster. One day while I was swinging high, a rope broke and I was thrown on my head. Brain fever ensued, and for a long time I hovered between life and death. Upon my recovery, malaria fastened upon me, and I have never been strong since.' The confining routine of office was impossible for him. Especially did he suffer from the heat, which put residence in Washington during the summer months out of the question.

Thus early and for various reasons he set aside the thought of a conventional political career; but his ambition, although unorthodox, was, as he admits, very real, and, even though he does not admit it, we shall see that he did much to satisfy it. He longed to play an influential if not a decisive rôle in politics, and from the beginning seems to have been inspired by the desire to improve political conditions. Through all his correspondence and papers runs this idealistic strain: to make of government a more efficient instrument for effecting the desires of the people; to inspire in the people a more sensible view of their welfare; to take a few feathers out of the wings of enthusiasm and insert them in the tail of judgment; above all, to hasten the advent of a system which would protect the weak, whether in the political or economic sphere, from exploitation by the strong. Even as a boy there was in him something of Louis Blanc and Mazzini, strictly controlled, however, by an acute sense of the practical that recalls Benjamin Franklin.

His ambition, furthermore, was determined by an ever-lively sense of proportion, which means sense of humor, that continually manifests itself in his papers. It led him to seek accomplishment rather than notoriety.

Careless of title or office, even had his health permitted him to seek them, yet determined to make of politics his real career, House faced the problem that confronts so many young idealists leaving college and anxious to serve their country and mankind. How to begin?

II

Mischance cut short the college career of House, for after two years at Cornell he was called back to Texas by the illness of his father, who died in 1880. The two had been close companions, and the younger man's sense of loss was acute and the deprivation of his father's aid and experienced counsel was a serious blow. 'My affection may blind me,' he wrote, 'and my judgment may have been immature, but he seemed to me then, as he seems to me now, among the ablest men I have ever known. . . . I owe more to my father than to any person, living or dead. He not only made it possible for me to pursue the bent of my inclinations by leaving me a fortune sufficient for all moderate wants, but he gave me an insight into the philosophy of life that has been of incalculable value. . . . While he devoted his life largely to commerce in various forms and while he acquired what seemed to Texas a large fortune, he taught me not to place a fictitious value on wealth. It was with him merely a means to an end.'

The year after leaving college, House married Miss Loulie Hunter, of Hunter, Texas, and after travelling in Europe for a twelvemonth, returned to make his home first in Houston and then in Austin, Texas. Cotton-farming and commercial enterprises kept him busy, but more and more he began to steal time from business to indulge his vital interest in public affairs. During what he calls 'the twilight years,' after he had achieved political success in Texas and before the opportunity for national service had opened, he indulged his taste for adventure by embarking upon various industrial schemes, some of which were obviously calculated to produce pleasure rather than profit for himself.

'In this connection I undertook the building of the Trinity and Brazos Valley Railway. The capital was raised by my friend, Thomas Jefferson Coolidge, Jr., of the Old Colony Trust Company of Boston, who occasionally visited me in Texas. I outlined the route and he accepted my judgment as to its feasibility.

'For two or three years, this gave me much pleasure and absorbed my entire interest. There was not a man connected with the building of this road, except the engineer, that had ever had the slightest experience with railroad building. I wonder now at the temerity of those Boston capitalists. My one thought was to have around me men capable and *honest*, and to this I attribute our success. My secretary, Edward

T. W. HOUSE
Father of Edward M. House

Sammons, than whom there is no better accountant, looked after the accounts; and William Malone, the manager of my farms, saw to it that we got such material as was paid for. I put but little money in the project, for I had but little; therefore I made but a small sum from it, successful as it was — some thirty thousand dollars. A larger share of the profits had been allotted me by the syndicate managers who had put up the money necessary to build the road, but I divided it with those friends in Texas, poorer than I, who aided in the actual work of building the road.

'It was a pleasure, though, to undertake to build a railroad honestly, without a dollar's profit to any one excepting to those who placed their money in the venture. The money was raised in advance and everything was paid for in cash, and no bonds were sold until after the road was a going concern and sold to another system.

'We undertook to lay down one cardinal principle which no road in Texas, up to that time, had deigned to do; and that was, to treat the public in such a way that they became friends of the road instead of enemies. If a farmer or any citizen along the route had a claim against the company, it was promptly and fairly adjusted. Notices were put up and circulars sent out that there would be no need to hire damage claim lawyers, when there was a claim against the T. and B. V. Railroad; that all honest claims would be adjusted immediately.

'The result was magical, and it was not long before the patrons of the road understood that we were acting in their interest as well as our own, and any attempt — and there were many — to blackmail us in the usual way that railroad corporations have been blackmailed, found no sympathy with any jury along the line of the road.'

During the eighties, Texas was just passing from the condition of a frontier where law was frequently enforced by the individual, according as his hand was quick and his eye true, and where order was a variable quantity. House speaks admiringly of 'those citizens of Texas who died with their boots on — a death which every citizen of Texas of those days coveted.'

We must picture him, accordingly, as a man who spent his early years not merely in Eastern colleges and schools, in cotton-farming, and politics, but as the companion and friend of the older generation — 'that intrepid band,' he calls them, 'that made Texas what she is to-day. I make obeisance to them! Nothing daunted them. They tore a principality from a sovereign state and moulded a trackless wilderness into a great commonwealth. These men were the heroes of my childhood; and now when I am growing old and have seen many men and many lands, I go back to them and salute them, for I find they are my heroes still.'

With the younger generation of frontiersmen, House was on close personal terms and for a while, after returning from college and beginning his business as planter, he lived their life. One of the oldest and perhaps the best of these friends was the noted and picturesque Ranger, Captain Bill McDonald, whose career House felt to be so typical of the Texas of those days that he could not rest until it was put into a book.

'I wanted to have Sidney Porter (O. Henry) do it. I had it in mind that he should write twelve stories, each representing some incident in Bill's life. I wrote to Porter, whom I had known while he lived in Texas; but the letter was held back by his mother-in-law until a few weeks afterwards, when she visited him at his summer home at New Ground, Long Island. In the meantime, not having heard from Porter, I got in touch with Albert Bigelow Paine through James Creelman, whom I knew, and he undertook the work. . . . I received a letter from Porter after Paine had undertaken the task, in which he said he would have liked to have done it, for it would have been a "labor of love."

'I was amused at Paine when Captain Bill arrived in New York. Paine and I were waiting for him at the New Amsterdam Hotel, at Fourth Avenue and Twenty-First Street, which was convenient to the Players' Club where Paine intended to stay while writing the memoirs. It was a cold, wet night, and Bill came in with his "slicker" and big Stetson hat. We went upstairs with him. He took off his coat, pulled from one side his .45 and from the other his automatic. He did this just as an ordinary man takes out his keys and knife. I explained to Paine that Bill had to carry his artillery in this way in order to be thoroughly ballasted — that he would have difficulty in walking without it.

'At this time, Paine was writing the life of Mark Twain and was living most of the time at Mark Twain's home, which was then in lower Fifth Avenue. Mr. Clemens invited us to dinner one evening. I could not go because of a previous engagement, but dropped in later. When I arrived, Mark and Bill were playing billiards and it was amusing to see Bill sight his cue just as if it were a rifle and, three times out of four, send his ball off the table. It entertained Mr. Clemens immensely. When we went upstairs Clemens ran and Bill ran after, as if to catch him, but did not do so. Bill winked at me and said, "I believe the old man really thinks I could not catch him." Bill is as lean and as agile as a panther.

'Another time Paine invited Bill and me to take dinner with him at the Players'. I found Bill in the lobby of the hotel without a collar. I said, "Bill, you have no collar on." He reached up his hand and replied, "That's so; I forgot it." However, he made no move to get one. Paine came in a few minutes later and asked if he were ready to go to dinner. Bill replied that he was. Paine then said, "Captain, you have no collar on." Bill remarked, "My God Almighty, can't a man go to dinner in New York without a collar?" Paine did not press the matter further and Captain Bill went to the Club just as he was, much to the amusement of everybody there.

'In my early boyhood I knew many of the Bill McDonald type, although he was perhaps the flower of them all. I knew personally many of the famous desperadoes, men who had killed so many that they had almost ceased to count their victims. . . .

'There were two types of so-called "killers" — one that murdered simply for the pure love of it, and others that killed because it was in their way of duty. Bill McDonald belonged to this latter class. So also did Blue-eyed Captain McKinney of the Rangers, whom I knew in my ranching days in southwest Texas.

'McKinney was finally ambushed and killed, as almost every sheriff of La Salle County was killed during that particular period. Whenever I went to our ranch, I was never certain that I would return home alive. Feuds were always going on, and in some of these our ranch was more or less involved.'

Fort Bend and Brazoria Counties, where the elder House's plantation lay, seemed to be the breeding-place for bad men.

'They were different from the ordinary desperado, and only killed upon insult or fancied insult. Duels were frequently fought on the plantation and were always deadly. I recall two in particular. George Tarver's brother and his room-mate had some slight quarrel concerning the bed they occupied in common. I think the room-mate put his muddy boots on the bedspread. "Here, you can't put those boots on the bed," said George's brother. "I can if I choose," was the reply. There was only one possible outcome to the debate. They went out, stood back to back, counted aloud, walking ten paces, wheeled, fired, and advanced upon one another. They fell dead almost in each other's arms, both having several mortal wounds. They were good friends a quarter of an hour before the duel.

'Another incident I remember. Jim Thompson fancied that some man, whose name I have forgotten, was making fun of him. He demanded that the man get his shotgun. The man hesitated and made a faint apology, which Thompson would not accept. The man then got his shotgun, stepped out of the house, both fired, and Thompson killed him instantly. Thompson was missed by a few inches. They were so close together when they fired that the buckshot went almost like a rifle ball, having no time to scatter.

'I asked Thompson why he was so insistent upon fighting. He said he knew that if he had not called the man to account, he would not have been able to live at Arcola and would have been branded as a coward. It was necessary, he thought, either to kill or be killed, and without further argument....

'I can hardly realize that so short a while ago we lived in an atmosphere where such things seemed proper and even a matter of course. I was often with men whom I knew would surely be killed soon, and perhaps at a time I was with them.

'Governor Hogg [1] did more than any executive in Texas to break up this habit of public killing.... He also broke up strikes during his administration. Captain Bill McDonald, of the Ranger Service, was the instrument he used. Hogg sent word to the leaders that if they continued to uncouple cars, or to do anything that might interfere with the movement of trains, he would shoot holes through them big enough to see through. When Bill conveyed this to the ringleaders and presented himself as the instrument through which it was to be done, lawlessness ceased.

'The nearest I ever came to killing a man was in Breckenridge, Colorado. It was in 1879, when the town was merely a

[1] Governor of Texas from 1890 to 1894.

mining camp. I had gone to Colorado at the request of Whitney Newton, a college friend who was in Breckenridge at that time buying gold dust and sending it to the Denver Mint by special messengers, the express companies refusing to carry it because of the danger of robbery.

'In going to Breckenridge in those days, one left the main line of the railway at the little station of Como, which at that time had but one house. A so-called stage carried one from there to the mining camp. There is no need to describe it, for it was like all other camps of that sort — rough men, and rougher women, gambling, drinking, and killing. I was in a saloon, talking to a man whom I had known in Texas, when the incident I speak of occurred. A big, brawny individual came into the room and began to abuse me in violent terms. I had never seen the man before and could not imagine why he was doing this. I retreated, and he followed. I had my overcoat on at the time and had my hand on my six-shooter in my pocket and cocked it. The owner of the saloon jumped over the bar between us. In five seconds more, I would have killed him. An explanation followed which cleared up the mystery. He had taken me for some one else against whom he had a grudge, and whom he had seen but once. I learned later that he was a popular ex-sheriff of Summit County and that if I had killed him I should have been lynched within the hour.

'It always amuses me when I see the bad men in plays depicted as big, rough fellows with their trousers in their boots and six-shooters buckled around their waists. As a matter of fact, the bad men I have been used to in southern Texas were as unlike this as daylight from dark. They were usually gentle, mild-mannered, mild-spoken, and often delicate-looking men. They were invariably polite, and one not knowing the species would be apt to misjudge them to such an extent that a rough word or an insult would sometimes be offered. This mistake of judgment was one that could never be remedied, for a second opportunity was never given.'

In later years House expressed intense amusement at the oaths and objurgations of Parisian taxi-drivers, which however violent never seemed to result in physical encounter. 'In Texas,' he said, 'it was the reverse. No words were wasted. Frequently the first symptom of mild disapproval would be a blow or revolver-shot. People praise us Southerners for our courteous demeanor; we learned it in a school of necessity.'

III

It would be a mistake to picture House's early life as merely that of the frontiersman. Quiet and unobtrusive as one of the mild-mannered desperadoes he describes, and as courageous, he loved to meet every variety of individual and he had a gift for bringing himself into touch with the Rangers and men of the back districts.[1] He loved the open country, the smell of the camp-fire, and the meal cooked over its embers. But his time was spent mostly in the towns and especially in the capital. He knew the business men of Texas, the editors, lawyers, and educators; later they tried to make him a trustee of the University of Texas. The Mayor of Houston writes to him as 'My dear Ed,' and the Governor signs himself 'Your friend.'

His father had bequeathed to him a social position in the State which he enjoyed maintaining and developing, so that, apart from the frequent journeys that he made to Europe, he came constantly in contact with persons of interest. The home in Houston was the place where nearly every distinguished visitor that came to Texas was entertained, Jeffer-

[1] S. V. Edwards, Captain of Rangers, wrote House, May 24, 1902: 'If you want anything in this new district all you have to do is indicate it. . . . I am with you to a finish in any old thing.'

son Davis among the rest. 'Father counted among his friends,' wrote House, 'the rich and the poor, the humble and the great.'

The younger House followed in his footsteps. After moving to Austin, he built a large house which became the focus of the social and political life of the region.

'The large veranda to the south [wrote House] was the scene, perhaps, of more political conferences than any similar place in Texas. It was there that the clans congregated. I had long made it a rule not to visit, and it was understood that if any one desired to see me, it must be at my home. I did this not only to conserve my strength, but because it enabled me to work under more favorable conditions. I had an office which I was seldom in, and latterly I refused to make any appointments there whatsoever. This necessarily led to much entertaining, and our house was constantly filled with guests. Those days and guests are among the pleasantest recollections of my life.

'Many distinguished people, passing through Austin, from time to time were our guests. Among those that I admired most was Dr. Charles W. Eliot of Harvard. His life and devotion to public service were a revelation to me. He seemed to regulate his life in a way to get the maximum of service for the public good.

'Baron d'Estournelles de Constant of France was another guest whose society I enjoyed while he was in Texas. I remember when leaving me at the station he remarked: "My friends in Paris would be amazed if they could hear me say I was leaving Austin, Texas, with keen regret."'

Apart from the interest which he took in men and in their activities, a further characteristic should be noted: constant and omnivorous reading. This fact is to be deduced less from his correspondence and papers than from the existence of a private library which he developed and enlarged without cessation. It is an illuminating instance of the man's real tastes that when, after the Paris Peace Conference, he had a book-plate made, he omitted in its composition all references to his diplomatic or political career; he chose as salient features above the horse, dog, and camp-fire, the gun and powder-flask, reminders of his early life — an open hearth and books. The books which he read were of all sorts, poetry and essays, but chiefly biography, history, and political science. The main strength of Colonel House in his later political career was, of course, his understanding of human nature, his ability to enter into friendly relations with all types; but it would be a mistake to overlook the strength he derived from books.

In such an atmosphere House began the career in politics which soon became his real vocation, and it was during those years that he underwent the political schooling that prepared him to assume a guiding rôle in national and international affairs. With all the cosmopolitan tastes which he developed by constant travel, and with every intention of entering the arena of national politics, he regarded his life in Texas as a necessary and delightful prologue. Before he could acquire national influence, he must win prestige in his own State. An ardent Democrat, he saw in Texas, with its tremendous influence in the party, an ideal spring-board. A liberal and progressive, he could throw himself into the fight for liberal and progressive legislation which Governor Hogg — 'the inimitable Hogg,' House calls him — was directing. He was ready for the opportunity, which was not slow to knock upon the door.

IV

The year 1892 was one of politico-social ferment in Europe and the United States; the forces of liberal progressivism were everywhere arrayed against reaction. In Texas the struggle was sharp. Governor Hogg, whose courage and force had made him a dominating influence in the State, was the centre of the storm; and because of his advanced ideas, many of which found incorporation in sweeping legislative reforms, he had aroused against himself a powerful group which protested against his nomination for a second term. The fight offered to the young House the opportunity for which he had been waiting. 'House was not nominally manager of the Hogg campaign,' writes T. W. Gregory, later Attorney-General, who was then active in Texas politics, 'but was chiefly responsible for the organization, and to him Hogg owed a large share of his victory.' [1] For ten years House had watched the mechanics of State politics, pondered the mistakes of politicians, developed personal contacts. Already he possessed the technique necessary for the conduct of a campaign, and it was infused with an enthusiasm for reform.

'When I found that the railroads and the entire corporate interests of Texas were combining to defeat Hogg [wrote House], I enlisted actively in his behalf. Although he had known me but a short time, we had many times discussed political ways and means, and he asked me and the then State Health Officer to take charge of his campaign. Later the burden of it fell on me. We selected a committee and got my good friend, General W. R. Hamby, to act as chairman. That campaign was a battle royal. We had no money, and every daily paper in Texas was against us. Hogg's opponent was Judge George Clark, of Waco. When the Clarkites found we had sufficient votes to nominate Hogg, they bolted the convention and nominated Clark. The Republicans endorsed him and we had another hard fight at the election, but Hogg won by a decisive majority. It was a bitter fight and

[1] Manuscript memorandum communicated to the author, August, 1924.

the wounds lasted many years. It was the first firm stand the people of any American State had taken against the privileged classes, and it attracted attention throughout the Union.

'I felt that Governor Hogg's confidence in me was a great compliment, because of my youth and, as far as any one knew, because of my lack of political experience.

'So in politics I began at the top rather than at the bottom, and I have been doing since that day pretty much what I am doing now; that is, advising and helping wherever I might.'

With the success of the Hogg campaign, the political position of House in Texas evidently became assured.

'From 1892 to 1902 [Mr. Gregory writes] House took continual interest in the elections and the administration of Texas.... From the first he displayed that quality which made him of such value to the successive Governors and to President Wilson, an almost uncanny ability to foretell the effects which any measure would have upon public opinion. He was offered by them and declined many positions of honor and power, and he might have been Governor himself....

'In 1894 he managed Culberson's successful campaign. He was again in charge when Culberson was reëlected in 1896. In 1898 and 1900 he directed the successful campaigns of Major Joseph D. Sayers. He was active in the Lanham campaigns of 1902 and 1904.'

Apart from the fact that House himself consistently refused office, one notes especially, in the first place, that he was invariably successful in his political ventures, and in the second place, that he did not rely upon a 'machine,' for House's candidate for Governor was almost invariably opposed by his predecessor. It was a curious manifestation of electoral skill, political judgment, or good luck, according as the reader may choose. Thus in 1894 Governor Hogg and House disagreed upon his successor. The Governor supported the veteran Senator Reagan, who had served in Jefferson Davis's Cabinet; House was behind the State's Attorney-General, Charles A. Culberson. Both were liberals. As always in Texas, the real struggle was at the Democratic Convention, where in addition to Reagan and Culberson two other candidates appeared — one of them as leader of the reactionary forces in the party which had been suppressed by Hogg. House pointed out the danger of division in the liberal camp. All the reform legislation of the past four years was threatened, and it could be saved only if one of the two liberals withdrew.

The final interview between the Governor and his recalcitrant adviser must have been picturesque. Hogg was immense, loud, commanding, with his 'Young man, you'll do as I tell you, if you know what's good for you.' House, of slight build and quiet manner, speaking almost in a monotone, was inflexible in his argument that liberalism in Texas depended upon the union of the progressive forces and that to secure it Reagan must withdraw. It ended with Hogg going to Reagan, who magnanimously agreed to retire in order to avoid the split in the liberal group. 'Texas never produced a nobler citizen than Judge John H. Reagan,' wrote House. 'He was honest, he was able, and he was fearless.'

Doubtless it was easier for House to pass this high estimate upon his erstwhile opponent, in that his retirement paved the way for the nomination of Culberson. Great was the astonishment of the convention when the man chosen to nominate Reagan, after beginning with the conventional eulogy of his subject, proceeded in the peroration to announce his withdrawal and to second Culberson himself. House stayed in the convention until his man had received a majority, then walked over to the club to congratulate him. It was characteristic of his foresight that he had by him the expert accountant, Major Edward Sammons, who could add fractions in his head, so that in the convention (where fractional votes of delegations are common) he knew the result some minutes before the clerks themselves. 'The truth is, as I told you,' wrote Culberson to House, August 17, 1894, 'I could not have won except through your splendid management.'

'This is the only time in my political career [wrote House] that I openly assumed the chairmanship of a campaign. It has been my habit to put some one else nominally at the head, so that I could do the real work undisturbed by the demands which are made upon a chairman.

'The public is almost childish in its acceptance of the shadow for the substance. Each chairman of the campaigns which I directed received the publicity and the applause of both the press and the people during and after the campaign had been brought to a successful conclusion. They passed out of public notice within a few months, or at most within a year; and yet when the next campaign came around, the public and the press as eagerly accepted another figurehead....

'In every campaign I have insisted that the candidate whose fortunes I directed should in no instance make any preëlection promises, either directly, indirectly, or otherwise. I pointed out that it was bad morals and worse politics. The opposition usually promised everything, and it was not infrequent that two men would meet that had been promised the same office.'

Four years later, a similar situation developed when Governor Culberson, after a second term, supported his Attorney-General, M. M. Crane, while House opposed him — largely on the ground that the Attorney-Generalship was becoming a stepping-stone to the Governorship. 'I did not believe it was a good precedent to follow,' he wrote, 'because it would cause an Attorney-General to become something of a demagogue, perhaps unconsciously but nevertheless surely.' He agreed, therefore, to direct the political fortunes of a Texas Congressman who during the entire campaign remained in Washington, Major Joseph Sayers.

'Culberson urged me not to do this [wrote House], declaring that defeat was certain. . . . I did not heed his advice. It looked as if it would be necessary to do what was done in the Culberson-Reagan fight four years before, and that was, to break down the organization which had been built up during the previous administration. This was not disagreeable to me, for I was never a believer in political machines.

'In the Culberson race I had to overcome the Hogg organization which I had helped to build up. In the Sayers-Crane campaign it was necessary to defeat the Culberson organization. . . . In justice to that organization, it pleases me to say that most of them came to offer their services in behalf of Sayers if I demanded it. This I did in no instance, advising them to go where their sympathies and interests lay.

'The two other candidates in this campaign were Lieutenant-Governor Jester and Colonel Wynne of Fort Worth. At the start I assumed that Crane had eighty per cent of the chances for success. However, there were no single counties in Texas he could call clearly his own, while there were many counties that could not be taken from Sayers.

'We had our friends in these Sayers counties call their primaries early. The Crane forces saw what we were doing, but were unable to respond in kind because they had no counties which they were absolutely certain of carrying. The result was that when county after county declared for Sayers and we had practically reached the end of our strength, Crane in a fit of depression withdrew from the race.

'The Dallas *News* called me over the telephone at twelve o'clock at night and said that Crane had sent in his written withdrawal. They asked me if I had any statement to make. I replied I would make one in the morning. I lay awake for nearly an hour, enjoying the victory, and then went back to sleep. In the morning before I arose I reached for one of my pockets, secured an old envelope, and wrote in pencil our opinion of Crane's withdrawal. I took occasion to compliment Crane upon his great patriotism in bowing to the will of the people, and I declared that it was certain that Mr. Jester and Colonel Wynne would not be lacking in as high patriotic motives and that the electorate of Texas could look forward with certainty to their early withdrawal. The result was that both Jester and Wynne began to deny they had any intention of withdrawing. But the deed was done, and Jester actually withdrew within a few weeks and Wynne did not stand the pressure much longer.'

Major Sayers displayed at the moment a gratitude and modesty which the elect of the people are not always prone to manifest.

'Your success in the management of my canvass [he wrote House, May 17, 1898] has been unprecedented in the history of political campaigns. You have taken a disorganized and probably a minority force at the outset and driven from the field the candidate of an organized majority. You have not only done this, but you have also held in line the lukewarm and trivial of our own party and have made them brave, vigorous, confident, and aggressive. Your generalship has indeed been superb, and considering that your own candidate was absent from the State and has not made a political speech outside of his own district in more than twenty years . . .

your success has been without a parallel in Texas politics. . . . I have felt that it would be wise in me to leave the entire matter to yourself.'

The situation was not less piquant in that Culberson, who opposed House's candidate for Governor, was himself running for the United States Senate and asked House to direct his campaign. The latter acceded, and the election of Culberson proved to be the beginning of a senatorial career that lasted a quarter of a century.

V

House's political activities in Texas were by no means confined to elections. Under both Hogg and Culberson he took a constant interest in legislation and gradually came to occupy the same position in the State as he was later to assume in national affairs. He believed first in the necessity of reform, and next in an intelligent and reasoned foundation for reform measures, and he spared no study or effort in the preparation of bills. His pride in the accomplishment of the Texas Governors was great, and perhaps not unjustified.

'House was always a progressive [writes Gregory], and in many respects a pronounced radical, almost invariably being more advanced in his ideas than the persons he was working with. This genuine interest in progressive legislation accounts to a large degree for his interest in politics. He wanted to see advanced ideas placed upon the statute books. It is interesting to note that, although rated as one of the wealthy men of Texas, he was invariably aligned politically on the side of the plain people and against most of those with whom he was socially intimate.'

'In Texas I worked, I think [wrote House], not only for Texas itself, but also in the hope that the things we worked for there would be taken up by the country at large; and in this I was gratified. The great measures which Governor Hogg advocated, like the Railroad Commission, the Stock and Bond law, were largely written into national law later. Texas was the pioneer of successful progressive legislation, and it was all started during Hogg's administrations. . . . I see it stated from time to time that California, Wisconsin, and other States were the first to impress the progressive movement upon the nation. This is not true; Texas was the first in the field, and the others followed.

'Even in municipal reform, Texas led the way. Galveston initiated the commission form of government, and nearly all the other Texas cities of importance followed. It was then taken up in Iowa and I often hear of the "Dubuque idea." As a matter of fact, they took over the idea from Texas.

'Governor Hogg, I think, we will have to place as the foremost Texan, giving Sam Houston the second place. He did not have the fine, analytical mind that Culberson has, but he possessed a force, vision, and courage to carry out, that few men I have known possess. With Hogg it was always a pleasure to enter a fight, for it was certain that there would be no compromise until victory crowned the effort. He was afraid of nothing and gloried in a conflict.

'It is a great pity that he did not go into national life when he left the gubernatorial chair. His proper place would have been in the House of Representatives, although he might have gone to the Senate had he so desired.'

House's relations with Governor Culberson were even closer than with Hogg. Many people have wondered how it was possible for the Colonel later to find a way to make himself indispensable to President Wilson and by what magic he maintained himself as the President's unofficial adviser. There was less of magic than of experience, for during his

Texas days he had been doing exactly the same sort of thing for the Governors.

'During Culberson's terms as Governor [he recorded] I devoted myself as constantly to his administration of public affairs as I have since to Woodrow Wilson's as President. I went to his office at the Capitol nearly every day, and sometimes continued my work there until nightfall.'

House's files are filled with letters like the following: 'Knowing that you have a great deal more influence with the Governor-elect than any one else, and as I ask nothing for myself, I venture to write you in behalf of a friend of mine. Etc.' And from the holder of an appointive office: 'I presume the crisis will approach very soon in matters political. When it comes, please remember me in your prayers.'

The Governor evidently relied upon House both as political confidant and personal friend. So much is made clear by the numerous letters that passed between them.

'You must take charge of things here [wrote Culberson] and organize the work. My room will be open to you at all hours.'

And at the opening of a legislative session:

'It is impossible for me to be in Austin prior to the organization of the legislature, and in fact I do not know when I can get there. This busy time I wish you would seek the Speaker, whoever he may be, and talk with him about the committees on taxation and revenue, finance and contingent expenses.'

'In my day [ran a letter from Culberson, dated February 1, 1895] I have had many friends, but you have been more

Charles A. Culberson

Joseph D. Sayers — James S. Hogg

THREE TEXAS GOVERNORS

than any to me. . . . There is nothing in the way of happiness and prosperity and honor good enough for you in my view, yet I hope for you all that is attainable.'

After Culberson entered the Senate, the friendship evidently persisted, for he writes to House: 'I wish I could see you to-day and have a long talk. I feel that way often these days. . . . Take a pencil and write me confidentially how I stand with the Democrats in the State now. Give me the thing straight, no matter how the chips may fall.' And when a certain bill came up in the Senate: 'What do you think of it? Write me fully and at your earliest convenience, because I want to study it.'

It was Governor Hogg who provided House with the title of 'Colonel,' by appointing him, entirely without the recipient's suspicion, to his staff. The staff officer's uniform could be, and was, bestowed upon an ancient and grateful darkey, but the title proved to be adhesive. There is a certain poetic justice, almost classical in character, to be seen in the punishment thus laid upon House, who spent his life in avoiding office and titles, and during the World War exercised as much ingenuity in escaping European Orders as in his diplomatic negotiations: henceforth, despite his protests, he became and remained 'Colonel House,' or even 'The Colonel.'

With the succeeding Governors, House's relations were not so close, but it is obvious that in 1902 his influence in Texas affairs still dominated. He was the directing spirit in the election of Lanham in that year, who wrote to him in gratitude for 'your discreet advice and promptness to suggest to me. Always say just what you think, for it will be received in the spirit tendered.' And again: 'The fact that your influence was for me has been of incalculable benefit to me. . . . The knowledge of your friendship for me will also deter other entries into the field. . . . I need and appreciate your counsel.' At the same period a letter from Congressman, later Postmaster-General, Burleson indicates that it had become a state tradition for House to draw up the party platform.

'I tender my congratulations upon the skill you have displayed in drafting the platform. . . . It is such a great improvement, from the standpoint of brevity, over those you have given us in the past, that I think the State is to be felicitated upon the prospects of its adoption.'

But the end of this phase of House's career was approaching. 'When another election drew near,' he wrote, 'I refused to interest myself in any way.' We find him asked by both candidates for his advice, which 'I gave to each of them — advice which in no way conflicted.' Apparently the one heeded the advice, while the other 'was so certain of success that he left his campaign to be run in the old slip-shod way, to find himself defeated.'

VI

'I had grown thoroughly tired of the position I occupied in Texas,' wrote House. He had, it is true, the satisfaction of participating in the administration of a great commonwealth; ten years of Texas success had been admirable preparation. They gave him the political experience and prestige he needed. But now he felt equipped for a broader field. 'Go to the front where you belong,' wrote Governor Hogg in 1900.

'During all these years [recorded House] I had never for a moment overlooked the national situation, and it was there that my real interest lay. In 1896 I was ready to take part in national affairs. My power in Texas was sufficient to have given me the place I desired in the national councils of the party.

'The nomination of Bryan in 1896 and the free silver issue made me feel the unwisdom of entering national party politics under such conditions. I therefore bided my time.'

He proved that he knew how to wait. Three national campaigns followed in which the Democratic Party was dominated by Mr. Bryan or by Eastern conservatives, and House stood aloof. In each campaign overtures were made with the purpose of giving him a responsible share in its management, but on each occasion he evaded them. The Democrats must embrace the liberal creed, he insisted, but it must be cleansed of the Bryan financial heresies. None the less, House came more and more into touch with the national Democratic leaders and with Bryan himself, and established a close personal friendship.

'Mr. Bryan's daughter, Grace, had not been well and he wished to spend a winter south. Governor Hogg and I undertook to arrange a home for the Bryans practically within the same grounds as ours. . . . So he, Mrs. Bryan, and the children lived there next to us during the winter, and I had many opportunities to discuss with him national affairs and the coming campaign. It was the winter, I think, of 1898 and 1899.

'I found Mrs. Bryan very amenable to advice and suggestion, but Mr. Bryan was as wildly impracticable as ever. I do not believe that any one ever succeeded in changing his mind upon any subject that he had determined upon. . . . I believe he feels that his ideas are God-given and are not susceptible to the mutability of those of the ordinary human being.

'He often told me that a man that did not believe in "the free and unlimited coinage of silver at 16–1 was either a fool or a knave." He was so convinced of this that he was not susceptible to argument.'

In 1900 Bryan went down to defeat for the second time. In 1904 the quarrels of the Eastern and Western Democrats would have ensured disaster even in the face of a weaker candidate than Roosevelt. 'I returned to Texas,' wrote House, 'discouraged over the prospects of the Democratic Party ever being able to rehabilitate itself.' In 1908 came the third Bryan candidacy and defeat.

But already the Democratic sun was about to rise. The difficulties in the Republican Party, which threatened under Roosevelt, became more obvious in the succeeding administration. They were intensified after Roosevelt's return from travel abroad by his own outburst of discontent at the policies adopted by Mr. Taft, whose selection as President he had himself demanded. The apparent control of the Republican Party by the Old Guard, alleged to be tied up to the 'interests,' the unsatisfied demand for measures of social reform, the threat of the new Progressive movement in the heart of the party itself, pointing to a possible split — all gave hope to the Democrats. That this hope was not entirely illusory seemed indicated by the state and congressional elections of 1910, when the political pendulum swung far in their direction.

Colonel House was watching the opportunity. The great problem was to find a leader. In 1910 he came East from Texas and, like Diogenes, sought a man.

'I began now to look about [he wrote] for a proper candidate for the Democratic nomination for President. In talking with Mr. Bryan, he had mentioned Mayor Gaynor of New York as the only man in the East whom he thought measured up to the requirements.

'I felt sure the nomination should go to the East, and I also felt it was practically impossible to nominate or elect a man that Mr. Bryan opposed. I therefore determined to look Mr. Gaynor over with the thought of him as a possibility.

'I used my good friend, James Creelman, to bring us together. Creelman was nearer to Gaynor than any other man. He arranged a dinner at the Lotus Club, at which only the three of us were present, and it was a delightful affair. The food and the wine were of the best, for Creelman was a connoisseur in this line. The dinner lasted until after twelve o'clock. I had been told that Gaynor was brusque even to rudeness, but I did not find him so in the slightest. He knew perfectly well what the dinner was for, and he seemed to try to put his best side to the front. . . . He showed a knowledge of public affairs altogether beyond my expectations and greater, indeed, than that of any public man that I at that time knew personally who was a possibility.

'I proceeded to follow up this dinner by bringing such friends as I thought advisable in touch with him.

'One day Creelman and I went to the Mayor's office by appointment, to introduce Senator Culberson and Senator R. M. Johnson, editor of the Houston *Post* and Democratic National Committeeman from Texas. . . . I got Culberson and Johnson to second my invitation to Gaynor to go to Texas during the winter and address the Texas legislature. Gaynor consented. When I went to Texas I asked some members of the legislature to introduce a resolution inviting him to address them. This was done and the invitation telegraphed to him. A newspaper reporter of one of the small Texas dailies sent Gaynor a telegram asking him about it. Gaynor telegraphed back something to the effect that he had no notion of coming to Texas to address the legislature and had never heard of any such proposal.'

Reasonable explanation of this surprising *volte-face* on the part of Mayor Gaynor has never been advanced. It may have been that he failed to appreciate the value of the support of Texas — a vital misjudgment, as the Baltimore Convention of 1912 proved. Or it may have been merely another example of the erratic and whimsical nature of the Mayor which did so much to vitiate his undeniably statesmanlike qualities. Colonel House felt certain, in any case, that Gaynor's blindness to the opportunity he had created, indicated a lack of political sagacity.

'I wiped Gaynor from my political slate [he wrote], for I saw he was impossible. I was confirmed in this resolution when Dix was nominated for Governor of New York, which I wanted Gaynor to accept. Some of the Mayor's other friends thought that it would be a mistake to accept the nomination, that to be Mayor of New York meant greater honor and more power than to be Governor of the State. I contended that the people would hesitate to nominate or elect a mayor of a city to the Presidency, but if he were elected Governor he would become the logical candidate.'

House continued his search. He had carefully considered Senator Culberson, and frequently discussed with him the possibility of the presidential nomination. But Culberson's health was poor. Furthermore, House believed that he was too purely a Southerner to make a successful race. The candidate must come, if possible, from the East; he must attract the West by his liberalism.

'I now turned to Woodrow Wilson [House wrote], then Governor of New Jersey, as being the only man in the East who in every way measured up to the office for which he was a candidate.'

House had never met Wilson, but his attention had been called to him by Wilson's ambitious reform programme in New Jersey and the success with which he was driving it through the legislature. He studied his background, which was admirable in that he had no political record and thus started with no political enemies, while his troubled career at Princeton seemed to label him as an opponent of aristocratic privilege. He studied his speeches, which he believed should be classed with the finest political rhetoric extant. There was obviously in him the capacity for moral leadership. Late in the year, House returned to Texas convinced that he had found his man, although as yet he had never met him. 'I decided to do what I could,' he writes, 'to further Governor Wilson's fortunes. I spoke to all my political friends and following, and lined them up one after another. This was in the winter of 1910–1911.'

Thereafter we find House making arrangements to bring the Governor to Texas, in clearing up doubts of his party regularity, in securing the aid of Culberson and striving for that of Bryan. A letter to E. S. Martin, editor of *Life*, makes it plain that House's support of Wilson as yet rested less upon his personal admiration for him than upon the conviction of Wilson's availability.

'The trouble with getting a candidate for President [he wrote, August 30, 1911] is that the man that is best fitted for the place cannot be nominated and, if nominated, could probably not be elected. The people seldom take the man best fitted for the job; therefore it is necessary to work for the best man who can be nominated and elected, and just now Wilson seems to be that man.'

Thus in his work for Wilson, House was serving the Democratic cause rather than the man, whom he had never seen.

One afternoon late in November, Governor Wilson called alone on Colonel House at the Hotel Gotham, where the latter was staying. From that moment began the personal friendship which was so powerfully to affect the events of the following years.

CHAPTER III

BEGINNINGS OF A FRIENDSHIP

It looks to me as if they depended too much upon speech-making and noisy demonstrations, and not enough upon organization.

House to Wilson, August 28, 1912

WOODROW WILSON and Colonel House first met on November 24, 1911, a year before the presidential election. Already House had decided definitely that circumstances made of Wilson the most available candidate, one who could arouse the enthusiasm of the voters in the electoral campaign, and one who, if elected, possessed the courage and the imagination to lead a vigorous reform administration. For these were the two qualities which the Colonel believed essential to a successful President.

Governor Wilson, in his turn, must have found his curiosity piqued by the friendly efforts of the unseen House, word of which had been brought to him during the summer. Without experience in national politics, he knew little or nothing of the career of House in Texas, nor of his relations there with the successive Governors and with Bryan. But he appreciated the skill with which House, working through Senator Culberson, had disposed of the attacks on Wilson's party regularity that threatened to destroy his candidacy even while in the embryonic stage; and he was impressed by the success of his address in Texas which House and Gregory had arranged.

This beginning of what Sir Horace Plunkett later called 'the strangest and most fruitful personal alliance in human history,' should properly have taken place under more dramatic auspices. The small hotel room where they met did not add glamour to the occasion and neither could guess what the political future held in store for them. But each evidently experienced an instinctive personal liking for the other which ripened immediately into genuine friendship. The first impressions of Wilson can only be deduced from the almost affectionate tone of the letters that he wrote to House after the interview. Those of the Colonel have been preserved in more definite form.

'He came alone to the Gotham quite promptly at four [recorded House], and we talked for an hour. He had an engagement to meet Phelan, afterward Senator from California, at five o'clock, and expressed much regret that he could not continue our conversation. We arranged, however, to meet again within a few days, when at my invitation he came to dine with me.

'Each time after that we met at the Gotham, as long as I remained in New York that autumn and winter and whenever he came to the city.

'From that first meeting and up to to-day [1916], I have been in as close touch with Woodrow Wilson as with any man I have ever known. The first hour we spent together proved to each of us that there was a sound basis for a fast friendship. We found ourselves in such complete sympathy, in so many ways, that we soon learned to know what each was thinking without either having expressed himself.

'A few weeks after we met and after we had exchanged confidences which men usually do not exchange except after years of friendship, I asked him if he realized that we had only known one another for so short a time. He replied, "My dear friend, we have known one another always." And I think this is true.'

It is curious to note that it was the personal amiability of Mr. Wilson, rather than his intellectual qualities or political ideas, which impressed House at the outset. He thus reported this first interview to his brother-in-law:

Colonel House to Dr. S. E. Mezes[1]

NEW YORK, *November* 25, 1911

DEAR SIDNEY:

I had a delightful visit from Woodrow Wilson yesterday afternoon, and he is to dine with me alone next Wednesday. . . .

I am glad that he has arrived, and we had a perfectly bully time. He came alone, so that we had an opportunity to try one another out.

He is not the biggest man I have ever met, but he is one of the pleasantest and I would rather play with him than any prospective candidate I have seen.

From what I had heard, I was afraid that he had to have his hats made to order; but I saw not the slightest evidence of it. . . .

Never before have I found both the man and the opportunity.

Fraternally yours

E. M. H.

Writing in November to Senator Culberson, House expressed his thorough satisfaction with Wilson as a candidate and solidified the support which the influential Texan Senator was already prepared to offer. 'The more I see of Governor Wilson the better I like him,' said House, 'and I think he is going to be a man one can advise with some degree of satisfaction. This, you know, you could never do with Mr. Bryan.'

Wilson's amenability to advice at this period permitted an important development which House suggested and carried through. The Governor had taken as his chief text for campaign speeches the political control of privileged interests under Republican Administrations. He had not, however,

[1] Then President of the University of Texas, later President of the College of the City of New York.

emphasized the importance of the real stronghold of privilege and the means by which it might be attacked. If Wilson were to pose as the champion of the 'common man,' he must not overlook the tariff.

'In reading the speeches he was making in 1911 [recorded Colonel House], I noticed he was not stressing the tariff. I called his attention to this and thought it was a mistake. Underwood and Champ Clark were making this a feature. I was sure Wilson could do it better than they, and, since it was becoming a prominent issue of the campaign, I advised striking a strong note on the subject in order at once to call attention to himself as a fit champion of the Democratic cause. I suggested that he let me invite D. F. Houston,[1] who had made a lifelong study of the question, to come to New York for consultation.

'The Governor agreed to the advisability of this move, and Houston came. I gave a dinner at the Gotham [December 7]. The others present besides Governor Wilson were Houston, Walter Page, McCombs, and Edward S. Martin. I seated Houston by Wilson and arranged it so they could talk afterwards. Before dinner I went over the data which Houston had prepared, and added to it and eliminated from it whatever seemed necessary. This data was afterwards given to Governor Wilson, who based his tariff speeches largely on it.'

The effect of Wilson's tariff speeches was destined to put him in the popular mind as the chief antagonist of Republican policies and therefore the natural representative of the Democratic point of view. The dinner at the Gotham also assured the enthusiastic support of Mr. Houston.

[1] Formerly President of the University of Texas; at this time Chancellor of Washington University, and later a member of Wilson's Cabinet.

Dr. D. F. Houston to Dr. S. E. Mezes

WASHINGTON UNIVERSITY
ST. LOUIS, *December* 11, 1911

MY DEAR MEZES:

. . . I have just returned from New York, where I saw a great deal of Mr. House and something of some other people. I will tell you all about it, including the Wilson part of it. Wilson is the straightest thinking man in public life, and can say what he thinks better than any other man. He may not be a great executive officer, but neither was Lincoln, and I am for him. Wilson is clean, courageous, and disinterested. It will be a liberal education to the community to have Wilson do the talking, such of it as he ought to do and will have to do.

I can't tell you how much I enjoyed my visit with Mr. House, especially on the train. He has a vision. I should like to make him Dictator for a while. . . .

Cordially yours

D. F. HOUSTON

II

The various booms for candidates were now beginning to assume definite form. The Wilson movement was regarded more seriously by the practical machine politicians than hitherto, but wiseacres believed that the final struggle would be between Underwood of Alabama and Harmon of Ohio. Both were regarded as representing conservative interests. Champ Clark of Missouri, esteemed a radical, was mentioned by those who realized the difficulty of success with a conservative standard-bearer and who feared that Wilson, after his fight with the New Jersey bosses, would not be inclined to accept the orders of any machine.

Both House and Governor Wilson understood that the approval of Bryan would be a factor essential to the success of Wilson's candidacy, and from the autumn until the time of the nominating convention, House worked ceaselessly to secure it. The intimacy with Mr. Bryan which he had developed in Texas now proved of inestimable value, for he knew exactly which of Wilson's qualities would attract Bryan and therefore deserved emphasis; he laid especial weight upon the fact that the reactionary forces in the Democratic Party were fighting both Bryan and Wilson.

'Before I left for Texas, in December, 1911 [wrote House], it was understood that I should nurse Bryan and bring him around to our way of thinking, if possible. Before Mr. Bryan left New York for Jamaica, he asked me to keep him informed concerning political conditions and to send him such clippings as I thought would be of interest. He said he was taking but few papers: the *World*, the Washington *Post*, I think he mentioned, because I wondered why he took either of them, since they were both so antagonistic to him.

'However, his request gave me an opportunity to send him such clippings as I thought would influence him most in our direction.'

As early as November, we find House writing to Senator Culberson: 'I saw Mr. Bryan just before he sailed for Jamaica and I think I removed several obstacles that were in his mind, and I got him in almost as good an attitude as one could desire.' Thereafter House called Bryan's attention to all the Wilson characteristics likely to attract his approval.

Colonel House to Mr. W. J. Bryan

New York, *November* 25, 1911

Dear Mr. Bryan:

... Governor Wilson called yesterday afternoon and was with me for an hour and a half.

I am pleased to tell you that when I asked him what he

thought of the Supreme Court ruling about which we talked when you were here, he replied in almost the exact terms you used to me. As far as I can see, your positions are identical.

He is also opposed to the Aldrich plan,[1] but I think you are both wrong there. You will have to convert me the next time I see you.

I am inclined to think that Aldrich is trying to give the country a more reasonable and stable system. It seems to me a long way in advance of the money trust which now dominates the credit of the nation.

There is some evidence that Mr. Underwood and his friends intend to make a direct issue with you for control of the next convention, and it looks a little as if they were receiving some aid from Champ Clark and his friends.

My feeling is that we can lay them low, but we must not lag in the doing of it. . . .

Faithfully yours

E. M. HOUSE

NEW YORK, *December* 6, 1911

DEAR MR. BRYAN:

. . . I was called over the telephone last week by a friend of Mr. Hearst, who made an appointment to see me. He said that Mr. Hearst had been out to his country place on Sunday and they had talked about enlisting me in his behalf for the presidential nomination.

I told him that I was thoroughly committed to Governor Wilson and that, even if I were not, I would advise Mr. Hearst to submerge himself for a while and work within the party for a season. After further conversation it developed that he was grooming himself for a dark horse.

[1] For a central bank. Wilson ultimately accepted House's arguments for centralized control of banking which materialized in the Federal Reserve Act. See Chapter VI.

I do not know what effect my talk had, but as yet he has made no formal announcement.

I learned, too, that he was favorable to Underwood or Champ Clark and was against Governor Wilson.

I took lunch with Colonel Harvey yesterday. It is the first time I have met him. I wanted to determine what his real attitude was towards Governor Wilson, but I think I left as much in the dark as ever.

He told me that everybody south of Canal Street was in a frenzy against Governor Wilson and said they were bringing all sorts of pressure upon him to oppose him. He said he told them he had an open mind, and that if they could convince him he was a dangerous man he would do so.

He said that Morgan was particularly virulent in his opposition to Governor Wilson. I asked him what this was based upon, and he said upon some remark Governor Wilson had made in Morgan's presence concerning the methods of bankers and which Morgan took as a personal reference.

He told me that he believed that any amount of money that was needed to defeat Governor Wilson could be readily obtained. He said he would be surprised if they did not put $250,000 in New Jersey alone in order to defeat delegates favorable to his nomination.

We are going to try to devise some plan by which we can use this Wall Street opposition to Governor Wilson to his advantage. If the country knows of their determination to defeat him by the free use of money, I am sure it will do the rest. . . .

If you can make any suggestions regarding the best way to meet the Wall Street attack, I would greatly appreciate it.

From now, letters will reach me at Austin, Texas.

With kind regards and best wishes for all of you, I am

Faithfully yours

E. M. HOUSE

There was in the foregoing letter a cleverness which might escape the too casual reader. In the form of simple narrative Colonel House underlined the activities of Hearst, who was anathema to Bryan, and emphasized Hearst's preference for Clark over Wilson; he then indicated the interest Wall Street exhibited in the defeat of Wilson; and he concluded by an assumption that Bryan would naturally align himself with the forces that stimulated the enmity of Hearst and Wall Street. Mr. Bryan evidently wavered. He had opposed Harmon from the first, as a rank reactionary, and he refused to consider Underwood. If Clark were to have the support of the New York group, Bryan might be drawn to Wilson.

Mr. W. J. Bryan to Colonel House

KINGSTON, JAMAICA
December 28, 1911

MY DEAR MR. HOUSE:

...Am anxious to get back and find out more of the political situation. I shall attend the Washington banquet on the 8th of January and will have a chance to learn how things are shaping up.

I am glad Governor Wilson recognizes that he has the opposition of Morgan and the rest of Wall Street. If he is nominated it must be by the Progressive Democrats, and the more progressive he is the better.

The Washington banquet will give him a good chance to speak out against the trusts and the Aldrich currency scheme.

Yours very truly

W. J. BRYAN

The Washington banquet, to which he referred, gave a good chance to Bryan himself to exhibit his personal generosity, for just before it Wilson's opponents published a letter which, while President of Princeton, he had written to

Mr. Adrian Joline, some five years previous. In the letter appeared this unfortunate sentence: 'Would that we could do something at once dignified and effective to knock Mr. Bryan once for all into a cocked hat.' It would have been only human nature if the Commoner had then and there forsworn Mr. Wilson and all his works. Instead, he did not permit himself to show any pique and at the dinner manifested the utmost cordiality to the Governor, who himself in a speech of rare discretion emphasized the admiration that all good Democrats felt towards Mr. Bryan.

It is possible that his friendliness towards Wilson was enhanced by the controversy between the Governor and Colonel George Harvey, which received much publicity as the result of a spirited exchange of letters between Mr. McCombs and Colonel Watterson. For Bryan distrusted Harvey as a representative of New York interests.

House appreciated keenly the part which Colonel Harvey had played in setting Governor Wilson on the road to political fortune. Harvey had encouraged him to give up his academic career and try the luck of politics; he had influenced the New Jersey machine to give him the nomination for Governor. From the first he had worked with the possibility of the presidential nomination in mind. But the fervor with which he supported Wilson in *Harper's Weekly* raised suspicions in the Middle West that the Governor, through Harvey, was putting himself under obligations to New York financial interests. This was so obvious that House had discussed with his friend E. S. Martin, editor of *Life* and also an associate editor of *Harper's Weekly*, the desirability of a less enthusiastic support of Wilson by the *Weekly*. After House left New York, Colonel Harvey put the question direct to Wilson, as to whether the Governor felt this support to be injurious; the reply of the latter was perhaps too brusque an affirmative. The affair might have passed as a minor incident, had it not been for the emotion displayed in the press by McCombs on the one side and Watterson on the other. It was a moment when the conciliatory influence of House, then absent in Texas, would have proved valuable.

Colonel House to Mr. E. S. Martin

AUSTIN, TEXAS, *January* 18, 1912

DEAR MARTIN:

What a mess we have made with the *Harper's Weekly*-Harvey-Wilson matter. I feel it is largely my fault, and yet I had no thought of it taking any such direction. I would rather be defeated for the Presidency than even be under the suspicion of ingratitude, and, according to Colonel Watterson, Governor Wilson was almost brutal. I hope this is exaggerated.

All I had in mind was for *Harper's* not to be so strenuous, but I never remotely considered wounding Colonel Harvey's feelings nor the breaking of the friendship between Governor Wilson and himself....

Faithfully yours

E. M. HOUSE

Both the Harvey episode and the publication of the Joline letter ultimately worked in favor of Mr. Wilson. In the Middle West and the South the impression became current that the Governor had braved the New York interests in refusing Harvey's support and had displayed honesty in telling Harvey that he did not want it. In Texas Mr. Gregory skilfully utilized a remark of Colonel Watterson, who had taken up the cudgels in favor of Harvey. Watterson spoke rather sneeringly of the 'austere truthfulness of the schoolmaster.' There was in Texas, a rural community, a great free school system and some forty thousand school teachers. Mr. Gregory at once gave full publicity to the phrase, asking whether Wilson should have lied in answer to Harvey's question and whether this was not a time when austere truthfulness was desirable even from a schoolmaster. The next day forty thousand Texan school teachers were behind Wilson.

Bryan, reassured by Wilson's quarrel with Harvey, obviously felt kindly toward him after his own magnanimous treatment of the 'cocked hat' incident. While still warm with the sense of having acted in a rather large way, he continued to receive the commendatory letters of Colonel House that always emphasized, directly or indirectly, the progressiveness of Wilson and the opposition of Wall Street to him.

Colonel House to Mr. W. J. Bryan

AUSTIN, TEXAS, *January* 27, 1912

DEAR MR. BRYAN:

... Another thing that has pleased me beyond measure is your treatment of the Joline-Wilson incident. Your friends all knew your bigness of mind and heart, but it was an object lesson to those who thought of you differently.

I am glad that you have taken the position that you have regarding the Wilson-Harvey controversy. I know a great deal about it, perhaps as much as any one, and I hope that I may have the pleasure of discussing it with you when you come to Texas. . . .

Faithfully yours

E. M. HOUSE

Colonel House to Governor Wilson

AUSTIN, TEXAS, *February* 2, 1912

MY DEAR GOVERNOR WILSON:

... Mr. Bryan is now on his Rio Grande farm, and I have asked him here before he leaves. In the meantime I will continue to keep in touch with him by correspondence.

Please let me know if there is anything you would like to

have suggested to him, for there can be no better place to do this than by the quiet fireside.

I am, my dear Governor,

Your very sincere

E. M. House

Colonel House to Mr. W. F. McCombs

Austin, Texas, *February* 10, 1912

Dear Mr. McCombs:

. . . Mr. Bryan has gone to Tucson to see his son, but he promises to stop over and see me at the first opportunity.

He says he did not stop in going through, on account of reaching Austin at four o'clock in the morning, which he thought a little early for me.

I sent him some clippings favorable to Governor Wilson, which he promises to use and asks for more. If you could think to have sent me things that you would like to have used in the *Commoner*, I am sure that I could arrange it.

I agree with you that Mr. Bryan's support is absolutely essential, not only for nomination but for election afterward; and I shall make it my particular province to keep in touch with him and endeavor to influence him along the lines desired.

He has evolved considerably in our direction, for when I first talked to him in October he did not have Governor Wilson much in mind.

Faithfully yours

E. M. House

Apart from his interest in winning Bryan to the Wilson cause, House directed his energies to the organization of Texas, the forty votes of which were bound to exercise a powerful influence at the Democratic Nominating Convention. As one looks back, it is easy to see that without Bryan and without the steadfast loyalty and enthusiasm of the

Texas delegates, Wilson could not have been nominated. That Colonel House realized this so long before the convention is an indication of the degree to which foresight affected his plans.

When he arrived in Texas, in December, 1911, he found that, despite the success of Wilson's Dallas speech, sentiment had not crystallized in his favor. An energetic campaign would have to be developed if Wilson delegates were to be chosen. 'That campaign,' writes Mr. Gregory, who played an important rôle in it, 'was the greatest work of organization that I remember. Colonel House had various pieces of his old political machinery lying around, which he soon brought together; but we had against us the political forces of the state. The Chairman and thirty of the thirty-one members of the State Executive Committee were opposed to Wilson, the Governor did not favor him, and Senator Joseph W. Bailey stumped the state against him. Only four of the Texas Congressmen favored him.'[1]

House mobilized his friends, who for three months stimulated Wilson sentiment in critical districts, without a blare of trumpets but none the less effectively, it would appear, for by the beginning of March the Colonel was willing to express the expectation of a solid Wilson delegation from Texas. He was the more optimistic in that the Harmon supporters devoted themselves to speeches rather than personal canvassing, a sure method, according to House, of making a noise and losing the fight.

Colonel House to Mr. W. F. McCombs

Austin, Texas, *March* 4, 1912

Dear Mr. McCombs:

. . . Confidentially, I have not been at all satisfied with

[1] Memorandum of T. W. Gregory. Subsequently Governor Campbell, a friend of Colonel House and later a member of the Texas delegation at Baltimore, supported Wilson vigorously in the National Convention.

our organization in this State; but I am glad to tell you that it is now getting in such shape that I feel I can say that you need have no further concern about Texas.

I will not go into details now, further than to let you know that it is in process of complete organization and that we find the sentiment largely for Governor Wilson.

Strangely enough, the opposition are doing practically nothing in an effective way, except to blow in the newspapers. . . .

Faithfully yours

E. M. HOUSE

Colonel House to Governor Wilson

AUSTIN, TEXAS, *March* 6, 1912

MY DEAR GOVERNOR WILSON:

I am pleased to tell you that we now have everything in good shape in Texas and that you may confidently rely upon the delegates from this State.

We may or may not have a presidential primary, but the result will not be changed.

In two or three weeks our organization will be perfected, and then I shall leave for the East where I shall have the pleasure of seeing you.

Faithfully yours

E. M. HOUSE

Mr. Wilson replied that House's news brought great cheer when he most needed it. The Governor had been discouraged by the news from Kansas and Michigan, where he felt the Wilsonian forces ought to have won, and he declared that the Colonel's success in Texas and the knowledge that he would soon be East to offer his counsel put him in heart again. Wilson was troubled by the suspicion of a combination against himself of Clark, Underwood, and Harmon, with a division of territory, and by what he regarded as evidence of its being financed from Wall Street. And he expressed the fear that the 'dear old party' might become the tool of reactionaries.

III

In April Colonel House returned to New York, satisfied that Texas was safe for Wilson, but disturbed by the failure of the Wilson forces to make the progress elsewhere that had been expected. For the political situation had changed since autumn. The conservative leaders, who favored Harmon or Underwood, appreciated the strength of liberal feeling in the party and realized that Wilson by assuming the leadership of the liberals might run away with the nomination. To defeat him the Harmon, Underwood, and Clark supporters combined to concentrate in each State upon the strongest candidate opposed to Wilson. The result was that the threat of Champ Clark, in particular, began to appear dangerous. Bryan had endorsed him as a liberal and the conservatives preferred him to Wilson, for he was a 'practical politician' with whom they could negotiate. At least he would serve to deadlock the convention against Wilson. 'Nobody regards Clark seriously,' wrote House to Gregory, 'except as a means to defeat Wilson.'

After a few days in the East, House recognized the strength of the combination that was putting Clark forward. Pennsylvania went for Wilson, but the South and the Middle West were cold. 'Illinois hit us a pretty bad jolt,' wrote House to Burleson on April 11. 'It was not that we expected to carry it, but we did not expect to lose by so heavy a vote.' A few days later, Nebraska declared for Champ Clark. The Colonel recorded that at the end of May it looked as if the anti-Wilson forces would triumph. Bryan remained neutral as between Clark and Wilson.

'I had seen Mr. Bryan in New York [wrote Colonel House]

almost immediately upon arrival in April, and had persuaded him to declare his belief that either Clark or Wilson would be an acceptable candidate. I could not get him to go further than this, although I pointed out that all his enemies were in the combination to defeat Wilson.

'Mrs. Bryan helped me in getting a favorable decision for Woodrow Wilson. I remember I breakfasted with the Bryans at the Holland House, and every argument I made in behalf of Wilson was supplemented by Mrs. Bryan.'

The Commoner refused as yet, however, definitely to commit himself, and Colonel House could not avoid the suspicion that Mr. Bryan regarded it as a good Democratic year and would not scorn the nomination.

Colonel House to Senator C. A. Culberson

NEW YORK, *May* 1, 1912

DEAR SENATOR:

... It looks to me as if the opposing candidates might again be Bryan and Roosevelt. In that event, I think Roosevelt would beat him. He would get his share of the progressive vote and most of the conservative vote. Bryan thinks he could beat Roosevelt, but in my opinion, he could beat Taft more easily.

Wilson's best chance now, I think, is the fear of many people that Bryan will be nominated and the further fear that Hearst may succeed in landing Champ Clark and then dominate the Administration.

Faithfully yours

E. M. HOUSE

As May passed, prospects appeared brighter; and the result of the Texas convention, which, as House had predicted, was wholly in Wilson's favor, gave impetus to the cause. The Colonel relied upon the forty delegates from Texas to stand firm, and his confidence was justified. He told them to consider no second choice. Mr. Gregory records that shortly before the convention, 'Tammany made an offer to the Texas delegation that, if they would drop Wilson, Tammany would support Culberson; but the delegation, which included Culberson himself, simply laughed at them.'

House also relied upon the fact that many delegates instructed for Clark or Underwood approved Wilson in their hearts and would vote for him as soon as it became obvious that their candidates could not be chosen and they were released from their pledges. He now advised Wilson to proceed carefully, for he felt that Bryan, influenced by his wife, was more favorable, and he feared the tactical mistake which at the last moment so frequently spoils a candidate's chances.

Colonel House to Governor Wilson

BEVERLY, MASSACHUSETTS
June 7, 1912

DEAR GOVERNOR WILSON:

I have a letter from Mr. —— this morning, telling me that he has suggested some things to you, which I hope you will not consider. . . .

In my opinion, everything is being done that should be towards influencing the delegates in your behalf. Plans for organizing them into an efficient and effective force at Baltimore are already under way, and will be much more potent than anything Mr. —— has suggested.

If I see the situation rightly, there has never been a time when your nomination seemed so probable as now, and if I were you I would move cautiously and do nothing further for the present.

I do not doubt but that a large part of your time has been taken up, as indeed has Mr. McCombs' and mine, by people giving advice which, if acted upon, would defeat our ends.

Do you recall what I told you concerning the conversation I had with Mrs. B.? I have a letter this morning from her containing this most significant sentence: 'I found Mr. B. well and quite in accord with the talk we had.' [1]

It encourages me to believe that Mr. Clark will never receive that influence and that you will. It also means that he [Bryan] will not want the nomination unless two Republican tickets are in the field.

If your engagements will permit, I hope that we may have the pleasure of seeing you here before the 25th.

Faithfully yours

E. M. House

Governor Wilson replied in a manner that would have surprised some of his later critics. He not merely thanked House for his advice, but confessed that he stood in need of it, for at first he had been inclined to follow Mr. ——'s suggestion. Not only did he admit he was wrong, but he promised not to act independently in the future.

IV

Colonel House was not at the Baltimore Convention which nominated Wilson. Because of his health he was accustomed to flee American summer heat, and even the importance of this particular crisis did not prevent him from following his regular habit, which was to spend the summer in Europe. When the convention met, he was on the ocean.

This absence did not eliminate his influence. In Texas he had been present at only three of the nominating conventions that chose the candidates he had supported; he was accustomed to lay his plans so carefully that they could be clearly understood and definitely executed by his lieutenants. Thus we find him, during the weeks that immediately preceded the convention, in close consultation with Mr.

[1] Evidently suggesting that Bryan was veering away from Clark.

McCombs and spending long hours with the leaders of the Texas delegation, which was promised the rôle of Old Guard in the approaching battle.

'On June 1 [the Colonel recorded] McCombs and I went to Beverly, Massachusetts, where we had taken a house for the summer. McCombs was so run down in health that I did not think he would be able to go to the Baltimore Convention on June 25. Governor Wilson thought I was mistaken about this and that he was tougher than his appearance indicated. I was sure, however, he needed the rest; and I was also sure he needed what suggestions and coaching I might be able to give him in regard to handling conventions, because he had never had any experience in such matters.'

In these consultations Mr. T. W. Gregory and Mr. T. A. Thomson of the Texas delegation played a prominent part. They were to hold the fort against Clark, who had already secured a majority of the delegates and who, if his strength did not weaken on the early ballots, threatened to gather enough more to obtain the necessary two thirds. Underwood was strong in the South, but among the Southern delegations there was bitter opposition to Clark which the Texans were able to capitalize.

'It looked to me [recorded House] as if Wilson had a good chance, but nothing more. I urged both Gregory and Thomson to use their influence with the Texas delegation to hold it as a unit and to stay in the fight in the same way we had been accustomed to do in Texas. The history of the Convention records the work of those forty delegates from Texas, without whose loyalty and intelligent support the President could never have been nominated.'

What House advised was to assign to each influential

member of the Texas delegation the task of working upon some other delegation with whom he had personal relations, and to secure mutual understanding that in no contingency would either yield to pressure from the Clark forces. This plan had evidently long been in Colonel House's mind, for as far back as December, 1911, he had written to a Southern friend, William Garrott Brown: 'It goes without saying that we will make no move adverse to Mr. Underwood in his own State, but we will expect our friends to see that delegates are selected there not unfriendly to Governor Wilson for second choice.' Mr. Gregory thus describes his own activities:

'Champ Clark had by far the largest convention vote of any of the candidates, and it was evident that he must first be disposed of before any of the other candidates would have a chance. In these circumstances the Wilson people made airtight agreements with a sufficient number of delegates instructed for candidates other than Clark, to the effect that under no conditions would any parties to the agreement vote for Clark; there was no agreement as to what would be done after Clark had been eliminated. The delegates involved in this agreement constituted more than one third of the convention vote, and against this stone wall the forces of Champ Clark battered in vain.'

Colonel House to Governor Wilson

BEVERLY, MASSACHUSETTS
June 20, 1912

DEAR GOVERNOR WILSON:

I am sorry beyond measure that it is my fate not to be able to be at the Baltimore Convention. Both my inclination and my deep interest in your success call me there, but I am physically unequal to the effort.

However, I have done everything that I could do up to

now to advise and to anticipate every contingency. I have had interviews with many delegates, and some of my warm personal friends on the Texas delegation will be here to-morrow in order to have a final word.

Colonel Ball, who is perhaps the most forceful man on the Texas delegation and the one best equipped for floor tactics, has wired me that he will be in Baltimore to-day.

I have told Mr. McCombs of those upon whose advice and loyalty he can lean most heavily, and now I feel that I can do nothing further excepting to send my good wishes.

If Mr. Clark's strength crumbles on the second and third ballot — which I hope may be the case — then I believe that you will be nominated forthwith; but if, on the other hand, his vote clings to him and he begins to get the uninstructed vote, he may be nominated.

We are sailing for England on the Cunard S.S. *Laconia* on the 25th at six o'clock, but Mr. McCombs has promised to tell me of the result by wireless; and if you are nominated I shall return almost immediately.

I shall at least have the benefit of the trip over and back, and that is one of the reasons I am going on the 25th rather than waiting until after I know the result. . . .

If you will permit me to act as your friend in an advisory capacity, it will give me pleasure to use my every effort in your behalf.

With kind regards and best wishes, I am

Faithfully yours

E. M. House

Beverly, Massachusetts
June 23, 1912

Dear Governor Wilson:

T. W. Gregory and T. A. Thomson, two of the delegates from Texas, have just left me.

I have never known two better organizers than they are,

and I have outlined to them in detail what to do at Baltimore with Mr. McCombs' approval.

I am afraid that if thorough organization is not had, we will find fifty of our friends working upon one delegation and perhaps no one attending to another delegation of equal importance.

I have suggested that the forty men from Texas be divided into four units of ten, and each given one of the doubtful Southern States. The same methods should be pursued with New Jersey, Pennsylvania, Wisconsin, and other loyal delegations. In this way the work becomes effective and good results follow.

I have urged them to make friends with the delegations to which they are assigned, to influence and entertain them in one way and another until the convention is ended. . . .

Faithfully yours

E. M. House

On June 25 Colonel House sailed, and on the same day the Democratic Convention met at Baltimore. Its history has been told many times and we may merely remind ourselves of the bitter struggle between the liberal and conservative forces, and of how Clark, originally put forward to break the Wilson movement, soon threatened to run away with the convention. His strength did not crumble, as House had hoped, after the first few ballots and, if we may believe Wilson's secretary, Joseph P. Tumulty, even McCombs despaired. At this juncture appeared the value of the plans made by House during the winter and spring. The Wilson delegates, at first in a small minority, stood firm, led by the band of forty from Texas. Gradually, as the cause of Underwood appeared hopeless, Wilson began to pick up votes from the delegations of which he was second choice; the Clark forces weakened. And at the critical moment the arguments that House had so constantly pressed upon

Bryan, during the winter and spring, bore fruit. The New York delegation, dominated by Tammany, attacked Wilson and supported Clark with such vigor that Bryan was finally convinced that Wilson must be the right man. His intervention proved decisive, and on the forty-sixth ballot Wilson received the nomination.

Colonel House had not yet reached England when the issue was determined.

'I received the notification of the nomination of Wilson by wireless, one day out from Liverpool. It was from H. H. Childers and read, "Wilson wins." It came at ten o'clock at night. Dr. Arthur Hadley of Yale and some others were playing cards at the time. I told Hadley that perhaps he would be glad to know that Woodrow Wilson had been nominated at Baltimore. I was sadly mistaken in my supposition that the knowledge of this would give him pleasure, for I never saw a man who evinced less enthusiasm.'

V

The real struggle of 1912 was for the nomination. It would have been far otherwise had the Republican Party remained united and presented its normal strength at the polls; in such a case the election of Wilson would have been difficult, if not impossible. But the dissensions which during the spring had already threatened Republican solidarity culminated in Republican disaster at the Chicago Convention, where Taft was nominated; for the adherents of Roosevelt bolted, organized the Progressive Party, and in August nominated their hero.

Most well-informed observers, while they conceded the personal popularity of Roosevelt, believed that the lack of an established organization would certainly prevent his election; nor did they believe that Taft, now deprived of the support of the most vigorous elements in the party, would prove a dangerous candidate. Wilson might count upon the approval of many regular Republicans who detested Roosevelt and who realized that the surest means of defeating him would be to elect Wilson. The issue proved the accuracy of such prognostications. Generalizations are usually misleading, but in this case the historian may venture the assertion that in 1912 Roosevelt put Wilson in the White House.

Colonel House was among those who believed that the result of the split in the Republican Party would be certain Democratic victory. Hence he did not cut short the travels that he had planned for the summer of 1912, which included Sweden, Finland, Russia as far east as Moscow, Germany, France, and England. In August, however, he returned ready to throw himself into the campaign, which soon captured all his time and energy. He was delighted with the liberalism and eloquence displayed in Wilson's speeches, which gained in effectiveness as the campaign progressed; and he found a double assurance of success in the vehemence with which Roosevelt emphasized the differences between Republicans and Progressives, in his virulent attacks upon Taft.

'In my opinion [he wrote Wilson, soon after his return] the greatest asset that we have is the scare that Roosevelt is giving the conservative Republicans, and I have found that my efforts in proselyting prominent Taft adherents have been successful whenever I have been able to show that a vote for Taft is a half-vote for Roosevelt.'

Colonel House to Governor Wilson

BEVERLY, MASSACHUSETTS
August 28, 1912

DEAR GOVERNOR WILSON:

... I am trying to get our friends to organize properly in Vermont and Maine. It looks to me as if they depended too much upon speech-making and noisy demonstrations, and not enough upon organization.

I have suggested that they get a committee in every precinct, whose business it shall be to get out the Democratic vote and influence as many of the Republican votes as possible.

Upon these committees I have suggested placing a Taft Republican who is supporting you for one reason or another, a progressive Republican who does not want to vote for Roosevelt and cannot vote for Taft, and the best Democratic organizer that can be obtained.

If this method is followed, not only in Vermont and Maine, but in every State in the Union, there will be nothing left of your opponents that will be worth while.

Your very sincere

E. M. HOUSE

What interested House chiefly was not so much the election of Wilson, which he regarded as certain, as the question of harmony between the Democratic leaders. Fortunately, the influence of Mr. Bryan was not among the disturbing elements. He was naturally satisfied with the part he played at Baltimore, where he had abdicated his own pretensions, and his attitude toward the candidate whose success he had done so much to assure was one of benevolence. Obviously he was not inclined to interfere with the management of the campaign.

Mrs. W. J. Bryan to Colonel House

FAIRVIEW, *July* 27, 1912

MY DEAR MR. HOUSE:

Have been in a mad struggle with mail lately — my desk is cleared and I celebrate by writing a line to you. Your letter was faithfully delivered by Mr. Thomson, and the correctness of your diagnosis was even then proven. I thought of you and Mrs. House several times while the fight was on. I knew how anxiously you were awaiting bulletins on shipboard.

Just between us three, it was a remarkable fight. I was never so proud of Mr. Bryan — he managed so well. He threw the opponents into confusion; they could not keep from blundering and he outgeneralled them at every point. After all their careful planning, he wrested the power from their hands. Under the circumstances I am sure the nomination went to the best place and am entirely satisfied with the result. Will said all the time he did not think it was his time, and when we found the way things were set up we were *sure* of it.

The people through the country regard him as a hero — he is filling Chautauqua dates in larger crowds than he has ever had, and is perfectly well. The mail! The secretary told me yesterday there are several thousand Baltimore letters still unopened, and it is almost impossible to handle the daily increase. I am not telling you these things to boast, but because I know you are interested to know how he is getting on since he has been 'buried' again.

As to the possibilities in case of Democratic success: I am not sure what he would do. I know he dislikes routine work exceedingly, but believe he would do anything to help the cause. . . .

Did you read the platform? Will got in a provision on national committeemen that will eliminate the whole ring four years from now. — This letter seems full of politics, but we are all interested. My best wishes for a safe return and kindest regards to Janet, Mrs. H. and yourself.

Sincerely yours

MARY B. BRYAN

Reassured by the friendly attitude of Mr. Bryan, Colonel House was none the less disturbed by the lack of organization in the Democratic campaign and the contentions that had arisen among the campaign leaders. 'They are making the usual campaign of speeches, publicity, and noisy demonstrations,' he wrote Mr. Houston, 'and if it were not for the split in the Republican Party the result would be fatal.' It was true that the Republicans and Progressives firmly refused to permit the Democrats to defeat themselves. But if the latter were so torn by discord at the moment of victory as to find it impossible to organize a harmonious administration, there would be small profit in victory.

Much of the difficulty resulted from the illness of Mr. McCombs, who had been chosen Chairman of the National Committee and who during the summer found himself unable to stay at Headquarters. Mr. McAdoo, Vice-Chairman, took active control of affairs. Feeling between the two men and their adherents became scarcely short of envenomed. It was the first news that reached House upon his arrival from Europe.

'We landed at Boston [he recorded] and motored to Beverly, where messengers began to come telling of discord and demoralization at Democratic Headquarters. Those that brought their tales first were adherents of McCombs, and my sympathy was largely with him.

'McCombs himself came from the Adirondacks to Boston for a conference with me. He told a story of perfidy that was hardly believable. McAdoo was the ringleader and he, McCombs, was the victim.'

For Colonel House the important matter was party harmony. Unable to decide exactly where the trouble lay, although to begin with he sympathized with McCombs, he was determined that the first Democratic Administration in twenty years should not be ruined at the outset by the scandal of a public quarrel. The initial step was to prevent the resignation of McCombs, which he threatened at regular intervals. The next was to come into touch with McAdoo.

Colonel House to Governor Wilson

BEVERLY, MASSACHUSETTS
September 2, 1912

DEAR GOVERNOR:

McCombs is seriously thinking of resigning, and may do so to-morrow.

There are reasons why his resignation at this time would be a serious blow to the cause. I cannot go into an explanation here, but you would readily understand the reason if all the facts were before you....

Mr. McAdoo has asked me to go to Maine, which I shall do to-morrow night or Wednesday morning; and when I return I should be glad to come to New York if you will let me know when you will be there.

Your very sincere
E. M. HOUSE

'I returned to New York [wrote Colonel House] as soon as the weather would permit, and had a conference with Woodrow Wilson. I asked if he knew of the feud that was going on between McAdoo and McCombs, and I indicated my sympathy for McCombs. At that time I knew McAdoo but slightly, having met him but twice. Wilson asked me not to make up my mind about the matter until I had learned the ins and outs of it by personal contact at Headquarters.

'I afterwards learned the wisdom of this advice, for I had not been in New York more than two weeks before I knew that there was another side. Later I found that it was almost wholly McCombs' fault and that McAdoo was scarcely to blame at all. McCombs was jealous, was dictatorial.... He was not well enough to attend to the campaign himself, and he could not sit by and allow McAdoo to carry on the work and get a certain amount of newspaper publicity. This latter was particularly galling to McCombs.'

At this moment (September 25, 1912), Colonel House began to make those detailed daily memoranda which, taken together, form a diary the historical importance of which can hardly be overstated. Every night, with rare exceptions, during the following seven years, he dictated his record of the events of the day, while his recollection was fresh and definite and with an astounding frankness of expression.

From the first of these memoranda it appears clear that during these weeks his main task was always the composing of quarrels. It was a function to which he had become accustomed from his days at school, where, according to a youthful friend, he loved to incite disputes between his schoolmates in order to have an opportunity to settle them.

In September and October there were not merely the difficulties between the leaders at National Headquarters which must be alleviated, but also the customary disagreement between the National Committee and Tammany Hall. The New York organization had fought the nomination of Wilson at Baltimore and would evidently not 'tote fair' in the election unless Wilson agreed actively to support the New York State ticket; and this Wilson would not do if it meant endorsing the Tammany boss, Charles F. Murphy. As always, there was the danger that Tammany would trade its support of the presidential candidate against Republican willingness to permit the election of the Democratic candidate for Mayor of New York City the year following. And this danger was increased by Wilson's attack upon the bosses and his refusal to approve the renomination of Governor Dix, which Murphy demanded.

At National Headquarters there were divided counsels. McAdoo, who may have himself hoped to be nominated for Governor, was willing to fight the bosses; McCombs, both because of his feud with McAdoo and his political affiliations, was willing to endorse them heartily. House disliked the bosses and wrote on September 28, 'I believe McAdoo would be good material for the Governorship.' But he held that an open breach with Tammany must be avoided at all costs.

'The New York situation is acute [wrote House, on September 25], and it is necessary for some definite policy to be decided upon. The break between Murphy and National Headquarters is becoming wider each day, and the newspapers are printing numerous false interviews which make it yet wider. I am anxious to hold the party together, so that every available means may be used for the common good. My dislike of Tammany and its leaders is perhaps stronger than that of Governor Wilson; yet, having had more political experience, I am always ready to work with the best material at hand. My idea is to have them decide upon some unobjectionable Tammany man for Governor of New York who would not bring discredit upon the party....

'There is much jealousy and back-biting at Headquarters, and tales are fetched and carried without number until all harmony is lost. McAdoo and others are anxious to give me a room for my personal use. I do not desire a room. They want to give me half of O'Gorman's.[1] Every one offers me some one else's room. McAdoo continues most cordial and belies the charges of his accusers....'

Wilson, fulminating against the bosses, was on the point of attacking Murphy and Dix by name and insisting that the New York nominating convention formally repudiate the control of Tammany Hall. It would have meant an open conflict between the National and the City and State organizations.

[1] United States Senator from New York.

'Governor Wilson [House wrote, September 28] came in last night from New England, leaving at twelve. He asked me to take him out in our motor for a conference. He was particularly anxious to discuss the State situation before making his speech at McCombs' dinner. McAdoo is urging him to come out actively against Dix and Murphy. I urged him not to do this. McCombs is the only link between the bosses and Wilson. The Governor's inclination is to go after them. He finally agreed to give out a letter Monday without mentioning either by name. . . .

'*October* 2: The New York situation is still in a muddle. . . .'

The solution finally discovered by Colonel House was not without its elements of humor. At least it prevented an open rupture between the National Democratic organization and the New York organization. Mr. Murphy, leader of Tammany, agreed to the demand of Wilson, edited by House, that no man should dictate to the nominating convention what it must do. Quietly he permitted the impression to percolate that Governor Dix need not be renominated. At the convention, he (according to a New York correspondent) 'once Boss Murphy, now metamorphosized by the talisman of college men's ideals into Leader Murphy, said nothing, gave no orders — when nominations for Governor were called reported himself "present, not voting!"' The convention, thus freed from the despotism of the bosses, repudiating Dix, proceeded to nominate the Honorable William Sulzer, the purest product of the New York City organization. 'The advocates of the bossless convention had won and nominated a Tammany brave.'

Thus House saved Wilson from the tactical mistake of a quarrel with Tammany, which would at this moment certainly have failed to dislodge the bosses and must have produced merely disorganization; at the same time he persuaded Murphy ostensibly to yield to Wilson's leadership.

Press reports gave him full credit: 'Just what the wise Texan whispered into the Princeton ears no man may know. But the club did not fall on the Tammany head. . . . The good ship is sailing strong and no breakers ahead. Without Tammany New York was gone. With Tammany New York City will give Wilson the largest vote ever recorded for a Democratic candidate. . . . The story of Democratic success is almost ready to be told. Only one thing can prevent — Wilson himself. If he makes no blunder! He almost did in the matter of New York — but Ed House is still here.' [1]

Later, when the leadership of Wilson in the party had been assured, House urged a vigorous assault upon Tammany; but a less propitious moment than the autumn of 1912 could not have been selected.

More difficult, however, was the situation caused by the physical and nervous condition of the Democratic Chairman. Much of House's time and energy was consumed in quieting the suspicions of Mr. McCombs, in persuading him to avoid indiscretions, and to forget enmities. It was not the first or the last occasion upon which Colonel House served the cause of harmony by assuming the ungrateful rôle of buffer.

'*October* 3: McCombs and McAdoo had an interview, and I hope that a more amicable relation will follow. The Governor was particularly anxious to have this brought about, and said he knew that I could do it if it could be done at all.

'*October* 8: I went to see McCombs. I do not like his affiliations or methods. He is very secretive and will only interview one person at a time, although he seems to have no secrets from me. He suggested getting rid of McAdoo by giving him the presidency of some railroad out West, which he said he could secure for him. . . .

'*October* 13: McCombs is very emphatic that no campaign promises, either direct or indirect, have been made.

[1] Press despatch by Pat Lay, New York, October 4, 1912.

I talked to Governor Wilson, urging him also not to make any promises. He says he has not, but he does not altogether trust McCombs in this direction....

'*October* 24: McCombs is in a panic, and believes there is a chance of losing New York, Illinois, and Wisconsin....

'*October* 25: I went to Headquarters at eleven and met McCombs as I was leaving.... He was countermanding everybody's orders, without regard to authority.... McAdoo tells me that the Governor thinks it best not to address him [McAdoo] in future, and McAdoo asked him not to consider him in any way. He said he would do the best he could until the campaign was over, and then he wished to be forgotten. I did not tell McAdoo that the Governor was doing this at my suggestion and because I am afraid of an open scandal between McCombs and himself....

'*October* 26: Very little is being done at Headquarters excepting routine work. I went over each department, after seeing McAdoo at nine at his hotel. McCombs is in conference most of the time with old-style politicians. The whole character of the callers has changed since he took charge, and for the worse. I fear Governor Wilson will have trouble on account of connections made at this time....

'*October* 31: McAdoo is not in evidence at all, and has almost effaced himself to secure harmony....'

VI

At the height of the campaign the country was shocked by the news that a fanatic had shot Mr. Roosevelt, who was on a speaking tour, and that, while he would recover from the wound, his personal campaign was at an end.[1] Colonel House, in opposition to the members of the Democratic

[1] Mr. Roosevelt, whose life was saved by the manuscript of his speech and his glasses' case in his breast pocket, recovered so rapidly that he was able to address an enthusiastic rally in Madison Square Garden just before the election.

Campaign Committee, insisted that Mr. Wilson should cancel his speaking engagements, for it did not seem quite sporting for him to continue his vigorous campaign so long as his most redoubtable adversary was laid low.

'*October* 18: Everything is upset to-day over the attempted assassination of Theodore Roosevelt. . . .

'I telephoned Governor Wilson at Princeton while Burleson was here, urging him to cancel all engagements until Roosevelt was able to get out again. Wilson was at first doubtful, but wrote out a statement, which he read to me over the telephone, following my suggestions as to what to say. All of the Campaign Committee were against me in this. They wanted the Governor to continue speech-making, and so advised him. My thought was that if he continued to speak after T. R. had been shot, it would create sympathy for T. R. and would do Wilson infinite harm. The situation is a dangerous one and needs to be handled with care. The generous, the chivalrous, and the wise thing to do, so it seems to me, is to discontinue speaking until his antagonist is also able to speak. I am glad Wilson sees it as I do. He suggested that we might delay a decision until to-morrow and get the opinion of the full Committee, but I disagreed with this and said that the delay would be disadvantageous. Then, too, it would make it embarrassing if the Committee differed from him, as they certainly would, for their individual opinions have already been expressed. Burleson thinks I took too much responsibility in advising contrary to the rest of the Committee. . . .'

The Colonel's opinion carried the day, and Wilson's speaking tour was abandoned. The effect of this gesture, combined with the exchange of cordial telegrams of sympathy and appreciation between Wilson and Roosevelt, was certainly not disadvantageous to Wilson's campaign.

'The best politics,' House used to say, 'is to do the right thing.'

The attack upon Roosevelt immediately drew House's attention to the danger of a similar attempt upon Wilson's life, and he bethought himself of his old Texas friend the Ranger, McDonald. Captain Bill would furnish complete protection and ideal company for the Governor. There was also the advantage that McDonald, as House well knew, would waste no time in discussion as to whether the trip from Texas were worth while or what preparations he ought to make.

Colonel House to Captain McDonald

[Telegram]

NEW YORK, *October* 15, 1912

Come immediately. Important. Bring your artillery.

E. M. HOUSE

Captain McDonald to Colonel House

[Telegram]

QUANAH, TEXAS, *October* 16, 1912

Coming.

McDONALD

Colonel House to Dr. D. F. Houston

NEW YORK, *October* 22, 1912

DEAR DOCTOR HOUSTON:

. . . I got the Governor to let me send for Bill McDonald after the T. R. assault. I merely wired Bill to come at once. . . . He thought I was in trouble, so he borrowed a shirt from one of his friends, boarded the train without money (which he borrowed on the way), and landed here in a little over two days after leaving Quanah.

I took him from the station to Headquarters, and it happened that Judge Parker and Norman Mack were in McCombs' rooms when I brought Bill in. He had on his big white Stetson and a four days' growth of beard, and I need not tell you he created a sensation....

Mrs. Wilson told me on Sunday that she had slept better Saturday night than at any time since T. R. was shot. They all seem pleased with Bill.

I arranged to keep him out of the papers, and he has refused to open his mouth to any one about anything. I told him when he came not to say a word to anybody, and he is carrying it out literally. I heard a reporter ask him who I was, and that is the only time I have heard him speak. He told the fellow that he was a stranger in New York and did not know.

The mayor and police of one town that I know tried to disarm Bill after he was out of the Ranger Service and had no right to carry arms, but they were unable to accomplish their purpose. I would like to see the New York police try it.

Faithfully yours

E. M. House

Wilson and his protector became fast friends. A fortnight after McDonald's arrival, House noted:

'I arose at seven and went over to see Governor Wilson and Captain Bill at the Hotel Collingwood. They were just leaving for the train, but we had a few minutes' conversation. Bill said the Governor was the finest fellow in the world, and the Governor seemed equally pleased with Bill and said he was taking good care of him.'

After the election McDonald returned to Texas, with keen appreciation of his Eastern experiences, but without reluctance to leave the hard city pavements. He once complained to Colonel House: 'Ed, I get awful tired of walking on these rocks.' He was not entirely uncritical of the protection provided eminent public servants by the Government.

'*November* 8: Old Bill arrived [recorded House], and after talking with him I think it is best for him to return home for the present. The Wilsons were sorry to see him leave. He looked over the secret service men to see if he thought them fit. He told me that they did well enough, but he did not like their carrying .38's. When he said this to the secret service men, they did not like it and replied: "A .38 will kill a man all right." "Yes," said Bill, "if you give him a week to die in." I find that he has talked much of me and my political work in Texas to Wilson. The Governor wanted to know whether I had been successful in all my political campaigns and what kind of men I had chosen.'

VII

The last days of the campaign were not marked by the customary excitement, for the result of the election had become a foregone conclusion. The contest between Roosevelt and Taft had split the anti-Wilson vote so effectively that a Democratic landslide in the electoral college appeared certain.

As election returns came in on November 5, it soon became clear that Democratic confidence in overwhelming victory was fully justified. Mr. Taft carried only two states, Roosevelt only 88 electoral votes. It is true that Wilson's popular vote was less than a majority, but his plurality in the electoral college was the greatest ever received by a presidential candidate, and he carried with him handsome Democratic majorities in the Senate and House of Representatives.

'I went to Headquarters [wrote House on the evening of election day], and saw a few people, but nothing of importance was going on. By half-past six o'clock it was evident that Wilson had won, so I sent him a telegram of congratulation. By seven o'clock returns were in enough to enable one to see that it was a Wilson landslide.

'I went down to the Waldorf Hotel, where McCombs had invited guests to hear the returns. He had taken nearly one side of the hotel, and there were about twenty-five people there....'

It was a season of triumph for McCombs, who as Chairman of the Committee received fervid praise. It was one of equal although less obvious triumph for Colonel House, whose share in the campaign only a few of the more keen-sighted realized. He held no office in the party organization, his goings and comings at Headquarters were unostentatious. But there was no thread in the campaign pattern which he had not touched, no symptom of party discord which had not evoked his genius for pacification.[1] The new Wilson Administration might have been wrecked at the moment of victory. This the President-elect understood and his gratitude to House was unfeigned.

Two days after the election, replying to House's note of congratulation, he declared that no small part of Democratic success must be ascribed to the counsels of the Colonel.

Whether or not the victory at the polls could be capitalized to ensure a positive programme of reform legislation, was the question of the future and to it Colonel House had already turned his attention.

[1] '"He would come into an office," explained a Democratic Committeeman, "and say a few words quietly, and after he had gone you would suddenly become seized with a good idea. You would put that idea forth and receive congratulations for it; it would work out first rate. Long after, if you thought the thing over, you would suddenly realize that the idea had been oozed into your brain by Col. House during a few minutes' quiet conversation. You did not know it and the Colonel did not want you to know it. As a matter of fact, before the campaign was over in his quiet way Col. House came near being the biggest man about the works, although he did not hold any position and would not take one."' — *Current Opinion*, vol. IV, no. 6, June, 1913.

CHAPTER IV

BUILDING A CABINET

You can never build a Cabinet to please everybody.... When you have about concluded that you have the proper man, some one will come along and condemn him so vigorously that it will make you doubt. Therefore, in the end, you will have largely to determine their fitness yourself.

House to Wilson, November 22, 1912

I

THE victory of 1912 was the first won by the Democrats in a presidential election since 1892, an even twenty years. This long exclusion from power laid a tremendous handicap upon the party and its leaders when they came to organize an administration; for in the United States the minority suffers as much materially from being the under-dog as the majority suffers morally from an over-long lease of control. The older men of the party which has been in opposition have developed critical rather than constructive faculties, and it is long since they have exercised executive functions; comparatively few younger men of capacity have been attracted to the party, and those few have had no administrative experience. What is worse, long political exile will have sharpened every one's appetite for office, and the first indication of success at the polls will sound like a dinner gong, gathering the ravenous horde of anxious place-hunters, whose ability is apt to be in inverse ratio to their eagerness.

Mr. Wilson did not conceal from himself the particular difficulties which he, as leader of the party and President-elect, must face. He was without political experience except for his brief tenure of the New Jersey governorship. Although he always maintained that a college president found ample opportunity to develop political genius, he did not, at this time certainly, overestimate his own ability. He was threatened, furthermore, by a flood of enthusiastic and contradictory advice. His two chief campaign leaders, McCombs and McAdoo, were at daggers drawn. The man who exercised strongest influence in the party, Mr. Bryan, Wilson regarded as impractical and notoriously mistaken in his personal judgments. Other leaders, such as Underwood and Champ Clark, he had fought vigorously in the pre-nomination campaign. Still others, in Congress, upon whom he must depend for the success of his legislative programme, were ex-Populists, such as Gore of Oklahoma, or machine politicians, such as Stone of Missouri; both types Wilson had attacked frequently and fearlessly, and their assistance in this juncture was at least questionable.

Each and all of them, furthermore, if not applicants for office themselves, marshalled a solid phalanx of deserving Democrats who had long and faithfully served the cause when there had been no hope of immediate reward and for whom places must be found. As early in the campaign as September 7, House wrote to Walter Hines Page: 'The wise man will not envy Governor Wilson even in success, for, as you say, the office-seekers will sorely beset him. They are cheerfully dividing up the honors now, and the numbers engaged in this pleasant pastime will increase as the campaign grows older.'

It was inevitable that Wilson should turn to Colonel House for assistance. Apart from the warm affection he had conceived for House, he knew the reputation for political sagacity which the Colonel had earned in Texas and he recognized the value of his services in the pre-nomination and electoral campaigns. House and Wilson, furthermore, were in close accord upon all important political issues. Both were ardent liberals, and Wilson's sympathy was not lessened by his realization that the Colonel's idealism was touched by a very real sense of the practicable.

The factor which counted most heavily in stimulating the confidence of Wilson was the obviously disinterested attitude of Colonel House. At the beginning he made it plain that he would ask nothing for his friends and wanted no office for himself. He was too much the philosopher to be attracted by the badge of public position, and he was convinced that he could serve the Administration more effectively out of office. 'I would not exchange the confidence and friendship that Governor Wilson seems to have for me,' he wrote in November, 'for any office in the land.' Nor would he give advice on appointments until the President demanded it.

Colonel House to Dr. S. E. Mezes

NEW YORK, *November* 4, 1912

DEAR SIDNEY:

... My mail is getting heavy with applications, but I think I know how to handle it. As a matter of fact, I do not care two whoops in Hades who gets the offices, and Governor Wilson knows it....

He has the opportunity to become the greatest President we have ever had, and I want him to make good. He can do it if the office-seekers will give him leisure to think, and I am going to try and help him get it....

The Governor spent practically all day with me Saturday, most of the time at the apartment. It would have done your heart good to have seen him walk in after we had finished lunch, and Loulie's expression when I asked him to join us. It is true that I took the food from under the servants' noses as they were about to eat it, but the Governor enjoyed what he had nevertheless....

Fraternally yours

E. M. HOUSE

Colonel House to Senator Culberson

NEW YORK, *November* 5, 1912

DEAR SENATOR:

... It is Governor Wilson's intention to leave in ten days for a four weeks' absolute rest, and during that time I suppose the boys will decide definitely upon what offices they will take.

As far as I am concerned, I am not interested in the office end of it.... I have urged Governor Wilson to leave these matters largely to his Cabinet, to the Senators and to the Congressmen, and let them be the buffer between himself and the hungry host. I rather think he will do this in his own defence, in order that he may have some leisure to consider the complex problems that will confront him....

It is that end of his Administration in which I am most interested. In other words, I am interested in measures and not in men, and what time I have I shall devote to helping him in that direction....

Your very faithful

E. M. HOUSE

With every one else trying to tell the President-elect what he ought to do and every one advising differently, and with Colonel House refusing to press any claims, Wilson characteristically put full trust in him. House was ready. Long before the election, regarding Wilson's victory as assured, he had prepared to help him in every way that he could; and he knew that the first call for advice would be upon the subject of appointments. However honest he might be in his interest in measures rather than men, the personnel of the new Administration was the first great problem to be faced.

'I am on constant watch for good material [he wrote on October 21] from which to select a Cabinet and other important places. I wish to be well informed if Governor Wilson should consult me.'

There was no danger that House would not be well informed of those who desired office. The applicants themselves saw to that. Party leaders already recognized the influence he had acquired and guessed that his approval might be the determining factor in an appointment. 'A tremendous mail arrived from all directions,' he wrote immediately after the election. 'Every one wants something.' All attempts to disguise the importance of the position given him by the President-elect proved fruitless, for Mr. Wilson's frequent visits to the small apartment on Thirty-Fifth Street were too well known. From October until the following spring, when in desperation he left for Europe, the assault upon the Colonel continued.

Colonel House to Dr. S. E. Mezes

NEW YORK, *October* 11, 1912

DEAR SIDNEY:

. . . It is not a pose with me, this keeping out of the lime-light; but it is my judgment that I can do far more effective work and accomplish the things I have in mind better by the methods I have heretofore followed.

I agree with you that it is going to be difficult to keep out of the papers. . . .

The trouble is, the fact that I am close to Wilson is becoming known; and, since everybody wants something, they are doing their best to please me and this is the way they think to do it.

A magazine is trying now to write me up and wants my photograph, but if they get it it will be when I have lost my head more completely than I think I have as yet.

Fraternally and hastily yours

E. M. H.

Pressure upon House was increased because Wilson had determined to go to Bermuda for a rest and before sailing was slow to confer with the politicians, who one and all feared that they were not going to find a place in the picture. The Colonel reassured them and urged patience, at the same time that he pointed out to Wilson the need of showing consideration for their sensibilities.

'I telephoned to the Governor [he wrote on November 14] and advised him to write a note to Mr. Bryan telling him that he would confer with him after his return from Bermuda. He said he would do so at once. I am to see the Governor Saturday morning and will advise him concerning other matters pending. In my opinion he is making a mistake in not calling for advice from political leaders, as they will become disgruntled.'

Two days later, before Wilson left, he and House drew up a tentative list for Cabinet positions and discussed the best means to satisfy those who, by their work in the campaign, felt that they had earned proper rewards. It was already agreed that Mr. Bryan must be given his choice of positions. As far back as September, House recorded that Wilson had accepted his argument that 'it would be best to make him Secretary of State, in order to have him at Washington and in harmony with the Administration, rather than outside and possibly in a critical attitude. Mrs. Bryan's influence, too, would be valuable.'

Whatever his capacity, Bryan had come to Wilson's rescue at Baltimore and might ask for political recognition. Furthermore, his influence in the party was such that, if hostile, he could effectively block the legislative programme and perhaps wreck the Administration. Nothing illustrates more clearly the exigencies of government under the party system. Mr. Wilson did not want Bryan in his Cabinet and did not believe him fitted for the Secretaryship of State; but it was undeniable that the new Administration could carry through its reform programme more effectively with Bryan in it. At least there would not be the danger to the public service that threatened in 1897, when McKinley, in order to provide a vacancy in the Senate which Mark Hanna might fill, appointed Senator Sherman Secretary of State.[1]

The claims of McCombs and McAdoo were placed in the forefront because of their campaign leadership. Wilson regarded the abilities of the latter highly, but he distrusted the former's capacity, although he had long had for him a personal fondness. McCombs was in ill-health, lacked evenness of temper, and was ready to make alliance with the type of old-fashioned politicians whom Wilson hated. He had done much to stimulate enthusiasm in the pre-nomination campaign, but the experience of the electoral campaign itself seemed to indicate that his appointment to a Cabinet position would not make for harmony, even if he possessed the requisite administrative capacity.

'*November* 16: Governor Wilson telephoned me early [recorded Colonel House] and asked if it would be convenient for him to come over [to House's apartment] at ten o'clock. He remained for an hour or more and we went over all matters in the most confidential way. Cabinet material was discussed.... We discussed what to do with McCombs and McAdoo. He said he would give the former a first-class foreign appointment in order to get rid of him. He said he would be willing to give him the Collectorship of the Port of New York if it were not that he could build up a formidable political machine. I told him McCombs would not

[1] William Roscoe Thayer wrote of this manœuvre: 'To force the venerable Sherman, whose powers were already failing, into the most important office after that of President himself, showed a disregard of common decency not less than of the safety of the nation.' (*The Life of John Hay*, II, 156.)

think of accepting the Collectorship. I suggested McAdoo as Secretary of the Treasury, Burleson as Postmaster General. He thought Daniels would be better for Postmaster General, but I thought he was not aggressive enough and that the position needed a man who was in touch with Congress. He agreed that this was true.

'We talked again of James C. McReynolds as Attorney-General. We practically eliminated Brandeis for this position.... He asked again about offering Mr. Bryan the Secretaryship of State or Ambassadorship to England, and I advised him to do so. He said that he would.'

II

With Wilson's departure for Bermuda, House set seriously to work investigating the claims and the capacities of the applicants for office, from lowest to highest. Much of the work was intensely uncomfortable.

'Visited Headquarters [he noted on November 18] and spent a disagreeable time with X and Y. Suggested to X the secretaryship of the Senate, which pays $6000 per year, but he scorns a position of this kind and wants something much better. Y is in the same frame of mind. Y abused McAdoo viciously. When I pressed him, he could not verify any of his statements. He says he will depend upon McCombs to look out for his interests. . . .

'I am overwhelmed with office-seekers who have probably seen notices of Governor Wilson having called on me on the 16th. I am busy getting up a list of Cabinet possibilities with data attached, to send the President-elect for his information. . . .'

Colonel House to the President-elect

NEW YORK, *November* 22, 1912

DEAR GOVERNOR:

. . . James C. McReynolds, of Tennessee, but more recently of New York, is worthy of consideration. Although a Democrat, Mr. Roosevelt made him special counsel for the Government in the suit against the Tobacco Trust and the Anthracite Coal Trust.

He won the Tobacco suit and he has won the suit against the Coal Trust as far as it has gone. It is now in the Supreme Court.

McReynolds severed his connection with the Government because of his disagreement with Mr. Wickersham regarding the dissolution of the Tobacco Trust. He contended that Wickersham's plan nullified the effects of the victory.

He is about fifty years old. He is considered radical in his views by a large part of the New York Bar.[1] His character and legal attainments are of the highest.

I lunched with Mr. Brandeis yesterday. His mind and mine are in accord concerning most of the questions that are now to the fore. He is more than a lawyer; he is a publicist and he has an unusual facility for lucid expression. . . .

A large number of reputable people distrust him, but I doubt whether the distrust is well founded, and it would perhaps attach itself to any man who held his advanced views.

Norman Hapgood [2] lunched with us and I found in him an enthusiastic admirer of Brandeis. They are both going to Hot Springs for a few days as guests of Mr. Charles R. Crane.

[1] This reputation doubtless resulted from the vigor with which he had prosecuted the suits against the trusts. As a member of the Cabinet Mr. McReynolds displayed no radical proclivities, and after he assumed his seat on the Supreme Court he was generally regarded as one of the most conservative of the Justices.

[2] Editor of *Collier's Weekly*, 1903–12; of *Harper's Weekly*, 1913–16; later appointed Minister to Denmark.

Franklin K. Lane, Democratic Interstate Commerce Commissioner from California, was with me a large part of yesterday. Lane is fine material, but he is contented with his present position and would not change it.

You will have some difficulty in selecting your Secretary of the Interior. The West wants him, but it would perhaps be a mistake to select him from there. In the first place, he could not maintain himself with his own people and satisfy the East. If he satisfied the East, the West would rend him.[1] It would also be well not to put an ultra-Eastern man in that position, for the West would resent such action.

As you know, the East is all for conservation and the Far West is for it in a limited way — that is, where it does not conflict with their material interests. The West is anxious to have the forests and mines opened up and used to an extent that would aid them commercially.

They are also largely wedded to the idea of state versus national control, which I think is wrong, but which we need not go into here.

There is one thing I want to say, and that is this: You can never build a Cabinet that will please everybody. When you seek advice you will find but few agreements, even amongst your friends. When you have about concluded that you have the proper man, some one will come along and condemn him so vigorously that it will make you doubt. Therefore, in the end, you will have largely to determine their fitness yourself.

Please do not bother to answer my letters unless there is something you want me to do.

Your very faithful

E. M. House

[1] Mr. Lane, who was ultimately appointed, belied this prophecy. Although a Westerner and retaining the confidence of the West, he was generally spoken of by the Eastern press as one of the most capable members of Wilson's Cabinet.

Mr. Wilson wrote from Bermuda, thanking House for his suggestions. He addressed him, as he had done since the summer of 1912 and continued to do for five years, as 'My dear Friend,' and signed himself 'Affectionately yours.' He expressed himself as able to rest with an equable mind if the kind American people would not unload their correspondence upon him, and encouraged House in a prospective trip to Washington.

Colonel House's visit to Washington was partly, as he expressed it, 'to find the lay of the land' so that he might wisely advise Governor Wilson upon his return from Bermuda, and partly to discover means to harmonize the discordant factions in the party. The differences that had arisen during the campaign were largely personal; those that now threatened were political and seemed likely to cause more serious difficulties. There was disagreement over the legislative programme, especially in the matter of currency reform; and a storm of greater or less severity seemed likely to arise over the question of the single term for President, which was warmly advocated by Bryan and to which Wilson was strongly opposed. House set himself to persuade the party leaders to take no step which might later bring them into conflict with the President. He worked unobtrusively. Mr. Burleson, a Democratic leader in the House, asked Senator Gore what he thought of the Colonel. 'Take my word for it,' replied Gore, 'he can walk on dead leaves and make no more noise than a tiger.'

His work was none the less effective in that it was quiet, and it does not spoil the story to say that in the end the currency and single-term problems were both settled in accordance with Wilson's wishes.

Colonel House to the President-elect

NEW YORK, *November* 28, 1912

DEAR GOVERNOR:

I spent two strenuous but interesting days in Washington. While there I had an hour with Chief Justice White, by appointment, and was with him at dinner later.

Among those that called upon me were Speaker Clark, Hoke Smith, Gore, Culberson, Bob Henry, Burleson, Carter Glass, and many others. I mention these by name, for each of them had something interesting to say.

Mr. Clark has not gotten over his defeat. He is inclined to be friendly with you, but his hatred of Mr. Bryan amounts to an obsession and it is not unlikely that there will be a personal difficulty between them when they meet.

Almost at the beginning, Clark asked me what you intended to do. I replied, 'About what?' He said, 'About anything or everything.' I told him that was a pretty leading question and asked him to be more specific. I finally told him that you intended to carry out the Democratic policies as far as you were able with the aid of such leaders as himself and others. Before he left, he was telling me the story of his life and we were on very cordial terms. I think he would like to be invited to see you when you return, and I believe it would be a wise thing to do. . . .

I had a most interesting hour with Mr. Glass. He candidly confessed that he knew nothing about banking or the framing of a monetary measure. I congratulated him upon this, for I told him that it was much better to know nothing than to know something wrong. He, too, indicated a willingness to do everything in his power to give as speedily as possible a sound economic bill, and upon lines advised by you. . . .

He expressed a desire to see you soon after your return, and I think the quicker you see him the better it will be. You will find him ready to coöperate with you to the fullest extent.

Harvey was there for the purpose of furthering his plan for a single term.

Mr. Taft favors this, and so does Mr. Bryan. Mr. Taft favors a six-year term, and Mr. Bryan leans to four years. Harvey told me that Bob Henry was working with Bryan along this line and that was going to be our first difficulty. He was very pessimistic. He said that no one knew your viewpoint concerning the matter and that your friends were apathetic, and that before they realized it a measure would be passed through both branches of Congress and be ready for submission to the people.

It does not require the signature of the President, but, if it did, Mr. Taft would sign it.

Harvey is mistaken about your friends not being alert in regard to it, because I talked to Burleson and others and told them to watch every move.

Harvey thought it would be a wise thing to compromise on a six-year term which would include you.

In talking with Gore about it afterwards, he said the difficulty there was that the Republican States would hesitate to lengthen the term of a Democratic President two years longer than was necessary. If the Republicans refused to lengthen the term of a Democratic President, then the Democratic States would in turn refuse to lengthen the term of a Republican President. . . .

The general consensus of opinion amongst those with whom I talked and who had met Bryan, was that he would work in harmony with your Administration if he went into the Cabinet, but they all thought that there were two difficulties which should be met at the outset: the question of a second term and the further question of currency reform. . . .

I obtained a great deal of valuable information from the Chief Justice. He talked to me frankly, with the understanding that what he said was to be repeated to no one excepting you.

He cheerfully slaughtered nearly all the gentlemen about whom I wrote to you in my last letter....

Your very faithful

E. M. House

With the return of Mr. Wilson, conferences multiplied, and the following six weeks House devoted to sifting the claims of importunate applicants and to a search for available but less vociferous candidates. A series of excerpts from his daily memoranda will illustrate the process. No letters were exchanged with Mr. Wilson during this period, since the two were in constant touch through the telephone.

'*December* 6, 1912: I had a long conversation with McCombs and Vick.[1] I believe if I had been authorized to offer McCombs a foreign embassy to-day, he would have accepted it. Office-seekers are driving him crazy. I suggested a foreign position and he said that he did not have sufficient money; but I told him that it would not take much. He asked where I would suggest his going — Vienna, Italy, or where? . . .

'*December* 11, 1912: Mr. David F. Houston came to dinner and spent the evening. We discussed the different Cabinet possibilities and other matters. He knows that I have suggested him to the President-elect for Secretary of Agriculture. He thought it would be better to defer legislation on currency and tariff until later, but I convinced him of the importance of passing such measures before all the patronage had been distributed....

'*December* 18, 1912: Governor Wilson came at half-past one. I talked to him about Morgenthau[2] and suggested him for Turkey. He replied, "There ain't going to be no Turkey,"[3] and I said, "Then let him go look for it." . . .

[1] Walter F. Vick, one of Mr. McCombs' chief lieutenants in the electoral campaign.

[2] Chairman of the Democratic Finance Committee and later appointed Ambassador to Turkey.

[3] Turkey in Europe seemed about to disappear as the result of the defeats administered by the Balkan League.

'I thought if I were in Wilson's place I would take only men I knew, that in making a selection it was like walking in the country — one could always imagine that something better was beyond, but upon reaching the given point the view was still in the distance like the rainbow.

'Bryan was also discussed freely. I advised him to offer Bryan the Secretaryship of State, but afterwards to suggest that it would be of great service if he would go to Russia at this critical time. He thought Bryan would want to discuss with him the personnel of his Cabinet and that they could never agree. I argued that there were many people and things that they could agree upon, as their object was really the same only their ways of getting at it were different. He might, I thought, mention the names of Burleson, Daniels, and others he was considering for the Cabinet who were also friends of Mr. Bryan.

'We discussed again the Attorney-Generalship. . . . We went back to McReynolds and I thought he seemed to understand the different phases of the situation better than any one I had talked to. He asked if I considered McAdoo suited for the Treasury, and I thought he was; under ordinary conditions I should say an Eastern man would be a bad choice, but that in this instance I heartily approved McAdoo.

'*December* 19, 1912: Governor Wilson called me over the telephone and said that McCombs was distinctly disappointed at the ambassadorial offer made him yesterday, and no decision was arrived at. He wanted to know again about Bryan and my advice about it. I advised being cordial in making the offer,[1] and to make it plain afterwards that he would appreciate his taking the foreign post [the Ambassadorship to Russia].

'B. M. Baruch, McCombs' friend, told Wallace that he had advised McCombs not to accept office, but to resign from the National Committee and to go into the practice of law

[1] Of the Secretaryship of State.

as soon as his health permits. McCombs seems terribly "cut up" over the fact that Governor Wilson has not offered him all that he desired and that he tendered him an Ambassadorship instead of a Cabinet place.

'I called up Governor Wilson to talk things over, and he asked if I still held to my advice about Mr. Bryan, and I answered "yes." This is the third or fourth time he has asked me this. It shows how distrustful he is of having Mr. Bryan in his Cabinet. . . .

'*December* 21, 1912: Tumulty telephoned about the Governor's and Bryan's interview. Bryan was in fine humor and everything was lovely.[1] He asked me to send a further list of men whom I thought it best for the Governor to see. I had already sent in a list several days ago to Trenton.

'McAdoo . . . is now anxious to go to Staunton, where the Governor is to attend some celebration given in his honor on the 28th, and some of McAdoo's friends are urging him to go, telling him he is effacing himself too much and will be forgotten. I advised to the contrary, but wished him to use his own judgment.

'*December* 23, 1912 [House and Colonel George Harvey taking lunch together]: Martin was also at lunch. Harvey told him that I was the best adviser the President-elect had, and that he thought I should be given the Secretaryship of the Treasury. Martin wanted to know, if my health permitted, would I take it? I replied, "Not if I were as strong as a bull!"; that, as it was, the Governor discussed everything frankly and without fear of misunderstanding, but that if I were an applicant for any position both he and I would feel the restraint. . . .

'The more I see of McAdoo, the better I like him. He is a splendid fellow, whole-souled, and generous, without a tinge of envy, and with it all he is honest and progressive.

[1] At this interview Mr. Bryan was offered the Secretaryship of State and tentatively accepted it.

'*December* 29, 1912: Tumulty was with me from five until half-past nine in the evening. We went over the situation in detail. He is very desirous of being Secretary to the President.

'I asked Tumulty how many letters of protest the Governor was receiving against himself for that position. He admitted that there had been five or six hundred. I inquired if he showed them to the Governor. He had not shown them all, but had always told him of the number received. He did not show him the letters which came that were favorable to him either....

'*January* 5, 1913: The Governor has invited Burleson, Palmer, Culberson, Gore, Hoke Smith, and Bob Henry, as I had suggested, to come to Trenton this week. Tumulty said the Governor did not want to invite them much, as he thought there was nothing that he wished to discuss with them. Tumulty explained to him that I thought he should see them in order to compliment them rather than to expect much help from their advice. He then consented to see them.

'*January* 7, 1913: McAdoo came at five and remained until seven o'clock. We discussed Cabinet possibilities. He wanted to know what my general idea was, and I told him that I thought the Governor had poor material to select from. McAdoo replied, "I believe you are right, and you may include me too." I disclaimed any thought or reference to him, but he cheerfully included himself. I explained that my reason for saying this was that the Democratic Party had been out of power so long that no one had been in training or in process of development for public office.

'X tells me that he understands from Thomas Nelson Page and others that Y is anxious for a reconciliation. Martin says Y has a plan for disposing of Bryan. I answered that a lot of people were busy with such plans, but I thought Governor Wilson and Mr. Bryan would be able to manage the matter themselves....

'*January* 8, 1913: I told him [Wilson] he was now leaving Texas out of the Cabinet. His reply was, "I want you to go in the Cabinet." ... He urged me not to give a definite answer for the present and said he very much wished me to be a member of his official family, that it seemed to coincide with the fitness of things.

'He generously asked me what place I would like, evidently leaving me to choose. I regard this as a very high compliment, for the reason that he has offered no one a place in the Cabinet up to now excepting Mr. Bryan, whom we agreed upon just after the election ... as a political necessity. Of course, I shall not take any office, although I would do much to oblige him and to be of service. My reasons are that I am not strong enough to tie myself down to a Cabinet department and, in addition, my general disinclination to hold office. I very much prefer being a free lance, and to advise with him regarding matters in general, and to have a roving commission to serve wherever and whenever possible.'

To such reasons for remaining out of office should be added one which Colonel House may not have definitely formulated, but which must have affected him at least subconsciously. His experience with the Texas Governors had taught him that, however much in sympathy he might be with their general policy, questions of detail must arise on which his opinions would be at variance from theirs. He believed that in essential matters he and Wilson would agree in principle, but they might conceivably disagree as to method. If he were in an official position such disagreement would compel his resignation, unless he were to be placed in the unpleasant position of carrying out a line of action which he disapproved. So long as he remained in a private capacity, he could give what advice he chose; and if the President did not follow it, House could shrug his shoulders and turn his attention to other matters in which Wilson might accept his guidance. 'Had I gone into the Cabinet,' House once said, 'I could not have lasted eight weeks.' Outside of the Cabinet he lasted for eight years.

III

The serious, although rather unconventional, responsibilities laid upon the shoulders of Colonel House during the process of drafting Cabinet possibilities, were not lightened by the political inexperience of the President-elect and his temperamental inability to develop confidential relations with the party leaders.

'Such men as Speaker Clark [so ran a despatch from Trenton to the New York *Herald*], Representative Oscar W. Underwood, Senator Hoke Smith, Senator Culberson, and many others of importance in the Democracy have journeyed to Princeton and gone away saying they had no more information than when they came. One of them said to me: "I know that Governor Wilson was elected President on November 5. I know that he will be inaugurated on March 4. Further than that I know nothing about what has happened or is going to happen." Several of the leaders frankly say, when asked what will happen after March 4: "You will have to ask either the President-elect or Colonel House."' [1]

As the days passed the politicians took their hopes and their ideas to House, who, somewhat embarrassed by his position, nevertheless worked steadfastly to make them feel less out in the cold. 'Making the suggestion through you,' wrote McCombs to House on January 2, of a proposition for Wilson's decision, 'is the only way I know of handling the matter.'

'*February* 17, 1913: X called at five o'clock [recorded

[1] *The Herald*, February 19, 1913.

House]. He wished to tell me many things, but particularly how very competent he was to be Secretary of the Treasury. He seemed hurt that Wilson had not called him into consultation, or sent for him, or noticed him in any way since the election. His position, he seemed to think, entitled him to great consideration. I explained that the President-elect had not called his friends into consultation, and those who had been with him had made the appointments themselves and had not come at his invitation. This was invariably the case, as far as I knew, with the exception of Mr. Bryan, Speaker Clark, Mr. Underwood, and some members of the Senate and House. He left in a fine humor, and promised to write me his views if I would convey them to the Governor. . . .

'*February* 19, 1913: Y came at half-past five. He complained bitterly of the way the Governor was treating him; that he did not consult with him or tell him about any of his plans. I asked if he knew of any one else that he consulted or to whom he told his plans. He confessed he did not, and I told him he had no right to complain. . . . He said there was a bitter feeling among the party leaders that they were not being consulted, and not taken into confidence. Of course he exaggerates this.'

It was all the more important that when it came to the composition of the Cabinet the wishes of the party leaders should be carefully considered; for if, after keeping his own counsel (or that of Colonel House), Mr. Wilson chose a Cabinet of independents, he would soon find a rebellious party in Congress. House was frankly troubled.

'Walter Page lunched with me to-day [the Colonel wrote on January 14]. I found that he had been advising Governor Wilson very much along the lines I have. . . .

'I tried him out as to the department in which he was most interested. If the Governor appoints him, I shall advise that he be given the Interior. I told Page that I was fearful that the Governor was thinking of appointing too many independents and that he was not looking for rock-ribbed Democrats.'

The Colonel struck the same note on the following day in a talk with Mrs. Wilson, whose influence with her husband he evidently counted upon.

'I told her that the men the Governor had in mind for his Cabinet were nearly all irregular party men and that most of them had voted for Taft four years ago. I cited —— as an instance. She spoke up immediately and said, "But you would not keep him out of the Cabinet on that account?" I replied no, not in his case, but I would not put in too many with the same sort of record, for the reason that the moment the Cabinet was announced their political records would be exposed.

'I thought that in twenty years from now no one would know how the different departments of the Government had been run and that the President's fame would rest entirely upon the big constructive measures he was able to get through Congress; and in order to get them through he had to be on more or less good terms with that body. This, I thought, was one of the most important things he had to consider, for his future reputation would rest almost wholly upon it.'

Of all the politicians, the one whose influence during the first legislative session would be most valuable was, of course, Mr. Bryan; and it was natural that House should suggest that he be given a voice in the composition of the Cabinet, or at least an opportunity to comment upon the tentative slate which Wilson had drafted by early January. The Governor agreed, House recorded on January 10, that it would be well for the Colonel to go to Miami, where Bryan was building a Southern home, and explain Wilson's plans. 'He said I could talk to him freely, but that it was to give him, Bryan, information and not to ask his advice.'

The newspapers of the East had taken unholy pleasure in picturing Mr. Bryan in a truculent frame of mind and inclined to dictate Mr. Wilson's policy and appointments. House discovered the reverse to be true. 'He is in a delightful humor,' the Colonel wrote Wilson on January 29. 'He likes the names suggested for the family gathering.' And as House developed his views he found Bryan careful not to press any specific appointments with undue ardor and surprisingly mild in his criticisms.

Colonel House to the President-elect

MIAMI, FLORIDA, *January* 30, 1913

DEAR GOVERNOR:

I had a long conference with our friend last night and again to-day. . . .

He is very earnest in his advice that a Catholic, and perhaps a Jew, be taken into the family. I told him T[umulty]'s appointment as Secretary would cover the one, but he thought not. He suggests Governor Higgins of Rhode Island as a possible choice. He shows a very fine spirit and is exceedingly anxious for your success. He also shows no disposition whatever to interfere, even in his own department. He says he would like to name his first assistant unless you have some one you want to place there.

He knows all the disadvantages to him of accepting place and mentions them in detail, but he says that those things must not be taken into account.

He thinks the Pacific slope should be recognized, but he does not seem to get beyond Phelan and Lane, although I do not think he would seriously object to any one excepting Teal.

For the first time, I think, he is finding out how difficult it is to form this body.

He likes the suggestion you made to me for Germany [Professor Fine of Princeton], but has no one in mind for England....

He has accepted all your conclusions so cordially that it has been a pleasure to me to discuss matters with him.

Your very faithful

E. M. HOUSE

'*January* 30, 1913: Mr. Bryan was as pleased with his new place [recorded Colonel House] as a child with a new toy. He is really a fine man, full of democratic simplicity, earnest, patriotic, and of a fervently religious nature. Mrs. Bryan is the "salt of the earth." She has all the poise and good common sense which is lacking in her distinguished husband....

'*January* 31, 1913: It was so warm that we did not go through the Everglades. Mr. Bryan came over in the evening and we had another political talk. He was much distressed when I told him that Governor Wilson had offered the Chinese mission to Dr. Charles W. Eliot. He thought it the poorest selection that could be made, for the reason that Eliot was a Unitarian and did not believe in the divinity of Christ and the new Chinese civilization was founded upon the Christian movement there. I asked him to state his objections in writing, not only as to Dr. Eliot, but as to any member of the proposed Cabinet. I said as far as Eliot was concerned, it was too late; but I did not believe Dr. Eliot would accept, for he had told the Governor that he would take it only if his wife approved and he was afraid she would not. Mr. Bryan was hopeful she would not.'

'He is only trying to help,' wrote House again to Wilson, 'and does not mean to urge.' 'Everything he said,' the Colonel noted later, 'showed a fine spirit in Mr. Bryan and seemed to me to be a hopeful sign for future harmony.' It appears from the terms of the following letter that Wilson left these negotiations entirely to House.

Colonel House to the President-elect

St. Augustine, Florida
February 6, 1913

Dear Governor:

Our friend has asked me many times whether I had heard from you in response to his suggestions. He wired me just before he left for Havana, asking the same question.

If I were you, I would send him a line indicating that you appreciated his interest and had found his suggestions helpful. He will be back in Miami next Thursday, and if he found a note from you awaiting him it would please him greatly. . . .

Your very faithful
E. M. House

IV

Upon Colonel House's return, early in February, Wilson felt himself prepared to make the definite appointments. It was already settled that Bryan should be Secretary of State. McAdoo had accepted the Treasury portfolio, and Burleson was to be offered that of Postmaster-General, two selections urged by House from the beginning. For Agriculture, Wilson had determined upon the distinguished economist, D. F. Houston, Chancellor of Washington University, another close friend of House. Josephus Daniels, a North Carolina editor, and W. B. Wilson, once a miner and an active albeit conservative labor leader, were to be given the portfolios of the Navy and of Labor respectively. There remained those of War, the Interior, Justice, and Commerce.

'*February* 8, 1913: The President-elect writes that he

needs to see me for a final conference about the official family. He asks me to sound Houston on the Secretaryship of Agriculture. On that case he is clear and his mind made up, but he thinks it best for me to open the matter with him. The Treasury has been offered and accepted as we planned.'

In the conferences between Wilson and House which followed, the latter urged the appointment of J. C. McReynolds and F. K. Lane, the first because of his record as special prosecuting attorney in anti-trust suits, the second because of his record on the Interstate Commerce Commission. Wilson did not know McReynolds, and on February 15 the Colonel recorded that the latter was invited to House's apartment while the President-elect was there, 'ostensibly to discuss the appointment of a District Attorney here. The Governor liked McReynolds.'

On the following day, Mr. Lane came over from Washington, for Wilson had asked House to sound him as he had already sounded the other appointees. The conference crystallized the Colonel's conviction that Wilson would make a mistake if he left Lane out of the Cabinet.

'I informed him of what we had in mind for him. The Interior, in his opinion, was the most difficult post in the Cabinet, but he would take it if we wanted him to do so. He said he would take anything we thought him best suited for, but that he was content to remain where he was as Chairman of the Interstate Commerce Commission.

'Feeling responsible for Lane, I drew him out upon all the leading questions, and I found that he has a remarkably strong, virile mind. My opinion of him increased materially, much as I had thought of him before. There will certainly not be a stronger or more dominant force in the Cabinet.

'Norman Hapgood came and I brought them together, and we had a fine hour. After Lane left, Hapgood expressed his enthusiastic admiration for him and said he thought he would suit the position for which we had him in mind wonderfully well. I asked that he write a letter to this effect, telling him I wanted him to share the responsibility with me because the President-elect had never met Lane and knew him only through me.'

The difficulties and complexities of political Cabinet-making are illustrated by the story of the succeeding days. One after the other, objections cropped up which seemed to destroy the availability of men Wilson wanted. His choice for Attorney-General was A. Mitchell Palmer, whose activity on the floor of the Baltimore Convention had gone far to decide Wilson's nomination. Opposition in certain quarters proved to be so strong that he was instead offered the Secretaryship of War. This, however, he felt he must decline, in deference to his Quaker principles. Inauguration day was approaching, was barely a fortnight away, and Wilson realized that no time could be lost if his Cabinet were to be completed by March 4.

'I asked him not to worry [wrote House], that the getting of Lane in the Cabinet was of much more importance than the losing of Palmer for Attorney-General; that Lane could take that place, if necessary, and fill it with distinction, and that we could keep Baker [1] for the Interior. . . .

'*February* 18, 1913: Newton Baker [recorded House] rang me up to say that he had arrived. When I was in Princeton, the Governor wrote him a note asking him to come to New York on Tuesday or Wednesday, as was most convenient, and to telephone me and that I would make an appointment for him to meet the Governor at my apartment. I asked Baker to dine with us at seven o'clock and I requested him not to let his presence in New York be known and, above all

[1] Newton D. Baker, reform Mayor of Cleveland.

things, not to let any one know he was coming to my apartment or was having an appointment with the President-elect. . . .

'I met Governor Wilson and brought him to the apartment. We had about forty minutes before Baker came, and we discussed the Cabinet and other appointments. . . .

'Baker came and we had a very delightful dinner; politics were not discussed at all, stories were told, Mark Twain and various other persons and matters were talked of. After dinner I left the Governor and Baker. . . .

'In about a half-hour, I returned. The Governor said he had offered Baker the Secretaryship of the Interior and that he was considering the matter. Baker finally decided he could not take it. He said there was no one to carry on the work in Cleveland which he had begun, and he thought the government of our American cities was the greatest disgrace to our citizenship; that Cleveland was emerging from that state and would soon be an example to her sister cities throughout the land.

'Both the Governor and I urged him to take a broader view of the situation and do the bigger work. He finally decided to take the matter under consideration for the night, and said if he changed his mind he would wire me to-morrow, quoting a line from Shakespeare which I would understand.'

The cryptic line from Shakespeare was never sent, and it was found necessary to look further for a Secretary of the Interior. Baker's refusal led Wilson definitely to decide that he would return to House's original suggestion of McReynolds as Attorney-General. The Colonel pointed out that Walter H. Page might be offered the Interior and Lane be shifted to the War Department. Wilson acceded and authorized House to see whether Page would accept. He at once called him upon the telephone, but learned that he had left town; he thereupon sent him a telegram asking him to call as soon as he returned.

Chance plays its part in history. Had Mr. Page been in town, he would have been offered and would have accepted the Secretaryship of the Interior, and he would not have gone to London as Ambassador. But before his return, the party leaders in Congress learned of the suggestion and objected strongly. Page, they pointed out, was a Southerner, and no Southerner should be Secretary of the Interior because of his control of pensions. In view of these objections, Wilson decided to keep Lane in the Interior and look for another man for War. House was left to explain his telegram to Page to the best of his ability when the latter returned. He proved equal to the interview, which might conceivably test his tact and powers of invention.

'*February* 24, 1913: Walter Page arrived in response to my telegram. When I wired him we expected to place him in the Interior and move Lane up to War, but in talking with the Governor last night it was decided best not to put a Southerner in that place.

'I told Page the reason we had summoned him was because there was likely to be a slip-up in some of the Cabinet places, and we wanted to know definitely whether he could be used in case it was necessary. I also told him the Governor wished me to discuss with him the material already gotten together. He suggested, and I advised, his going at once to Trenton to take the matter up with the Governor.'

A few weeks later, House told Page how near he had been to becoming Secretary of the Interior, a story which excited in Mr. Page more amusement than regret.

The final choice for the portfolio of War was delayed until the last moment. Colonel House had strongly recommended Mr. H. C. Wallace, who later became Ambassador to France. Mr. Wilson approved the selection and offered the post to Wallace. But the latter found it impossible to accept. The ultimate decision was made on the spur of the moment. During the morning of February 24, House recorded: 'Tumulty suggests, and we are going to look up, a New Jersey man, Vice-Chancellor Garrison, and see whether he will fill the bill.' Wilson evidently lost no time, for in the evening:

'Tumulty telephoned while Page was here, saying that the Governor had sent for Vice-Chancellor Garrison and was very much pleased with him, and had offered him the post of Secretary of War.'

The reader can hardly escape a shock of surprise at the apparently nonchalant manner in which the President-elect chose his Cabinet. In reality he had received an immense quantity of carefully sifted information, and the eligibility list of possibilities was drafted with care. But he made his final selection with a suddenness of decision that startled House himself.

'The thing that impresses me most [he recorded] is the casual way in which the President-elect is making up his Cabinet. I can see no end of trouble for him in the future unless he proceeds with more care.'

The Cabinet, as finally selected, was a *mélange* of administrators selected because of personal ability and of political leaders whose influence demanded recognition. The number of purely political appointments was less than is customary, a tribute to Wilson's original determination to consider ability alone in his appointments. Because of this fact and also because of his consistent refusal to discuss the Cabinet intimately with any one but House, the wiseacres were largely at fault in their prognostications. Ten days before the Inauguration, the New York *Herald* announced 'Rifts in Cabinet Secrecy.' But the list which it published of the probable Cabinet proved to be far from accurate.[1] Of the ten final appointees, only four were recognized beforehand by the *Herald* as possibilities.

The publication of the official family aroused more surprise than enthusiasm. In Republican circles the new Cabinet was naturally regarded as inferior, and by the country as a whole it was looked upon as mediocre. This was inevitable, since Wilson's choice was limited not merely to Democrats but to radicals who would approve of the drastic reforms he contemplated. For half a century the Democratic party had been out of power, except for the two terms of Cleveland's Presidency; and during that period there had been a steady gravitation of men of practical ability into the opposite political camp, which was more and more affiliated with the great money and business interests.

'It has thus come about [a New York paper pointed out] that most of the men eminent in the administration of national affairs have become defenders of existing conditions, in spite of the growing importance of a newly awakened national consciousness of intolerable wrongs in the political and economic life of the country. . . . Such men as seem to give promise of solid ability and administrative success lack importance in the public mind. . . . [Mr. Wilson] expects the country to be surprised by the absence of commanding or distinguished figures in his selection, but feels that the men he is to call into power will in time develop reputations that will justify him.' [2]

Colonel House himself was satisfied rather than enthusi-

[1] See Appendix to chapter.

[2] *Evening Mail*, New York, January 17, 1913.

astic, and in meeting the criticism of his friends emphasized the difficulties of the problem more than the innate strength of the Cabinet.

'Walter Page [he noted on February 24] came after dinner and told of his trip to Trenton. He regretted that it was too late to keep Daniels out of the Cabinet. The President-elect had already written him. I knew this, because he told me he intended writing McReynolds, Daniels, and Burleson notes on Sunday. . . . He said to Page, "You do not seem to think that Daniels is Cabinet timber." Page replied, "He is hardly a splinter."

'In discussing the Cabinet, Page thought it distinctly mediocre and thought the country would so regard it. I asked him how he could better it; and when he attempted to do so, like all the rest he failed signally. . . . I think, in all the circumstances, we have done well.'

APPENDIX

	The Herald list of February 22	*The Cabinet as appointed*
Secretary of State	W. J. Bryan	W. J. Bryan
Secretary of the Treasury	W. G. McAdoo	W. G. McAdoo
Secretary of War	Charles R. Crane	Lindley M. Garrison
Attorney-General	A. Mitchell Palmer	J. C. McReynolds
Postmaster-General	Josephus Daniels Albert S. Burleson	Albert S. Burleson
Secretary of the Navy	Lewis Nixon	Josephus Daniels
Secretary of the Interior	Alva Adams Edward L. Norris	F. K. Lane
Secretary of Agriculture	Obadiah Gardiner	D. F. Houston
Secretary of Commerce and Labor	Louis D. Brandeis	W. C. Redfield W. B. Wilson (Labor)

CHAPTER V

THE SILENT PARTNER

The source of his power was . . . the confidence that men had in his sagacity and unselfishness.

E. S. Martin, in 'Harper's Magazine,' February, 1912

I

'MR. HOUSE is my second personality. He is my independent self. His thoughts and mine are one. If I were in his place I would do just as he suggested. . . . If any one thinks he is reflecting my opinion by whatever action he takes, they are welcome to the conclusion.'

Such was the reply given by President Wilson to a politician who asked whether House represented him accurately in a certain situation. It indicates the degree of confidence which he placed in the Colonel. The President made it clear that, although House had refused official position of any kind, he was determined that the Administration should not lose the political services which House was qualified to perform. On the very day of his inauguration he asked and summarily accepted his recommendations for important appointive posts.

'The President-elect telephoned [Colonel House wrote on March 4] and asked Loulie and me to meet his family party at the Shoreham Hotel at 9.45, in order to accompany them to the Capitol for the inauguration ceremonies. I took Loulie to the Shoreham and left her with the Wilsons, but I did not go to the Capitol myself. I went instead to the Metropolitan Club and loafed around with Wallace. Functions of this sort do not appeal to me and I never go.

'Mrs. Wilson invited us to the White House to see the

fireworks. When we arrived we found the President was over in his office. I went there and was with him for a few minutes in order to tell him that I had investigated John H. Marble for Interstate Commerce Commissioner, in place of F. K. Lane, and had found him satisfactory. The President had never met Marble and had made no inquiries concerning him further than mine. He said he would send his name in to-morrow, along with the names of his Cabinet. He made the appointment in this way in order to avoid the great pressure which would be made upon him by candidates for this important office. . . .'

'*March* 8, 1913: The President asked me to be at the White House this morning at nine.

'The offices were nearly deserted at so early an hour. The President was dressed in a very becoming sack suit of grey, with a light grey silk tie. It was rather an informal-looking costume, but very attractive. I sat with him for nearly an hour and we had a delightful talk. We discussed the Cabinet mainly, and he laughingly told me his estimate of each one and how they acted at the first meeting. . . . The President spoke finely of Bryan and said their relations were exceedingly cordial. . . .

'The President suggested that we could have a cypher between us, so when we talked over the telephone or wrote we could discuss men without fear of revealing their identity. He took a pencil and started out with Bryan, saying, "Let us call him 'Primus.'" McAdoo is already known as "Pythias," McCombs being "Damon." Garrison he suggested as "Mars," McReynolds "Coke," Burleson "Demosthenes."'

Thus began House's career as Silent Partner.[1] It was a relationship which rested chiefly upon the political coöperation of the Colonel in meeting the problems of government.

[1] The appellation was first used by Peter Clark Macfarlane in an article in *Collier's*, and soon became general.

His labors were of the most varied kind, and he sought every opportunity to ease the load that bore upon the President, to bring him information, to work out details of policy. There was, however, an essential personal basis to the relationship, since it would have been impossible for a man of Wilson's temperament to put full political confidence in a man who did not evoke his affection as an individual.

'I have an intimate personal matter to discuss with you [he said to House in the summer of 1915]. You are the only person in the world with whom I can discuss everything.[1] There are some I can tell one thing and others another, but you are the only one to whom I can make an entire clearance of mind.'

The letters of Wilson to House invariably displayed an intensity of personal feeling that would have astounded those who attributed to him about the same degree of warmth as that of a Euclidean proposition and failed to realize the human qualities that lay concealed under his armor of exterior austerity. He wrote him frequently of his desire to talk with him and the need and desire for his advice on many a complicated matter. At the end of the first legislative session, he put his feeling into emphatic language.

'Your letter on the passage of the Tariff Bill [the President said] gave me the kind of pleasure that seldom comes to a man, and it goes so deep that no words are adequate to express it. I think you must know without my putting it into words (for I cannot) how deep such friendship and support goes with me and how large a part it constitutes of such strength as I have in public affairs. I thank you with all my heart and with deep affection.'

[1] This was after Mrs. Wilson's death and before the President's remarriage.

The friendship between the two, however rapidly it bloomed, was progressive. It is not uninteresting and is perhaps significant to trace its development through the forms of salutation used by the President in his letters. They met in November, 1911, and until the following spring Wilson addresses him as 'Dear Mr. House.' But after his nomination, in August, 1912, he begins to address him as 'Dear Friend,' signing himself 'Faithfully yours,' or 'Sincerely yours.' After his election in November, 1912, he signs himself 'Affectionately yours,' and this is constant with the salutation of 'Dear Friend,' for two and a half years. In moments of great emotion, as at the time of Mrs. Wilson's death, he addresses him as 'My dear, dear Friend.' In the summer of 1915, at the period of the *Arabic* crisis when he was torn by doubt and worry, the President begins to address him as 'Dearest Friend,' a salutation which remains invariable until after his reëlection in November, 1916. In January of 1917 the President reverts to the form of address, 'My dear House,' although he continues the conclusion, 'Affectionately yours.' Otherwise it is impossible to detect in Wilson's letters any change of tone. It is certain that the political relationship between the two men remained as close during the two years that followed; but it is possible that their personal friendship was most intense between the years 1912 and 1917.

Close spiritual communion was not dependent upon physical propinquity, for the heat drove Colonel House far from Washington in the spring and frequently several months would pass without their meeting. Separation seems to have made no difference in their understanding. 'I never worry when I do not hear from you,' wrote House. 'No human agency could make me doubt your friendship and affection. . . . I always understand your motives.' At the end of each summer, enterprising and ill-informed newspapermen would regularly feature a 'break.' 'You are a little behind your schedule this year, my friend,' said House to a reporter one September day, after the publication of the annual story.

During the cool months, however, Wilson and House saw much of each other, for the latter made frequent trips to Washington, and on each of these trips Wilson devoted long hours to intimate discussions with his adviser. The President lacked the capacity and inclination for meeting and entertaining varied types of people which, under the Roosevelt régime, made the White House a magnet for explorers, littératteurs, pugilists, and hunters — every one who had an interesting story to tell. Wilson had the college professor's love of a quiet evening by the fireside with the family, and an early bed, varied by a visit to the theatre, preferably a simple vaudeville.

House was one of the few admitted to the small family circle. 'At night,' said Herbert Corey in the *Commercial Advertiser*, 'after Mr. Wilson had wound the clock, and put out the cats and politicians, House stayed for a little further talk.' To the President's study House brought the impressions he had formed of public opinion, gathered from his numerous contacts with office-holders, business men, and editors, and there Wilson gave free vent to his political theories, his aspirations, and his fears. There, too, the President found relaxation in reading poetry and essays to his friend.

'*May* 11, 1913: I spoke to the President about conserving his strength, and suggested various means by which it could be done. I thought it was essential. He said it looked as if the people were trying to kill him, and he spoke of the loneliness of his position, in a way that was saddening....

'I spoke of his probable renomination and reëlection. He replied, "Do not let us talk about that now. My dear friend, if I can finish up my legislative programme, I do not desire reëlection." I urged him to keep up his courage, for if he ever faltered in the slightest he would lose his leadership and influence. He realized this and declared he would maintain his courage to the end.

'*October* 16, 1913: One thing the President said, which interested me, was that he always lacked any feeling of elation when a particular object was accomplished. When he signed the Tariff Bill he could not feel the joy that was properly his, for it seemed to him that the thing was over and that another great work was calling for his attention, and he thought of this rather than the present victory.

'*November* 12, 1913: He [Wilson] said he believed in the Executive becoming the leader in putting into law the desires of the people. He thought there was no danger in this course for the reason that unless a President had the force of public sentiment back of him, he could never get a law through. That the reason he himself had been successful with the tariff and the currency bills was because the people demanded them, and Congress knew it. It was not the pressure from him, but the pressure of the nation back of him.

'He read some extracts from his works on government, in order to define better his views. He expressed himself as being in sympathy with the movement for amending the Constitution with less difficulty than at present. . . .

'He said he had not slept well the night before; that he had nightmares, and that he thought he was seeing some of his Princeton enemies. These terrible days have sunk deep into his soul and he will carry their marks to his grave.

'*December* 22, 1913: At dinner there was no one present but the family, and the conversation ran along general lines. I asked the President how high he ranked Lincoln's Gettysburg Address. He said, *very, very high.* He had also noticed that great orations and great poems, when spoken or written under deep emotion, were simple in language. He mentioned Burke as an example. Some member of the family took exception to this opinion and cited Browning and also suggested that Shakespeare made his heroes say grandiloquent things under stress of great emotion. . . .

'I spoke of his success, and he said his Princeton experience hung over him sometimes like a nightmare; that he had wonderful success there, and all at once conditions changed and the troubles, of which every one knew, were brought about. He seemed to fear that such a dénouement might occur again. . . .

'It was twenty minutes to twelve when we left his study for bed. He was solicitous of my welfare and came into my room to see that everything was properly arranged.

'*April* 27, 1914: The President spoke of not feeling at home anywhere now; that is, he had a feeling that he had no home. He said he felt the same way when he was at Princeton and occupied the house of the President; that while he was perfectly comfortable and happy in his surroundings, yet he always had that unsettled feeling as if he had no permanent abiding-place.

'*April* 28, 1914: At breakfast I spoke of Edward S. Martin's delicious humor, and I thought he was not only humorous but had as much good sense as any one I knew. The President replied that "humor and good sense go together." . . .

'I asked if he would like to be editor of a daily paper. He replied that nothing would appeal to him less, for the reason that no one could write every day an opinion of value. It was difficult enough to do this once a week, but impossible to do it each day. He said he enjoyed *Punch* very much. That "while there were no laughs in it, it was full of smiles."

'*May* 11, 1914: No one dined with us excepting Grayson,[1] and after dinner he left us. The President read poems to me for nearly an hour. It was Wordsworth, Matthew Arnold, Edward Sill, and Keats. What he particularly liked was "A

[1] Dr. Cary T. Grayson, physician to the President.

Fool's Prayer" by Sill, and "A Conservative" by Gilman. When he finished reading, I took out my budget.[1]

'*August* 30, 1914: The last morning I was with the President [in the country] he planned to play golf early enough to get back for lunch and leave on the 2.40 train for Washington. It was my intention to leave . . . when he started for the golf field. This necessitated our getting up early and about the same time. He arose a half-hour earlier than was necessary, merely to give me the uninterrupted use of our common bathroom. This illustrates, I think, as well as anything I could mention, his consideration for others and the simplicity of the man. I notice, too, in his relations with his family that he is always tender, affectionate, and considerate.

'*September* 28, 1914: We talked much of leadership and its importance in government. He has demonstrated this to an unusual degree. He thinks our form of government can be changed by personal leadership; but I thought the Constitution should be altered, for no matter how great a leader a man was, I could see situations that would block him unless the Constitution was modified. He does not feel as strongly about this as I do.

'*November* 7, 1914: There were no outside visitors for dinner, but the President artfully evaded getting alone with me in his study. He was afraid I would renew the McAdoo-Tumulty controversy. However, he need not have worried. We had a delightful evening. He began by talking about German political philosophy and how wrong their conclusions usually were. He spoke of himself as a disciple of Burke and Bagehot. This is literally true, for he is always quoting from one or the other, mostly from Bagehot.

'He began to speak of a flexible or fluid constitution in contradistinction to a rigid one. He thought that constitu-

[1] Meaning the items of political business that demanded the President's attention.

tions changed without the text being altered, and cited our own as an example. At the beginning, he thought, there was no doubt that there was no difference of opinion as to the right of the States to secede. This practically unanimous opinion probably prevailed down to Jackson's time. Then there began a large sentiment for union which finally culminated in our Civil War, and a complete change of the Constitution without its text being altered.

'Just then the ladies came in the sitting-room where we were, and I got him to read some poems, something he very much likes to do. He read William Watson's "Wordsworth's Grave," and afterward, at my request, Gray's "Elegy." He also amused himself with any number of limericks. We did not go to bed until around 10.30.

'*December* 19, 1914: As usual, no one excepting the family was present at dinner. After we had finished the President read aloud for nearly two hours, "The Adventures in Arcadia of the Idle Rich."'

When President Wilson came to New York, he almost invariably stayed with Colonel House. The two would motor in the country, often to Piping Rock, followed by the secret service automobile and three cars of newspapermen who hovered around the President 'like birds of prey,' the Colonel wrote, to be ready in case of an accident. More pleasant were the evenings spent in the small apartment on Thirty-Fifth Street and later on Fifty-Third Street. House disconnected the telephone, barred the door, and left to the President the blessed choice between going to bed or a talk upon some subject unconnected with politics — literature, ethics, the immortality of the soul.

Like Napoleon, Wilson enjoyed suddenly descending upon his friends.

'*November* 14, 1914: Last night Loulie and I went to dinner and theatre with the Bertrons. He had the Belgian Minister and Madame Havenith. The play was "The Only Girl," which I found amusing. Upon my return to the apartment I found a call from the White House. In answering it, they told me the President would arrive at six o'clock this morning and would expect me to breakfast at six-thirty. This changed my plans and I had to notify the Police Commissioner and several others, so it was well after midnight before I went to bed, and I arose at half-past five.

'The matter of entertaining a President within such confined quarters as our little apartment is not an easy undertaking, especially since I have no clerical force excepting my one secretary.

'*October* 8, 1915: To-day started off with the usual bustle incident to a visit from the President. Telegrams, telephone calls, secret service men, newspaper reporters, notes, etc., etc. However, the confusion will cease the moment the President arrives, for I do not permit the telephone to ring and we are undisturbed by letters, notes, telegrams, or visitors. When he is once here, everything appears as peaceful as if there were no such things as noise and confusion in the world.'

II

House's admiration for the President's qualities was as keen as his personal affection was deep. He regarded Wilson's power of leadership as supreme, and in certain respects he placed a high estimate upon his intellectual qualities.

'I have seen a great deal of the President on this visit [he wrote April 17, 1914], and we have opened our minds to one another without reserve. I am impressed by the analytic qualities of his mind and the clearness with which he expresses his thoughts. I have come in contact with minds of greater initiative and imagination, but never one that had more analytical power and comprehension.

'*November* 14, 1914: The President . . . is efficient in his manner of working. For instance, when we were discussing his message to the people concerning the Belgian Relief funds he said: "Now let us decide what points are best to cover." He took a telegraph blank having lines on it, and began to take down in shorthand the different points, he making some suggestions and I making others. There were about five points to be covered, and he asked me to think if that were all. When we concluded, there was nothing more; he called his stenographer and dictated the message in full.

'He has one of the best ordered minds I have ever come in contact with, although he is always complaining of forgetfulness.'

On the other hand, Colonel House was too objective not to observe certain qualities in the President which weakened him as an executive and the effects of which might ultimately seriously endanger his influence.

'One peculiar phase of the President's character develops itself more fully from time to time [he wrote, November 22, 1915]; that is, he "dodges trouble." Let me put something up to him that is disagreeable and I have great difficulty in getting him to meet it. I have no doubt that some of the trouble he had at Princeton was caused by this delay in meeting vexatious problems.

'Another phase of his character is the intensity of his prejudices against people. He likes a few and is very loyal to them, but his prejudices are many and often unjust. He finds great difficulty in conferring with men against whom, for some reason, he has a prejudice and in whom he can find nothing good.

'*July* 10, 1915: I am afraid that the President's characterization of himself as "a man with a one-track mind" is all too true, for he does not seem able to carry along more than one idea at a time. I say this regretfully, because I have the profoundest admiration for his judgment, his ability, and his patriotism.

'*December* 8, 1915: The President, as I have often said before, is too casual and does the most important things sometimes without much reflection.'

An example of such casualness is to be found in Mr. Wilson's speeches, which at times he delivered almost impromptu. He had the power of arranging in his head, at short notice, the order of the topics he would treat and even of constituting the phrases he would use. On May 11, 1914, he came from Washington to deliver a memorial speech at the Brooklyn Navy Yard as tribute to the sailors who had died in the capture of Vera Cruz. House met him at the station and asked him about the speech. 'He had not prepared anything,' wrote the Colonel, 'but he would think it out *en route* from the Battery to the Navy Yard. It is his way of doing. Sometime he will make a serious blunder. It is an occasion for something great, and he may or may not rise to the occasion.'

Unfortunately, President Wilson lacked the power to conceal his prejudices and he was not equipped by temperament or experience to appear a good 'mixer.' A Senator passed the word to House that 'the Senators are in an ugly mood and critical of the President. One grievance is that when they go to the White House for conferences, they are offered nothing to drink excepting water and nothing to smoke.' 'The President,' House commented, 'does not drink excepting occasionally at meals and he never smokes; consequently he does not offer such things to his guests.'

More serious was the fact that the President did not convey the impression of great respect for the Senators, either individually or as a body. 'Senator ——,' he hazarded, 'is the most comprehensively ignorant man I have ever met.'

And later, referring to the same statesman, Wilson said to House, 'Some one wanted to know the other day if I didn't think So-and-So the most selfish man in America. I replied, "I am sorry, but I am already committed to Senator ——."' Such remarks, frequently as apt as they were indiscreet, did not tend to promote cordial relations between the two branches of government.

Mr. Wilson, however, evidently felt that the criticism passed upon him for aloofness and cold self-confidence was quite unjustified.

'*December* 22, 1913 [conversation between House and Wilson]: I said my long experience with public officials had made me fearful of any one after they were elected to office; that the adulation of friends and partisans and the position itself, seemed to go to their heads and they did not do rational things. . . . He thought there was no fear of this with him; that his long university training had shown him how necessary it was to confer about important matters; that he seldom went into a conference and came out with the same ideas as when he went in.

'*April* 15, 1914: I asked [Wilson] whom he considered the greatest man in the early days of the Republic. He thought Alexander Hamilton was easily the ablest. We spoke of Washington and how much he depended upon Hamilton's advice. I thought this in itself indicated Washington's greatness. The fact that he was able to pick out Hamilton from among his associates, as his guiding mind, and that he used him in this way, showed a breadth of view that was remarkable. I told him that all the really big men I had known had taken advice from others, while the little men refused to take it. . . .

'At another time in our conversation, he remarked that he always sought advice. I almost laughed at this statement, for McAdoo had just been telling me to-day that he was at

White Sulphur with the President and his family when the despatch came from Admiral Mayo concerning his demand of Huerta to salute our flag, and he said the President never even mentioned the matter to him. The President does get a lot of information and suggestions from others, but it mostly comes gratuitously and not by his asking. McReynolds, Houston, Lane, and all the others have the same story to tell. . . .

'*April* 18, 1914: Houston and I lunched with Martin [recorded House]. Henry Watterson was also there. He spoke kindly of the President and said they did not differ regarding his policies, but he was a man that he, Watterson, could not successfully coöperate with, indicating that the President was cold and indifferent. I told him that as far as my own experience had been, he was just the opposite, for I had never had a sweeter, kinder, or more affectionate friend than Woodrow Wilson. . . .

'*June* 27, 1914 [in London]: I lunched with Page.[1] Afterwards we went into the private park in front of his house and talked for an hour or more. He asked me to bring to the attention of the President the fact that he, the President, was not seeing enough business men and was not talking to them, as he expressed it, "in their language." He thought the President had a broad and philanthropic view of the situation, and that everything he was doing for the country was absolutely right, but he failed to give proper assurances to the business world that he had their welfare at heart and was not unfriendly as they thought. He suggested that the President should invite some of them to lunch and show them some marked social attention. I did not think he would do this — he was not constituted that way; that I had been at the White House a great deal, but, with the exception of seeing Cleveland Dodge there once, I had not met any one other than the immediate family.

[1] Walter Hines Page, Ambassador to the Court of St. James's.

'I told him, too, how very tired the President was and how he had to conserve his strength, and that we must take him as he was and not as some people would like to have him. He said a prominent American told him the other day that the President did not confer with any one excepting me; . . . he thought a President should not confine himself to a single individual. Page asked how he knew this was true. He replied that it was a matter of common knowledge in America.

'I told Page the President consulted with the individual members of his Cabinet about their departments, but he did not consult with them on matters affecting their colleagues, and I thought he was right. If he did this, he would soon have every Cabinet officer meddling with the affairs of the others, and there would be general dissatisfaction.'

Keenly aware of the wave of criticism that threatened the President because of his retired habits, and realizing that Wilson's strength lay in the formulation and exposition of policy rather than in the despatch of business through personal conference, House set himself to the labor of innumerable interviews and multifarious correspondence, which might offset the criticism and lighten the burden of detail that weighs upon every President. He intercepted importunates on their way to the White House and promised to arrange their business with the President more rapidly than they could themselves. He sifted applications for appointments. He discussed industrial relations with capitalists and labor leaders. He advised the chiefs of industrial corporations how to settle their difficulties with the Government. And afterwards, reporting the gist of these interviews to the President, he brought him into touch with the currents of opinion and affairs.

'*March* 22, 1913: Mr. Frick came at eleven. He wished to know whether I thought it was possible to settle the United

States Steel Corporation suit outside of the courts. He declared that he came of his own initiative and no one knew he was doing so. He wanted the matter kept confidential, excepting the President and Attorney-General. We discussed the matter at some length. I pointed out the difficulties, with which he concurred. He seemed fair. I promised to mention the matter and to see what could be done. . . .

'*March* 24, 1913: I told him [Wilson] about Mr. Frick's call and his suggestion in regard to the United States Steel Corporation suit. Before the President replied, I said, "You had better let me tell Frick that you referred me to the Attorney-General and suggested that whatever proposal came to you should come through the Attorney-General's Office." The President smiled and said, "You may consider it has been said."

'We discussed it at some length. The President thought that the Steel Corporation should have the same consideration as any other, neither more nor less, and that they should be allowed to make a proposition for an agreement as to a decree of court in the suit. . . .

'*April* 18, 1913: I went to the White House early and met the President on his way to the memorial service held for the late President of the Honduras. I found a large number of people waiting, Mitchell Palmer being one of them. I asked if I could not attend to his matters for him, explaining how busy the President was and how uneasy we were for his health if the pressure continued. He said he wanted to know about Guthrie's chances for an ambassadorship. I was able to tell him that the President had him down for Japan. I asked, "What next?" He wished to know about Berry for Collector of the Port of Philadelphia. I was able to tell him that McAdoo and I had threshed that out the day before and we would both recommend his appointment.

'After that he wanted to know about Graham, who wishes to go in the Attorney-General's Office. I told him that Mc-

Reynolds and I had discussed that the day before and that he intended to appoint him. This satisfied Palmer and he went back to the Capitol.

'Jerry Sullivan from Iowa was waiting to see the President, and I treated him as I did Palmer. He had just been appointed on the Appraisers' Court in New York. . . . He was uncertain as to whether he ought to leave Iowa and wished to know how much time he could have to decide. . . . I asked him not to bother the President, but to take it up with me and I would thresh it out with the Attorney-General and take it to the President in concentrated form. He had several other desires, which I advised him to put in writing and to send to me at his convenience.

'I wish I could always be here to do these things for the President and give him time to devote himself to the larger problems which confront the country. . . .

'*August* 2, 1913: John Mitchell, President of the Federation of Miners, and Timothy Healy, President of the International Brotherhood of Stationary Firemen, lunched with me to-day. I talked to them earnestly concerning the future of labor. I urged upon them the necessity of taking a broad view, and not letting the unimportant things of to-day interfere with the larger ones which are to come. . . .

'*November* 19, 1913: I lunched with Charles Grasty of the Baltimore *Sun*. The other guest was Mr. Daniel Willard of the Baltimore and Ohio. I found Willard had a clear knowledge of railroad rates. Many of the facts given me by Secretary Lane, Commissioner Marble, and Frank Trumbull are misleading. Mr. Willard is very agreeable. He used the tablecloth instead of paper to make diagrams and to illustrate his points, and he ate no lunch to speak of, but talked all the time, though not tiresomely. . . .'

Not the least important function taken over by the Colonel was that of receiving complaints against the Administration — which his personal friends, who frequently did not share his admiration for the President, passed on to him with a rugged disregard for his peace of mind. With journalists and editors he kept always in close touch, and they seemed to find in him a man to whom it was worth while to send criticism.

Mr. E. S. Martin to Colonel House

May 18, 1915

Dear House:

. . . Cass Gilbert was at lunch. I said to him: 'The most that I shall do to-day will be to send clippings to House. Why do people do such things for House?' And then we went on to discuss House.

Well! I hope House is pretty well and that the swivel in his honorable neck is working easily, so that when his head is turned with consortations with the mighty he can twist it back without too much effort.

Good luck!

E. S. Martin

1914

Dear House:

I commend to your thoughtful consideration the story I read in the paper, that in some districts in India where they held a bee and cleaned out the tigers, the wild pigs so multiplied that they ruined the crops.

Are the wild pigs going to . . . devour us when we pass the anti-trust bills with the labor union exemptions and muzzle the railroads and skin the millionaires?

I think that is quite a parable about the tigers and the wild pigs.

The I.W.W.'s, the laborites, the socialists, all the cranks and all the hoboes, they are the wild pigs.

Yours

E. S. M.

May 11, 1915

DEAR HOUSE:

. . . Woodrow, after a three-day conference exclusively with himself, made a short speech yesterday which I didn't like; but no matter. I wished he had talked to himself and conferred with some one else. They say he has not conferred one single lick with Bill Bryan . . . and that is good. So we profit by the virtues of Woodrow's defects. . . .

I think Wilson will do right, but if he gets sloppy I'm going to get right in with the Powers of Darkness [Roosevelt and his followers] and help drive the Bryan and Daniels crowd out into the wilderness. This I say, not that it is true, but to enable you to feel the temper of the public. . . .

Good luck.

E. S. M.

Mr. George W. Wickersham to Mr. E. S. Martin (forwarded to Colonel House)

NEW YORK, *February* 3, 1914

MY DEAR MARTIN:

Your editorial for February 11 is very sane. The trouble with Mr. Wilson is that he lives in an imaginary world. He fancies that a thing should be so, and it *is* so. Which is all very well until a large enough number of people begin to inquire, 'Is it so?' Then, like 'the unsubstantial fabric of a vision,' it vanishes. Unlike it, it *does* leave a mark behind.

Yours faithfully

GEORGE W. WICKERSHAM

Mr. James Speyer to Colonel House

NEW YORK, *March* 12, 1914

MY DEAR COLONEL HOUSE:

I am glad you are coming back soon! I am satisfied that the gentlemen in Washington do *not* realize the seriousness of the financial situation through the general impairment of railroad credit. The Interstate Commerce Commission shows no disposition to hurry its decision, as to an advance in rates; on the contrary, they have again extended the time for hearings and are asking more questions, etc. Meantime gross and net earnings are declining and the weaker roads like the Erie, Southern Railway, Chesapeake and Ohio, etc., cannot sell their bonds except at bankruptcy figures, *if* at all. I can only repeat that in my opinion, which I do *not* express publicly, we are face to face with the possibility not of *one* but of *several* receiverships of the big railroad systems. And you know how harmful that would be and how slow the recovery. Mr. Rea's statement of which I enclose a copy is absolutely true and so is the enclosed article from the *Railway Gazette*.

Something must be done and *done soon*, in a big and courageous way, to stop these attacks by Government agencies both Federal and State, if disaster is to be averted. We need a practical and constructive policy and measures.

I wish I could write more cheerfully, but even I am not sufficiently optimistic to close my eyes to existing conditions.

With kind regards

Sincerely yours

JAMES SPEYER

Major Henry L. Higginson to Colonel House

BOSTON, MASSACHUSETTS
January 13, 1915

MY DEAR COLONEL HOUSE:

. . . It does not seem clear to Washington that the action there and in the States is keeping business men on pins, and that, having lost considerable money and lost almost entire confidence, they are not willing to risk their credit. They have simply withdrawn their money in a large way from active business, and are waiting to see whether it is safe for them to pledge their names and their honor in carrying out either old or new enterprises. . . . It is not what Mr. Wilson's

Administration has wished; it is not his intention or that of Congress, no doubt, but they do not see, they do not realize how people feel.

I was glad to vote for Mr. Wilson, and have liked a great deal that he and Congress, with his guidance, have done; but this shipping bill is a terrible mistake. If we can only have peace and nothing new, trust placed in railroad directorates and in other great concerns, we shall go on very well. . . .

Perhaps these matters could be laid before influential men and do some good, and perhaps not.

With kind regards, I am

Very truly yours

H. L. HIGGINSON

Mr. E. S. Martin to Colonel House

NEW YORK, *February* 10, 1915

DEAR HOUSE:

Your press agent is still working overtime.

Who is he, anyhow?

Here are a few clippings.

Our poor country is working along under shortened sail since you left.[1] I don't know any more than I can help about what is going on, and read the papers through smoked glasses. I understand that your friend W. W. has clenched his teeth through the remnants of the shipping bill and means to hold on. He has a heroic bite. I am afraid it is his destiny finally to adhere to something that will sink with him. But who can tell? We are all in the Lord's hands and should be hopeful however anxious. . . .

Yours

E. S. MARTIN

House received the complaints cordially, explained the situation, and promised to do what he could to better it. To

[1] For six months in Europe.

members of the Cabinet he passed on the criticisms and insisted upon the need of meeting the factors that produced them.

'*November* 7, 1913: Bishop Brent came at half-past five to tell of conditions in the Philippines. He says they have a very wrong impression of the Administration, believing that the Democratic Party's advent to power means immediate self-government for them. He does not believe it possible to give them self-government until the school children of to-day become old enough to take an active part in public affairs.

'I complimented him upon the work he is doing, and suggested that any time he wished to reach the President or to accomplish something which he could not accomplish through the ordinary channels, he could communicate with me.'

Colonel House to Mr. William Garrott Brown

New York, *April* 10, 1913

Dear Mr. Brown:

Martin tells me that you think too many Southerners are being given office under this Administration.

You are quite right, but it is hard to help it. The best material that has been suggested for office comes from the South, and it is almost as hard to get satisfactory Democrats from the North as it would be for a Republican Administration to get satisfactory Republicans from the South.

In naming Mr. Page for England the President went into the subject carefully, and by process of elimination Mr. Page seemed to be the most available. And so it has been in every instance....

It seems to me that we will have to assume the burden of responsibility and let it go at that. If the Administration succeeds, as we now hope, then it will be a great tribute to the South; and if it fails, we must necessarily shoulder a larger part of the blame. . . .

With warm regards and best wishes, I am

Faithfully yours

E. M. House

Mr. E. S. Martin to Colonel House

New York, *October* 21, 1915

Dear House:

It uplifted me very much to talk to you.

It always does.

You must be a hypnotizer. Anyhow you always make me feel that we're going to do our duty.

Here's next week's *Life* with a good cartoon.

More power to your elbow!

E. S. M.

Colonel House to Secretary McAdoo

Austin, Texas, *March* 7, 1914

My dear Friend:

I am enclosing you two letters from Colonel Nelson of the Kansas City *Star*, which I think it would be well to have the President glance over.

Every day some complaint of this sort reaches me. I never tire of reading the generous chorus of praise of the President's first year in office, and no one knows better than we how richly he deserves it. However, long experience has taught me how quickly this may turn in other directions. If this should happen, I feel sure it will not be from any act of the President himself, but because those of us whom he has trusted on the watch tower have failed in their duty toward him. . . .

Faithfully yours

E. M. House

III

The extraordinary position of Colonel House, without office and yet an integral part of the Administration, was made possible not merely by the personal regard of the President and the infinite variety of services which House performed for him, but by the intimacy of relations he maintained with the Cabinet. He carried on constant correspondence with them, sometimes personal, sometimes political, always cordial in character. Each time that he visited Washington he evidently took pains to study the problems of their departments and to acquire for them whatever information he could. Brief selections from his memoranda indicate the informality of their intercourse.

'*March* 20, 1913: From Burleson I went to call upon the Secretary of the Interior, and spent a very pleasant quarter of an hour. After that I returned to the Cosmos Club, where I met McAdoo and Houston. They immediately began to berate me for having put them in the Cabinet. They wanted to know what they had done to have such jobs imposed upon them. Houston said he had work enough to do for six healthy men....

'*April* 13, 1913: Secretary Lane came an hour before the time set for the dinner to be given Ambassador James Bryce. He desired to talk of his department and to outline some plans for the future....

'*November* 24, 1913: We arrived at the Bryans' at nine and went almost immediately to bed. It was understood that we were to have breakfast at half-past seven, but, much to our relief, Mrs. Bryan knocked on our doors a few minutes later and announced that Mr. Bryan would take his horseback exercise before breakfast, so we would not have it until half-past eight — an unusually late hour for the Bryan household....

'*November* 25, 1913: To-day was Cabinet day, and I remained to meet the different members as they came in, for there was something I had to say to each. . . .

'*December* 12, 1913: Houston and Burleson came around to see me. I first took up with them the question of Cabinet officers not making speeches without the President's permission, and perhaps not making any speeches unless the President had something in particular for them to say to the country about their departments. I thought the present habit of members of the Cabinet making indiscriminate speeches was very bad, and often embarrassing. I suggested that if the President would designate them to speak upon certain subjects at certain times, what they said would have much weight and would be almost equal to a presidential utterance.

'I found there was some feeling among the members of the Cabinet because the Friday Cabinet meetings had been discontinued. I agreed to mention it to the President and ask him to resume them. Later in the day I did this, and the President consented to do so.

'The President was pleased when I told him I had spoken to a sufficient number of the Cabinet to ensure the adoption of my suggestion that no speeches should be made in the future without his consent, and only when he thought the occasion demanded it. . . .

'*November* 15, 1915: Last night the Secretary of War sent a special messenger from Washington, bearing a letter for me concerning his report. He desired me to discuss with the President the advisability of putting his report out in advance of handing it to the President. The President does not wish him to do so, and I am to convey to Garrison this unpleasant information. Mr. Bryan has wired requesting that I ask the President to appoint a friend of his as Marshal here. This he also declined to do, because he said the man was not fit for that particular place. . . .

'*December* 22, 1913: McAdoo's carriage met me [upon arrival in Washington] and I drove to his home for breakfast. He came to my room in his pajamas, half asleep. He had been up practically all night so as to be in touch by telephone with the House and Senate Conference Committee, which did not reach a conclusion until five o'clock this morning.

'During the morning I remained in McAdoo's private office, telephoning some of the Cabinet members and making some memoranda of things I desired to discuss with the President. . . .

'*December* 23, 1913: I walked with McAdoo to the Cabinet meeting and saw the others as they assembled. Redfield was particularly anxious to show me some statistics regarding our exports, which he considered interesting. . . .

'*January* 16, 1914: I spoke to each member of the Cabinet as they came in, and talked to Lane about the conservation of our radium deposits, strongly urging it. . . .

'*April* 28, 1914: McAdoo and I went back to the White House, as there was to be a Cabinet meeting. There I met all the Cabinet, but had no conversation with any of them excepting Houston. I advised him that the President felt he could not spare him from the Department of Agriculture for the present, but later would probably place him on the Federal Reserve Board. . . .

'*May* 8, 1914: From the Treasury I went to the White House Offices in order to see members of the Cabinet before they convened. McReynolds, Burleson, Lane, Garrison, and others each held me for a moment. Lane was anxious to know whether I thought it advisable for him to go to California at this time to take the LL.D. degree which the University of California has offered him. I advised taking it up with the President and being governed by his wishes. . . .'

No more striking example of the cordial feeling of Cabinet members towards Colonel House can be found than the offer made by the Postmaster-General and the Attorney-General to resign, if their withdrawal would make it easier for the President to appoint House Secretary of State. This occurred in the early autumn of 1915, after Bryan's resignation.

'Burleson and Gregory [noted House on June 20, 1915] thought perhaps I was refusing to become Secretary of State because it would give Texas three men in the Cabinet and all from Austin. They therefore offered to send in their resignations if I would accept.

'When I told the President about Burleson and Gregory offering to resign so as to leave me free to accept the Secretaryship of State without embarrassment to him, he said, "I am glad you told me, for it is something I shall always remember with pleasure."'

Colonel House to Postmaster-General Burleson

ROSLYN, LONG ISLAND
June 21, 1915

DEAR ALBERT:

Gregory has given me your message, and nothing has ever touched me more deeply.

There is no consideration, I think, that would influence me enough to make me accept an office. My endeavor must always be in the path I have so long followed. If I could be brought to think of it at all, it would be to serve my friends and not to accept sacrifices from them.

You and Gregory have made me feel that life is worth living and that all I have tried to do has not been in vain.

Your friend always

E. M. HOUSE

To House, members of the Cabinet brought the most varied problems. He responded with an unsparing expenditure of time and energy and, like Kipling's hero, frequently showed them a quiet and safe way round, out, or under. They evidently relied upon his judgment in matters of appointments. 'Will you kindly have this pair looked up,' wrote McAdoo, 'and tell me what is thought of them?' And two days later: 'Please hurry up report on Mr. Vernon [appointments].' And again, still later: 'Here is a sample of my troubles. Will you be good enough to look into the character of this man and let me hear from you quickly?'

'*May* 10, 1914: Attorney-General McReynolds lunched with me [recorded House]. We went over much the same ground covered in Washington. We discussed a vacant Federal judgeship... and I insisted upon his making an immediate appointment. The docket is becoming clogged and there is no reason for his delay. I had X to see him this morning in order that he might look him over. His only objection to him was that he had no chin. The two men I sent him last week as candidates for United States Marshals seemed to be all right excepting that they were too fat. I have another suggestion to make for an appointment, but the man has a large mole on the back of his ear. I shall ask him to be careful not to expose that side of his head.

'Later in the day, Gregory and I were laughing at this eccentricity of McReynolds. Gregory says he is such a big, fine-looking fellow himself that he cannot get it through his head that any one has any ability that is not built upon the same lines.'

Attorney-General McReynolds to Colonel House

NEW YORK, *May* 11, 1914

DEAR MR. HOUSE:

I've devoted some time to the judgeship, and this is the way it lies in my mind:

X is well recommended and would not be a bad appointment; neither will he ever make more than an ordinary judge. He did not make a good impression on me personally.

Y made a better impression, but I do not regard him as the very best kind of material. If I should act wholly on my own impressions, I'd guess in favor of Y.

However, if you gentlemen think it wisest to select X, I will recommend his appointment and take the chance. He said that he was not certain about acceptance if tendered. We ought to know whether he will, before any formal tender is made to him.

Will you see that the rest is done?

Called you on the 'phone, but you were reported out with the President.

Sincerely

McReynolds

House's opinion was finally approved.

With Gregory, who succeeded McReynolds when the latter was appointed to the Supreme Court, Colonel House's association was even more intimate. The Colonel discussed frankly with him the relations of a Cabinet member with the President, and gave him the benefit of his own experience:

'Never to go into long-winded arguments upon any subject, but to state his position in brief terms and never repeat. That when he and the President agreed upon a matter, never to give him reasons for so agreeing, as the President was too busy to listen to unimportant details. I was sure he would always be able to see the President whenever necessary if he did not burden him with unimportant and unnecessary verbiage. . . .

'Gregory is very able and has been exceedingly successful with New Haven affairs, but it has not spoiled him in the least. He is one of the few that I have ever met who, I believe, would never get "the big head" no matter how suc-

Albert S. Burleson David F. Houston

Thomas W. Gregory

THREE TEXAS CABINET-MEMBERS

cessful he became. He is not only able, but is as loyal as the Legion of Cæsar.'

Colonel House to Attorney-General Gregory

PRIDE'S CROSSING, MASSACHUSETTS
August 20, 1914

MY DEAR FRIEND:

. . . I am so eager for your success and so anxious it may be brought about without any impairment of your strength that there are many suggestions that have come to me since our last talk.

Do be careful about making appointments too soon. Take your time about them and do not let friendship have any undue influence upon you. . . .

Affectionately yours
E. M. HOUSE

On his side, Mr. Gregory wrote continually to House, evidencing invariably the strongest affection both for him and for the President. 'How can I ever repay such confidence or justify it,' he wrote on August 22, 1914. 'How can I ever even up matters with you, who have given him so exaggerated an idea of my ability?' And four days later: 'Come to Washington soon, give us all the suggestions you can spare, and do not doubt that I know you to be, as you have been for years, my very best friend.'

Apparently the Cabinet counted on House not merely to discover available material for appointments, but also to inform unsatisfactory office-holders that they need not expect reappointment or continuance. The function could not have been attractive. House writes to McAdoo: 'I am always ready to meet any suggestion that you make, but if you know Mr. X at all you would know that it would be utterly impossible for me or any one else to notify him "in a tactful way" and "in a way not to hurt his feelings" that his services were to be discontinued. I would as soon undertake to square the circle or to prove the fourth dimension.'

Mr. X, who was evidently a gentleman to be handled diplomatically, seems to have made difficulties, for some time later Mr. Gregory wrote as follows to the Colonel:

Attorney-General Gregory to Colonel House

WASHINGTON, *November* 25, 1914

MY DEAR FRIEND:

I went to the White House last night and had a long talk with the President about X. I do not think the President will agree to appoint him to the —— position, although a final conclusion was not reached. The President made a memorandum of X's case and is going to make an effort to provide for him in some way, and I will keep the matter in mind.

I do not want X, however, to be eternally bombarding my private secretary and me with telegrams demanding his immediate appointment to the place, and I must say that he is making a nuisance of himself. I wish you would get this idea conveyed to him in some diplomatic way....

Sincerely and affectionately yours

T. W. GREGORY

Much more interesting and congenial was the task which Colonel House set himself whenever in Europe — that of studying all sorts of reforms so as to be able to pass on new ideas to the heads of departments in Washington.

'This afternoon [he wrote in London, June 20, 1913] Sir Horace Plunkett came to call and remained for an hour. We discussed the betterment of the farming class along the lines of more effective farming, farming credits, coöperative marketing, and the making of country life more pleasant and desirable. He wished me to come to Ireland and visit him for three days before we sail, and I have promised to go. I am much interested in this phase of governmental work. I want to see what has been done in Ireland under his direction so that I may take some practical knowledge of it to the President and to Secretary Houston for their information.'

House knew of the lifetime of service which Plunkett had devoted to the science of agricultural improvement and to its application to Ireland, of his friendship with Roosevelt, and his love for America. He looked upon him as among the most eminent of living British statesmen, and he hoped to win his interest and help in the solution of American agricultural problems. Plunkett, on his side, had been on the watch for a chance to come into contact with the new Democratic Administration and was delighted to find in the President's adviser a congenial spirit, between whom and himself sprang up an enduring companionship. 'Thus began,' said Plunkett, twelve years later, 'this precious friendship of my later years.' [1]

Sir Horace Plunkett to Colonel House

WASHINGTON, D.C., *October* 16, 1913

MY DEAR COLONEL HOUSE:

You leave me wondering how you can show such extraordinary kindness to a stranger in the land, of whom you know so little, and how I can ever repay such hospitality and help. Yesterday morning and last night will long remain delightful memories. You gave me the opportunity I badly needed to explain things to Mr. Houston, and in this, judging by his kindness to me to-day, I think I must have had some success. I had a most useful time with him and others at the Department this morning and shall probably resume my studies to-morrow. I paid my respects to the President and was

[1] Conversation with the author, August 1, 1925.

shocked to see him looking so worn. The change since January last is terribly marked, and you ought to try and force him to take a week's complete rest the moment the strain is relaxed — even at the sacrifice of some public business.

You will be glad to know that already the atmosphere at the Department of Agriculture has noticeably changed. I am going to think quietly over what I have learned and shall probably write you from Battle Creek a suggestion for a line which, if taken by the President in his first annual message, might greatly assist the Agricultural Department. You would know whether to mention it to the President. Any suggestions I may have from time to time for the Department I shall send direct to the Secretary. . . .

With renewed thanks and kind remembrances to Mrs. House, I am

Sincerely yours

HORACE PLUNKETT

Most characteristic is the following letter, which suggests the remarkable position held by Colonel House. Mr. Lane had in mind resigning from the Cabinet in case a certain other high office should be opened to him. Quite obviously he regarded House's approval as necessary, and yet his fondness for the Colonel was such that he was unwilling to embarrass him by approaching him directly.

Secretary Lane to Dr. S. E. Mezes

WASHINGTON, *July* 4, 1916

MY DEAR SID:

. . . Now don't think me importunate or cheeky or impatient. I'm here to do my 'bit.' I'll stand guard all night without a whimper. All I want is for you, in that superlatively tactful way of yours, to find out if my chances are worth considering at this time — and if they are, will the

Colonel make them something better than mere chances. If they are not, I shall continue sawing wood, and whistling most of the time.

I am not asking for what Ned calls 'bull-con' or for any pat on the back. If you can give me a tip, I shall be obliged; if not, I shall be as always your most devoted and sometimes humble servant,

F. K. L.

P.S. Treat this rather frivolous epistle upon a most important subject as entirely between *us*. I wouldn't for a good right leg want Colonel E. M. to think me to be butting in.

IV

The activities of Colonel House were not confined to assisting the National Administration. We find him in consultation with the Boston city authorities when appointments were to be made, and the New York City and State Democrats looked to him for counsel and aid. An infinite number of lesser problems were cheerfully deposited upon his doorstep by friends, acquaintances, and strangers. He soothed disgruntled journalists, and discussed the plans of inventors who would save the Republic from material destruction in the next war and social enthusiasts who would preserve its soul during the peace.

'I have had as fine a collection of cranks to-day [he wrote on October 20, 1913] as it has been my lot to meet for a long time. Mr. Bryan sent one, Secretary Daniels sent another, and I inherited yet another from the President. The talk has ranged all the way from office-seeking to the control of the planetary system. . . .'

'*October* 23, 1914: My, my, what a busy day! Commencing with Governor Glynn, McAdoo, Dudley Malone, Commissioner Adamson, former Corporation Counsel Archibald

Watson, Stuart Gibboney, Clarence Shearn, Montgomery Hare, Francis Lynde Stetson, McAneny, and so many others I cannot even think of them. Every phase of the New York State election has been referred to me to-day. Telegrams, party notices, arrangements for meetings, have all passed up for visa. I am literally tired out and shall be glad when the election has come and gone. . . .

'*May* 23, 1914 [on an Atlantic liner]: I had several wireless messages, one from Mrs. ——, who desires her husband, who is now Consul at ——, appointed to the vacancy in London. Even at sea there is no rest from the office-seekers. . . .

'*November* 4, 1914: Loulie and I took the 12.08 for Washington. Major-General —— went with us by invitation. I shall be more careful next time, for he literally talked me to death. If he can fight as hard as he can talk, no enemy in the world could resist him. . . .'

Colonel House regarded his position in public affairs with philosophical eye and not without a touch of humor. 'The funny part of it is,' he wrote to his brother-in-law, 'that people seem to think that I have done something unusual, when as a matter of fact it is only because the newspapers have begun to say extravagant things about me. Such, however, is the stuff of which fame is made.'

The interest of the Colonel's life was beyond question, but none the less it must have proved wearying. The more people realized the difficulty of reaching President Wilson personally, the more strenuous were the efforts they made at least to reach House.

'The Governor comes in again this afternoon [wrote House to Dr. Mezes] to spend the night with me and go to the theatre. It is an exceedingly pleasant diversion to have him, but you have no idea how much work it entails.

'As soon as the papers blaze forth in the morning, my

troubles immediately begin anew and I receive communications from unheard-of quarters as well as from friends who have been lost for many years....'

And later:

'... I am suffering from the after-effects of the President's visit. All the latent cranks in the country are at me. Some to kill,[1] some to amuse, but most of them to instruct concerning what is best to be done in every phase of government....'

House also asked himself what would be the effect of his growing reputation upon the mind of the President and others in official positions. The rôle of *éminence grise* was one that demanded a never-failing tact. It may have been flattering to be so placed that every one should regard his consent to a proposal as equivalent to success, but it was politically perilous as well as physically tiring.

Colonel House to Dr. S. E. Mezes

New York, *April* 24, 1913

Dear Sidney:

... I was in Washington ten days, and when I returned I literally had to wade through mail to get to my desk. Every office-seeker and every crank in the United States is on my trail, and I get photographs from all sorts and conditions of people who think in this way they can impress their identity more securely upon me.

It all comes from the newspaper notoriety, and the end is not yet. The next edition of *Collier's*, I believe, is to do the

[1] The following, although belonging to a later period, is typical of the threatening letters House received: 'Sorry I missed the President when he left your home. I had a nice bullet for him for a wedding present! I get him yet and you to, because you are a facker. A friend of Justice.'

thing in grand style. The article is to be entitled 'The President's Silent Partner.' I urged them to name it anything but that, but nothing but that would satisfy them. They said that title had much more punch in it than any other. I agree to that, but I am afraid that I will get some of the licks.

I do not know how much of this kind of thing W. W. can stand. The last edition of *Harper's Weekly* spoke of me as 'Assistant President House.' I think it is time for me to go to Europe or take to the woods.

Fraternally yours

E. M. House

House decided to go to Europe, where he spent the summer of 1913. But he returned to find his influence undiminished and his energies engaged in a succession of major problems, at first domestic and then international in character.

CHAPTER VI

THE ADMINISTRATION STARTS WORK

President Wilson has brought his party out of the wilderness of Bryanism. It has been a great exhibition of leadership.

New York Tribune, December 24, 1913

I

'THE main thing, I think [wrote House to Wilson, July 31, 1915], is always to do the job better than any one else has ever done it, and the political end will take care of itself. This has always been my theory, and I have found it satisfactory and successful.'

This note, which recurs continually in House's letters, would doubtless have surprised many persons who, without adequate information, looked upon the Colonel primarily as a political manager and an expert in party tactics. Another misconception lay in the belief that House acted as a brake upon the President, constantly restraining him from overenthusiasm in reform and urging caution in speeches and legislative measures. His papers by no means bear out this supposition. One may deduce from them, indeed, the definite conclusion that the Colonel was the more radical of the two and was ever in fear lest this Administration, like so many others, once it came into power should be content merely to govern and forget to pave the path for progress. House always insisted upon the need of courage and of radical reform. A clear example of his feeling is found in two conversations, almost a year apart, between House and the President. The first occurred at the moment when tariff lobbyists were threatening the political annihilation of Wilson if he persisted in driving through the Tariff Bill without regard to the demands of special interests. The second took place when reactionary forces were stirring feeling against him because of his proposed anti-trust legislation.

'*May* 11, 1913: Captain Bill McDonald once told me that he attributed his still being alive to the fact that he had never hesitated the fraction of a second, but had always gone straight towards the point of danger, and the courage of the other fellow had always failed. I urged this attitude upon the President as strongly as I knew how, and told him it was the *most essential thing of all.* . . .

'*April* 27, 1914: We talked of the desirability of pushing the progressive cause forward. I thought unless we did this, we could not justify being in the position we were. We spoke of the political results of such a course, and came to the conclusion that it was best not to consider that aspect at all, but to go resolutely forward with the reform programme and let the future take care of itself.'

The extent of Colonel House's influence upon the legislative plans of the Administration may be gathered from a remarkable document which deserves some attention. In the autumn of 1912, immediately after the presidential election, there was published a novel, or political romance, entitled 'Philip Dru: Administrator.' It was the story of a young West Point graduate, incapacitated for military service by his health, who was caught by the spirit of revolt against the tyranny of privileged interests. A stupid and reactionary Government at Washington provokes armed rebellion, in which Dru joins whole-heartedly and which he ultimately leads to complete success. He himself becomes dictator and proceeds by ordinance to remake the mechanism of government, to reform the basic laws that determine the relation of the classes, to remodel the defensive forces of the republic, and to bring about an international grouping or league of powers, founded upon Anglo-Saxon solidarity. His reforms accomplished, he gives effect once more to representative institutions as formulated in a new American Constitution, better fitted than the old for the spirit and conditions of the twentieth century.

As a romance, the book was not notable, for the effort of the anonymous author had evidently been spent upon the careful working-out of the political and social ideas of the young Philip Dru rather than upon its literary form. Certain reviewers, however, were piqued by the daring and the ingenuity of these ideas and, treating the book as a political manifesto rather than a novel, acclaimed it as a remarkable publication. Speculation as to the personality of the unknown author, who was described merely as 'a man prominent in political councils,' naturally followed. There seemed to be general agreement that he could not belong to either of the two older parties. 'We trust he is to be found among the Democrats,' wrote one reviewer, 'but we greatly fear he is of the New Party.' Another reviewer was of similar opinion: 'We trust that the author's counsel and assistance will be available at Washington, if not during the present Administration, surely when the Progressive Party assumes control.' There were, indeed, numerous suggestions that Mr. Roosevelt himself was the author.

Five years after its publication an enterprising bookseller, noting the growing influence of House in the Wilson Administration, wrote with regard to the book: 'As time goes on the interest in it becomes more intense, due to the fact that so many of the ideas expressed by "Philip Dru: Administrator," have become laws of this Republic, and so many of his ideas have been discussed as becoming laws.' And he ends with the question, 'Is Colonel E. M. House of Texas the author? If not, who is?'

Colonel House was, in truth, the author; to his other occupations he had added that of novelist. He tells us himself in a brief memorandum how, in the autumn of 1911, he conceived the idea of writing a novel as a medium to express his economic and political theories. That winter in Austin he was seriously ill.

'When I began to convalesce at home, and before I was able to get about, I wrote "Philip Dru: Administrator." I was surprised at the rapidity with which I wrote, for I was not certain when I began that I could do it at all....

'I was also surprised to find how much I was interested in doing this kind of work. I had written platforms, speeches, etc., for different candidates and officials, and newspaper articles for campaign purposes, but this was an entirely new departure. I did not spend more than thirty days upon the first draft of the book. Mezes read and approved it, and I sent it to Houston to look over, largely with the view of getting his judgment as to the economic features of it.

'He kept the manuscript until I passed through St. Louis on my way East. He declared his belief that it was economically sound, but held that the fiction in it was so thin that he advised rewriting it as a serious work, as he had suggested originally.'

Colonel House to Dr. D. F. Houston

AUSTIN, TEXAS, *March* 12, 1912

DEAR DOCTOR HOUSTON:

... I expect to elaborate somewhat concerning the functions of the National Government.

I particularly want to make it clear that the Executive and his Cabinet will be more nearly akin to the English Premier than to the French, inasmuch as I want him to have the right to propose measures directly and without referring them to a committee.

If you have any suggestions along this or any other lines, please let me have them.

I have done some padding — as, for instance, the story of

the tenement fire — which I expect to take out later and put in more serious stuff.

It is not much of a novel, as you will soon discover; at the same time, unless it were known by that name its audience would be reduced at least ninety-nine per cent. If it was called what I really mean it to be, only those who think pretty much as I do would read it, and those I am trying to reach would never look at it.

Faithfully yours

E. M. House

But this was the spring of 1912, and all of House's energies were taken up with the pre-convention campaign that ended with the nomination of Wilson. The early summer he spent in Europe. Evidently not wishing to give the time necessary to putting it into the form that Mr. Houston advised, by elimination of the romance, and fearing that a scientific essay would not reach a large public, he decided merely to smooth it out so far as possible while on the Atlantic.

'I worked assiduously on "Philip Dru" all the way over and all the way back, but had no time for it in Europe. . . . We returned early in August, and the first thing I did was to shake myself clear of "Philip Dru."

'E. S. Martin read the manuscript and wanted me to rewrite it, saying that "some of it was so good that it was a pity that parts of it were so bad." I had no time, however, for such diversions, for the political campaign was engrossing my entire time and the publisher was urging me to give him the manuscript so it might be advertised in the autumn announcements.

'I was so much more interested in the campaign than I was in the book that I turned it over to the publisher, having determined to let it go as it was.'

Whatever the literary merits of 'Philip Dru,' it gives us an insight into the main political and social principles that actuated House in his companionship with President Wilson. Through it runs the note of social democracy reminiscent of Louis Blanc and the revolutionaries of 1848: 'This book is dedicated to the unhappy many who have lived and died lacking opportunity....' 'The time is now measurably near when it will be just as reprehensible for the mentally strong to hold in subjection the mentally weak, and to force them to bear the grievous burdens which a misconceived civilization has imposed upon them.' Government, accordingly, must be inspired by the spirit of charity rather than the spirit of ruthless efficiency. Especially must privileged interests be excluded from governmental influence, for by the nature of things their point of view is selfish.

Through the book also runs the idea that in the United States, government is unresponsive to popular desires — a 'negative' government, House calls it — for it is at more pains to do nothing with safety than to attempt desirable reforms which might disturb vested interests and alienate the voters. 'We have been living under a Government of negation.' The theory of checks and balances has developed so as to reënforce this negative character of government; closer coöperation between the President and Congress, perhaps in the direction of parliamentary methods, is necessary if the tendency of American government is to be made active and positive.

The specific measures enacted by Philip Dru as Administrator of the nation, indicated the reforms desired by House.

The Administrator appointed a 'board composed of economists and others well versed in matters relating to the tariff and internal revenue, who ... were instructed to work out a tariff law which would contemplate the abolition of the theory of protection as a governmental policy.'

'The Administrator further directed the tax board to work out a graduated income tax....'

Philip Dru also provided for the 'formulation of a new banking law, affording a flexible currency bottomed largely upon commercial assets, the real wealth of the nation, instead of upon debt, as formerly.... Its final construction would completely destroy the credit trust, the greatest, the most far-reaching, and under evil direction the most pernicious trust of all.'

'He also proposed making corporations share with the Government and States a certain part of their net earnings....'

Such were some of Dru's plans which shortly found actual life in Wilsonian legislation. No wonder that Cabinet members like Mr. Lane and Mr. Bryan commented upon the influence of Dru with the President. 'All that book has said should be,' wrote Lane, 'comes about.... The President comes to "Philip Dru" in the end.' [1]

Other excerpts indicate the extent of House's progressiveness.

'Labor is no longer to be classed as an inert commodity to be bought and sold by the law of supply and demand.'

Dru 'prepared an old-age pension law and also a laborer's insurance law covering loss in cases of illness, incapacity, and death.'

'He had incorporated in the Franchise Law the right of Labor to have one representative upon the boards of corporations and to share a certain percentage of the earnings above the wages, after a reasonable per cent upon the capital had been earned. In turn it was to be obligatory upon them [the laborers] not to strike, but to submit all grievances to arbitration.'

[1] *Letters of Franklin K. Lane*, p. 297.

To such an extent had Colonel House formulated his ideas upon national problems before the election of Wilson. 'In regard to "Philip Dru,"' wrote House in 1916, 'I want to say that there are some things in it I wrote hastily and in which I do not concur, but most of it I stand upon as being both my ethical and political faith.'

II

Four great legislative problems confronted Wilson, and their solution constitutes his chief claim, in matters of domestic politics, to the title of statesman. They concerned the revision of the tariff, with the introduction of an income tax law, the creation of the Federal Reserve banking system, the control of trusts, and the regulation of industrial relations. In meeting them Wilson displayed the inspiring leadership essential to success; he showed himself as convincing and sympathetic when he dealt with Congress as a whole, as he was reserved in his dealings with individual Congressmen. By the end of the special session which passed both the Tariff and Currency Acts, his moral supremacy was firmly established and his mastery of the party was complete. He was hailed as the Moses who had led the party out of the legislative ineffectiveness supposedly characteristic of all Democrats.

In each of the great problems House took deep interest. He brought to the President the variety of opinions which he culled from his numerous personal contacts, he utilized his relations with party leaders to assist the passage of the bills through Congress. But it was in the currency question that he took chief interest, for this he had long studied and from its solution might be expected positive, tangible benefits in a short time. As cotton planter and one-time banker in Texas he appreciated the dangers of an inelastic currency, and as a liberal he distrusted the financial power which certain metropolitan banking firms were able to wield over national commerce and industry.

Organized capital, 'Wall Street' in popular parlance, had secured a control of banking credits which, if it were extended, might place the industrial life of the country in the power of private and at least partially irresponsible interests. Against this so-called 'credit trust' Mr. Bryan had protested in 1896: 'Let the Government go out of the banking business,' the financial magnates had cried; to which Bryan retorted, 'Let the banks go out of the Government business.' If private individuals could release or withhold credits at will, it meant a control of industry and inequality of opportunity at complete variance with traditional American principles.

Colonel House to Senator Culberson

MAGNOLIA, MASSACHUSETTS
July 26, 1911

DEAR SENATOR:

. . . I think Woodrow Wilson's remark that the money trust was the most pernicious of all trusts, is eminently correct.

A few individuals and their satellites control the leading banks and trust companies in America. They also control the leading corporations; and if they are to be permitted on the one hand to use the corporations as a bar against loss to any speculation which they may make, and to use on the other hand the banks and trust companies to borrow all the funds they may need for such speculations, the stockholders of the corporations which they dominate and the business world that depends upon funds from the trust companies and banks which they dominate, are bound to suffer. . . .

Faithfully yours

E. M. HOUSE

During the autumn of 1912 and the spring of 1913, even in the midst of the campaign and the process of forming a Cabinet, House worked constantly on the currency problem, in order to be prepared to assist the President when he should meet the congressional committees. The task which Colonel House set himself was primarily to prevent the President-elect from committing himself to any one scheme until the problem had been thoroughly studied; later he guided the measure so that it was left in the control of experts and preserved from the heresies of political incompetents. The Colonel was the unseen guardian angel of the bill, constantly assisting the Secretary of the Treasury and the Chairmen of the Senate and House Committees in their active and successful labor of translating it into law. Wilson, who was accused of a tendency to avoid advice, proved himself in fact to be far from the self-confident doctrinaire pictured by his opponents, and in the matter of currency reform he was determined that the bill should be founded upon expert opinion.

'The greatest embarrassment of my political career [he said to an enthusiast on this subject] has been that active duties seem to deprive me absolutely of time for careful investigation. I seem almost obliged to form conclusions from impressions instead of from study, but I intend to go much more thoroughly into this matter before saying anything about it; and I heartily agree with you that this, the most fundamental question of all, must be approached with caution and fearlessness and receive dispassionate and open-minded treatment. I wish that I had more knowledge, more thorough acquaintance, with the matters involved. All that I can promise you is sincere study. I wish that I could promise you a constructive ability.'

Colonel House was indefatigable in providing for the President the knowledge that he sought. He collected in his study the banking laws of every nation of Europe. He gathered reports and abstracts from college professors of economics and banking. But he laid chief stress upon his frequent conferences with the bankers themselves, especially those who had had practical experience in drafting previous bills for Republican Administrations.

'*December* 19, 1912: I talked with Paul Warburg over the telephone regarding currency reform. I told of my Washington trip and what I had done there to get it in working order; that the Senators and Congressmen seemed anxious to do what Governor Wilson desired and that I knew the President-elect thought straight concerning the issue.

'*February* 26, 1913: I went to the Harding dinner and talked with the guests invited to meet me. It was an interesting occasion. I first talked to Mr. Frick, then with Denman, and afterwards with Otto Kahn.

'*March* 13, 1913: Vanderlip and I had an interesting discussion regarding currency reform.

'*March* 27, 1913: Mr. J. P. Morgan, Jr., and Mr. Denny of his firm, came promptly at five. McAdoo came about ten minutes afterwards. Morgan had a currency plan already formulated and printed. We discussed it at some length. I suggested that he should have it typewritten and sent to us to-day.' [1]

'The Governor [recorded Colonel House on January 8, 1913] agreed to put me in touch with Glass, Chairman of the Banking and Currency Committee, and I am to work out a measure which is to be submitted to him.

'He spoke of his fear that Bryan would not approve such a bill as I have in mind. I said it was better to contend with Mr. Bryan's disapproval and fail in securing any bill at all, than it was to get one which was not sound.

'*March* 24, 1913: I had an engagement with Carter Glass at five. We drove, in order not to be interrupted....

[1] Typewritten, in order to avoid the impression that might be given by a printed plan that Morgan's were so sure of their financial power that they could impose a cut-and-dried plan.

'I urged him not to allow . . . the Senate Committee to change what we had agreed upon in any of the essential features. He promised to be firm. I advised using honey so long as it was effective, but, when it was not, I would bring the President and Secretary of the Treasury to his rescue.

'I spoke to the President about this after dinner and advised that McAdoo and I whip the Glass measure into final shape, which he could endorse and take to Owen [1] as his own. My opinion was that Owen would be more likely to accept it as a presidential measure than as a measure coming from the House Committee on Banking and Currency.'

The Currency Bill was brought into the House of Representatives early in the extra session, its main features unchanged from the first drafts decided upon by the President, McAdoo, and the Chairmen of the House and Senate Committees. The initial difficulties threatened by certain elements in the party which tended toward economic free-thinking, were safely passed. There remained, however, the opposition of a number of Senators, behind which lay the dislike of the bill expressed by prominent Eastern bankers, who evidently feared that it meant a weakening of Wall Street's power and an amateur or political control of national financial problems. House spent much of his summer in defending the bill and more of his autumn in securing political support for it.

'*July* 23, 1913 [conversation with Josiah Quincy, former Mayor of Boston]: I tried to show him the folly of the Eastern bankers taking an antagonistic attitude towards the Currency Bill. The Administration is endeavoring to serve the country as a whole, and it is the better part of wisdom for the Eastern bankers to join hands in working out a measure for the general good.

[1] Chairman of the Senate Committee.

'Quincy wanted to know what I thought the result would be of their threat to withdraw their national bank charters and take out state charters. I thought the threat was puerile, and not to be discussed, and that the bill would be passed no matter what action they took in that direction.'

On the following day, House dined with the members of the Boston Clearing House Association to discuss the bill. He went in no optimistic frame of mind. 'I have a feeling,' he wrote, 'that they are not coming for the purpose of discussing the measure with open minds, but are antagonistic to it. I shall be alone to defend the measure.'

His forebodings were apparently realized, for he noted after the dinner: 'I found the bankers singularly barren of suggestions. They seem to stand upon the general proposition of being against the Administration bill, but without any constructive suggestions looking to its betterment.'

House found more consolation and satisfaction in a long talk with Major Henry L. Higginson, at the end of August.

'I can well understand [wrote House] why he is considered by many, Boston's first citizen. We talked of the currency question and I found that he had a breadth of view unusual amongst those of his calling. He seemed to want what was best for the entire country, and not something for his particular locality and profession. I explained with what care the bill had been framed. Just before he arrived, I had finished a review by Professor Sprague of Harvard of Paul Warburg's criticism of the Glass-Owen bill, and will transmit it to Washington to-morrow. Every banker like Warburg, who knows the subject practically, has been called upon in the making of the bill. Major Higginson seemed thoroughly satisfied with the endeavors the Administration have made to construct a good and beneficent measure.

Colonel House to Mr. E. S. Martin

BEVERLY, MASSACHUSETTS
September 2, 1913

DEAR MARTIN:

...The Currency Bill should go through the House next week, but it will have a harder road in the Senate. I have been working upon it assiduously. McAdoo has been here three or four times, and it seems to me that I have seen every banker and political economist in the East.

The bankers, sad to relate, know next to nothing about it, and none of them agrees as to what is best. The only unanimity of opinion amongst them is that the bill should be made for them and be operated by them, and they cannot understand that the manufacturers, merchants, railroads, farmers, and others have any rights in the premises.

I think the bill is getting in good shape. Houston was with me last week and he says that in his opinion, and in the opinion of ninety per cent of the political economists throughout the country whose opinions are of value, it is the best bill that has ever been constructed — infinitely better than the Aldrich Bill....

Faithfully yours
E. M. HOUSE

'*October* 19, 1913: I saw Senator Reed of Missouri in the late afternoon and discussed the currency question with him. He says the President seems to be more concerned in regard to haste than he does as to the measure itself. In this, of course, he is mistaken. The President is satisfied with the measure approximately as it is, and he knows that Reed and the other Democratic Senators who are delaying it are doing so from a failure to study the measure as it has progressed through the House, and he is impatient in consequence.

'*October* 31, 1913: Paul Warburg was my first caller, and he came to discuss the currency measure. There are many features of the Owen-Glass Bill that he does not approve. I promised to put him in touch with McAdoo and Senator Owen, so that he might discuss it with them.

'Senator Murray Crane [1] followed Warburg. He has been in touch with Senators Weeks and Nelson of the Currency Committee, and urged them to bring about quick action in order that the business community could have done with this uncertainty and could go ahead with the renewed hope a proper currency measure will give them. He telephoned me later that he had been in communication with Washington, and he advised that we bring some pressure upon the Democratic insurgents of the Committee. I called up McAdoo immediately and asked him to convey this information to the President and to gently start the pressure. I also arranged for him to meet Warburg here on Monday.

'*November* 17, 1913: Paul Warburg telephoned about his trip to Washington. He is much disturbed over the currency situation and requested an interview, along with Jacob Schiff and Cleveland H. Dodge. Mr. Dodge came in advance of the others. He said he felt obliged to come at their request, because they had just given him a substantial subscription for the Y.M.C.A. fund. He had a feeling that the President knew what he was doing and did not need any more advice than he was getting from the channels he himself selected. I told him I shared this view and that, since all the experts disagreed, it left one in doubt as to what to do.

'Mr. Schiff and Mr. Warburg came in a few minutes. Warburg did most of the talking. He had a new suggestion in regard to grouping the regional reserve banks, so as to get the units welded together and in easier touch with the Federal Reserve Board. Mr. Schiff did not agree as to the advisability of doing this. He thought the regional reserve banks should be cut down to four and let it go at that.

'They wanted me to go to Washington with Mr. Warburg

[1] Republican Senator from Massachusetts.

and Mr. Dodge, Mr. Schiff saying I was the Moses and they would be the Aarons. He asked if I knew my Bible well enough for this to be clear to me. I told him I did. I combated the idea that the President was stubborn in his stand upon the currency measure. I thought he had to be firm and had to make up his mind as to what was good and what was bad in the innumerable suggestions that came to him, and that was all he was doing. I advised against going to the President with new suggestions. I thought they should be taken to Secretary McAdoo, Senator Owen, and Mr. Glass; if they agreed as to the advisability of accepting them, the President would probably also accept them.'

Pressure from both sides and from above, as exercised by the President, finally compelled the acquiescence of the opposing Senators; and on December 20, 'a gala day' House called it, the Federal Reserve Bill passed the Senate. It was hailed generally as a greater triumph for Wilson even than the Tariff Act, and in the Colonel's matured judgment was the most important single legislative act of the entire Wilson Administration. Even the strongly Republican New York *Tribune* could not withhold words of commendation: 'President Wilson has brought his party out of the wilderness of Bryanism. It has been a great exhibition of leadership.'

Few persons suspected the share taken by Colonel House in the formation and passing of the Federal Reserve Act, and he said nothing that might enlighten the public. Towards the end of December, 1913, after the Senate had approved the bill, House was discussing it with two outstanding journalists, Lawrence of the Associated Press and Price of the Washington *Star*. 'I wish you would let me tell about your activities in making the bill,' said the latter. But the Colonel was obdurate in his insistence upon silence. 'Will you stay over to see it signed?' asked Lawrence. But now that the main job was accomplished, House admitted he lacked sufficient interest in any mere ceremony to keep him in Washington.

III

As events developed, Colonel House's connection with the Federal Reserve Act was by no means ended when it became law, for there remained the problem of the appointment of the five Governors of the Federal Reserve Board who, with the Secretary of the Treasury and the Comptroller of the Currency, act as the coördinating body of the system. The personnel of the Board was obviously a matter of the first importance, not merely for the sake of administrative efficiency, but also because the easiest way to win public confidence in a measure which has been questioned is to appoint men whom the public admires and trusts.

Colonel House acted in much the same capacity when it came to the appointment of the Board as he did in the selection of the Cabinet; that is, he gathered lists of possibilities, interviewed them, culled opinions about them, sifted the names and passed them on to President Wilson and Secretary McAdoo. The following excerpts are typical:

'*January* 19, 1914: Mr. X came to lunch. I had a very frank talk with him, saying I had thought of him in connection with the Federal Reserve Board and intended to present his name to the President provided I did not find some one else whom I thought better fitted for the place. The more I see of him, the more I like him. He is not the biggest mentality I have met, but he has good sense and has many fine qualities.

'Mr. Y came to be looked over for the Federal Reserve Board. He differs from X inasmuch as he is an applicant, while I sought X out myself without any suggestion from any one. . . . He is older and has had more experience, but he is not so fine a type. I played the part of schoolmaster, as usual, and questioned him closely about himself and his business career.

'*January* 21, 1914: After dinner we [Wilson and House] went to the President's study as usual, and began work on the Federal Reserve Board appointments. I insisted that it was the most important constructive legislative measure that had been passed since the foundation of the Republic and thought its success or failure would largely depend upon the personnel of the Board. He replied, "My dear friend, do not frighten me any more than I am now." I saw no need for alarm, because for this particular Board there was plenty of good material to choose from. . . .

'In discussing the Federal Reserve Board, there was one man whose name I presented by saying that he had been getting his friends to endorse him and had secured many eminent people to ask for his appointment. The President replied to this, "Let us eliminate him without further discussion."'

Secretary McAdoo to Colonel House

WASHINGTON, *February* 15, 1914 [?]

DEAR COLONEL:

. . . I wish some people would quit trying to put over political appointments on the Board! That is the most insidious and difficult thing to deal with. I am firmly opposed to making these banks political instrumentalities, and yet I am going to offend many of my best friends because they can't see the importance of eliminating politics absolutely from the organization of the banks. Of course this doesn't apply to you! I'm speaking of politicians.

With warm regards, always

Cordially yours

W. G. McADOO

Colonel House to the President

AUSTIN, TEXAS, *February* 21, 1914

DEAR GOVERNOR:

I find that Mr. X of Dallas is too old to be considered, so he will have to be eliminated.

Burleson, who is here to-day, tells me that Doctor Y, of whom you speak, is a crank of the first water and would not do.

I do not know Mr. Z, and the objection to him might be that he is not sufficiently prominent for his appointment to carry weight. That is something to be considered in this Board if it is to be thought of in the same sense as the Supreme Court.

I can think of some men that I am sure would be equal to the job, but they would not carry confidence and therefore would be poor appointments.

If the elder Simmons were appointed for the two-year term, you could replace him by Houston afterwards, if you desired. Then, with Miller from the Pacific Coast and Wheeler or some one else from Chicago, you would have the West taken care of....

If Z does not bear inspection, then your suggestion of Gregory [1] would not be bad. Gregory is something of the same type as Carter Glass, and, while he knows nothing of the matter now, yet within six months he would be as well-informed upon the subject as Glass was after that period of time.

Call me when you need me, for I am always under orders.

Yours with devotion

E. M. HOUSE

P.S. Any recommendation made by members of Congress should be *prima facie* evidence of unfitness, and I would not take any suggestions from that quarter without the most

[1] T. W. Gregory, later Attorney-General.

careful investigation. What I mean is that their recommendations would be political, and therefore largely worthless.

'*March* 25, 1914: Houston, McAdoo, Williams, and I [wrote House] discussed the division of the country into districts and the location of the regional reserve banks.

'In the evening the President and I dined alone and went immediately to his study to have an old-time business session in regard to the Federal Reserve Board. I found he had added no names to those I had given him before I left for Texas. We concluded, however, that I should get up some new material and submit it to him next week, when he hopes to be able to visit me in New York.'

Colonel House to the President

NEW YORK, *April* 3, 1914

DEAR GOVERNOR:

I am terribly disappointed that you could not come this week, and more particularly since Mrs. Wilson's condition is the cause.

I have been working assiduously towards getting a list of suggestions to submit to you for the Federal Reserve Board. Since you are not coming, I am enclosing them in this.

If Richard Olney would take the two-year term, it would be fine, for Houston could then be appointed to succeed him. I have asked a number of people whose opinions are worth while, in regard to Olney, and they all approve it. I do not know whether he would accept, but I have been told that he might do so.

There are a number of names on the list that seem to me admirable, but they would need a little more looking into. If you will indicate the ones that appeal to you, I will investigate further....

Affectionately yours

E. M. HOUSE

During the following weeks, McAdoo and House had many conferences, as a result of which the President was ready by the end of April to make his appointments. House would have been pleased to have Houston appointed Governor of the Federal Reserve Board, but Wilson would not consent to his leaving the Cabinet at this time. 'I wish there were two Houstons instead of one,' he had told House on February 18. 'I really do not see how I can spare him from the Secretaryship of Agriculture, particularly at this juncture when we are considering rural credits and when we are just beginning to be able to guide the farmers in new directions. We have not yet entirely convinced them of our usefulness.'

Instead, the President accepted House's suggestion of offering the post of Governor to Richard Olney of Boston, Secretary of State under President Cleveland and one of the most distinguished figures of the party. Paul Warburg of New York, because of his interest and experience in currency problems under both Republican and Democratic Administrations, and W. P. G. Harding as a leading banker of the South, had always been sponsored by House and were accepted by the President. To represent the Middle West and the Pacific Coast, H. A. Wheeler of Chicago and A. C. Miller of California had finally been selected. Warburg, Harding, and Wheeler were professional bankers, Olney a lawyer, and Miller a college professor whose distinction in the field of economics had brought him into the Department of the Interior. Political affiliations were not a factor in their appointment; but of the five two were Republicans, two Democrats, and the fifth an independent.

Notes made by House of conversations with Wilson in April throw light on the final process of appointment.

'*April* 15, 1914: We motored for an hour and a half and had a delightful talk. We discussed the Federal Reserve Board at length, and McAdoo's attitude toward the different names proposed. I had taken the precaution to thresh these matters out with McAdoo and could tell the President his state of mind. I am anxious for this Board to administer the currency law successfully, for I am certain the President's reputation in history will rest largely upon its success or failure.

'*April* 28, 1914: After dinner we went to the office for the President to sign his mail. We read the Mexican despatches together and afterward got down to the real finish of the Federal Reserve Board. He took his pen and wrote down their names: Richard Olney first, then Paul Warburg, Harding, Wheeler, and Miller. He turned to me and said, "To whom would you give the ten-year term?" I advised giving it to Miller, which he did. He gave Olney the two-year term, Warburg four years, Harding and Wheeler the six and eight-year terms.

'I told him McAdoo preferred Hamlin.[1] He replied, "But I prefer Olney and I happen to be President." He also said, "McAdoo thinks we are forming a social club." This, of course, was because McAdoo had consistently urged a Board that would work in harmony with him.'

Olney, however, found it impossible to accept. He wrote the President that he had undertaken trusts which he could not resign and that the provision requiring each member of the Board to give his entire time to its work would prove an insuperable obstacle to his acceptance. 'You can hardly be sorrier than I am,' he said, 'that I am able to do so little in aid of an Administration whose first year of achievement makes it one of the most notable the country has ever known.' The appointment was therefore given to Mr. Hamlin, according to McAdoo's wishes.[2]

[1] Mr. Hamlin was an Assistant Secretary of the Treasury whom McAdoo desired to take out of the Department and put upon the Board.

[2] A further change in the original composition of the Board resulted from Mr. Wheeler's inability to serve. After some delay the place was given to F. C. Delano of Chicago.

IV

The close of the first legislative session of the Wilson Administration was a season of triumph for the Democratic Party. Two of the major problems had been met with vigor and honesty, and settled, in principle at least, to the satisfaction of the nation. The income tax provisions of the Tariff Act and the Federal Reserve System of the Currency Act established a solid basis upon which national finances could rest securely during the days of stress that followed the outbreak of war in Europe. The triumph of the Administration was the greater in view of the failure of the preceding Republican Administrations to settle the currency problem. The main principles of the solution finally carried through by Wilson, the Republicans had advocated, individually or collectively; but they had lacked either the courage or the strength to write them into law.

Wilson's success justified largely the inclusion of Mr. Bryan in the Cabinet. The Commoner's sense of loyalty had kept him from an attack upon the Federal Reserve Act which, it would appear, he never entirely understood; but had he been outside the Cabinet, with his influence in the party, he could have destroyed the measure which failed to accord with his personal doctrines.

Ambassador W. H. Page to Colonel House

LONDON, *December* 20, 1913

MY DEAR HOUSE:

. . . I've just read of the passage by the Senate of the Currency Bill. What a record that is! The Tariff Act and the Currency Act at one sitting. I don't know the final form of the currency measure, but no matter. The getting of it through is an unmatched achievement. . . . It's all wonderful; and I'll be proud to do or to endure anything for the man at the helm who steers the old ship in this fashion. If I'd lived a hundred years ago I'd have said, 'There's the hand of God in this.'

Yours

W. H. P.

Mr. Jacob W. Schiff to Colonel House

NEW YORK, *December* 23, 1913

MY DEAR COLONEL HOUSE:

I want to say a word of appreciation to you for the silent, but no doubt effective work you have done in the interest of currency legislation and to congratulate you, that the measure has finally been enacted into law. We all know that an entirely perfect bill, satisfactory to everybody, would have been an impossibility and I feel quite certain fair men will admit that unless the President had stood as firm as he did, we would likely have had no legislation at all. The bill is a good one in many respects, anyhow good enough to start with and to let experience teach us in what directions it needs perfection, which in due time we shall then get. In any event you have personally good reasons to feel gratified with what has been accomplished, and trusting that this feeling may increase your holiday spirit,

I am with good wishes

Faithfully yours

JACOB W. SCHIFF

Secretary Lane to Colonel House

WASHINGTON, D.C., *December* 25, 1913

MY DEAR COLONEL:

. . . This should be a glad time for you. I know of no one who has more fully realized his ambition or who may with more justification take pride in the good he has done.

I was sorry not to see you when the President signed the

Currency Bill. He made a speech in all ways worthy of himself — which is saying much. . . .

Sincerely yours

FRANKLIN K. LANE

The fact that he had had some share in the legislative accomplishment of these months was the reward that House sought for the pains and effort he had given to help in making Wilson's Administration a success. To a friend who wrote complaining that House's aversion for holding office would deprive him of the public credit that belonged to him, the Colonel replied: 'I am satisfied with the consciousness of having taken part in things that are worth while.'

The sentence was not entirely accurate, for, although Colonel House was obviously careless of the fact that the extent of his activities was not widely suspected, he wanted to exercise his energy in a broader field. He was wearied by the details of party politics and appointments; even the share he had taken in constructive domestic legislation did not satisfy him. From the beginning of 1914 he gave more and more of his time to what he regarded as the highest form of politics and that for which he was peculiarly suited — international affairs. They shortly became his main preoccupation, and it is in this field that he rendered his greatest services.

CHAPTER VII

ASPECTS OF FOREIGN POLICY

If some of the veteran diplomats could have heard us, they would have fallen in a faint.

Sir William Tyrrell to House, November 13, 1913

I

Nothing is more strange than the chain of circumstances which finally brought President Wilson to play a rôle of supreme importance in the affairs of the world, and to centre his whole being upon a policy of international service. At the beginning of his political career, and even during his first two years as President, diplomatic questions were of far less interest for him than his legislative programme; he was slow to develop what might be called a definite policy, and he left his Ambassadors to work out their problems themselves. Shortly after the appointment of Mr. Page as Ambassador to St. James's, Colonel House reports that he asked Wilson 'if he had given Ambassador Page special instructions.... He had not, but took it for granted that he would be diplomatic and conciliatory.'

This seems casual, but we may remind ourselves that neither the traditions of the Democratic Party nor the background of Mr. Wilson could lead to the expectation of keen interest in other than domestic matters. The Democratic platform touched on foreign affairs only in a brief reference to the Philippines, and Wilson himself in his first inaugural address confined himself entirely to questions of social and industrial reform.

For Colonel House, on the other hand, foreign problems were always of the first interest and importance. When he says that he shaped his early career so as to prepare him and permit him to satisfy his penchant for politics, he interpreted the word 'politics' in its broadest sense, and included international relations. During his career in Texas he had never ceased to study current diplomacy; and running all through his varied activities as the President's adviser in 1913 there is obvious the desire to free himself from details of domestic politics and to find time to help in the formulation of a positive foreign policy. With the passing of the legislative programme of 1913, he felt convinced that the moment had come for Wilson to lay its broad foundations. A year and a half later, on June 24, 1915, he wrote: 'To my mind, the President has never appreciated the importance of our foreign policy and has laid undue emphasis upon domestic affairs. I thoroughly approved this up to the end of the special session of Congress, when the tariff, banking, and such other measures were involved....'

However slow to formulate a positive policy, President Wilson was acutely aware of the danger that always menaces American interests abroad when a change of administration occurs, and to his credit be it said that he fought constantly against the threatened intrusion of the spoils system. His first choices for the more important diplomatic posts were President Eliot, Richard Olney, Professor Fine of Princeton; and before his inauguration he expressed to House his desire to elevate 'the foreign service by appointments as nearly akin to that of Dr. Eliot as he could find favorable material.' The problem was not a simple one, in view of the difficulty of discovering distinguished Americans with the necessary combination of intellectual background and material resources, and also in view of the purely partisan influences which regarded the foreign service as primarily designed to furnish occupation for political supporters. The invincible good-nature of Mr. Bryan made it hard for him to refuse an application for a diplomatic or consular appointment, especially when made by some loyal adherent of 16–1 in '96. Surely such a one had earned his reward![1]

House was entirely of the President's opinion. He urged that even the highest consular offices should be kept under Civil Service Regulations, and it was at his insistent recommendation that *diplomates de carrière*, such as William Phillips and H. P. Fletcher, who had proved their ability under Republican Administrations, were brought back into the diplomatic service or promoted. And he warned the President against appointments that might seem connected with business interests.

'*April* 18, 1913: I told Mr. Bryan [recorded House] of my conversation with the President regarding the question of keeping the Consuls under the Civil Service. . . . The President stated that he would hold to Roosevelt's executive order in regard to Consuls. Mr. Bryan is a spoilsman and is in favor of turning the Republicans out and putting in Democrats. He argued strongly and eloquently for his position. I remained quiet, for my sympathy is with the President's policy even though it keeps some of our very good friends from their desires.

'*January* 16, 1914: We discussed the President's Civil Service views [House wrote of a later conversation with the Secretary of State], which, of course, do not agree with Mr. Bryan's. I can see some feeling developing between them . . . on the question of patronage. Mr. Bryan has no pa-

[1] Thus the Secretary of State wrote to the Receiver of Customs in San Domingo, who had been appointed through the influence of Mr. McCombs: 'Now that you have arrived and are acquainting yourself with the situation, can you let me know what positions you have at your disposal, with which to reward deserving Democrats? . . . You have had enough experience in politics to know how valuable workers are when the campaign is on; and how difficult it is to find rewards for all the deserving. . . . Let me know what is requisite, together with the salary, and when appointments are likely to be made.' (Letter dated August 20, 1913, and published in the New York *Sun*, January 15, 1915.)

tience with the Civil Service. He said the President told him I had recommended ——, and the President desired to appoint him. Mr. Bryan said, "Of course he can do as he pleases, but I am certain —— is one of those supercilious persons who will be constantly looking down upon me."'

Colonel House to the President

NEW YORK, *October* 8, 1914

DEAR GOVERNOR:

One or two people have asked me to suggest X for the Mexican Embassy.

I hardly think it is necessary to caution you about this, but I feel that perhaps I had better do so.

X, I have always been told, was a part of the Y, Z Oil Company and a bosom friend of Z. The fact that you offered him Argentina makes them feel that he would have a chance for this place, which I have no doubt he would accept quickly enough.

When this appointment is made, I would be certain that the appointee was chemically clean from oil or ore.

Affectionately yours

E. M. HOUSE

When it came to the more important diplomatic appointments, Wilson appealed constantly to House for information and advice. At one moment the President commissioned him to discover an applicant's attitude on religion, as he was being considered for China and the President wanted to know whether or not he was an orthodox Christian.[1] House undertook the delicate task, and the following day put the presumptive candidate through an examination on religious principles. 'He did not seem to have any worth while,' re-

[1] This interest upon the part of Mr. Wilson was dictated by Mr. Bryan's insistence that none but an orthodox Christian could be appointed as Minister to China.

corded the Colonel, and the appointment was not made. With House the President discussed at length the choice of men for St. James's, Berlin, Rome, Vienna, and Paris.

For the Court of St. James's, Wilson expressed himself as anxious to find a man who could continue the traditions established by Adams, Bayard, and Hay. But first President Eliot, and then Richard Olney, declined the post. Colonel House, who was himself frequently suggested for this position, urged Walter Hines Page. The latter was personally magnetic, possessed a genial and discriminating wit, and could boast of a distinguished journalistic career. On March 20, House, recording a conversation with the President in which Mr. Wilson expressed his discouragement at the lack of material for the important ambassadorships, wrote: 'I think he will eventually offer the London mission to Walter Page.'

'*March* 24, 1913: We first took up foreign appointments [House noted of a later conversation with Mr. Wilson]. He thought that Walter Page was about the best man left for Ambassador to Great Britain. I was not only the first to suggest Page for this place, but, since Eliot and Olney declined it, I have advocated him earnestly. He asked if I thought Page would take it. I assured him that he would, and promised to find out definitely to-morrow.

'We discussed a great number of other people for foreign appointments. . . . I thought Thomas Nelson Page should have Italy, and he agreed. . . .

'*March* 26, 1913: I called up [Walter] Page and said, "Good morning, Your Excellency." He wanted to know what it meant. I replied it meant a great deal. He seemed quite agitated and asked whether I was not joking. I replied that I was not, for the President had authorized me to ask him if he would accept the Ambassadorship to the Court of St. James's. We arranged for him to call at 4.30.

'Page arrived promptly. He was excited over the news I had conveyed. He asked me to tell him exactly how it happened. I told him I had suggested his name to the President two months ago.... I had talked to the President from time to time about the matter, and when I dined with him on Tuesday he had authorized me to find whether he, Page, would accept.

'He was immensely pleased with the compliment, but expressed doubt as to his ability to fill the place. It was so entirely different from anything he had previously done....

'*March* 28, 1913: Walter Page telephoned around nine o'clock: "I have decided to turn my face towards the East," which meant he would accept the post to Great Britain. I felicitated him and expressed my pleasure. He wished to know the next move. I told him I would notify the President and that he would write him a formal note offering him the Ambassadorship.

'I called up the President at Washington a little after nine, to tell of Page's acceptance. He replied, "That is fine; I am very glad." He promised to write him at once.

'I telephoned Page to let him know how pleased the President was. He expressed great appreciation for what I had done....'

Having confided to House the mission of informing Mr. Page of his choice, the President thought little more about it and was apparently in no hurry to communicate himself with the appointee — an attitude which surprised and troubled the new Ambassador and recalls the manner in which Secretary Houston had been appointed to the Cabinet:

'*March* 30, 1913: Walter Page and Secretary Houston came to dinner [wrote House], and we had a delightful time. Houston and I tried to make Page feel happy in his new field of endeavor. He seems fearful lest he might not be able to maintain himself, and yet he said he had enough sporting blood to undertake it. He was somewhat disturbed because he had not heard from the President, and asked me whether I thought it was actually settled.

'Houston then told of his experience. He said, "I have never to this good day received any notification of my appointment as Secretary of Agriculture, excepting that which I received from Mr. House." And further, "I was uncertain whether I should come to Washington, but I concluded I had better do so. I came, and I had no notification there. Finally some cards were sent to my wife and to me, inviting us to lunch at the White House after the Inauguration. We went, the President shook hands with me and said he was glad to see me, but nothing else. The President's Secretary sent me word that the President expected me at the White House at eleven o'clock the next day for an informal meeting of the Cabinet. I felt that matters were getting warm and I was getting nearer my job. I went to the informal meeting and, since I seemed to be expected, concluded that in due time I would be notified; but I never was. Then I read in the newspapers that my name had gone to the Senate, and finally I received my commission." . . .

'*April* 12, 1913: I lunched at the White House [recorded House]. Loulie, Mr. and Mrs. Page, and Mr. and Mrs. Wallace were the other guests. Soon after lunch I rang up Mr. Bryan to tell him that Mr. Page desired to pay his respects. He asked us to come over to the State Department at once. Bryan was very gracious to Page, which pleased him because he has not said many kindly things of Mr. Bryan. Page hoped Mr. Bryan would place him in the kindergarten and teach him as rapidly as possible the essentials of his work. Bryan laughingly replied, "I will have to learn myself first." . . .'

These were busy days for Colonel House. It was the period

when he was trying to concentrate upon the framing of the Federal Reserve Act; but on the one hand the President, and on the other every one who desired a diplomatic post, assailed him for advice and assistance.[1]

'*March* 10, 1913: Another stream of callers all day, and long distance telephones from Washington and elsewhere. This job of being "adviser to the President" may have its compensations, but it certainly has its drawbacks. . . .

'*March* 11, 1913: Again another day of office-seekers. Thomas Nelson Page called. He did not mention his own aspirations, but I brought up the subject myself. I told him that it had been the President's intention to appoint him either to France or Italy, but I was afraid now that he [Mr. Wilson] had reached Washington he would be stormed by those desiring the appointments for others.

'Page said he would prefer Italy to France, though France was a greater honor. . . .

'*April* 12, 1913: The dinner to the French Ambassador, Monsieur Jusserand, was interesting. I talked with Senator Lodge. He wants a man from Nahant retained in the Boston Custom House, and I promised to try and arrange it if he was competent.

'Thomas Nelson Page was at the dinner, and I informed him that if no change was made he would go to Italy. I advised him to keep away from the President. . . .

'*April* 16, 1913: A Colonel who would be a Brigadier-General, and a Secretary of Legation who would be transferred from Japan to France, caught me at breakfast. The diplomat is wealthy, so I requisitioned his motor and had him take me from place to place until lunch time. . . .

'*April* 20, 1913: Justice Gerard came to see me about his chances for ambassadorial honors. I thought they were

[1] The character and the amount of the work carried on by Colonel House suggests the advisability of including in the Cabinet a member without portfolio.

slight, but they were better now than they had been. He laughed and said, "I do not believe that until right recently I had any chances at all." That, I replied, was true. I told him, furthermore, if McCombs and Morgenthau were given foreign appointments that five out of the nineteen major places would have gone to New York, which was out of all proportion to her share. He saw the point. He did not believe McCombs would accept. He evidently does not know McCombs; he is as likely to do one thing as another. . . .

'*September* 29, 1913: X is sitting on the doormat again. Rumors that McCombs is not to take the Ambassadorship to France have started his hopes afresh. . . .'

II

Because of his interest in foreign affairs and diplomatic appointments, House was brought into close touch with the Ambassadors, and the cordial relations that resulted went far to facilitate the special missions which he undertook in Europe during the war. Thomas Nelson Page wrote after his appointment:

'Neither letter nor cable can in the least convey the appreciation I have of your kindness to me since our first acquaintance. I am just going to let the debt stand as it is, and reckon ourselves as old friends whose community of feeling and sentiment does away with any count of mere time.'

Brand Whitlock wrote from Brussels:

'My dear friend, I hope it's only *un petit au revoir*. . . . Your last letter brought me joy. . . . It increased, if that were possible, my desire to see you and to have again one of those long chats. . . . I have need of such sympathetic intercourse.'

Willard at Madrid, Penfield at Vienna, Morris at Stockholm wrote frequently to him, and House evidently spared neither time nor effort in keeping them informed of political developments at home.

The Colonel's correspondence with Gerard at Berlin and Walter Page at London was voluminous.

'I told Gerard [recorded House] that he would get very meagre information from the State Department concerning the happenings in Administration circles, and I promised to keep him measurably well-posted in order that he might confer without embarrassment with the Kaiser or the Minister for Foreign Affairs. In turn, he said he would write me every ten days.'

Colonel House's relations with Mr. Gerard became of great political importance in the stirring days that were to come, for the Ambassador kept his promise. His war letters to House were pungent and prophetic, and through them President Wilson was to be informed accurately of the complicated forces that governed Germany. Nothing is further from fact than the legend that the President lacked available and authentic information of the political underworld on the continent of Europe. Mr. Gerard was excelled by none in the dignity and capacity with which he maintained the interests and furthered the policy of his Government in the most trying diplomatic situation of the war zone. He knew how to establish cordial relations with the Berlin Government, and he gave thought to the details that make for friendliness. But he never forgot Bismarck's aphorism: 'A good Ambassador ought not to be too popular in the country to which he is accredited.'

Ambassador Gerard to Colonel House

BERLIN, *November* 4, 1913

MY DEAR COLONEL:

Now that I have presented my letters to the Kaiser, I have something to report.

Pursuant to your suggestion I stopped in London to see Page, and had to wait nearly a week for him, as he was in Scotland with Carnegie. I found him a most agreeable and attractive man, and, from all I heard in London, he is a great success.

I spent the remainder of my time in Paris, principally in furniture shops, but arrived here the 6th October. . . . The Kaiser was away and I was not received until last Wednesday.

The Kaiser has permitted me to wear ordinary clothes, which disposes of the infernal uniform question, so there I am now better off than Page who has to wear knickers to Court functions.

Before seeing the Kaiser I called on the Imperial Chancellor, von Bethmann-Hollweg — a very tall, pleasant, Abraham Lincoln sort of man. He is one of the few officials who does not speak English, but we got on very well in French and some German. The Minister of Foreign Affairs is away, but his substitute, Zimmermann, is a very jolly sort of large German who was once a Judge, which made us friends at once. The rest of my time I put in at Embassy work, of which there is plenty, and in calling on the various Ambassadors and calling on others who call on me. I think I have the house question settled and will take an old quiet-looking house formerly owned by Prince Hatzfeld, then by the von Schwabachs . . . and just now bought by an adjoining bank. It will cost me a good deal to put it in repair, but, as it is large enough for the Embassy offices, if I get the same allowance as heretofore made, I shall pay much less rent than the Paris man or than Page in London, who, by the way, has secured a most suitable and 'fashionable' house in Grosvenor Square.

I have taken up a lot of things which former Ambassadors did not. I am taking an active part in the American Benevolent Society, the American Church (where Lanier and I sit every Sunday in the front pew), the American Institute, and the American Lunch Club, the American Association of Commerce and Traders, etc., and my wife will become President of the American Woman Club, a very worthy charity which takes care of the numerous girl students in Berlin.

We must have made a wonderful sight when we were presented to the Kaiser; they sent the Royal carriages for us with footmen standing behind in powdered wigs, outriders, etc., though we looked rather dismal in our dress suits. In the glass carriages we must have looked like a funeral. The Kaiser is a much more majestic-looking man than I expected. . . . We mostly talked business and sport, and he asked why we didn't have an Embassy building in Berlin and congratulated me on at last housing the Embassy in a decent house. When I presented the staff to him, he asked why we did not all ride in the Thiergarten and I told him we would challenge any Embassy in Berlin to any known form of sport.

Friday I went to Potsdam by train in a Royal military carriage and was driven to the new Palace, where I was presented, alone, to the Empress. She is a tall, fine-looking woman, and we talked of nothing in particular, just 'white conversation.'

I made a speech at a German art banquet and have been doing a good deal of work for the Panama Exposition. There is an agreement between England and Germany that neither shall exhibit unless both do. . . .

Yours ever

James W. Gerard

With Walter Hines Page, as with Gerard, Colonel House maintained constant and intimate relations. The new Ambassador to St. James's was pleased to have a correspondent to whom he might write frankly and through whom he might influence the President. When House came to London in June, 1913, Page greeted him warmly and shared with him his hopes and difficulties.

'I dined with Page last night [wrote Colonel House on June 19] and remained with him until half-past twelve.... He finally walked home with me to our hotel.

'He had many curious and interesting experiences to relate and he was much disturbed at some of his social blunders. The one which distressed him most was at the Duke of Norfolk's the other evening. He took Princess —— in to dinner and afterward, when they were in the drawing-room, he left her without being dismissed. The reason he did this was that he had been reminded that he was the one to leave first, and for the moment he forgot that with a member of the Royal Family the reverse course was proper.

'He considered taking a duchess or royalty out to dinner was hard sledding. They refused to exert themselves in the slightest to keep up the conversation, and he said it was the hardest work he had yet encountered in his Ambassadorial duties. He spoke particularly of the Duchess of ——. She was a woman of good sense, he understood, but she kept it quietly to herself when he was with her. He had gotten quite "chummy" with the Duke of Connaught, and was doing all he could to make himself agreeable to the important people in England.

'He asks me to aid him in formulating some constructive policy that will make the President's Administration and his notable in the annals of this Embassy. He said of all men, I could help him most in this regard. He is always generous in his praise of me. I shall try to outline some plan before I leave, for I have some things in mind which I think may redound to the advantage of both countries.'

Mr. Page had great success in winning the regard and respect of the British people and the Government to which he was accredited. His *bonhommie*, his transparent honesty of purpose and method, his evident anxiety to discover means of promoting Anglo-American friendship, soon placed relations between the two Governments upon a cordial personal basis, which Page, like House, believed to be the only firm foundation for intercourse between nations. The Ambassador and his wife had won the hearts of the British even before the trying months of the war, in which Page's hatred of German militarism intensified British affection for him. On July 12, 1914, Colonel House noted of a conversation with the English journalist, Sidney Brooks:

'In speaking of the Pages, Brooks said Mrs. Page had made the greatest success of "any Ambassadress within his memory." This is delightful to hear.'

Mr. Page, however, as he himself confessed, was subject to moods, 'I sometimes think,' he wrote to House, 'they are the dominant moods of my life, when I feel that I don't want any official position at all.... I have so long been entirely free and so independent that official restraint is yet unnatural.' He found it hard to sink his individual convictions in carrying out instructions from Washington. He enjoyed his work, but the difficulties always attaching to the life of an American Ambassador abroad galled him, and his sensitive nature suffered under vexations which some of the other Ambassadors hardly noticed. To House he poured out his soul. In a letter of December 12, 1914, he concluded: 'I didn't mean to write you all these things.... But I must once in a while blow off to somebody. You have the misfortune to be the only man to whom I *can* blow off.' With characteristic frankness, the Ambassador let the Colonel understand with some definiteness that he regarded the conduct of the State

Department under Mr. Bryan as worse than unfortunate. And yet at the conclusion of almost every long letter came the assurance that in the main he was enjoying his task, and the intimation that the vexations were minor by-products. 'As for this Embassy,' he wrote April 27, 1914, 'we're getting on better. We now get answers to questions, and if I had ever been disposed to complain, there's no excuse for complaining now.'

All the difficulties with which the State Department had to contend, House explained: the need of a period of experience, the pressure of political factors, the lack of funds. 'Please bear in mind too,' he wrote to Page, 'that just now the State Department is working day and night and is all too short of help. They expect a bill of relief from Congress shortly, and then you will get more secretaries and they will get more help.' With serpentine wisdom, he replied to Page's criticism of individuals in Washington by repeating complimentary remarks which those very individuals had recently passed regarding the Ambassador. Thus, on October 29, 1914, in a letter to Page: 'Your criticism of X came to me the day that Wallace was telling me of a talk he had with him the day before, in which he, X, said: "Y and Z together have not done as much as Walter Page, and yet they advertise themselves so well that the American people think that comparatively no one else has done anything." This is to be forgotten.'

The relations of House with the American Ambassadors abroad were paralleled closely by those which he maintained with foreign diplomatists in Washington. Before the outbreak of the war he was on intimate, almost confidential, terms with Spring-Rice and Bernstorff, Jusserand and Dumba. He was thus admirably equipped to study plans for developing the positive foreign policy upon which he hoped President Wilson would soon embark.

III

Colonel House's conception of such a policy was far-reaching. He believed that the time had passed when the United States could pose effectively as the protector of all the American states, and he wanted to bring about a definite friendly understanding with the great South American states upon the basis of an equal partnership. He realized acutely the feeling in South America, hostile to the United States and based upon the consciousness that the Monroe Doctrine (as they interpreted it) was thoroughly one-sided and accordingly distasteful to Latin-American sensibilities. If it could be transformed into a common policy and a common responsibility in which all American states participated, it would, House insisted, benefit the United States no less materially than morally. Such a partnership, he believed, might develop into a league for the preservation of peace and tranquillity in the Americas, and would be of the utmost service in handling situations such as had arisen in Mexico.

This ambitious plan, reminiscent of Blaine's Pan-American proposals, carried another, even more ambitious, as its inevitable consequence. A general Pan-American Pact was bound to interest the European Powers, some of which, such as the British Empire, were also American Powers. House was one of the few persons in the United States who realized before the war how thoroughly the previous thirty years had altered our relations with Europe and made of the United States, intellectually and economically, one of the family of World Powers. Political companionship, he was convinced, must follow. Never lacking in boldness, he was willing to accept the consequences; and just as he felt that the mythical protectorate of the Monroe Doctrine should be transformed into an American partnership, so he believed that the legend of political isolation from Europe was the outworn remnant of an age that was past. What he wanted was some sort of coöperative understanding with the great European Powers that might help to preserve the peace of the world, in which the United States had vital material interest. This conviction was not lessened by his realization that the European situation was critical and might at any moment result in a general European war.

Such a policy implied a frank recognition that the factors upon which American traditions rested had disappeared. If it were to be developed successfully, a working understanding with Great Britain would be necessary, both because the presence of the British in Latin America could not wisely be ignored and also because the imperial power of Great Britain was necessary to any feasible plan of international coöperation.

Anglo-American relations were not unfriendly at the beginning of the Wilson Administration, but a cordial and intimate understanding could not be reached until two clouds were removed, of which the most important, at least in the public mind, concerned the Panama tolls controversy. During the last year of Mr. Taft's Administration, Congress had passed an act exempting vessels engaged in coastwise trade of the United States from Panama Canal tolls, notwithstanding a clause in the Hay-Pauncefote Treaty of 1901 which provided that the Canal should be open to ships of all nations on 'terms of entire equality.' Feeling in the United States, especially in Irish districts, favored such exemption warmly, on the ground that it was 'reasonable,' and made an 'open canal.' A plank in the Democratic platform approved it. Feeling in Great Britain supported with equal warmth the contention that, reasonable or not, such exemption directly contravened engagements taken in 1901; the issue was not one of logic, but simply whether the United States would keep its word.

Even before Wilson assumed office, he and House seem to

have agreed that, despite the overwhelming majority in Congress that favored exemption, the American contention ought not to be upheld.[1] It was of supreme importance to emphasize international ethics by an insistence upon the sanctity of treaties. On January 24, 1913, House discussed the matter with Wilson:

'I asked him concerning his views in regard to the Panama Canal tolls controversy with Great Britain. I was glad to find that he took the same view that I have, and that is that the clause should be repealed.'

Action could not be taken by the President during the extra session of Congress. It was first necessary that he establish firmly his leadership, for what he planned was nothing less than a complete conversion of the party upon an issue intensely troubled by the strong anti-British feeling characteristic of many Democratic strongholds. The topic was therefore not raised during the extra session. Ambassador Page did not fail to call constant attention to the importance of the question, indulging in promises of the benefits of repeal that might be regarded as exaggerated.

Ambassador W. H. Page to Colonel House

LONDON, *August* 28, 1913

MY DEAR HOUSE:

... If the United States will ... repeal the Canal toll discrimination, we can command the British fleet, British manufacturers — anything we please. Till we do these things, they'll regard us as mean and stingy and dishonorable on occasion and, therefore, peculiar and given to queer freaks;

[1] 'The repeal of the tolls exemption was opposed by nearly all of the Democratic leaders in Congress. To drive the repeal through the House and the Senate, Wilson was compelled to have recourse to Cabinet members, especially Burleson and McAdoo.' (Note by E. M. H.)

they like *us*, but don't know what to think of our Government. Our Government, they don't trust or admire. . . .

Heartily yours

WALTER H. PAGE

If the British felt they had cause of complaint with the American Government over the matter of the Canal tolls, the American Government, on the other hand, felt that the British were hampering Wilson's policy in Mexico. The British Ambassador in Mexico, Sir Lionel Carden, was known to be an advocate of Huerta and was supposed to represent the British oil interests of Lord Cowdray. Huerta was believed to have made extravagant promises of concessions to those interests in the event that his régime became firmly established. The American Government assumed that the British Foreign Office stood behind the British oil interests and that the British provisional recognition of Huerta meant that they would fight Wilson's policy of non-recognition.

Obviously the difficulties with the British resulted largely from misunderstanding and misinformation on both sides. What was necessary was a frank interchange of views, and House welcomed the opportunity given him in the summer of 1913 to approach the British Foreign Secretary, Sir Edward Grey.

It was on July 3, 1913, that the two first met, at a small luncheon given by Sir Edward at his house, 33 Eccleston Square. The only others present were Ambassador Page and Lord Crewe, then Secretary for India. Colonel House doubtless looks back upon the luncheon as an event in his career, since he came to have for Grey an affection and a respect unsurpassed in his relations with foreign statesmen. This feeling resulted in large measure from a singular community of personal tastes and ideals, which from the moment they met made a deep impression upon Colonel House. He found in Sir Edward a philosopher, like himself careless of conventional honors, with no apparent sense of his own importance, driven, over-hard perhaps, by what he felt to be his duty and taking no credit therefor. As statesman, moreover, the British Foreign Secretary approached House's ideal, supremely distinguished as he was by sincerity of purpose and honesty of method; above all a diplomat who did not regard diplomacy as a mysterious intrigue, but rather as a means by which the representatives of different states could discuss frankly the coincidence or the clash of national interests and reach a peaceable understanding. House was then and always convinced that foreign policy should be conducted like personal business, from which it differed only in degree of importance; and he wanted to introduce into diplomacy the characteristics of personal intercourse, with its code of individual honesty and friendliness. In Grey he discovered a man with whom he could treat upon this basis. We shall find them discussing the most delicate points of national policy with the frankness that officials of the same department of a government might use.

Their first conversation was of importance, for it led in the autumn to an understanding on the two vexatious questions at issue. House explained Wilson's Mexican policy and attitude on the tolls exemptions; Grey intimated that British support of Huerta was neither definite nor final.

'*July* 3, 1913: While Lord Crewe and Page were discussing the eradication of the hookworm in India and other countries [recorded House], Sir Edward and I fell to talking of the Mexican situation. I told him the President did not want to intervene and was giving the different factions every possible opportunity to get together. He wished to know whether the President was opposed to any particular faction. I thought it was immaterial, as far as our Government was concerned, which faction was in power, if order was maintained. I thought our Government would have recognized

Huerta's provisional Government if they had carried out their written promise to call an election at an early date and abide by its decisions.

'Sir Edward said his Government had not recognized the Huerta Government excepting as a provisional one, and that if Huerta undertook to run for President in spite of his promise not to do so, their recognition of him would come up again as an entirely new proposition. He intimated that in those circumstances they would not recognize him.

'He wished to know what would happen if we intervened, and suggested that perhaps the same condition would prevail as in Cuba. I replied that this was a question for the future, but personally I did not believe intervention would be as serious as most people thought.

'We then drifted to the Panama Canal tolls question. He said his Government intended to put two propositions squarely up to our Government; i.e., whether we desired to take up the discussion of the treaty as it stood, or whether we would prefer arbitration. His Government have no objection to our Government giving free passage to coastwise vessels, so long as it did not interfere with British shipping or was not unfavorable to it; but just what plan could be devised to bring this about, he did not know. However, he was willing to take up the discussion with our Government in the event the free tolls were not abolished by the bill now before our Senate.

'I suggested that the matter should not be pressed for the moment, but be left open for the long session of Congress beginning in December. I explained that the President was exceedingly anxious to get through his legislative programme at the extra session; that a reduction of the tariff and the reform of our currency system were almost vital to the success of his Administration, and that in the Senate he had only a narrow margin on the tariff and he did not wish to press anything else until these measures were through.

'Sir Edward said he quite understood the President's position and sympathized with it, and his Government were perfectly willing to allow the matter to rest as suggested.'

Ambassador W. H. Page to Colonel House

London, *July* 8, 1913

Dear Mr. House:

I had an interview to-day with Sir Edward Grey about a matter of state business; and, when I rose to go, he followed me to the door and stopped me and said that he owed me much for the pleasure I had given him in making him acquainted with you; and he wished me to tell you that he should expect to see you whenever you should come to London: 'I was much interested in what he told me — a man that I'm glad to know,' said he.

I send you this while it is still hot in my mind. . . .

It was a duchess last night — an easy and friendly one; to-night it's a bishop, quality yet unknown; to-morrow night, the Russian Ambassador, a fine old Slav whom I know.

Yours heartily

W. H. P.

Thus, at the moment when Anglo-American relations threatened to become clouded by popular feeling over Panama tolls, the personal intervention of Page and House went far to secure complete official cordiality. Grey was evidently assured of the friendliness of the President, as manifested through his personal adviser. On the other hand, the forbearance of the British in not pressing the tolls question convinced Wilson of what House and Page insisted upon; namely, that Grey was anxious to work with the United States and that a cordial understanding was possible if only outstanding issues could be frankly discussed.

That Sir Edward was impressed by the value of his talk with House is indicated by his decision to send his secretary,

Sir William Tyrrell, to the United States to canvass the whole matter of Anglo-American relations with the President and his adviser. This was the more important in that the new British Ambassador, Sir Cecil Spring-Rice, was ill and unable to take up his duties actively. Tyrrell proved to be an ideal selection. He shared the complete confidence of Grey and his views on international relations, so that not merely could he give to Wilson Grey's exact ideas, but he might claim from the President an equal frankness. No one understood better the ins and outs of Continental politics, or realized more acutely how great an asset to the British American sympathy might become in case of trouble in Europe. He possessed, moreover, an almost boyish enthusiasm for the task in hand, which completely won the affection of the Colonel and the confidence of the President. He came in doubt as to the willingness of the Americans to coöperate with Grey. He returned convinced that they would play the game. 'Tyrrell's back,' wrote Ambassador Page to House, in December, 'a changed man. He says that you and the President and Houston did it. That's all to the good.'

House took pains to come into touch with Sir William immediately after his arrival, and explained to Wilson the importance of his mission.

'*November* 11, 1913: The President saw me at once, although I had no appointment. I expressed concern in regard to Mexico and explained more in detail about Sir William Tyrrell. In talking to Sir William we were practically talking to Sir Edward Grey, and I thought it would be foolish not to utilize the opportunity in order to bring about a better understanding with England regarding Mexico. I told him of my luncheon engagement at the British Embassy on Wednesday, and thought if he would give me a free hand I might do something worth while. He authorized me to talk to Sir William as freely as I considered advisable....

'*November* 12, 1913: I suggested again that in my talk with Sir William Tyrrell it would be well to urge him to get England to bring the other Powers to exert pressure upon Huerta in order that he might eliminate himself.

'The President asked me to come to the White House and remain with him overnight. I told him I had counted upon returning home, but my going depended upon the success of my interview with Sir William. I promised to get in touch with him, the President, as soon afterward as it was convenient to him, provided anything worth while developed. He said he had wished to get with me yesterday. He also told of how very tired he was. . . .'

Colonel House had met Sir William in New York, but the decisive interviews took place in Washington, at the British Embassy and the White House.

'*November* 12, 1913: At one o'clock [recorded House], I lunched with Lady Spring-Rice at the British Embassy. . . .

'Sir Cecil Spring-Rice was not well enough to appear, and sent me words of regret. After lunch, Sir William Tyrrell and I went into another room and discussed the questions uppermost in the minds of both. He began by showing me despatches from his Government and his own replies. He declared Lord Cowdray had no concessions from Huerta, and if he could get them in the future, his Government would not recognize their validity. He thought a deliberate attempt was being made to connect Cowdray with these matters in order to create a sentiment for intervention. He said Sir Lionel Carden was not antagonistic to America; he was fair and would do in spirit, as well as in act, just what he was told to do by his Government. He admitted he was very pro-British, but, other than that, no criticism could be made of him.

'I replied that both the President and Mr. Bryan held very

different views of Lord Cowdray and Sir Lionel Carden, and I was glad to hear the other side. He spoke of Sir Edward Grey's desire to bring about a cessation of armaments, for he thought our present civilization would eventually be destroyed upon that rock. He thought, too, that an armament trust was forcing all Governments not only to pay excessive prices, but was creating war scares — they being the only people having any interest in having the different Governments keep up large expenditures for war purposes.

'We talked of the Panama tolls question. Sir William said Sir Edward Grey's idea was that no possible good came to nations if either the letter or the spirit of a treaty were broken. He said the English people felt keenly upon this subject, and no one more so than Sir Edward himself; and the only reason he held office was his desire to promote the peace of nations.

'I replied that the President felt as keenly as Sir Edward did about the inviolability of treaties, and I thought when he talked with him, the President would make his position clear. I expressed the desire immediately to bring the President and Sir William together, and he was delighted to have the opportunity....'

President Wilson was not generally expansive in conferences with persons whom he met for the first time, and House was somewhat surprised and even more pleased that the interview developed the degree of frankness that characterized it.

'*November* 13, 1913: The President received Tyrrell in the Blue Room. He had on a grey sack suit, while Sir William wore a cutaway. They both appeared a little embarrassed. The President opened the conversation by saying I had told him of my conversation with him yesterday; and then outlined the purpose of our Government regarding Mexico, very much as I had done the day before. Sir William replied much as he had to me. The President spoke frankly and well; so did Sir William. It was an extremely interesting discussion.

'The President, of his own volition, brought up the arbitration treaty and the Panama tolls question and, much to my surprise, told Sir William what he had in mind, not only as to his views, but also how he expected to put them into force. He asked him to convey to Sir Edward Grey his sympathy with the view that our treaty with England should remain inviolable, but to ask him to have patience until he had time to develop the matter properly. He thought an overwhelming majority of our people held his views, but there was an opposition composed largely of Hibernian patriots, both in the Senate and out, that always desired a fling at England.

'We talked of the necessity of curbing armaments and of the power of the financial world in our politics to-day. Sir William was just as earnest in his opinion regarding this as either the President or I. . . . The President said, "It is the greatest fight we all have on to-day, and every good citizen should enlist."

'The hour was up, and the President had to leave for other engagements. . . . I talked with Sir William for a moment after the President left. He was pleased with the interview and thanked me cordially. He said he had never before had such a frank talk about matters of so much importance. We all spoke with the utmost candor and without diplomatic gloss. He said, "If some of the veteran diplomats could have heard us, they would have fallen in a faint." Before leaving, we agreed to keep in touch with one another. He is to telephone me whenever he receives despatches which he thinks I should see, and I am to go to Washington when necessary.'

IV

The basis of House's diplomacy was always complete frankness whenever he negotiated with men who were willing to place their cards on the table; and the relations he developed with the British through Sir William Tyrrell were intimate. Tyrrell responded readily. 'You will forgive, I know,' he wrote to House on January 20, 1914, 'the frankness of my utterance, but that is the basis of our relationship, isn't it?' As a result of this intimacy, a quite informal, but none the less significant, understanding was reached.

The British Foreign Office made plain to Sir Lionel Carden that he must not take steps to interfere in any way with Wilson's anti-Huerta policy in Mexico. Tyrrell on November 26 showed to House despatches from Grey, plainly indicating this; and henceforth the Administration profited by the British influence. It is hardly an exaggeration to say that the abdication and flight of Huerta, in July, 1914, was directly related to the withdrawal of British support. Huerta's elimination was the first and perhaps the only diplomatic triumph won by Wilson in his Mexican policy, and it is right that future historians should understand that something of it was due to British coöperation.

On the other hand, President Wilson promised to push the repeal of the clause exempting American coastwise shipping from the Canal tolls, provided the British would not hurry him. To this they gladly agreed, and on December 13, House wrote to Page: 'Sir Cecil Spring-Rice will leave the Panama tolls question entirely in our hands.' The conversation with the British Ambassador to which House refers is interesting in view of the events of 1914, for it indicated how thoroughly Sir Edward Grey was determined to base his foreign policy upon the principle of the sanctity of treaties.

'*December* 11, 1913: I lunched at the British Embassy. I was the only guest. Sir Cecil Spring-Rice and I talked of the Panama tolls question, and he agreed to leave the matter alone and let us take it up at our leisure and handle it in the way we thought best. He said that as far as the monetary end of it was concerned, the British Government would perhaps lose something more by their interpretation of the treaty than by ours; but the thing they had most in mind was maintaining inviolable treaty obligations. He said in southern Europe that question was constantly to the fore; and the next time it arose after the United States had violated the Hay-Pauncefote Treaty, the fact would be thoroughly threshed out, and it would be said that Britain made no objection to the violation of a treaty where the United States was concerned, but when one of the smaller nations of eastern Europe did so a great hue and cry was raised.'

House had taken up the tolls problem with Wilson in October, at a time when the President's legislative programme seemed to be nearing completion, and he found Wilson determined to force repeal of the exemption upon Congress, although he recognized that it would test his party leadership more than any question that had thus far arisen. The President thought 'that trouble would be encountered in the Senate, particularly in the opposition of Senator O'Gorman, who constantly regards himself as an Irishman contending against England rather than as a United States Senator upholding the dignity and welfare of this country.'

The Colonel, according to his habit, preferred to persuade the opposition before open debate began, rather than fighting out the issue in Congress. He brought the situation to the attention of Senator O'Gorman's son-in-law, Dudley Malone, a warm supporter of the Administration, who had just resigned from the State Department to become Collector of the Port of New York.

'*November* 26, 1913: Malone and I discussed the Panama tolls question. He indicated that Senator O'Gorman would make a strenuous fight to uphold his position on this subject. I diplomatically showed him reasons for this country to keep on good terms with Great Britain. I explained how the President's hands would be tied in Mexico if he did not have the sympathy of Great Britain in his plans. Malone saw the point and agreed to help in bringing Senator O'Gorman around to a more reasonable view. He promised to start upon this at once, and I agreed to confer with O'Gorman later and try to persuade him to accept the President's policy....

'*January* 21, 1914: We [Wilson and House]... decided it was best to bring the matter to the attention of Congress immediately, so that the British Government would have something to go on when Parliament convened February 10. We decided it was best not to see Senator O'Gorman alone, but to call the Senate Foreign Relations Committee in as a whole, Republicans and Democrats alike, and explain the situation to them; that it would be well to tell them how important it was at this particular time that our relations with Great Britain should be undisturbed; that it was better to make concessions in regard to Panama rather than lose the support of England in our Mexican, Central and South American policy.

'The President has called the Committee for Monday. I shall look forward with some anxiety to the outcome. I suggested that a poll be taken of the Senate in advance, in order to find what support he would have. Senator James was decided upon for this work. Senator Stone would have been selected, but he has not been well and is in the South for the moment.

'The President said one of the strangest things that had come about was that he and Stone had become good friends and that the Senator seemed to have a positive affection for him....'

It proved impossible to push the matter forward as rapidly as House had hoped, for the opposition was still strong in both Committee and Senate. It yielded, however, before Wilson's insistence. On March 5, the support of the Senate Committee apparently assured to him, the President in a message to Congress formally asked the repeal of the clause exempting from tolls vessels engaged in coastwise trade. He based his demand chiefly upon the fact that everywhere, except in certain quarters of the United States, opinion held that the clause violated the Hay-Pauncefote Treaty.

'Whatever may be our own differences of opinion [said Wilson to Congress] concerning this much-debated measure, its meaning is not debated outside the United States. Everywhere else the language of the treaty is given but one interpretation, and that interpretation precludes the exemption I am asking you to repeal. We consented to the treaty; its language we accepted, if we did not originate; and we are too big, too powerful, too self-respecting a nation to interpret with too strained or refined a reading the words of our own promises just because we have power enough to give us leave to read them as we please. The large thing to do is the only thing that we can afford to do. . . .'

The President also had in mind, of course, the value of British influence in meeting the Mexican problem, and to this he made veiled reference which excited endless speculation and of which he himself never gave public explanation. 'I ask this of you,' he said, 'in support of the foreign policy of the Administration. I shall not know how to deal with other matters of even greater delicacy and nearer consequence if you do not grant it to me in ungrudging measure.' The other matter of great delicacy was the elimination of Huerta and the understanding with Great Britain.

The obvious determination of the President, the sense of loyalty to his leadership in the Democratic Party, and the active labors of Burleson and McAdoo, who had charge of getting the measure through House and Senate respectively, finally bore fruit. In June the repeal of the special exemption became law. From this time forward, the United States Government could count upon the sympathy of Sir Edward Grey.

'*June* 27, 1914 [London]: I lunched with Sir Edward Grey, Sir William Tyrrell, and Walter Page [wrote Colonel House]. We talked from 1.30 until 3.30. . . . Sir Edward and I did practically all the talking, Page and Sir William only occasionally joining in.

'We spoke first of the Panama tolls repeal bill. Sir Edward expressed pleasure at the fine way in which the President did it and without any negotiations between the two Governments in regard to it. He spoke of his having done it of his own volition because of his high sense of justice. He purposes paying this tribute to the President in Parliament when a fit opportunity occurs.'

The fit opportunity did not occur, for only a month later the European war broke out and the mind of Sir Edward was caught by problems that were nearer home. But the sentiment of American friendliness lingered in the Foreign Office even during the vexatious discussions regarding blockade and neutral rights. Through his insistence upon the sanctity of international engagements, furthermore, Wilson was able to assume a tone in his controversy with Germany which would have been impossible if he had yielded to the dictates of expediency in the question of Panama tolls.

CHAPTER VIII

A PAN-AMERICAN PACT

It will be such a great accomplishment that there will be nothing he [Wilson] can ever do afterward that can approach it in importance.

Ambassador Naon to Colonel House, December 29, 1914

I

THE success with which President Wilson forced the repeal of the Panama tolls exemption upon an unwilling Congress, thus securing the good will of the British as well as vindicating the good faith of the United States, was followed almost immediately by the flight of Huerta from Mexico. This diplomatic victory was of even less significance than the fact that, by refusing to intervene actively in Mexico and by calling for the mediation of the A.B.C. Powers, he had given a powerful stimulus to the cordiality of South American feeling. Mr. Fletcher, Minister to Chile, wrote enthusiastically to House of 'the President's success in the Mexican difficulties — turning, as he did, a situation fraught with difficulties and danger to our American relations into a triumph of Pan-Americanism.'

Colonel House was anxious to capitalize the advantage of the moment, in order to develop a positive and permanent Pan-American policy, based upon the principle of conference and coöperation. The world had witnessed the bankruptcy of European diplomacy, which the outbreak of the Great War made manifest in August, 1914, and which, in House's opinion, resulted primarily from the lack of an organized system of international coöperation. Such a system he was anxious that Wilson should develop for the Americas; and when the President visited him in November he laid his plans before him.

'*November* 25, 1914: I advised him [recorded the Colonel] to pay less attention to his domestic policy and greater attention to the welding together of the two western continents. I thought the Federal Reserve Act was his greatest constructive work and was the thing that would stand out and make his Administration notable. Now I would like him to place beside that great measure a constructive international policy, which he had already started by getting the A.B.C. nations to act as arbitrators at Niagara. I thought the time had arrived to show the world that friendship, justice, and kindliness were more potent than the mailed fist.

'He listened attentively to what I had to say, and asserted that he would do it and would use his speech at San Francisco, when he opened the Exposition, to outline this policy.'

A few days later, so eager was he to see such a policy developed while circumstances were propitious, Colonel House permitted himself a rare luxury — that of enforcing his verbal advice by a letter.

Colonel House to the President

New York, *November* 30, 1914

Dear Governor:

. . . As I said to you when you were here, I feel that the wise thing for you to do is to make your foreign policy the feature of your Administration during the next two years.

The opportunity to weld North and South America together in closer union is at your hand; do you not think you should take some initiative in this direction before your speech at the Panama Exposition? You might take that occasion to amplify it, but in the meantime there are many things that might be done to give it further acceleration. . . .

Affectionately yours

E. M. House

Some weeks later, the plan had taken more definite form in the Colonel's thoughts and he decided that he would go to Washington to impress it upon the President — a still more unusual step on his part and one that indicated how much importance he attached to the scheme. What Colonel House had in mind was nothing less than a rather loose league of American states which should guarantee security from aggression and furnish a mechanism for the pacific settlement of disputes.

The reader will doubtless observe that what House planned bears a close relationship to the League of Nations which Wilson ultimately advocated for the world at large. Especially significant is the account which the Colonel gives of the following conversation with the President, for it indicates that at this moment was born almost the exact wording of Article X of the League of Nations Covenant.

'*December* 16, 1914: I then explained the purpose of my visit to Washington. I thought he [Wilson] might or might not have an opportunity to play a great and beneficent part in the European tragedy; but there was one thing he could do at once, and that was to inaugurate a policy that would weld the Western Hemisphere together. It was my idea to formulate a plan, to be agreed upon by the republics of the two continents, which in itself would serve as a model for the European nations when peace is at last brought about.

'I could see that this excited his enthusiasm. My idea was that the republics of the two continents should agree to guarantee each other's territorial integrity and that they should also agree to government ownership of munitions of war. I suggested that he take a pencil and write the points to be covered.

'He took a pencil, and this is what he wrote:

'"1st. Mutual guaranties of political independence under

republican form of government and mutual guaranties of territorial integrity.[1]

'"2nd. Mutual agreement that the Government of each of the contracting parties acquire complete control within its jurisdiction of the manufacture and sale of munitions of war."

'He wished to know if there was anything else. I thought this was sufficient, taken in conjunction with the Bryan Peace Treaties which had already been concluded between the republics of the two continents.

'He then went to his little typewriter and made a copy of what he had written, and handed it to me to use with the three South American Ambassadors with whom it was thought best to initiate negotiations. We discussed the method of procedure, and it was agreed that it should be done quite informally and without either himself or the Secretary of State appearing in it until after I had sounded the different Governments at interest. We did this for another reason, and that was not to hurt Mr. Bryan's sensibilities. It was agreed that I should explain the matter to Mr. Bryan and should tell him why it was thought best for me to do it rather than the President or himself.

'The President was evidently somewhat nervous about Mr. Bryan's attitude. It was easy to see that he did not want him to interfere in any way with my procedure, and yet he was afraid he might be sensitive regarding it. I thought I could work it out satisfactorily, for Mr. Bryan is generous and big-minded in matters of this sort. . . .

'*December* 17, 1914: I arranged for an interview with Mr. Bryan at 9.30 this morning. I outlined the plan the Presi-

[1] Cf. Article X of the League of Nations Covenant: 'The members of the League undertake to respect and preserve as against external aggression the territorial integrity and existing political independence of all Members of the League. In case of any such aggression or in case of any threat or danger of such aggression the Council shall advise upon the means by which this obligation shall be fulfilled.'

dent and I were preparing for the linking of the Western Hemisphere and showed him what the President had written, explaining why it was thought best that I should do it. He acquiesced in a most generous way, which proved my forecast to the President was correct.... After but a few minutes' conversation upon the subject of this proposed league, he began to discuss the Venezuela Minister's proposal concerning the calling of a convention of belligerent and neutral nations, for the purpose of securing the rights of neutrals. He also discussed the Russian treaty, which had been tentatively suggested as being possible at this time. After that he got off on prohibition, and I was glad to take him to his office and proceed to other business. ...'

Mr. Bryan, in truth, appeared to take but little interest in this Pan-American policy, for he had complete confidence in the 'cooling-off' treaties he had arranged, which provided for a period of investigation, in case of dispute, before hostilities could be started. Some days later, after House had reported progress to the Secretary of State, the Colonel recorded:

'*December* 20, 1914: Mr. Bryan seemed pleased with what had been done, but drifted off into the question of patronage and the best way to "do up Senator X." ... He followed me all the way to the automobile, bareheaded in the cold bleak wind, to get in as much as he could upon that subject.'

II

Given a free hand, Colonel House proceeded with surprising rapidity. On December 19, he saw the three Ambassadors of the A.B.C. Powers and was much encouraged by their attitude. What he planned was obviously to the advantage of the South American States, in that it would bring them into equal partnership with the United

States and would transform the Monroe Doctrine from a protective assurance on the part of one state into a mutual covenant. Whether or not a Pan-American Pact of the kind he suggested would prove an effective guaranty of peace might be doubtful; but it would certainly eliminate the implication of inferiority which South America deduced from the traditional form of the Monroe Doctrine. To secure such moral advantages, however, the South American States must renounce all aggressive designs. Would they prove equal to the opportunity offered them? The plan assumed also that the smaller Latin-American States had attained a degree of political stability which would permit them to maintain the promises which they made. The assumption was at least questionable.

'*December* 19, 1914: Justice Lamar telephoned that the Argentine Ambassador was back. I made an engagement with him at half-past eleven. I hurriedly gathered together what data I could get concerning Argentina and upon Naon himself. When the Justice introduced me, he excused himself for a moment and took Naon aside to inform him how thoroughly I represented the President. He then took his leave.

'I began the conversation by complimenting Naon upon the advanced thought in his country, particularly in regard to penal reform. I considered the Argentine fifty or one hundred years ahead of Europe and the United States in that direction. I marvelled at the statesmanship that saw as long ago as 1864, when they had their war with Uruguay, that a victorious nation had no moral right to despoil the territory of the vanquished. After I had made these few remarks, I had fertile soil upon which to sow the seeds of my argument.

'Naon took the typewritten memorandum which the President had given me and warmly approved both sentences one and two. He was tremendously impressed with the significance of the first article, and said it struck a new note and would create an epoch in governmental affairs. When I told him the President had written the memorandum on the typewriter himself, he asked permission to keep it, saying it would become an historical document of much value.

'I urged him to communicate with his Government by cable and to give me an answer by Monday or Tuesday. He felt confident the reply would be favorable. He took my address in New York and said he would communicate with me without delay. I let him understand that when the South American Governments had acted upon the matter and it had been pretty well buttoned-up, I would step aside and have the President and Mr. Bryan act officially. When I left, he followed me to the door and said he considered it a joy to work toward the consummation of such a policy as "your great and good President has promoted." . . .

'At lunch I reported to the President the substance of my conversation with the Ambassador from the Argentine, and he was delighted. Naon thought I would have more difficulty with the Brazilian and Chilean Ambassadors.

'The President said in talking with them I could go very far, and he was emphatic in the statement that the United States would not tolerate . . . aggression upon other republics.

'In the afternoon I saw them both. Da Gama [1] was easy of conquest and with practically the same argument I used with Naon. Suarez [2] was more difficult because he is not so clever, in the first instance, and, in the second, Chile has a boundary dispute with Peru. He asked if I knew of this, and I told him I did, but we would arrange in the final drawing of the agreement to cover such cases, since there were other boundary disputes which would have to be adjusted, like

[1] The Brazilian Ambassador.

[2] The Chilean Ambassador.

that between Costa Rica and Panama. They both agreed to cable their Governments and strongly recommend the ratification of the proposal.'

This was rapid work for the first day of negotiations and Colonel House, who knew something of diplomatic delays, did not conceal his satisfaction. He was pleased still more by the speed with which the Ambassadors of Brazil and Argentina extracted replies to his suggestion from their Governments. Brazil was the first to respond, less than a week after the original suggestion of the Colonel had been offered.

Ambassador da Gama to Colonel House

WASHINGTON, *December* 24, 1914

MY DEAR COLONEL HOUSE:

I have just received the answer from my Minister of Foreign Affairs to the telegram I sent him on Saturday, 19th, transmitting the two propositions of the President's project of convention.

The answer was delayed pending further information that I sent on Monday and then consultation with our President, who gladly authorizes me to declare that both points of the President's proposal are agreeable, it being understood that only American territories are contemplated in the first of those paragraphs.

I suppose that the sounding having proved favorable, the formal overture of the negotiations will soon follow. This will be an epoch-making negotiation.

Yours sincerely

DA GAMA

Colonel House to the President

NEW YORK, *December* 26, 1914

DEAR GOVERNOR:

I am enclosing you a copy of a letter from da Gama which I have just received and which I know will please you as much as it has me.

As you know, I had a telephone talk with Naon; but he spoke such broken English and the connection was so bad, that I could not gather the sense of his message. He promised to write, but I have nothing from him yet. I gleaned enough to know that he wanted to have another conference; therefore I told him I would be in Washington early next week.

This is a matter of such far-reaching consequence that I feel we should pay more attention to it just now than even the European affair, for the reason that, if brought to a successful conclusion, the one must have a decided influence upon the other. . . .

Affectionately yours

E. M. HOUSE

Three days later House went again to Washington, where he had a gratifying conference with the Argentine Ambassador. Naon handed to him the following despatch, which had just come in from Buenos Ayres: 'The Government receives with sympathy the proposition with the understanding that such a proposition tends to transform the one-sided character of the Monroe Doctrine into a common policy of all the American countries.'

'*December* 29, 1914: Naon was very enthusiastic [House recorded] over the entire proposal and said, ". . . It will be such a great accomplishment that there will be nothing he [Wilson] can ever do afterward that can approach it in importance."

'He thought Chile would hesitate to come in. . . . He had talked with the Chilean Ambassador since I was in Washington and had not received much encouragement. I told him that the United States would not favor the acquisition of territory by the other republics, either by war or otherwise, and that Chile might as well accept that condition in a formal convention. He replied that Argentina held the same view, and would not willingly permit territorial aggrandizement in South America.'

The Colonel returned to the White House to report to Wilson.

'We discussed the best means of buttoning-up the South American proposition, and it was agreed that he should see Senator Stone immediately upon his return; and we again discussed whether it would be advisable to bring the matter before the entire Senate Committee on Foreign Relations, or before the Democratic members of it. He would not discuss anything of importance with Senator —— for the reason that he immediately gave it to the press; in this instance it was necessary to have the matter presented to the country properly when they first heard it, and not get a garbled or distorted account from a political opponent.

'I told him Naon desired to know whether it was our purpose to make twenty-one different treaties or a single convention. I had replied that it was the intention to make a single convention, which the President thought was right. Naon suggested, I told him, that the A.B.C. Powers and ourselves should first thresh out the terms to a satisfactory conclusion before bringing in the smaller republics. This, too, the President agreed to.

'*December* 30, 1914: We had breakfast, as usual, at eight. The President and I talked a few minutes afterward and laid out the business that I should attend to. I made an engagement with the Chilean Ambassador for eleven o'clock.

'I found he had not heard from his Government. He gave a change of ministry as the reason, and was sure he would receive a favorable reply. I could not see how he could fail to do so. This was not really in accordance with Naon's statement to me, but I found Naon wrong in the first estimate of the manner in which Brazil and Chile would receive the proposals.

'*January* 13, 1915: I found the Chilean Ambassador very cordial, but he had not heard from his Government regarding the President's proposal. I told him the Senate would adjourn in about sixty days and would not meet again for nearly a year, and that it was important for him to get into communication with his Government again and ask them to send a response. I informed him of the favorable responses from both Brazil and Argentina; but before proceeding to a further discussion of the convention we wished to hear from Chile. The President requested me to say to him that he had approached Senator Stone of the Foreign Relations Committee and had found him sympathetic, and he felt sure there would be no difficulty from that source....

'I went... to see the Brazilian Ambassador to inform him also that the President had taken the matter up with the Senate Foreign Relations Committee, and he would soon call them together for a more intimate discussion of the details of the convention. Da Gama was pleased with this procedure and thought it was wise for the President to get the Senate in line before any public announcement was made.

'I returned to the White House for lunch, and while the President was dressing for his golf I told of my morning's work.'

Chile was slow in responding, but on January 21, 1915,

Colonel House received the following letter from Ambassador Suarez:

Ambassador Suarez to Colonel House

WASHINGTON, *January* 19, 1915

MY DEAR SIR:

. . . I wished to inform you that I have since two days the expected reply from Chile. It is favorable in principle and praises the idea as a generous and pan-american one.

Although it is sometimes not a little difficult to find the proper expressions to render an idea agreeable to several parties, I hope we shall succeed when the moment of discussing the development of our first accord comes.

Mr. Bryan has told me lately to be in full acquaintance with the matter; and under this understanding I assume I can communicate with him in your absence.

I am, my dear Mr. House,

Very sincerely yours

EDO. SUAREZ

This was ambiguous, but House, who was on the point of leaving for Europe, to be engaged upon quite different but equally important affairs, urged the President to accept the letter at its face value and push the agreement through.

Colonel House to the President

NEW YORK, *January* 21, 1915

DEAR GOVERNOR:

I am enclosing you a copy of a letter which has come from the Chilean Ambassador this morning.

Everything now seems to be in shape for you to go ahead. I believe the country will receive this policy with enthusiasm and it will make your Administration notable, even had you done but little else. . . .

Affectionately yours

E. M. HOUSE

III

Colonel House left for Europe on January 31, 1915. Henceforth his time and his energies were chiefly occupied with the problems that arose from the European war, but his interest never flagged in the Pan-American policy which he had done so much to inaugurate. He insisted upon its general value as an example, which might later be followed in Europe, of international organization in place of international anarchy; he emphasized its special value in view of the persistent uneasiness resulting from the always unsettled Mexican problem. For the elimination of Huerta had not led to any diminution of disorder; attacks upon American lives and property continued, and American public opinion, at least in certain circles, called for a positive policy that might end the crisis.

House himself was constitutionally unable to approve a purely negative line of action, and, while he realized the dangers of forcible intervention in Mexico by the United States alone, he believed that with the coöperation of the South American Powers, the mediation of which had already been utilized in 1914, the Mexican problem could be settled. Such a step would fit in perfectly with the plan for a Pan-American Pact. Just before leaving for Europe he urged it upon the President and the Secretary of State.

'*January* 24, 1915: I suggested [to Wilson] that the Mexican problem could best be solved now by calling in the A.B.C. Powers and ourselves. The President thought this an excellent idea and that it was merely a question of when to put it in operation. I offered to see the Ambassadors to-morrow if he thought well of it. He believed this would be too soon, for conditions were not quite ready in Mexico for such a move, and he was afraid the A.B.C. Ambassadors would not want to move so quickly. . . .

'*January* 25, 1915: I talked to Mr. Bryan of my suggesting a commission form of government for Mexico, with the A.B.C. Powers and ourselves acting jointly. He thought fairly well of it, but was not as enthusiastic as the President. I talked of the South American concord and many other matters.'

Colonel House to the President

PARIS, FRANCE, *March* 15, 1915

DEAR GOVERNOR:

Since I have been over here, every now and then Mexico raises its head.

It would be of enormous advantage to your prestige if you could place that problem well on the road to settlement before this war ends. I have heard it time and again — not directly, but through others — that the belligerent Governments will become insistent that order be restored there.

Winslow [1] tells me that he hears it constantly in Berlin. I have wondered whether you have taken the matter up with the A.B.C. Powers, as you contemplated when I left. This seems to me to be the wisest solution. I think you have now given them [the Mexicans] every chance to work it out themselves, and help should be offered them and insisted upon....

Affectionately yours

E. M. HOUSE

President Wilson, however, was unwilling to take so decided a step at this time. Three months later he himself drew a graphic picture of conditions in Mexico: 'Her crops are destroyed, her fields lie unseeded, her work cattle are confiscated for the use of the armed factions, her people flee to the mountains to escape being drawn into unending bloodshed, and no man seems to see or lead the way to peace

[1] Lanier Winslow, attaché in Berlin.

and settled order.... Mexico is starving and without a Government.' Even so, he hesitated to take any positive action.

Colonel House was in Europe from January to June. On his return he found that, despite the cordial approval given by Argentina and Brazil, no progress had been made by Wilson or Bryan in pushing the Pan-American Pact to a definite conclusion. Clearly, much of the delay might be attributed to the hesitations of the Chilean Ambassador, but it seemed plain also that the Secretary of State had not taken up the matter with energy. He lacked the sort of ability necessary to translate ideas into facts. Mr. Bryan had imagination and foresight; many of his ideas which began as subjects of ridicule ended by becoming laws, but, except in rare instances, not through his own efforts.

'The most important event of the day [recorded House on June 18, 1915] was a visit from Henry P. Fletcher, our Ambassador to Chile. We discussed the South American situation as it related to the proposal I made the President before I left, concerning the welding of the two continents. I find nothing has been done in this matter during my absence. The Chilean Ambassador and Government have been the cause of the delay. They evidently do not want to tie themselves to a non-aggressive policy.... I do not feel, however, that the situation has been handled to the best advantage; and I shall take it up with the President again and suggest some means by which it may be expedited.

'Fletcher thought if we got the A.B.C. Powers to declare for the Monroe Doctrine it would be sufficient. I told him that this would in no way be sufficient and that he did not grasp the idea or scope of it. We desired to see the Americas knitted together so as to give the world a policy to be followed in the future. Haste was necessary for the reason that the European war made the time opportune, and, if it did not go through before the end of the war, it might never do so.

'I suggested to Fletcher the advisability of his visiting the different South American countries to further the proposal. I thought if Chile continued to obstruct, we should go ahead without her. The smaller republics would agree and, with Argentina and Brazil, it made but little difference whether Chile came in or remained out.'

With the appointment of Mr. Lansing as Secretary of State, in July, 1915, following Bryan's resignation, new impetus was given to the proposals which House had initiated. 'I am again urging action in that direction,' the Colonel wrote on July 18 to Thomas Nelson Page. A week later, Mr. Lansing came up to the North Shore to spend the day with him.

'*July* 24, 1915: Secretary and Mrs. Lansing arrived on the 10.30 train. Lansing and I at once went into executive session and talked continuously until lunch. There was much to go over. I wished to tell him of European conditions, as I found them, and to give him an insight into what had been done in the Department concerning some important matters.... The South American proposal was one. I was surprised to find that Lansing was ignorant of what had been done. He said, as far as he knew there was nothing on file in the Department. I was surprised, too, that the President had not talked with him more freely and given him fuller information concerning pending matters....

'We took up the Mexican situation and he is getting under way the arrangement to have the A.B.C. Powers join us in composing the difficulties there. He did not know the suggestion was mine and was made as far back as January and lying dormant until now. I do not think the President can altogether relieve himself of blame in this delay, for, while he would probably have gone ahead with it if . . . he had had as Secretary of State a better executive, yet it might have been done even under the unfavorable circumstances with which he had to contend. . . .

'I find him [Lansing] thoroughly familiar with the machinery for such designs, and he seems to be energetic and ambitious to make a record.'

Practical effects of this conference were not slow to appear. In the first place, Mr. Lansing took up at least part of the suggestion that Colonel House had made the preceding January and which the President and Secretary Bryan had not pushed forward; namely, that the South American Powers should be called in to assist in the settlement of the Mexican problem. In August, upon the invitation of Mr. Lansing, the diplomatic representatives of Argentina, Bolivia, Brazil, Chile, Guatemala, and Uruguay met at Washington to discuss the Mexican settlement. From this conference there resulted an invitation to the different Mexican leaders to meet in pacific conference to arrange for general agreement and orderly elections. All the leaders, with the exception of the chief of the Constitutionalists, Carranza, agreed to the invitation, and yet it was Carranza who seemed to exercise the widest powers in Mexico and whose coöperation was essential. Wilson did not deceive himself into the belief that Carranza was friendly to the United States, but both the President and House recognized in Carranza's lieutenant, Obregon, certain qualities which might prove equal to the problem of Mexican pacification.

'*September* 23, 1915: We breakfasted at eight [wrote House]. After breakfast Tumulty talked to me for nearly an hour. The President rescued me and took me up to his study. We discussed Mexico. He laughingly said that Carranza had once or twice put it over us and in a very skilful way.

He thought when the A.B.C. Conference resumed on the 8th of October, we would perhaps have to recognize Carranza. We were both of the opinion that General Obregon was responsible for the accelerated fortunes of Carranza and that he would perhaps finally turn out to be the "man of the hour" in Mexico. We agreed that if Carranza was to be recognized he must first guarantee religious freedom, give amnesty for all political offences, institute the land reforms which had been promised, give protection to foreigners, and recognize their just claims.'

Despite the steady negative returned by Carranza to the invitation to meet with the other Mexican leaders, the conference of American states at Washington refused to be snubbed; in October it decided that the Carranza régime constituted a *de facto* government in Mexico and recommended its recognition. This recognition was granted by the United States Government on October 19.

The Mexican problem was not thereby settled, but general opinion would probably have agreed with that of Ambassador Gerard, who wrote Colonel House in October: 'Carranza has his faults, like most of us, but it seems to me that it is the proper thing to recognize him and a good solution of a bad situation.'

Once again the method of solution was of more importance than the result. Students of the Latin-American situation insisted that it was of the first significance that the United States should have taken this step in conjunction with and upon the recommendation of the chief South American states. President Wilson did not fail to capitalize the friendly sentiments aroused in South America when he delivered his annual message:

'The moral is that the states of America are not hostile rivals, but coöperating friends, and that their growing sense of community of interest, alike in matters political and alike in matters economic, is likely to give them a new significance as factors in international affairs and in the political history of the world.'

Under the influence of this display of the United States' desire to coöperate rather than to control, Mr. Lansing found it possible to continue discussions on the definite Pan-American Pact. On October 19, House wrote to Walter Hines Page: 'Lansing is pushing the South American proposal. The President, Lansing, and I went into this thoroughly some two weeks ago and decided upon a course of action which we believe will accelerate matters and perhaps bring it to a conclusion before Congress meets.'

As a result of long discussion, the original proposition made by House had been revised so as to eliminate one obvious source of practical difficulty; namely, the veto upon the private manufacture of arms. For reasons which the League of Nations Commission later were to find cogent, the abolition of private manufacture was deemed not feasible. Indeed, the new draft of the Pact carried merely a provision for an automatic embargo on munitions in case of revolutionary attack upon an existing government. Articles providing for investigation and arbitration in the settlement of disputes were added. The first and most important article, guaranteeing 'territorial integrity' and 'political independence under republican forms of government,' was retained.

Secretary Lansing to Colonel House

WASHINGTON, *November* 18, 1915

MY DEAR COLONEL HOUSE:

I enclose a revision of the four propositions for the proposed Pan-American Convention.[1] Possibly the President has already sent you a copy, but I am doing so on the supposition that he has not.

[1] See Appendix to chapter.

Before Ambassador Naon sailed, I submitted to him the propositions and he was entirely satisfied with them.

This morning I saw the Brazilian Ambassador and he also approved. This afternoon I asked the Chilean Ambassador to come and see me, and after a long discussion of the whole question he changed his views in regard to the convention and said that he could see no reason why Chile could not accept the propositions as redrafted. I urged on him the advisability of speedy action and he agreed that he would at once communicate them to his Government and ask that the new Cabinet, which comes into office on December 20th, would act immediately and cable him instructions accordingly.

I feel convinced that the Ambassador will do all he can to secure favorable action by his Government.

I thought you would be interested to know the present status of the negotiations and when I see you will explain more fully the substance of my conversation with Mr. Suarez.

I hope to be in New York at the Army-Navy football game on the 27th and shall stay over until Sunday night. Possibly I may have an opportunity to see you then if you are not in Washington before that time.

With warm regards, I am

Cordially yours

ROBERT LANSING

IV

As in the case of the League of Nations Covenant three years later, Colonel House was less interested in the wording of the draft than in the spirit behind the agreement and in securing definite and unanimous acceptance. 'I think you have now gotten the four propositions down to the best possible form,' he wrote Mr. Lansing on November 20. And he urged the President to get the business 'buttoned-up.' Indeed, the matter seemed so close to completion that on January 6, 1916, Mr. Wilson, in his address to the Pan-American Scientific Congress, stated publicly the gist of the proposals.

But more delays intervened. House again left for Europe in December, remaining abroad until March; and, apparently, during his absence little progress was made in overcoming the final difficulties. While in Europe, although engaged on complex and even more far-reaching business, the Colonel did not forget the Pan-American Pact and took what occasion he might to assist it. It was the subject of discussion between him and the Chilean Minister to Great Britain, Señor Eduardes, and also members of the British Cabinet. He was hopeful of British support, and even considered the possibility of the participation of Canada in the Covenant.

'*February* 20, 1916: I had a conference with the Chilean Minister before lunch [he wrote]. He said his Government was pleased with the proposed pact between the American republics. He mentioned the fear Chile had of Japan. He spoke of the advantage Chile could be to the United States because of her coastline as a base, and because of her nitrate and copper deposits. He believed that Chile during the coming year would take second place among copper-producing countries. While talking with him, it occurred to me it would be a good time for Great Britain to indicate that she was in sympathy with the Pan-American Pact; and I told Eduardes I would suggest to Sir Edward Grey to-morrow that he have some member of the House of Commons put a question to him asking if the Government was cognizant of this Pact, how they regarded it, and what effect it would have upon Great Britain. I shall suggest that Grey reply that Great Britain views it sympathetically; that, being one of the largest American Powers, she looks with favor upon any arrangement which will make for a closer union of American states.

'Eduardes was delighted with this suggestion. Later in the day I proposed it to Lansdowne.[1] He was startled, and said it was a matter needing careful consideration because Japan might consider it was directed at her. I thought Japan should be taken at her word. She has repeatedly said she had no designs in the Western Hemisphere, and Great Britain need only accept her assurances at their face value. Lansdowne favored the proposal, but declared it of such importance that careful thought should be given it.

'*February* 21, 1916: The first question I took up with Grey was the suggestion which came to me yesterday regarding the Pan-American Pact. I told Grey I had mentioned it to Lansdowne and he thought it a great move, provided it was so guarded as not to offend the Japanese. Grey took the same attitude I did, that the Japanese could not possibly consider it directed at them. He enthused over the idea and asked me to dictate the question I thought should be put to him in Parliament. I did so, while he wrote it down. It was, whether the Government was taking cognizance of the Pan-American Pact recently announced, guaranteeing the political and territorial integrity of the American republics, and what effect it would have upon the British Dominions in America.

'The thought then occurred to me, and I expressed it to Grey, that after this was done and after I had consulted with the President, the British Government might join the American guaranty as far as their American colonies were concerned. This, I told him, was one way [for Great Britain] to bring about a sympathetic alliance not only with the United States, but with the entire Western Hemisphere. In my opinion, it was an opportunity not to be disregarded and its tendency would be to bring together an influence which could control the peace of the world.

'Grey . . . thought it should be done. I afterward cabled

[1] Minister without Portfolio.

the President, telling him what I had proposed to Grey, but without giving details. . . .

'I gave Loreburn [1] a summary of what I had told Grey concerning the Pan-American Pact and what Grey had promised to do in the House of Commons provided the Canadian Prime Minister approved. Grey felt that a matter appertaining solely to American affairs should first be submitted to the Canadian Government, and this was being done by cable.

'I suggested to Loreburn that he prepare a speech in advance, without saying anything to Grey, so when the announcement was made in the Commons he could give it his warm approval in the House of Lords. He was eager to do this, for he said it presented to his mind a magnificent prospect.

'*February* 22, 1916: He [Grey] told me that Bonar Law was of the opinion it would be somewhat hasty to have the question asked in the House of Commons, and an answer given just now, about the Pan-American Pact. He has cabled the Canadian Prime Minister and the matter will be brought out at the time considered most opportune.'

Returning to the United States on March 5, House heard from Grey soon afterwards that the British thoroughly approved of the Pan-American Pact and were interested in the plan of affiliation with it, but evidently feared to make any public statement before its consummation seemed better assured.

Sir Edward Grey to Colonel House

FOREIGN OFFICE, *March* 23, 1916

DEAR COLONEL HOUSE:

Soon after you left, the Chilean Minister volunteered a statement to Sir M. de Bunsen [2] of his conversation with you about the Pan-American proposal.

[1] Lord Loreburn, an advanced Liberal and former Lord Chancellor.

[2] British Ambassador to Austria until 1914; appointed Special Ambassador to States of South America in 1918.

In consequence of what Sir M. de Bunsen told me I thought it desirable to see the Chilean Minister before saying anything in public. I found him pleased with what you had said to him, but insisting very carefully that the idea of partnership must be emphasized and that of tutelage suppressed.

He admitted that you had done this, but he made it clear that if I made any public statement it must be evident that I was founding myself not only on what President Wilson had said, but on the feelings of the A.B.C. countries in South America as well.

I asked him to send me a statement which he said the President of Chile had made favourable to the idea, so that if I had to say anything in public I might refer to it as well as to what President Wilson had said.

The Canadian Government were quite willing that I should say what I thought of saying in favour of it, but finding I should be on rather delicate ground as regards the A.B.C. countries, I think I will wait till the matter comes up in the Press again before making any public utterance.

I made it clear to the Chilean Minister that we were favourable to the plan as put before him by you, and that you had spoken to me in exactly the same way as to him, but I said nothing of having discussed with you the question of a public statement here.

Yours sincerely

E. Grey

Notwithstanding the cordial protestations of the Chilean Minister in London, House soon discovered that the attitude of Suarez in Washington was not encouraging and that, as a result of the hesitations of Chile, the early enthusiasm of Brazil was beginning to evaporate. The situation was complicated by a new Mexican crisis. On March 8, Villa, in revolt against Carranza and pursuing the temporarily profitable career of bandit under the diaphanous guise of liberal patriot, crossed the frontier and murdered sev American citizens at Columbus, New Mexico. The pu expedition under Pershing which was sent after him the border, led to verbal and military retaliation on th of Carranza which threatened to produce formal warfare between Mexico and the United States. The atmosphere during the spring and summer months was by no means favorable to the completion of the Pan-American Pact. Furthermore, Mr. Fletcher, who had been given charge of the negotiations, discovered an unwillingness to settle upon details that nullified the agreement upon the principle which the South American states had professed.

The differences were slight on the surface, but they proved sufficient to delay and finally to prevent signature of the Pan-American Pact. It was impossible for the United States to urge action, without arousing the suspicions of Chile that the Pact in reality was to serve our special interests rather than those of the Americas in general. On August 8, Frank Polk, then Under-Secretary of State, wrote to Colonel House that the Pact 'seems dead for the moment.'

On the following day, Mr. Fletcher reported that progress had stopped. Señor Naon desired delay in order that the tense feeling aroused by the crisis in Mexico and the dispute with Carranza might subside. The attitude of Chile became increasingly aloof.

'In view of the check put on the negotiations by Mr. Naon's unwillingness to sign [wrote Fletcher to House], I could not open out the treaty to the other republics. So the matter rests *in statu quo*. Chile is definitely and decidedly opposed to the treaty. . . . I feel sure that if we go on without Chile, that is, isolating her from the American concert, she will turn naturally elsewhere in finance and trade and that gradually a spirit of hostility against the United States will be engendered.'

Thus the summer dragged along. In September, following the subsidence of the Mexican crisis, the Argentine Ambassador declared himself ready to sign; but Chile still held off and Brazil tended to follow her example. The last reference in Colonel House's papers for 1916 to the plan which he had started nearly two years before, is dated October 1:

'Fletcher called to report on the Pan-American Peace Pact. He did not go further with Ambassador Naon, who is willing to sign for Argentina, because Lansing had promised Dr. Müller, Brazilian Secretary of State for Foreign Affairs, that he would not move actively in the matter until the 15th of November, which would give Müller time to return to Brazil and ascertain the will of his Government. Müller has been in the United States for the past six weeks at a health resort.'

The weeks that followed were filled first with election activities and then with the negotiations that succeeded Germany's first peace note. The Pan-American Pact was pushed to one side and, with the entrance of the United States into the European war in the spring of 1917, it slipped into a forgotten grave.

The failure to carry through the plan to its completion must have brought harsh disappointment to Colonel House, who followed the progress of negotiations with invariable interest, although he ceased to retain active direction of their course. But even unfulfilled, the plan occupies a position of historical significance. It was designed not merely to bring the American states more closely together, but also to serve as a model to the European nations when they had ended the war. Both in its specific language and in its general intent, the Pan-American Pact is the immediate prototype of the Covenant of the League of Nations. By the summer of 1916 Colonel House could see its failure with greater equanimity because his eyes already caught the vision of the United States entering and vivifying a larger concert than that of purely American states. The development of our relations with Europe, forced by the war, brought upon the horizon the need of a world organization into which the Americas might conceivably be drawn.

Even before the war House realized that the traditional separation of the United States from Europe in matters political could not be maintained indefinitely and that the time had come when political events of moment in Europe must inevitably prove of direct importance to the United States. It was this realization that led him to give over the active direction of the Pan-American scheme while his chief interest was caught in the European situation. It led him to visit the Kaiser in June, 1914, and thus to enter upon an adventure that determined the course of his main activities during the following six years. Nothing with which he had hitherto been connected, whether of a diplomatic character or in the field of domestic politics, compares in importance with the European mission he undertook in the early summer of 1914, to which we must now turn our attention.

APPENDIX

Pan-American Pact — Revised Draft

ARTICLE I

That the high contracting parties to this solemn covenant and agreement hereby join one another in a common and mutual guaranty of territorial integrity and of political independence under republican forms of government.

ARTICLE II

To give definitive application to the guaranty set forth in Article I, the high contracting parties severally covenant to endeavor forthwith to reach a settlement of all disputes as to boundaries or territory now pending between them by amicable agreement or by means of international arbitration.

ARTICLE III

That the high contracting parties further agree, First, that all questions, of whatever character, arising between any two or more of them which cannot be settled by the ordinary means of diplomatic correspondence shall, before any declaration of war or beginning of hostilities, be first submitted to a permanent international commission for investigation, one year being allowed for such investigation; and, Second, that if the dispute is not settled by investigation, to submit the same to arbitration, provided the question in dispute does not affect the honor, independence, or vital interests of the nations concerned or the interests of third parties.

ARTICLE IV

To the end that domestic tranquillity may prevail within their territories, the high contracting parties further severally covenant and agree that they will not permit the departure from their respective jurisdictions of any military or naval expedition hostile to the established government of any of the high contracting parties, and that they will prevent the exportation from their respective jurisdictions of arms, ammunition, or other munitions of war destined to or for the use of any person or persons notified to be in insurrection or revolt against the established government of any of the high contracting parties.

November, 1915

CHAPTER IX

THE GREAT ADVENTURE

The situation is extraordinary. It is militarism run stark mad. . . . There is some day to be an awful cataclysm. . . .

House to Wilson, May 29, 1914, *from Berlin*

I

At the beginning of Wilson's Administration there were few citizens of the United States who professed a knowledge of, or an interest in, European politics. The traditions of the nineteenth century still held the public mind — traditions which laid down, as the primary principle of American policy, a complete abstention from the political affairs of Europe. They had their origin in sound judgment. During the early days of the Republic, as both Washington and Jefferson realized, entanglement in foreign alliances would have meant that the United States, lacking material strength, must have become the catspaw of an alien power. On the other hand, Nature had provided a wonderful opportunity if the independent colonists would turn their backs upon the Atlantic and devote themselves to developing the resources of their own land.

Thus during the early nineteenth century the young country spent its energy upon domestic problems: an aggressive extension of the frontier, a fierce wrestle with the backwoods, a struggle for political unity, the building of transportation lines, the creation of an industrial system. The people knew and cared little of what went on across the Atlantic.

But by the beginning of the twentieth century, conditions had changed. Not merely had the Pacific coast been reached and the intervening territory conquered, but through the merchant and the missionary American interests had been established in the Orient, and the fortunes of war had brought the Philippines under the United States flag. Our Government claimed a position of equality with the European Powers in the Far East and, under the direction of Hay, had entered into close coöperation with them there. The acquisition of Porto Rico, the control of Cuba, the cutting of the Panama Canal, assured predominance in the Caribbean. Almost unconsciously, the country had become a world power, and it was certain that political contacts with Europe must become more frequent and close, for the great European states were also world powers and their interests touched ours at many points. Economic and intellectual intercourse with Europe was intimate and constant; political intercourse was henceforth inevitable.

This fact had been realized by President Roosevelt, who insisted that responsibility must accompany power. So keen was his sense of responsibility that in 1905 and 1906 he took an active, albeit unguessed, part in the negotiations that led to the Algeciras Conference, which averted the threat of a European war. This was a crisis in which the United States had no direct interest, and one which concerned purely European states. Roosevelt participated in the negotiations merely because of his conviction that the United States must fulfil its duties to the rest of the world in the cause of peace. In such a cause he was willing to scrap the tradition of isolation.

The war clouds of 1906, however, continued to hang low over Europe. The reconciliation of France and Great Britain, consummated in the Entente of 1904, had disturbed the Germans, who saw in it an encouragement to the French political renaissance and to the active foreign policy of the French Foreign Minister, Delcassé. They had hoped to break the Entente by raising the Moroccan issue, but failed. In 1907 they were still more disturbed by the Anglo-Russian reconciliation. It seemed to them that an iron ring was being drawn about Germany. They feared especially the development of an aggressive Russian policy in the Balkans that would destroy Germany's ally, Austria, and cut off the road to the southeast. Once more, in 1911, they tried to break the Entente, now the Triple Entente, and again they failed.

Counsels in Germany were evidently divided. There were those, such as the Chancellor, von Bethmann-Hollweg, an amiable but anæmic personality, who hoped to find a solution in a peaceable understanding — especially with the British, without whose help Russian plans in the Near East could not succeed. But there were others who insisted that Germany must precipitate a war at the first favorable moment, before Russia was ready. The aggressive spirit had been taught for a generation by the professors, it was rampant in military circles, and it had caught the naval officers.

The temper of these groups, who doubtless did not represent exactly the ruling opinion of the nation, would have been a less serious factor, if it had not been supported by the widespread conviction that the Entente was planning to close in on Germany. In this case, as so often, fear proved to be the mother of recklessness. Should the control of German policy be captured even temporarily by the firebrands, backed by a panicky public sentiment, the danger of a decision to risk everything on a sudden attack was very real. And because of the complexity of the diplomatic groupings, such an attack would mean a general European war.

In England the peril was realized acutely, but the Government faced an unpleasant dilemma. The rapid development of German sea-power could not but be regarded as a threat to British security, which naturally led to the keenest sort of naval competition. Any slackening in British naval preparation would be flying in the face of Providence. In view of the engagements which the British had made with France, which however informal were none the less morally binding, military preparation was also necessary. Such preparation, on the other hand, could only intensify the diplomatic crisis, by increasing the fears of Germany and giving a lever to the German militarists who desired war.

In Russia and in France military development was the order of the day. There were many who looked upon the general war as inevitable; the Dual Alliance must get ready and must omit no step which might increase its diplomatic and military weight. Any other policy would lay those in control open to the charge of criminal negligence. But each step taken seemed to transform the Dual Alliance from a defensive to an offensive combination and inevitably stimulated the fears and the belligerence of Germany.

Europe thus prepared for war and, as William Graham Sumner used to say, 'What you prepare for you get.' It is true that in 1913 the immediate danger seemed to pass when the efforts of Sir Edward Grey brought a pacific solution to the Balkan crisis. For a few months a *détente* in Anglo-German relations, assisted by the offer of British coöperation in German plans for the Bagdad Railway, appeared to provide a means for ending the conflict of alliances. But as the British Premier later wrote, the diplomats were conscious that they 'were skating on the thinnest of ice and that the peace of Europe was at the mercy of a chapter of unforeseen and unforeseeable accidents.' [1]

II

Like Roosevelt, House was convinced that a European war must necessarily attain such proportions that every part of the world would be touched, and that it was both the duty and the interest of the United States to do all in its power to avert it. The days had passed when America was isolated from the Eastern Hemisphere; she had much to fear from European trouble and she could do much to appease it.

Even before the inauguration of President Wilson, House

[1] Asquith, *Genesis of the War*, 166.

planned a policy of coöperation which should include the United States, Great Britain, and Germany. He saw that the crux of the danger lay in the animosity of Germans and British, and he hoped that it might be allayed by getting the two countries to work towards a common end. Germany's expansive energy, he thought, might be turned into more useful channels than Krupp factories and dreadnoughts.

'*January* 22, 1913: Martin lunched with us [Colonel House recorded]. . . . I told him that I wanted to get Governor Wilson to let me bring about an understanding between Great Britain, this country, and Germany, in regard to the Monroe Doctrine. . . .

'I also told him that it would be my endeavor to bring about a better understanding between England and Germany; that if England were less intolerant of Germany's aspirations for expansion, good feeling could be brought about between them. I thought we could encourage Germany to exploit South America in a legitimate way; that is, by development of its resources and by sending her surplus population there; that such a move would be good for South America and would have a beneficial result generally.'

During the first year of the Wilson Administration, the pressure of domestic problems left the plan only half formed in House's mind. But he kept turning it over and, as occasion offered, he raised the subject with persons whose influence and information might prove useful.

'*April* 23, 1913: I have a letter from James Speyer [he wrote] asking me to meet at lunch downtown Count von Bernstorff, the German Ambassador, who has expressed a desire to know me. I never go downtown, and declined. . . .

'*April* 25, 1913: James Speyer telephoned and again asked

if I would lunch with the German Ambassador uptown instead of downtown, and I promised to do so. . . .

'*May* 9, 1913: I lunched at Delmonico's with the German Ambassador, Count von Bernstorff, and Mr. Speyer.

'The Count talked rather more freely than I anticipated a diplomat of his training would. He spoke of Mr. Bryan and of the different assistants in the State Department with a good deal of freedom. He also criticized ex-Secretary Knox and Huntington Wilson, his First Assistant.

'The most interesting part of his conversation was after lunch, when Mr. Speyer left us and Bernstorff and I walked down the Avenue alone. I suggested, that it would be a great thing if there was a sympathetic understanding between England, Germany, Japan, and the United States. Together I thought they would be able to wield an influence for good throughout the world. They could ensure peace and the proper development of the waste places, besides maintaining an open door and equal opportunity to every one everywhere.

'Much to my surprise, he agreed with me. He said the understanding between Germany and England was much better of late, and if they had some mutual field of endeavor he thought a good understanding could finally be brought about between them. He suggested that perhaps China was the most promising field at present for concerted action, for the United States could work there with Germany and England. . . .'

Two months later, in London, House discussed the broad lines of this plan with the American Ambassador. Page sympathized thoroughly with House's scheme of utilizing the force of nations for purposes other than military or naval. 'It is a time,' he wrote to House, 'for some great constructive, forward idea — an idea for action. If the great world forces could, by fortunate events and fortunate combinations, be united and led to clean up the tropics, the great armies might gradually become sanitary police, as in Panama, and finally gradually forget the fighting idea and at last dissolve. . . .'

But Page felt that the Europeans were too traditionally minded to embark upon such a plan, which had in it something suggestive of the Secretariat of the League of Nations. 'On the Continent of Europe,' he wrote, 'the Kaiser is probably the foremost man. Yet he cannot think far beyond the provincial views of the Germans. In England, Sir Edward Grey is the largest-visioned statesman. Yet even he does not seem to have a definitely constructive mind.'

House did not force his ideas upon the British at this time, but he discovered that in Sir Edward Grey he would deal with a man who may have lacked imagination, but who was sincerely desirous of attempting any scheme that might lead towards the maintenance of peace. On July 3, 1913, Colonel House had lunch with Grey, Lord Crewe, and Page.

'We discussed the feeling between Germany and England. Sir Edward remarked that the great cause of antagonism between nations was the distrust each felt for the other's motives. Before leaving this subject I told him of my luncheon with Count von Bernstorff, German Ambassador at Washington, and that I had been surprised to hear him say he believed that good feeling would soon come between England and Germany. My purpose in repeating this was to plant the seeds of peace.'

On his return to the United States, House was caught in the swirl of appointments and the passage of the Federal Reserve Act. But whenever he had the opportunity, he returned to his study of the European problem.

'*September* 1, 1913: I have had some interesting conversations with Dumba,[1] particularly in regard to some phases of the political situation in southeastern Europe. He was at one time Minister at Bucharest and, of course, knows the Balkan situation thoroughly.'

In November arrived Sir William Tyrrell, Grey's secretary, with whom House found it possible to discuss in all candor every sort of international question. After arranging with Tyrrell the understanding as to Wilson's Mexican policy and Panama tolls, the Colonel proceeded to impart his new plan, which he had formulated with some definiteness. The existing crisis he hoped to tide over by an understanding that would lead to a limitation of armaments. If this succeeded, he would follow it up with the plan he had already suggested to Bernstorff — a coöperative policy of developing the waste places of the world.

'*December* 2, 1913: I told him [Tyrrell] the next thing I wished to do was to bring about an understanding between France, Germany, England, and the United States, regarding a reduction of armaments, both military and naval. I said it was an ambitious undertaking, but was so well worth while that I intended to try it. He thought it one of the most far-reaching and beneficent things that could be done. He thought if we continued as at present, ruin would eventually follow, and in the meanwhile it would prevent us from solving the vexatious industrial problems we are all facing. He considered I had "a good sporting chance of success."

'I asked him to suggest my procedure, and we discussed that at length. He thought I should go to Germany and see the Kaiser first, and afterward the Ministers of Foreign Affairs and Finance. He said I would find them responsive to the idea, but that the Minister of Marine, von Tirpitz, was a reactionary and largely responsible for the present German policy.

[1] Austro-Hungarian Ambassador.

'He did not think it necessary for me to take any credentials. He advised having our Ambassador in Germany whisper to the Kaiser that I was "the power behind the throne" in the United States. That if this were done, I would have to warn our Ambassador to tell official Berlin I did not care for "fuss and feathers"; otherwise I would have red carpets laid for me all over Berlin.

'He thought I should proceed quietly and secretly, but should secure an audience with the Kaiser and say to him, among other things, that England and America "had buried the hatchet" and there was a strong feeling that Germany should come into this good feeling and evidence their good intention by agreeing to stop building an extravagant navy, and to curtail militarism generally.

'Sir William assured me that England would coöperate with Germany cordially, and had been ready to do so for a long while. He saw no cause for difference between them. With England, United States, France, and Germany [agreed], we both thought the balance of the world would follow in line and a great change would come about. He said the Kaiser was a spectacular individual and partook more of French qualities than he did of German. He likened him to Roosevelt.

'Sir William promised to give me all the memoranda passed between Great Britain and Germany upon this question of disarmament, in order that I might see how entirely right Great Britain had been in her position.'

Ten days later, House discussed the plan with President Wilson and received his approval. 'I might almost say he was enthusiastic,' wrote House to Page. It was decided that in the early summer the Colonel should go directly to Berlin and take the plan to the Kaiser. If he proved complaisant, House would go to England.

During the winter and spring he made his preparations.

In January he wrote to Gerard to make sure of the Kaiser's plans; he learned that Wilhelm II would be in Corfu in the late spring, that he would return to Potsdam, go on to Kiel for the races, then on a cruise in Norwegian waters, and later to his estates on the Rhine.[1] House chose the earliest moment available and cabled Gerard to arrange the interview for June, after the Kaiser's return from Corfu.

The Colonel felt himself already in such close touch with the situation in Great Britain that he believed the chief task he must undertake would be a study of current German psychology and especially the character of William II. In January we find him taking lunch with Benjamin Ide Wheeler and quietly extracting information.

'*January* 1, 1914: We had a delightful time together. He is just back from Germany and has seen much of the Kaiser, not only this time but upon former visits. He visits him in the most informal manner and spends many hours with him and his family. He gave me nearly all the information I need regarding the Kaiser and his *entourage*. Wheeler is also a close friend of Roosevelt's, and I was interested in his comparison of the two men. He considers them very alike, particularly in regard to memory and impulsiveness, but they are dissimilar inasmuch as the Kaiser has a religious turn of mind and is more cultured in his manners.

'In order to obtain the information I desired, I had to disclose my object in questioning him; and he encouraged me to believe that I might have some chance of success in bringing the Kaiser around to an agreement for disarmament. He thought the Minister of Marine would be the obstacle, just as Sir William Tyrrell had pointed out. He

[1] House to Gerard, January 1, 1914; Gerard to House, February 11, March 15, 1914. The matter is of historical interest, since it has been asserted that the Kaiser sailed to Norway as a blind to cover German war plans. It is clear that his itinerary was arranged long before the murder of the Archduke.

said the Kaiser had told him that his object in building a navy was not to threaten England, but to add prestige to Germany's commerce upon the seven seas. He had spoken of how impossible war should be between England and Germany, or, in fact, how utterly foolish any general European war would be. He thinks the coming antagonism is between the Asiatics and the Western peoples and that within twenty years the Western peoples will recognize this and stand together more or less as a unit.

'Wheeler told of how narrowly a general European war was averted last March over the Balkan embroglio, and how the Emperor thinks he saved the day by his suggestion of creating the State of Albania.[1] The Kaiser told Wheeler that he had warned Russia if they attacked Austria, he would strike them immediately. The Kaiser also told him he felt kindly toward England and that he was Queen Victoria's favorite grandchild.

'In his talks with the Kaiser, he said the Kaiserin seldom joined in the conversation, but would sit quietly knitting and only entered the discussion when it fell upon domestic problems.

'Another difference between the Kaiser and T. R. was that the Kaiser was a good listener when necessary, and is courteous in doing so.'

Colonel House spent most of the winter in Texas. But as soon as he returned to the East in March and notwithstanding the time and effort he was giving to the Federal Reserve appointments, he continued preparations for his European venture. In April he had long conferences with

[1] After the defeats of the Turkish army by the Balkan League in the autumn of 1912, Austria protested against the acquisition of any part of the Adriatic littoral by Serbia. A conference of the Great Powers was held at London, where Great Britain and Germany worked for a compromise and where the independent State of Albania was created. Serbia acquired Macedonia, thus precipitating a quarrel with Bulgaria.

Irwin Laughlin, Counsellor of the American Embassy at St. James's.

'*April* 9, 1914: We fell to talking about my plan for decreasing armaments. Laughlin was three years First Secretary of the American Embassy at Berlin. During that time he talked with the German Chancellor regarding disarmament, and he did not believe there was one chance in a million of my getting Germany to consent to a naval holiday.

'I surprised him by telling him of the direct information I had of the Kaiser himself — none of which, though, was favorable to my plan, but rather coinciding with Laughlin's views. But what impressed him was the method I had in mind of accomplishing results. I explained my purpose not to take it up from a sentimental or purely ethical viewpoint, but to try and prove that it would be of material advantage to Germany.

'I went into some detail as to giving Germany a zone of influence in Asia Minor and Persia, and also lending a hope that they might be given a freer hand commercially in the Central and South American republics. I changed his views as to the desirability of making the effort, but he wanted time to think it over and promised to let me know his conclusions later. Laughlin knows the Germans well, and he told me of the difficulties of reaching the Emperor under right conditions. . . .

'*April* 10, 1914: Mr. and Mrs. Irwin Laughlin lunched with us. Laughlin and I went into my disarmament plan at some length. I used him as a dummy, as it were, knowing he would catch me if I tripped at any point. I discussed my intentions thoroughly, and talked to him as I would talk to the Kaiser were we to meet.

'After thinking of the matter overnight and hearing my plans more in detail, Laughlin believes I should make the effort. . . .

'*April* 16, 1914: At half-past nine I left to go to the Borden Harrimans' in order to meet the guests, since Mrs. Harriman had told them I would do so. Prince Münster, Prince Paul Troubetskoy and his wife, Ambassador Dumba, General Wood, and several others were there. I talked with Prince Münster for a while about the German Emperor, in order to get more information about him. . . .

'*April* 28, 1914: I spoke to the President about what I was doing in regard to Germany and the Kaiser, and he remarked, "You are preparing to make the ground fallow." I asked again whether he was certain that he wished me to go at this particular time. He replied, "The object you have in mind is too important to neglect." . . .

'*May* 7, 1914: Hugh Wallace saw Count von Bernstorff and told him I was going to Germany on the sixteenth day of May. Von Bernstorff said the German Foreign Office had already informed him I was coming and had asked him to give them a report upon me, which he had sent. He said he intended sending another, which I thought was perhaps inspired by Wallace. . . .'

Thus Colonel House set forth on his extraordinary mission, a private American citizen whose only relevant title was 'personal friend of the President,' a single individual hoping to pull the lever of common sense that might divert the nations of the Old World from the track of war to that of peace. To inject himself successfully into the core of the European maelstrom demanded as much courage as diplomatic deftness. These qualities he possessed, as well as a sense of proportion which caused him often to laugh at the stark humor of the odds against him. But the stake for which he played was tremendous. It was the peace of the world. If he failed no harm was done. And if he succeeded —!

He called his mission the Great Adventure.

III

Colonel House to the President

AMERICAN EMBASSY
BERLIN, *May* 29, 1914

DEAR GOVERNOR:

I was fairly well informed as to the situation here when I reached Germany. Prince Münster and the Count von Moltke were fellow passengers, and I came to know von Moltke well.[1]

Münster is what we would call a reactionary, and I let him do all the talking. Von Moltke, on the contrary, is perhaps the only noble in Germany who has a detached point of view and sees the situation as we do. He gave me valuable information, which merely tended to confirm my opinion as to the nearly impossible chance of bettering conditions.

I have not seen the Kaiser, but have been invited to lunch at Potsdam on Monday. Just what opportunity there may be to talk with him is an uncertainty....

I have had long talks with von Jagow, Minister for Foreign Affairs, and Admiral von Tirpitz. Jagow is a clever diplomat without much personality. Von Tirpitz is the father of the greater navy and is forceful and aggressive. Neither has ability of the highest order.

I was told not to talk to von Tirpitz, because of his well-known opposition to such views as we hold; but, finding that he is the most forceful man in Germany excepting the Kaiser, I concluded to go at him. We had an extremely interesting hour together, and I believe I made a dent. Not a big one, but sufficient at least to start a discussion in London.

I am careful always not to involve you. Opinions and

[1] This Count von Moltke was a nephew of the great Field Marshal and a cousin of the German Chief of Staff during the invasion of Belgium and France who was superseded by Falkenhayn after the failure of the German offensive.

purposes I give as my own, and you come in no further than what may be assumed because of our relations.

The situation is extraordinary. It is militarism run stark mad. Unless some one acting for you can bring about a different understanding, there is some day to be an awful cataclysm. No one in Europe can do it. There is too much hatred, too many jealousies. Whenever England consents, France and Russia will close in on Germany and Austria. England does not want Germany wholly crushed, for she would then have to reckon alone with her ancient enemy, Russia; but if Germany insists upon an ever-increasing navy, then England will have no choice.

The best chance for peace is an understanding between England and Germany in regard to naval armaments, and yet there is some disadvantage to us by these two getting too close.

It is an absorbing problem, and one of tremendous consequence. I wish it might be solved, and to the everlasting glory of your Administration and our American civilization.

Your faithful and affectionate

E. M. House

What Colonel House soon realized was that in Germany there was a sense of fear as well as aggressiveness, the fear of the man tortured by uncertainty and ready to jump at the throat of the first who seemed to move. Conscious of the enmity which it had aroused, Germany kept its revolver cocked and would let it off at the least whisper.

'*May* 27, 1914: I had insisted before coming [recorded House] that we should not be entertained. There are only a few people I desire to meet. However, the Gerards did not literally follow our desires and we had several people every day. On Tuesday they gave a dinner of twenty-four covers, at which were Admiral von Tirpitz, Minister of Marine, von Jagow, Minister for Foreign Affairs, Sir Edward Goschen, the

British Ambassador, and Count and Countess von Moltke, who were invited at our request.

'Von Tirpitz and I left the dining-room together and we stood in one of the drawing-rooms and talked for an hour. He evidenced a decided dislike for the British, a dislike that almost amounted to hatred. One of the things that amused me most was his suggestion that the English "looked down upon Germans and considered them their inferiors."

'Von Tirpitz spoke of the anti-German feeling in the United States and cited our newspapers in evidence of it. He also spoke of Admiral Mahan's articles which have a pro-British leaning. I assured him our newspapers did not indicate our real feeling, and asked him whether the press of Germany represented the feeling of the Germans toward us. He replied, "Not at all." He said the Government had absolutely no control over the German newspapers, but in England, he noticed, the English brought their papers around to the Government point of view whenever the situation required it.

'I spoke of the courage and character of the President. This I illustrated by different incidents — one being his insistence in taking part in the funeral parade of the Vera Cruz sailors, and another his refusal to be intimidated or coerced into recognizing Huerta. I drew clearly the distinction between the President and Mr. Bryan. I wanted official Germany to know that if any international complications arose between our two countries, they would have to deal with a man of iron courage and inflexible will.

'Von Tirpitz and I talked largely of armaments, I pleading for a limitation in the interest of international peace and he stating vigorously the necessity of Germany's maintaining the highest possible order of military and naval organization. He disclaimed any desire for conquest and insisted it was peace that Germany wanted, but the way to maintain it was to put fear into the hearts of her enemies.

'I pointed out the danger in this programme, for, while Great Britain did not desire to see Germany crushed because it would leave her to reckon alone with her ancient enemy, Russia, at the same time she could not view with equanimity the ever-increasing naval strength of Germany combined with her large and efficient standing army. If it came to a decision as to whether Germany should be crushed or be permitted to have a navy sufficient to overcome British supremacy at sea, their policy would clearly be to let Germany go under.

'I thought an understanding could be brought about between Germany and England. He hoped so, but he did not trust England, because the English were not "reliable." Von Tirpitz was the most anti-English of any of the German officials with whom I talked. I am giving my conversation with him very fully, for it indicates the general trend of my conversations with others.

'Among other things we did was to go to the Aviation Field and see what they were doing in that direction. I found it difficult to get any estimate of the aërial strength of Germany. One of the airmen was brought up to the club by the German Major in charge and introduced to us. He then went up and did some spectacular flights for our benefit. He came directly over our heads and looped the loop several times. He performed all sorts of dangerous and curious manœuvres. I was glad when he came down, for I was afraid his enthusiasm to please might result in his death. The Major told me that thirty-six had already been killed on that field.

'The airman was named Fokker, and he told me he was a Dutchman and had recently come from Holland at the request of the German Government.'

Thus was Colonel House, before the war, given a glimpse of the aviator whose name was to become terribly familiar.

IV

Not without difficulty and the exercise of diplomatic adroitness, Ambassador Gerard had arranged that House should have a private talk with the Kaiser. Official Berlin protested. The Foreign Office was perfectly willing that the Colonel should receive the satisfaction of an interview, but they insisted that some member of the civil Government must be present. House was equally definite in his insistence that it must be a *tête-à-tête* or nothing. 'If that is not possible,' he had written Gerard, 'then please do not bother about it at all.' He wanted to be sure that the frankness of the conversation should not be impeded by official red tape. Later he wrote: 'It was a bluff on my part, but I declined to see him unless it could be arranged that I could see him alone.'

Whatever the magic influence may have been, and House ascribes it to the diplomacy of Ambassador Gerard,[1] the bluff accomplished its purpose, and Gerard finally received word that if he and House would come to Potsdam on June 1, an occasion would be made for the latter to talk alone with the Kaiser. On that day took place the ceremonies of the *Schrippenfest*,[2] a gorgeous presentation of devotional militarism in the Prussian style, such as the Kaiser loved dearly.

[1] House wrote later, 'I cannot state too strongly my appreciation of the part the Ambassador played in finessing with Wilhelmstrasse in order to bring about the desired result.'

[2] The *Schrippenfest*, literally the 'White Roll Feast' (a *Schrippe* being a roll of white bread), was held annually on Whit-Monday for the model Battalion, in Potsdam. Traditionally it was the one occasion of the year when the common soldier received white instead of black bread, and when he was also treated to such luxuries as meat courses, stewed prunes, and wine. The feast was given by the Kaiser, who invited foreign military and naval attachés, ambassadors, and distinguished strangers. It was attended by the Kaiserin and the younger members of the imperial family. The outstanding feature of the ceremony was the Kaiser's presence at the table, sitting in the midst of his troops, eating their white rolls, and drinking from a glass already used by one of the common soldiers.

House and Gerard, in their black evening dress suits, provided a grotesque sombreness quite out of keeping with their surroundings — 'like two black crows,' as the Kaiser himself described them with more pungency than politeness.

'*June* 1, 1914: Gerard and I [recorded House] set forth for Potsdam at half-past nine. We arrived too early and wandered about until nearly eleven, and then entered the Palace. We found ourselves to be the only guests invited to the *Schrippenfest*.

'We were taken through a beautiful sweep of rooms, running across the park front, until we came to a side entrance. Here we waited a few minutes until the Kaiser was announced. He came up and shook hands and passed out with his suite into the park. We followed after the royal party, which consisted of the Emperor, the Empress, and the Princes and their wives. We were given a position near the royal family.

'After religious exercises came the parade, then the decorations were given, and afterward we went across to the other Palace, where the soldiers were having their lunch. During this time I was largely with Herr Zimmermann, Under-Secretary of State for Foreign Affairs and Acting Secretary while von Jagow is absent [on his honeymoon]. I found him quite responsive to my ideas concerning a sympathetic understanding between Great Britain, Germany, and the United States. We discussed every phase of the present European situation.

'We lunched in the famous Shell Hall ['probably the ugliest room in the world,' remarked Gerard].[1] The table was crescent-shaped and was beautifully decorated. Gerard and I were seated directly opposite the imperial party. On my right was the Minister for War, General von Falken-

[1] The walls of the room were composed of sea-shells which encrusted the plaster.

hayn;[1] the man to my left was some general from Saxony, but I did not catch his name. The Emperor talked across the table with our party, mostly with General von Falkenhayn. . . . The food was delicious and the meal not long, perhaps fifty minutes. . . .

'I had cautioned Gerard before coming to Berlin not to use the title of "Colonel" when referring to me or when introducing me after I arrived. This did not serve my purpose, for Bernstorff had cabled of my coming, so I became "Colonel" immediately. Most of my time at luncheon was used in explaining to my neighbors the kind of Colonel I was — not a real one in the European sense, but, as we would say in America, a geographical one. My explanation finally reached Falkenhayn's consciousness, but my neighbor from Saxony was hopelessly befuddled and continued until the last to discuss army technique. . . .

'Afterwards we adjourned to one of the larger drawing-rooms, where I was presented to the Empress. We talked of Corfu, the beauty of Germany in the spring, and other generalities. When this formality was over, the Kaiser's Aide-de-Camp came to say that His Majesty was ready to receive me on the terrace. . . .

'I found that he had all the versatility of Roosevelt with something more of charm, something less of force. He has what to me is a disagreeable habit of bringing his face very close to one when he talks most earnestly. His English is clear and well chosen and, though he talks vehemently, yet he is too much the gentleman to monopolize conversation. It was give-and-take all the way through. He knew what he wanted to say, so did I; and since we both talk rapidly, the half-hour was quite sufficient.

'Gerard and Zimmermann stood in conversation some ten

[1] Falkenhayn became later Chief of Staff and directed the German offensive of 1916 against Verdun. Following the failure to take Verdun, he was succeeded by Hindenburg.

or fifteen feet away, quite out of hearing. At first I thought I would never get His Majesty past his hobbies, but finally I drew him to the subject I had come to discuss.... I found him much less prejudiced and much less belligerent than von Tirpitz. He declared he wanted peace because it seemed to Germany's interest. Germany had been poor, she was now growing rich, and a few more years of peace would make her so. "She was menaced on every side. The bayonets of Europe were directed at her," and much more of this he gave me. Of England, he spoke kindly and admiringly. England, America, and Germany were kindred peoples and should draw closer together. Of other nations he had but little opinion....

'He spoke of the folly of England forming an alliance with the Latins and Slavs, who had no sympathy with our ideals and purposes and who were vacillating and unreliable as allies. He spoke of them as being semi-barbarous, and of England, Germany, and the United States as being the only hope of advancing Christian civilization....

'I thought Russia was the greatest menace to England and it was to England's advantage that Germany was in a position to hold Russia in check, and that Germany was the barrier between Europe and the Slavs. I found no difficulty in getting him to admit this.

'He spoke of the impossibility of Great Britain being able to make a permanent and satisfactory alliance with either Russia or France. I told him that the English were very much concerned over his ever-growing navy, which taken together with his enormous army constituted a menace; and there might come a time when they would have to decide whether they ran more danger from him and his people making a successful invasion than they did from Russia, and the possibility of losing their Asiatic colonies. I thought when that point was reached, the decision would be against Germany.

'I spoke of the community of interests between England, Germany, and the United States, and thought if they stood together the peace of the world could be maintained. He assented to this quite readily. However, in my opinion, there could be no understanding between England and Germany so long as he continued to increase his navy. He replied that he must have a large navy in order to protect Germany's commerce in an adequate way, and one commensurate with her growing power and importance. He also said it was necessary to have a navy large enough to be able to defend themselves against the combined efforts of Russia and France.[1]

'I asked when he would reach the end of his naval programme. He said this was well known, since they had formulated a policy for building and, when that was completed, there would be an end; that Great Britain had nothing to fear from Germany, and that he personally was a friend of England and was doing her incalculable service in holding the balance of power against Russia.

'I told him that the President and I thought perhaps an American might be able to better compose the difficulties here and bring about an understanding with a view to peace than any European, because of their distrust and dislike for one another. He agreed to this suggestion. I had undertaken the work and that was my reason for coming to Germany, as I wanted to see him first. After leaving Germany it was my

[1] In a memorandum made later, House recorded: 'I forgot to say that I asked the Kaiser why Germany refused to sign the "Bryan treaty" providing for arbitration and a "cooling-off period" of a year before hostilities could be inaugurated. He replied: "Germany will never sign such a treaty. Our strength lies in being always prepared for war at a second's notice. We will not resign that advantage and give our enemies time to prepare."'

Had Germany signed this treaty, it would not have been possible for the United States to enter the war on the submarine issue until after the lapse of a twelvemonth, except on the ground that German use of submarines constituted acts of war against the United States.

purpose to go directly to England, where I should take the matter up with that Government as I had done with him.

'I explained that I expected to feel my way cautiously and see what could be accomplished, and, if he wished it, I would keep him informed. He asked me to do this and said letters would reach him "through our friend Zimmermann here in the Foreign Office." . . .

'I talked to the Kaiser on the terrace for thirty minutes and quite alone. Gerard and Zimmermann stood some ten feet away. There was a special train scheduled to leave Potsdam at three o'clock, and the time was growing perilously near and every one was becoming uneasy. The Empress herself came upon the terrace at one time for the purpose of breaking up our conversation, and, prior to that, she had sent one of her sons for the same purpose. Neither, however, approached us, for they saw the earnest and animated manner in which we were talking. She finally sent the Grand Chamberlain, who approached in a halting and embarrassed way, and told the Emperor of the difficulty. He scarcely noticed him and dismissed him curtly and continued our conversation for at least ten minutes more.

'By this time I had said all I cared to and was ready to leave myself; therefore I stopped talking and was very quiet in order to indicate that I, at least, was through. This had the desired effect and we bade each other good-bye. Gerard told me afterward that there was the greatest amount of interest displayed concerning what the Kaiser and I were discussing, and that all Berlin was talking of the episode and wondering what the devil we had to say to each other for so long and in such an animated way.'

V

Colonel House left for Paris in the evening that followed his memorable interview with the Kaiser. He was evidently well pleased with the reception that his plan had met, for although the Emperor made no promises, he left House with sufficient encouragement to proceed in taking up matters with the British. 'I am glad to tell you,' he wrote Wilson from Paris, 'that I have been as successful as I anticipated. . . . I am very happy over what has been accomplished and I am eager to get to London to see what can be done there. I have a feeling that the soil will be much more fallow.'

What impressed House chiefly in Germany was not so much a will to war based upon any definite plan, but an unreasoning nervousness which might at any moment result in a reckless attack, and a complete inability to approach the problem with intelligent poise and capacity for compromise.

'I find that both England and Germany [he wrote the President] have one feeling in common, and that is fear of one another. Neither wants to be the first to propose negotiations, but both are agreed that they should be brought about, though neither desires to make the necessary concessions.'

In the meantime President Wilson, whose attitude toward the European situation had originally been not far from indifferent, began to appreciate the possibilities of the Great Adventure. He wrote House of the thrill of pleasure he experienced on receiving the Colonel's report and of his confidence that House had begun a great thing and was carrying it through in just the right way with characteristic tact and quietness.

In Paris discussions proved to be impossible. France was caught by a Cabinet crisis and the capital would think of nothing but the shooting of Calmette by Madame Caillaux and all the political consequences thereof. Following his custom when conditions seemed unpropitious, House retired into his shell, whence for a few days he continued merely to observe.

'*June* 8, 1914: I have spent a quiet week in Paris, my most arduous duty being to dodge Americans and others wanting to see me. We have had many invitations to dinner and luncheon, all of which have been declined, although one came from our Ambassador.

'I called on Herrick,[1] it having been understood that I would do so when I was ready to talk with him. Mr. Roosevelt had been with him the day before, and he told me something of T. R.'s mental and physical activities. Herrick made the prediction that T. R. was getting ready to go back home and to give the Democrats a thoroughly unhappy time. I replied that I was sure he could do nothing that would distress us so much as it would his fellow Republicans.

'Herrick read passages from his forthcoming book upon rural credits and told me that within a short time he would have it finished and ready for publication. He would then like to return to America. . . .

'*June* 12, 1914 [London]: I came from Paris on the 9th. I lunched with Page on the 10th and he lunched with me yesterday, so we have had an exchange of ideas. He was kind enough to say that he considered my work in Germany the most important done in this generation. I thought before making an estimate we would have to see how far I could get with it here. He replied I would find this Government very sympathetic and he felt a beginning was as good as accomplished. We decided to approach Sir Edward Grey first and leave it to his judgment whether to bring in Asquith and the King. . . .'

House arrived in London at the height of the season, and there was no possibility of securing political results with speed. Social affairs held sway, and it was not until a full week after the Colonel's arrival that Ambassador Page could find a free day for the lunch with Sir Edward. In the mean-

[1] The American Ambassador.

time House followed his habit of seeing people of interest and information — chatting with Sir Horace Plunkett and Lord Bryce, lunching at the Embassy with Roosevelt and other notables, and meeting such varied types as Lord Curzon and Henry James, the Bishop of London and John Sargent, dining at Burdett-Coutts' palatial home in Piccadilly and discussing its art treasures and manuscripts, and reckoning the wealth of nations with Sir George Paish, of the *Statist*.

On June 17, House, Sir Edward Grey, Sir William Tyrrell, and Page had lunch together. The Colonel told of his visit to Germany and his proposition to the Kaiser.

'Sir Edward was visibly impressed [recorded Colonel House], and we discussed every phase of the European situation, particularly as it applied to Germany and England. He agreed with me that the French statesmen had given up all idea of revenge and of the recovery of Alsace and Lorraine, and that they would be content with the position of France as it now is. . . .

'We spoke of the difficulties of bringing about negotiations. I suggested that the Kaiser, he, and I meet at Kiel in some way; but this was not gone into further.

'The relations between Russia and the British Empire were talked of freely and with the utmost candor. Sir Edward explained that Great Britain and Russia touched at so many points in the world that it was essential for them to have some sort of good understanding.

'I thought they should permit Germany to aid in the development of Persia. He said it might be a good move to play the one against the other, and yet the Germans were so aggressive it might be dangerous. Sir Edward was very fair concerning the necessity for Germany to maintain a navy commensurate with her commerce, and sufficient to protect herself from Russia and France. I told of the militant war

E. Grey.

spirit in Germany and of the high tension of the people, and I feared some spark might be fanned into a blaze. I thought Germany would strike quickly when she moved; that there would be no parley or discussion; that when she felt that a difficulty could not be overcome by peaceful negotiation, she would take no chances but would strike. I thought the Kaiser himself and most of his immediate advisers did not want war, because they wished Germany to expand commercially and grow in wealth, but the army was militaristic and aggressive and ready for war at any time.

'I told him there was a feeling in Germany, which I shared, that the time had come when England could protect herself no longer merely because of her isolated position; that modern inventions had so changed conditions that the Germans believed she would be within striking distance before long, just as were her Continental neighbors. Sir Edward replied, "The idea, then, is that England will be in the same position as the Continental Powers." I said, "Quite so."

'I gave my opinion of the German aërial strength and what they might accomplish even now. I explained the part we desired to play as pacificators and why I felt we could do this better than they could do it themselves. I warned him that the present Chancellor of Germany might go at any time and be replaced by von Tirpitz, and a solution would then be a much more difficult undertaking.

'I feel that my visit has been justified, even if nothing more is done than that already accomplished. It is difficult for me to realize that the dream I had last year is beginning to come true. I have seen the Kaiser, and now the British Government seem eager to carry on the discussion. It is hard to realize, too, that every government in the world may be more or less affected by the moves we are making and every human being may be concerned in the decisions reached from day to day.

'I told Sir Edward the Kaiser had said when his name was

mentioned that he, Sir Edward, had never been on the Continent and therefore could not understand Germany. Sir Edward replied that while this was not literally true, it was nearly so; a great many years ago he went to India and crossed the Continent of Europe, though practically without stopping, and the other day he was in Paris with the King for several days.'

Colonel House to the President

LONDON, *June* 17, 1914

DEAR GOVERNOR:

... I found Sir Edward a willing listener and very frank and sympathetic. I am to stay the week-end with Tyrrell, and lunch with Sir Edward next Wednesday. In the meantime he will doubtless discuss the matter with his colleagues....

I find here everything cluttered up with social affairs, and it is impossible to work quickly. Here they have their thoughts on Ascot, garden parties, etc., etc. In Germany their one thought is to advance industrially and to glorify war. In France I did not find the war spirit dominant. Their statesmen dream no longer of revenge and the recovery of Alsace and Lorraine. The people do, but those that govern and know, hope only that France may continue as now. Germany already exceeds her in population by nearly fifty per cent, and the disparity increases year by year. It is this new spirit in France which fills me with hope, and which I used to-day to some advantage. France, I am sure, will welcome our efforts for peace.

Your faithful and affectionate

E. M. HOUSE

LONDON, *June* 26, 1914

MY DEAR FRIEND:

I had a very interesting luncheon with Sir Edward Grey Wednesday. The other guests were the Lord Chancellor,[1] the Earl of Crewe, and Sir William Tyrrell. Page had to go to Oxford to take his degree and could not be with us.

I did not go into the details of my trip to Germany again, for I took it for granted that Sir Edward had given them to both Haldane and Crewe.

I gave it as my opinion that international matters could be worked out to advantage in much the same way as individuals would work out private affairs, and I thought that most of the misunderstandings were brought about by false reports and mischief-makers, and if the principals knew of the facts, what appeared to be a difficult situation became easy of solution.

I illustrated this by mentioning the service Sir William Tyrrell performed in America last autumn and the consequent cordial relations between our two countries.

The conversation lasted two hours, and it was agreed that it should be renewed at a later date. In the meantime, the general idea was accepted; that is, that a frank and open policy should be pursued between all the parties at interest.

They told me that there was no written agreement between England, France, and Russia, and their understanding was one merely of sympathy and the determination to conserve the interests of one another. . . .

Sir Edward was in a most delightful mood and paid you a splendid tribute. At our last meeting, he said it was his purpose, at the proper time, in the House of Commons to say publicly what he thought you had done for international morals.[2]

I breakfasted with Lloyd George yesterday and had a

[1] Lord Haldane.

[2] A reference to the repeal of the Panama tolls exemption.

most interesting conversation with him. I found him peculiarly ill-informed regarding America and its institutions. I will tell you more of this when we meet.

I am lunching with the Prime Minister on Thursday of next week, and I will write you again when anything further of importance follows. . . .

Your faithful and affectionate

E. M. House

House not merely emphasized the negative aspect of the problem, the necessity of removing the factors that threatened war in Europe, but also urged the importance of a positive policy of international coöperation with a constructive purpose. It was the same plan he had discussed with Page and Bernstorff, a plan designed to bring the Great Powers of the world into a general undertaking for the development and protection of the backward regions of the world, and it contained the germ of the mandatary scheme later worked out in the League of Nations. He suggested the plan one cool evening as he sat with Sir Cecil Spring-Rice and Sir William Tyrrell before the open fire in Tyrrell's country home. Spring-Rice and Tyrrell approved, and House carried his plan to Grey.

Colonel House to the President

London, *June* 26, 1914

Dear Governor:

There is another matter I have taken up, which I hope may have your approval. I have suggested that America, England, France, Germany, and the other money-lending and developing nations, have some sort of tentative understanding among themselves for the purpose of establishing a plan by which investors on the one hand may be encouraged to lend money at reasonable rates and to develop, under favorable terms, the waste places of the earth, and on the other hand to bring about conditions by which such loans may be reasonably safe.

I suggested that each of these countries should tell its people that in the future usurious interest and concessions which involve the undoing of weak and debt-involved countries would no longer be countenanced; that the same rule must hereafter prevail in such investments as is now maintained in all civilized lands in regard to private loans.

I brought this matter up at luncheon on Wednesday, and Grey, Haldane, and Crewe were equally cordial in their discussion of it. I told them I wanted to get their views so that they might be laid before you when I returned.

If this can be brought about, it will not only do away with much of the international friction which such things cause, but it will be a step forward towards bringing about a stable and healthful condition in those unhappy countries which are now misgoverned and exploited both at home and abroad.

Your faithful and devoted

E. M. House

When Colonel House put a project before President Wilson, he did not expect affirmative commendation. He evidently took the President's silence for consent, for, as he once said, 'If the President did not object, I knew that it was safe to go ahead, for he rarely agreed in words; while if he disagreed, he always expressed himself.' With House the opposite was true; we find many phrases, in his memoranda, such as 'I showed by my silence that I did not agree.'

In the present case, receiving no dissenting cable from Wilson, the Colonel proceeded to elaborate his plan. On July 3 he gathered the American Ambassadors to St. James's and Italy, the British Ambassador to the United States, and Sir William Tyrrell. Spring-Rice had prepared a memorandum for Sir Edward Grey, giving the main points of House's proposal, so that the Foreign Office might be fully informed of its bearing.

Colonel House to the President

LONDON, *July* 4, 1914

MY DEAR FRIEND:

. . . Sir Cecil Spring-Rice, Sir William Tyrrell, Walter Page, and Thomas Nelson Page, who is now here, took lunch with me yesterday to go into a more detailed discussion. . . .

Tyrrell told me that Sir Edward Grey was deeply interested [in the suggestion] and approved entirely its general purpose, and that you could count upon this Government's coöperation.

It was the general consensus of opinion that a great deal of friction in the future would be obviated if some such understanding could be brought about in this direction, and that it would do as much as any other one thing to ensure international amity.

The idea, of course, is based entirely upon your Mobile speech, and it is merely that we are trying to mould something concrete from what you have already announced in general as your policy. I suggested that it would be well to keep the matter absolutely confidential until after I had talked it out with you and you had decided how best to bring all the other Governments into agreement, if at all. I do not think it wise to have it known that England was the first to accept the proposal.

Tyrrell thought that after we had worked out a plan here which was acceptable to this Government, I could take it to you for your approval and further suggestion. You could then, if your judgment approved, take it to the other Governments through Jusserand — ostensibly because he is the dean of the Diplomatic Corps at Washington, but really because the Central and South American republics would feel more kindly towards a proposal coming from a Latin nation.

Tyrrell, Spring-Rice, and I meet again on Wednesday to bring the matter into final form. Page may or may not be present. I think perhaps he had better not be, for the reason that it would lend something of an official character to it, which we wish to avoid.

I touched lightly upon this subject to the Kaiser and I feel sure he, too, will approve. This was fortunate, for the reason that it can be said it was brought to his attention first.

Your faithful and affectionate

E. M. House

P.S. As Page puts it, this is a concrete example of what may be accomplished if a better international understanding can be brought about.

Sir Edward Grey's personal response to the suggestions of House was enthusiastic, for he was as sincerely anxious to do all that lay in his power to convince Germany of the peaceful intentions of the British, as he was to lay the foundations for a permanent system of international coöperation. He may or may not have realized that quick action was desirable. Unfortunately quick action did not seem possible. He had to consider the sensibilities of the French and Russians, and Tyrrell reported to House that Grey was meditating methods of coming into touch with the Germans without offending the other members of the Entente. Such were the vices of the pre-war system of alliances which made impossible straightforward conversations. Grey was evidently not willing to go to Kiel as House had suggested. Furthermore, the major interest of the Cabinet lay in the Irish crisis, and it was difficult to persuade them that the international situation demanded immediate attention if the explosion were to be prevented.

House chafed at the delay, but philosophically continued

his round of social engagements which might later be turned to diplomatic advantage. Sidney Brooks, of the *Times*, asked him whether he wished to meet 'politicians or gentlemen,' and it was with him that House breakfasted with Lloyd George.

'*June* 25, 1914: Sidney Brooks called at nine o'clock this morning [recorded House], and we went to the Chancellor of the Exchequer's for breakfast. We were a trifle late and Lloyd George was waiting for me. There were also at breakfast Governor Clifford of the Gold Coast country, and Lloyd George's daughter. It was a most informal affair, each of us going to a side table and helping himself to whatever desired, as is the usual English custom. The choice of food consisted of fried sole, sausage, ham, eggs, fruit, coffee and tea. George ate a very hearty breakfast....'

A week later he lunched with the Prime Minister and Mrs. Asquith.

'*July* 2, 1914: After the ladies left the table, Asquith asked me to come and sit by him so that we might talk, which we did earnestly for fifteen or twenty minutes. I did nearly all the talking. We first discussed the merits of Cabinet officers sitting in Parliament or Congress, as the case may be.... I expressed the feeling that it was better they should have seats, and he also was inclined to this view.... I felt very much at home in London now, for the reason that his Government was being abused in exactly the same terms and by the same sort of people as were abusing the Wilson Administration in the United States. This amused him. I thought the purposes of the Liberal Government and of the Democratic Party were quite similar; that we were striving for the same end, but if the Conservatives of the two countries had their way, the end would probably be that many of them would be stripped of their wealth and hanged to lamp-posts. He agreed to this.

'Mr. Asquith cast the usual slur upon Mr. Bryan. I explained why the President had taken him into his Cabinet. He understood that the President had acted wisely and yet he considered it extremely unfortunate that the necessity existed. This is the usual comment I hear everywhere, in Germany, in France, and here. They do not do Mr. Bryan justice, but it is absolutely useless to fight his battles, because in doing so you discredit the purpose you are striving for.'

VI

While House waited for Grey to give some definite word which he might pass on to the Kaiser, the spark was struck that ignited the pile of combustible material which the diplomatic conflict of a decade had heaped up. On June 28, the Archduke Franz Ferdinand, heir apparent to the Austro-Hungarian throne, was murdered by a Serb nationalist in Serajevo, chief city of Bosnia. Presumably few Englishmen had ever heard of the Archduke and fewer still could locate the provincial capital on a map, yet such was the diplomatic net in which Europe was caught that within six weeks British soldiers were meeting death on the Belgian border.

The news of the Archduke's assassination reached London at the height of the Irish crisis and the feminist agitation, and it created no more audible effect than a tenor solo in a boiler-shop. Some days later the Foreign Secretary expressed a sense of anxiety as to the situation in Southeastern Europe, but domestic politics continued to hold the attention of the Cabinet. In Berlin the danger of a political crisis was openly discussed in the papers, and privately the sanction of the German Government was given to Austria for any retaliatory and repressive measures that Vienna might choose to put into effect against Serbia. But apparently there was little suspicion that the *carte blanche* so carelessly vouchsafed would end in world war and the destruction of the Empire. The higher officials of the army and navy were not recalled to Berlin; the Foreign Secretary remained on his honeymoon; plans for the Kaiser's cruise were not interrupted. Ambassador Gerard wrote cheerfully to House of his return to the United States in August.

Ambassador Gerard to Colonel House

BERLIN, *July* 7, 1914

MY DEAR COLONEL:

. . . Have been on A.'s yacht at Kiel, and Mrs. Gerard is still there. I came up for our Colony celebration of the 4th of July.

Dined with the Kaiser and lunched with von Tirpitz before the news of the murder of Franz Ferdinand came. They were both most enthusiastic about you. Von Tirpitz thanked me for giving him the opportunity to meet you. We have about decided to go to U.S.A., sailing August 12th on *Vaterland* — and I shall certainly report to you, wherever you are, before my return.

Kaiser had asked me to sail a race on his racing yacht with him at Kiel, but the murder in Bosnia prevented my thus spending a day with him.

Tennis is responsible for this almost illegible handwriting.

When do you sail? . . .

Berlin is as quiet as the grave. . . .

Yours ever

JAMES W. GERARD

What more sinister, in the light of after events, than the last sentence: 'Berlin is as quiet as the grave.' It was the eve of Armageddon.

Ironically enough, precisely at this moment when Austria

planned her attack upon Serbia, and Germany blindly approved, while the wheels of war were already being geared, the British Foreign Office made definite albeit rather belated response to the suggestions of House. On July 3 the Colonel heard from Tyrrell that Grey wanted him to let the Kaiser know of the peaceable sentiments of the British in order that further negotiations might follow. House at once wrote a long letter to His Imperial Majesty.

Colonel House to the President

LONDON, *July* 3, 1914

MY DEAR FRIEND:

. . . Tyrrell brought word to me to-day that Sir Edward Grey would like me to convey to the Kaiser the impressions I have obtained from my several discussions with this Government, in regard to a better understanding between the nations of Europe, and to try and get a reply before I leave. Sir Edward said he did not wish to send anything official or in writing, for fear of offending French and Russian sensibilities in the event it should become known. He thought it was one of those things that had best be done informally and unofficially.

He also told Page that he had a long talk with the German Ambassador here in regard to the matter and that he had sent messages by him directly to the Kaiser.

So you see things are moving in the right direction as rapidly as we could hope.

Your faithful and affectionate

E. M. HOUSE

Colonel House to the Kaiser

AMERICAN EMBASSY
LONDON, *July* 7, 1914

His Imperial Majesty,
Emperor of Germany,[1] King of Prussia,
Berlin, Germany.

SIR:

Your Imperial Majesty will doubtless recall our conversation at Potsdam and that with the President's consent and approval I came to Europe for the purpose of ascertaining whether or not it was possible to bring about a better understanding between the Great Powers, to the end that there might be a continuation of peace, and later a beneficent economic readjustment, which a lessening of armaments would ensure.

Because of the commanding position Your Majesty occupies, and because of your well-known desire to maintain peace, I came, as Your Majesty knows, directly to Berlin.

I can never forget the gracious acceptance of the general purpose of my mission, the masterly exposition of the world-wide political conditions as they exist to-day, and the prophetic forecast as to the future which Your Majesty then made.

I received every reasonable assurance of Your Majesty's cordial approval of the President's purpose, and I left Germany happy in the belief that Your Majesty's great influence would be thrown in behalf of peace and the broadening of the world's commerce.

In France I tried to reach the thoughts of her people in regard to Germany and to find what hopes she nursed. My

[1] The Kaiser was 'German Emperor' and not 'Emperor of Germany.' He always aspired to the latter title, which the jealousy of the German Princes forbade. Is this unconscious or intentional flattery on the part of Colonel House? On the copy of the letter is an endorsement in House's handwriting: 'I wrote this letter and submitted it to Irwin Laughlin, Counsellor of the Embassy, and he advised its stilted style, which I very much dislike. E. M. H.'

conclusion upon leaving was that her statesmen have given over all thought of revenge, or of recovery of the two lost provinces. Her people in general still have hopes in both directions, but her better-informed rulers would be quite content if France could be sure of her autonomy as it now exists.

It was then, Sir, that I came to England and with high hopes, in which I have not been disappointed.

I first approached Sir Edward Grey, and I found him sympathetic to the last degree. After a two hours' conference, we parted with the understanding that we should meet again within a few days. This I inferred to mean that he wished to consult with the Prime Minister and his colleagues.

At our next conference, which again lasted for two hours, he had, to meet me, the Lord Chancellor, Earl Crewe, and Sir William Tyrrell. Since then I have met the Prime Minister and practically every important member of the British Government, and I am convinced that they desire such an understanding as will lay the foundation for permanent peace and security.

England must necessarily move cautiously, lest she offend the sensibilities of France and Russia; but, with the changing sentiment in France, there should be a gradual improvement of relations between Germany and that country which England will now be glad to foster.

While much has been accomplished, yet there is something still to be desired in order that there may be a better medium created for an easy and frank exchange of thought and purposes. No one knows better than Your Majesty of the unusual ferment that is now going on throughout the world, and no one is in so fortunate a position to bring about a sane and reasonable understanding among the statesmen of the Western peoples, to the end that our civilization may continue uninterrupted.

While this communication is, as Your Majesty knows,

quite unofficial, yet it is written in sympathy with the well-known views of the President, and, I am given to understand, with the hope from His Britannic Majesty's Government that it may bring a response from Your Majesty which may permit another step forward.

Permit me, Sir, to conclude by quoting a sentence from a letter which has come to me from the President:

'Your letter from Paris, written just after coming from Berlin, gives me a thrill of deep pleasure. You have, I hope and believe, begun a great thing and I rejoice with all my heart.'

I have the honor to be, Sir, with the greatest respect, Your Majesty's

Very obedient servant,

EDWARD M. HOUSE

Thus was a last opportunity given to the Kaiser, who had the assurance of a disinterested outsider that if Germany sincerely desired peace she would have the active assistance of the United States and the coöperation of Great Britain. It was a definite answer to the allegation that Grey's policy aimed at the encirclement and isolation of the Germans. Alas! By the time Colonel House's letter reached Germany, Wilhelm II was already on his cruise in Norwegian waters whence he was recalled by the Austrian ultimatum to Serbia and the war-clouds that immediately gathered.

The Great Adventure had ended in failure. But House's attempt to prevent the war was perhaps less barren of consequences than superficial consideration would suggest. His experience during these months in Europe that ended with the sudden descent of the horror he feared, taught him the need of international organization and confirmed his belief in the necessity of some positive purpose to be followed by this organization. He was already, in essence, an advocate of a league of nations, and his influence with Wilson in this respect was to be an historical factor of vital importance. Among House's papers there is a significant memorandum which he made of a conversation with the President soon after the beginning of the war.

'*August* 30, 1914: I explained my plan about the backward nations and how enthusiastically it was received by the British Government, and how much they thought it would do toward bringing about a better understanding between the Great Powers. I believed if we had had an opportunity to put this into effect, in all human probability such a war as this would not have occurred — because with the Powers meeting at regular intervals, and with such a concrete example of the good that might be accomplished by concerted action, a conflagration such as was now going on would have been impossible.'

NOTE. — ' "The visit of Colonel House to Berlin and London in the spring of 1914," Emperor William remarked to me at Doorn, "almost prevented the World War." ' — GEORGE SYLVESTER VIERECK.

CHAPTER X

WILSON AND THE WAR

He [Wilson] goes even further than I in his condemnation of Germany's part in this war....

Extract from Diary of Colonel House, August 30, 1914

I

Colonel House sailed on July 21 and arrived in Boston eight days later. Immediately before he left, word was carried to him that the British Foreign Office had awakened to the serious character of the international situation.

'*July* 20, 1914: Tyrrell brought me another message from Sir Edward Grey, which was to the effect that he wished me to know before I sailed that the Austro-Serbian situation was giving him grave concern.'

The forebodings which the Colonel had experienced in Berlin were indeed in process of realization. On July 23, Austria sent to Serbia an ultimatum designed to provoke war, and five days later, brushing aside the Serbian reply as unsatisfactory, began the bombardment of Belgrade. The civil rulers of Germany appreciated suddenly the peril of the path down which they were being dragged by their Austrian ally and their own military clique; stupidly, they refused to accept the conference suggested by Grey, which would have permitted a cooling-off period; and as the crisis intensified with the mobilization of Russia in support of Serbia, the army leaders seized control at Berlin. As House had prophesied, they wasted no time but struck immediately. Diplomatic and military complexities produced this paradox: that a Russo-German war set in motion by an Austro-Serbian quarrel must begin with a German attack upon France, prefaced by the cynical and brutal onslaught upon Belgium. Great Britain, committed to the defence of Belgium by legal, and to that of France by moral, engagements, impelled by her own national interest, could not stand aside. It was the general war.

House reached Boston and went up to the North Shore while the issue of the crisis was yet undetermined. He still hoped that the assurances he had sent William II of British good feeling might strengthen the Kaiser's peaceful inclination, and that England and Germany might work together for a pacific solution, as they had in 1913. If only the British had been less deliberate in their consideration of House's proposals, an understanding might have been reached before the murder of the Archduke.

Colonel House to the President

PRIDE'S CROSSING, MASSACHUSETTS
July 31, 1914

DEAR GOVERNOR:

When I was in Germany, it seemed clear to me that the situation, as far as a continuation of peace was concerned, was in a very precarious condition; and you will recall my first letter to you telling of the high tension that Germany and southern Europe were under.

I tried to convey this feeling to Sir Edward Grey and other members of the British Government. They seemed astonished at my pessimistic view and thought that conditions were better than they had been for a long time. While I shook their confidence, at the same time I did not do it sufficiently to make them feel that quick action was necessary; consequently they let matters drag until after the Kaiser had gone into Norwegian waters for his vacation, before giving me any definite word to send to him.

It was my purpose to go back to Germany and see the

Emperor, but the conservative delay of Sir Edward and his confrères made that impossible.

The night before I sailed, Sir Edward sent me word that he was worried over conditions, but he did not anticipate what has followed. I have a feeling that if a general war is finally averted, it will be because of the better feeling that has been brought about between England and Germany. England is exerting a restraining hand upon France and, as far as possible, upon Russia; but her influence with the latter is slight.

If the matter could have been pushed a little further, Germany would have laid a heavy hand upon Austria and possibly peace could have been continued until a better understanding could have been brought about.

Russia has a feeling, so I was told in England, that Germany was trying to project Austrian and German influence deep into the Balkan States in order to check her. She has evidently been preparing for some decisive action since the Kaiser threw several hundred thousand German troops on his eastern frontier two years ago, thereby compelling Russia to relinquish the demands that she had made in regard to a settlement of Balkan matters. . . .

Your faithful and affectionate

E. M. House

Pride's Crossing, Massachusetts
August 1, 1914

Dear Governor:

There are one or two things that would perhaps be of interest to you at this time and which I shall tell you now and not wait until I see you.

Sir Edward Grey told me that England had no written agreement with either Russia or France, or any formal alliance; that the situation was brought about by a mutual desire for protection and that they discussed international matters with as much freedom with one another as if they had an actual written alliance. . . .

The great danger is that some overt act may occur which will get the situation out of control. Germany is exceedingly nervous and at high tension, and she knows that her best chance of success is to strike quickly and hard; therefore her very alarm might cause her to precipitate action as a means of safety.

Please let me suggest that you do not let Mr. Bryan make any overtures to any of the Powers involved. They look upon him as absolutely visionary, and it would lessen the weight of your influence if you desire to use it yourself later. . . .

If I thought I could live through the heat, I would go to Washington to see you; but I am afraid if I reached there, I would be utterly helpless. I wish you could get time to take the *Mayflower* and cruise for a few days in these waters so that I might join you.

Your faithful and affectionate

E. M. House

Even as House was writing these letters, the act which he feared took place. Assailed by technical arguments which he could not controvert, the Chancellor was carried away by the military influence and threw up his hands. Germany despatched to Russia the ultimatum that made war inevitable and flung into Belgium the vanguard of the army designed to conquer France.

Herr Zimmermann to Colonel House

Berlin, *August* 1, 1914

My dear Colonel:

I beg to inform you that I laid the letter which you addressed to His Majesty the Emperor from London before His Majesty. I am directed to convey to you His Majesty's sincere thanks.

The Emperor took note of its content with the greatest interest. Alas, all His strong and sincere efforts to conserve peace have entirely failed. I am afraid that Russia's procedure will force the old world and especially my country in the most terrible war! There is no chance now to discuss the possibility of an understanding, so much desired, which would lay the foundation for permanent peace and security.

With assurances of my high regard, I remain, my dear Colonel,

Sincerely yours

ZIMMERMANN

From Ambassador Page in London there came a veiled but emphatic reference to the efforts which House had made to prevent the war. Mr. Page issued the following announcement to the press:

'One thing I want to make clear that a great many people have talked to me about. Many seem to have the impression that the United States missed a great opportunity. The United States did everything possible to avert war. If ever a job was done right up to the hilt, it was that.'

On the other hand, Sir Cecil Spring-Rice, the British Ambassador in Washington, went so far as to intimate that, while it was the information that House brought from Berlin which had opened Grey's eyes to the seriousness of the situation, the Colonel's endeavors might have been one of the causes which precipitated that crisis. 'You came so near making a general war impossible,' he told House, 'that the war party in Berlin and Vienna became alarmed. They probably knew why you were in Berlin and what you said to the Kaiser. They also probably knew why you went to England, and they undoubtedly knew the contents of your letter to the Kaiser. That, together with Sir Edward Grey's conversations with the German Ambassador in London, alarmed the war party and they took advantage of the Archduke's murder and the Kaiser's absence to precipitate matters, believing they were coming to the end of the passage and that it was now or never.'

The hypothesis is interesting, not entirely conclusive.

Eight months afterwards House made a private memorandum, the gist of which accords in general with the opinions of later historians who were able to study the German official documents.

'*April* 15, 1915: I am often asked my views as to the cause of the war [he wrote], and, while I never give them, I might as well record them here.

'It is clear to me that the Kaiser did not want war and did not actually expect it. He foolishly permitted Austria to bring about an acute controversy with Serbia, and he concluded that by standing firm with his ally, Russia would do nothing more than make a vigorous protest, much as she did when Austria annexed Bosnia and Herzegovina. The rattling of the scabbard and the shining armor were sufficient in that case and he thought they would be in this, for the reason that he did not believe Great Britain would go to war concerning such a happening in the Southeast. He had tried England twice in the West and had found that he himself must give way, and there was not much danger of his trying it again where England was involved. But in this instance he thought Germany's relations with England had improved to such an extent that she would not back Russia and France to the extent of making war on Germany.

'And he went so far in what might be termed "bluff" that it was impossible at the last moment to recede because the situation had gotten beyond him. He did not have the foresight to see the consequences, neither did he have the foresight to see that the building up of a great war machine must inevitably lead to war. Germany has been in the hands of a group of militarists and financiers, and it has been to conserve their selfish interests that this terrible situation has been made possible.'

II

Wilson had to meet the political crisis at a moment when he was overwhelmed with domestic trouble, for his wife was at the point of death. 'His burdens are heavier than any President's since Lincoln,' wrote House to Page on August 6. 'He has grown enormously in popularity within the last ten days and there is scarcely a dissenting note throughout the country. I believe he will live in history as one of the greatest Presidents, if not the greatest, that this country has brought forth.'

Such eulogistic phrases must have been inspired by House's general feeling of admiration for the President rather than by what he did in the crisis, for there was little he could do. Urged by the Senate resolution and against House's judgment, Wilson issued a formal appeal to the belligerents, offering his services in the cause of mediation. But it was, as might have been expected, without effect.

Colonel House to the President

Pride's Crossing, Massachusetts
August 5, 1914

Dear Governor:

... If a statement is made, let me suggest that you make it clear that what you have done was at your own instance. If the public either here or in Europe thought that Mr. Bryan instigated it, they would conclude it was done in an impracticable way and was doomed to failure from the start.

I hate to harp upon Mr. Bryan, but you cannot know as I do how he is thought of in this connection. You and I understand better and know that the grossest sort of injustice is done him. Nevertheless, just now it is impossible to make people think differently.

It may interest you to hear that Olney expressed regret that he did not accept your tender of the Ambassadorship to London. He said he had no idea it would mean anything more than social activity.

My heart is full of deep appreciation for your letter of August 3. I never worry when I do not hear from you. No human agency could make me doubt your friendship and affection. That my life is devoted entirely to your interests, I believe you know, and I never cease from trying to serve you.

Your faithful and affectionate

E. M. House

The President's offer of mediation was merely an expression of willingness to act. As sent to the monarchs of the belligerent Powers, it read:

Sir:

As official head of one of the Powers signatory to the Hague Convention, I feel it to be my privilege and my duty under Article 3 of the Convention to say to Your Majesty in a spirit of most earnest friendship, that I should welcome an opportunity to act in the interest of European peace either now or at any time that might be thought more suitable as an occasion, to serve Your Majesty and all concerned in a way that would afford me lasting cause for gratitude and happiness.

Woodrow Wilson

A fortnight after this offer, President Wilson issued an appeal to the citizens of the Republic, requesting their assistance in maintaining a state of neutrality. It was later to draw upon the President the virulent attacks of pro-

Entente elements, especially on the Atlantic seaboard, but at the moment, as Colonel House indicates, general articulate opinion seemed to approve it heartily. Wilson based the appeal, not upon indifference to the war, but upon the danger that might arise for the United States if factions should take form supporting the one or the other of the belligerent groups.

'It will be easy to excite passion [said the President], and difficult to allay it. Those responsible for exciting it will assume a heavy responsibility, responsibility for no less a thing than that the people of the United States, whose love of their country and whose loyalty to its Government should unite them as Americans all, bound in honor to think first of her and her interests, may be divided in camps of hostile opinion, hot against each other, involved in the war itself in impulse and opinion if not in action. . . . Every man who really loves America will act and speak in the true spirit of neutrality, which is the spirit of impartiality and fairness and friendliness to all concerned.'

Colonel House to the President

PRIDE'S CROSSING, MASSACHUSETTS
August 22, 1914

DEAR GOVERNOR:

Thinking that I might see you soon has caused me to hope that I might tell you in person of how splendidly I think you are meeting the difficult situations that come to you day by day.

Your Address on Neutrality is one of the finest things you have ever done, and it has met with universal approbation. Every day editorials of the Republican press speak of you as if you were of their party instead of being the idol of ours.

The food investigation, the shipping bill, the war risk insurance bill, and everything else that you are doing give the entire nation cause for constant congratulation that you are at the helm and serving it as no other man could.

Of course the war continues to be a most disturbing and uncertain element. I am sorry that Japan injected herself into the general *mêlée*, for it will place an additional strain upon us not to become involved.

The saddest feature of the situation to me is that there is no good outcome to look forward to. If the Allies win, it means largely the domination of Russia on the Continent of Europe; and if Germany wins, it means the unspeakable tyranny of militarism for generations to come.

Fundamentally the Germans are playing a rôle that is against their natural instincts and inclinations, and it shows how perverted men may become by habit and environment.

Germany's success will ultimately mean trouble for us. We will have to abandon the path which you are blazing as a standard for future generations, with permanent peace as its goal and a new international ethical code as its guiding star, and build up a military machine of vast proportions.

Your faithful and affectionate

E. M. House

President Wilson was harshly criticized in the following year for not having adopted a more positive policy at this time. As signatory to the Hague Convention, his critics averred, the United States should have protested against the German invasion of Belgium and the President should have made plain that in sympathy, at least, the country stood on the side of the Entente Allies. Such criticism disregards the fact that the opinion of the whole country was by no means crystallized at this time, and that the issuance of protests or expressions of sympathy would be worse than futile, unless the Government intended to abandon its attitude of neutrality.

Few persons dared to suggest at that time that the United

States should enter the war. Theodore Roosevelt, who was to become one of the most outspoken of those who later demanded participation, writing in the *Outlook*, congratulated the country on the separation from Europe which permitted its neutrality.[1] Ambassador Page, who himself a few months later insisted that the United States must break relations with Germany, wrote to House on August 28, 1914: '...What a *magnificent* spectacle our country presents! We escape murder, we escape brutalization; we will have to settle it; we gain in every way.' And the British Ambassador, Sir Cecil Spring-Rice, wrote to the Colonel on September 12, 'I hope and believe that at any rate *one* part of the world will keep out of it.'

One of the rare Americans who at the moment had the courage to suggest that the United States should adopt a positive policy in order to ensure the defeat of Germany, was President Charles W. Eliot. His suggestion is the more interesting in that Dr. Eliot displayed then, as always, a mental poise which prevented him from criticizing Wilson when the latter refused to take action. Eliot admitted that neither he nor any American could know enough of the facts to insist upon the course he first advised, and he also admitted that Wilson could not be sure that public opinion in the United States would support positive action. It even appears that Eliot himself, after second thought, reached the same conclusion as the President.

The historian may well ask, however, whether the policy first advised by Dr. Eliot would not have shortened the war

[1] 'Our country stands well-nigh alone among the great civilized Powers in being unshaken by the present world-wide war. For this we should be humbly and profoundly grateful. All of us on this continent ought to appreciate how fortunate we are that we of the Western world have been free from the working of the causes which have produced the bitter and vindictive hatred among the great military Powers of the Old World.... It is certainly eminently desirable that we should remain entirely neutral and nothing but urgent need would warrant breaking our neutrality and taking sides one way or the other.' — *Outlook*, September 23, 1914.

by many months and perhaps have saved the need of an American expeditionary force. Would it not also have been a direct step toward a league of nations? President Wilson was so far impressed by his arguments that he read the earlier letter to his Cabinet and discussed the suggestion carefully with House. He wrote to Eliot, however, that he did not regard it as practicable.

Dr. Eliot to the President

ASTICOU, MAINE, *August* 8, 1914

DEAR PRESIDENT WILSON:

I have hesitated three days to mail the enclosed letter to you, and should still hesitate to forward it while you are overwhelmed with sorrow, did I not recall that under such circumstances there is comfort and relief for the sufferer in resolving that he will thereafter do everything in his power to help other people who are suffering or bereaved.

At this moment millions of men are apprehending death or agonies for themselves or poverty and desolation for their families, and millions of women are dreading the loss of lovers, supporters, and friends; and perhaps you have the power to do something to stop these miseries and prevent their recurrence.

In such an effort you would find real consolation.

With deepest sympathy in your affliction, I am

Sincerely yours

CHARLES W. ELIOT

ASTICOU, MAINE, *August* 6, 1914

DEAR PRESIDENT WILSON:

Has not the United States an opportunity at this moment to propose a combination of the British Empire, the United States, France, Japan, Italy, and Russia in offensive and defensive alliance to rebuke and punish Austria-Hungary and Germany for the outrages they are now committing, by enforcing against those two countries non-intercourse with the rest of the world by land and sea? These two Powers have now shown that they are utterly untrustworthy neighbors, and military bullies of the worst sort — Germany being far the worse of the two, because she has already violated neutral territory.

If they are allowed to succeed in their present enterprises, the fear of sudden invasion will constantly hang over all the other European peoples; and the increasing burdens of competitive armaments will have to be borne for another forty years. We shall inevitably share in these losses and miseries. The cost of maintaining immense armaments prevents all the great Powers from spending the money they ought to spend on improving the condition of the people, and promoting the progress of the world in health, human freedom, and industrial productiveness.

In this cause, and under the changed conditions, would not the people of the United States approve of the abandonment of Washington's advice that this country keep out of European complications?

A blockade of Germany and Austria-Hungary could not be enforced with completeness; but it could be enforced both by sea and by land to such a degree that the industries of both peoples would be seriously crippled in a short time by the stoppage of both their exports and their imports. Certain temporary commercial advantages would be gained by the blockading nations — a part of which might perhaps prove to be permanent.

This proposal would involve the taking part by our navy in the blockading process, and, therefore, might entail losses of both life and treasure; but the cause is worthy of heavy sacrifices; and I am inclined to believe that our people would support the Government in taking active part in such an effort to punish international crimes, and to promote future international peace.

Is it feasible to open *pourparlers* by cable on this subject? The United States is clearly the best country to initiate such a proposal. In so doing this country would be serving the general cause of peace, liberty, and good will among men.

This idea is not a wholly new one to me. The recent abominable acts of Austria-Hungary and Germany have brought to my mind again the passages on the 'Fear of Invasion,' and the 'Exemption of Private Property from Capture at Sea,' which I wrote a year ago in my report to the Carnegie Endowment for International Peace, entitled *Some Roads Toward Peace*, pp. 16–17. The outrageous actions of the last fortnight have reënforced the statements I then made, and have suggested a new and graver application of the doctrines therein set forth.

I offer this suggestion in entire submission to your judgment as to its present feasibility and expediency. It seems to me an effective international police method, suited to the present crimes, and the probable issues of the future, and the more attractive because the European concert and the triple alliances have conspicuously failed. It, of course, involves the abandonment by all the European participants of every effort to extend national territory in Europe by force. The United States has recently abandoned that policy in America. It involves also the use of international force to overpower Austria-Hungary and Germany with all possible promptness and thoroughness; but this use of force is indispensable for the present protection of civilization against a savagery, and for the future establishment and maintenance of federal relations and peace among the nations of Europe.

I am, with highest regard,

Sincerely yours

CHARLES W. ELIOT

Asticou, Maine, *August* 20, 1914

Dear President Wilson:

In revising a letter I had written you on August 17th, amplifying the proposal contained in my letter of August 6th, I have come to the conclusion that it would not be desirable 'to open *pourparlers* by cable on this subject' at the present moment, even if it were feasible. Two considerations have led me to this conclusion: (1) We apparently do not possess full information on the real purposes and objects of either Russia or Germany; at least the thinking American public does not possess this information, and therefore cannot justly fix on Germany the chief responsibility for the present cataclysm. The extreme rashness of Germany's action cannot but suggest that elements of the situation, still unknown to the rest of the world, were known to her. I do not feel the confidence I then felt in the information accessible when I wrote my letter to you of August 6th. (2) Communications between our Government and the Governments of France and Great Britain, which would necessarily be secret, are undesirable at the present stage of the conflict. Indeed secret diplomacy is always to be disliked, whether used by free governments or despotic. These are sufficient objections to the *pourparlers* I suggested.

I am inclined to give new weight to certain reasons for holding to our traditional policy of neutrality in conflicts between other nations: (1) It seems probable that Russia, Great Britain, and France together can inflict ultimate defeat on Germany and Austria-Hungary — the only tolerable result of this outrageous war. (2) It seems possible that the seven nations now at war can give the much-needed demonstration that the military machinery which the last half of the nineteenth century created all over Europe cannot be set in motion on a large scale without arresting production to a very dangerous degree and causing an intolerable amount of suffering and misery. The interruption of production and commerce which has already taken place since July 31st is unexampled in the history of the world; and yet the destruction of life and property has hardly begun. If seven nations can give this demonstration, the other nations had better keep out of the conflict.

On reflection, I have also come to think that much public discussion of the interest of free governments in the reformation of the military monarchies of Europe will be necessary before American public opinion will sanction forcible opposition to outrages committed by those monarchies on weaker and freer neighbors.

I remain of the opinion that, in the interests of civilization and peace, neither Germany nor Austria-Hungary should be allowed to succeed in its present undertakings.

Your address to your countrymen on the conditions of real neutrality is altogether admirable in both form and substance.

Sincerely yours

CHARLES W. ELIOT

ASTICOU, MAINE, *August* 22, 1914

DEAR PRESIDENT WILSON:

My letter to you of August 20th crossed in the mails yours of August 19th to me. Yours came to hand yesterday, the 21st. I had already come to your conclusion. . . .

I am, with highest regard and confidence,

Sincerely yours

CHARLES W. ELIOT

III

That President Wilson adopted a policy of neutrality from a feeling of tenderness for Germany and from a failure to appreciate the moral issues involved in the war and in the German attack upon Belgium, is an assertion which has been frequently put forward. It rests upon supposition or prejudice, and not upon evidence. So much is plain from House's account of his visit to the President's summer home at Cornish at the end of August, 1914.

'*August* 30, 1914: I was glad to find the President situated so delightfully [recorded the Colonel]. The house reminds one of an English place. The view is superb, and the arrangement and furnishings are comfortable and artistic. The President showed me my room himself. It was the one Mrs. Wilson used to occupy and was next to his, with a common bathroom between. We are in one wing of the house and quite to ourselves. A small stairway leads down to his study, and it was there that we sat and discussed matters until after one o'clock when lunch was announced.

'I told of my experiences in Europe and gave him more of the details of my mission. He was interested in the personalities of the people who are the Governments' heads, and later said my knowledge of these men and of the situation in Europe would be of great value to him.

'The President spoke with deep feeling of the war. He said it made him heartsick to think of how near we had come to averting this great disaster, and he thought if it had been delayed a little longer, it could never have happened, because the nations would have gotten together in the way I had outlined.

'I told in detail of my suggestion to Sir Edward Grey and other members of the Cabinet, that the surest guaranty of peace was for the principals to get together frequently and discuss matters with frankness and freedom, as Great Britain and the United States were doing. He agreed that this was the most effective method and he again expressed deep regret that the war had come too soon to permit the inauguration of such procedure. He wondered whether things might have been different if I had gone sooner. I thought it would have made no difference, for the reason that the Kaiser was at Corfu and it was impossible for me to approach him sooner than I did. . . .

'I was interested to hear him express as his opinion what I had written him some time ago in one of my letters, to the effect that if Germany won it would change the course of our civilization and make the United States a military nation. He also spoke of his deep regret, as indeed I did to him in that same letter, that it would check his policy for a better international ethical code.

'He felt deeply the destruction of Louvain, and I found him as unsympathetic with the German attitude as is the balance of America. He goes even further than I in his condemnation of Germany's part in this war, and almost allows his feeling to include the German people as a whole rather than the leaders alone. He said German philosophy was essentially selfish and lacking in spirituality. When I spoke of the Kaiser building up the German machine as a means of maintaining peace, he said, "What a foolish thing it was to create a powder magazine and risk some one's dropping a spark into it!"

'He thought the war would throw the world back three or four centuries. I did not agree with him. He was particularly scornful of Germany's disregard of treaty obligations, and was indignant at the German Chancellor's designation of the Belgian Treaty as being "only a scrap of paper."

'I took occasion here to explain to him Sir Edward Grey's strong feeling upon the question of treaty obligation, and his belief that he, the President, had lifted international ethics to a high plane by his action in the Panama tolls question.'

But although the personal feeling of the President was with the Allies, he insisted then and for many months after, that this ought not to affect his political attitude, which he intended should be one of strict neutrality. He felt that he owed it to the world to prevent the spreading of the conflagration, that he owed it to the country to save it from the horrors of war. There was also some truth in the popular impression that he looked upon the war as a distant event, terrible and tragic, but one which did not concern us closely in the political sense. He had not yet come to realize that his great opportunity was to lie in foreign affairs.

Colonel House saw in the war a great chance to bring about a revolution in international organization by impressing upon the public mind the need of a new standard of international morals. The code of conduct for nations should be as high as that for individuals and, if public opinion could be brought to realize this necessity, House believed that a new spirit would inform international affairs. He tried to show the President how much he might do by preaching this doctrine, which later became the soul of Wilson's international policies. 'He did not have a hopeful outlook,' recorded House, August 30. 'I tried to make him see that reforms were going forward with much more celerity than heretofore, for man desired the commendation of his fellow man more than anything else, and with public opinion set toward higher purposes, individuals would naturally strive to obtain the good opinion of society.'

Some weeks later House expounded his creed to his friend Edward S. Martin, in whom he found a sympathetic auditor. It was henceforth the *leit-motiv* running through all his diplomatic experiences.

'I lunched with Martin to-day at the Century Club [wrote House]. He had just written one of his illuminating editorials for *Life*, and we fell to philosophizing upon international morals and governmental affairs. I did most of the talking, trying to point out the fundamental error in international morals, inasmuch as they are upon a different level from individual morals. No high-minded man would think of doing as an individual what he seems perfectly ready to do as a representative of a State. It has been thought entirely legitimate to lie, deceive, and be cruel in the name of patriotism. I endeavored to point out that we could not get very far toward a proper international understanding until one nation treated another as individuals treat one another. We see the wreck individuals make of themselves by devoting all their time to selfish interests, and, while they may acquire things that seem to them worth while, in the end they lose the regard of their fellow men and find themselves unhappy because of them.'

House believed that the United States should lead in a crusade for such a revolution in international morals. He found the President difficult to stir. Wilson was profoundly interested in domestic problems and was still slow to formulate a positive foreign policy. He seemed to feel that he had already accomplished his great work.

'*September* 28, 1914: The President [House noted] declared if he knew he would not have to stand for reëlection two years from now, he would feel a great load lifted from him. I thought he need not accept the Presidency unless he wished to, even if the Democratic Party demanded it, though I could understand why he would feel it a duty to do so provided his health permitted. I could not see what else he could do in life that would be so interesting. He replied that the thing that frightened him was that it was impossible to make such an effort in the future as he had made in the past, or to accomplish anything like what he had accomplished in a legislative way. He feared the country would expect him to continue as he had up to now, which would be impossible. I thought the country would neither expect it nor want it. There were other things he could do which would be far more delightful in accomplishment, and would add even more to his fame. I referred particularly to his foreign policy which, if properly followed, would bring him world-wide recognition.

'I find the President singularly lacking in appreciation of the importance of this European crisis. He seems more interested in domestic affairs, and I find it difficult to get his attention centred upon the one big question.

'Congress will adjourn now within a few days, and when it is out of the way it is my purpose to make a drive at the President and try to get him absorbed in the greatest problem of world-wide interest that has ever come, or may ever come, before a President of the United States.'

A month later House noted again:

'*October* 22, 1914: I am sorry to say, as I have said before, that the President does not seem to have a proper sense of proportion as between domestic and foreign affairs. I suppose it is the Washington atmosphere that has gripped him as it does every one else who lives there, and the work of the day largely obscures the tremendous world issues that are now before us.'

Wilson's lack of appreciation of the opportunity for a positive policy in foreign affairs accounts in some measure, perhaps, for his failure to perceive the immediate necessity of developing the military and naval strength of the nation. Colonel House, on the other hand, had taken great interest in what came to be called 'preparedness,' even before the outbreak of the European war, and he seems to have been on terms of intimacy with the outstanding apostle of the movement, Leonard Wood.

'*April* 16, 1914: I had a long talk with General Wood

about the army's preparedness. We discussed the international situation, particularly regarding Japan and the possibility of trouble there, and what would be necessary to be done. He said Manila was now so fortified that we could hold it for a year at the minimum, and that within a short while Hawaii would be in a similarly impregnable position. He thought the Panama Canal was so near completion that it could be used in twenty days in the event of an emergency. We promised to keep in close touch with one another from now on.'

If, as House hoped, the United States were to take the lead in an international movement to prevent future war or to render it less likely, it was of vital importance that the moral influence of America should be based upon an adequate material force, especially a strong army and navy. There was even the possibility that if the nation were placed on a war footing as rapidly as possible, the United States would be in a position to insist that the belligerents stop fighting, by a threat of entering the war against the side that refused reasonable terms. And with Europe on the road to exhaustion, the combined economic and military strength of America would permit her to decide what were reasonable terms.

There was also the danger of a German victory, in which case the United States, if unarmed, would find herself facing an aggressive power capable of carrying through by force an expansive policy in South and Central America that might touch closely and adversely our most important interests. In any event, it seemed the part of wisdom to prepare a force sufficient to support the diplomatic demands we might be compelled to make upon the belligerents, should either side disregard our rights as a neutral.

Because of such factors Colonel House found himself in complete agreement with the preparedness crusade, and he urged that immediate steps be taken to strengthen both army and navy. He found the President cold. Wilson did not visualize the rôle America might play in the same fashion as House; he believed that the United States should give an example of pacific idealism which was at the other pole from military preparation, and he felt himself supported by the mass of public opinion which, until aroused by the peril and the opportunity of the situation, opposed the sacrifices necessary to preparedness.

'*November* 3, 1914: Loulie and I [recorded House] lunched with General and Mrs. Leonard Wood at Governor's Island. I wished to see the General before I went to Washington. I am strongly of the opinion that it is time for this Government to adopt some system, perhaps the Swiss, looking toward a reserve force in the event of war. I found General Wood receptive. He is to send me, at the White House, memoranda and data to hand the President for his information.

'Wood is desirous of going to the war zone, and I told him I would try to arrange it for the reason that we have no military man who has had any experience in the handling of large bodies of troops. . . .

'*November* 4, 1914 [conference between Wilson and House]: We passed to the question of a reserve army. He baulked somewhat at first and said he thought the labor people would object because they felt that a large army was against their interests. He did not believe there was any necessity for immediate action; he was afraid it would shock the country. He made the statement that no matter how the great war ended, there would be complete exhaustion; and, even if Germany won, she would not be in a condition seriously to menace our country for many years to come. I combated this idea, stating that Germany would have a large military force ready to act in furthering the designs which the military party evidently have in mind. He said she would not have the men. I replied that she could not win unless she had at least two or three million men under arms at the end. He evidently thought the available men would be completely wiped out.

'I insisted it was time to do a great constructive work for the army and one which would make the country too powerful for any nation to think of attacking us. He told me there was reason to suspect that the Germans had laid throughout the country concrete foundations for great guns, similar to those they laid in Belgium and France. He almost feared to express this knowledge aloud, for, if the rumor got abroad, it would inflame our people to such an extent that he would be afraid of the consequences. General Wood has the matter under investigation, and he asked me to caution Wood to be very discreet.[1]

'I spoke of General Wood's desire to be sent abroad and asked him to let him go in order that we might have at least one man in our army with some experience. He said they would not accept him. I replied that Wood thought otherwise and it was something for him to work out in his own way.

'In speaking of the building-up of our army, I thought if the Allies were successful there would be no need for haste; but if the Germans were successful and we then began our preparations, it would be almost equivalent to a declaration of war, for they would know we were directing our preparations against them. I therefore urged that we start without delay, so that we might be ready and avoid being placed in such a position. . . .

'*November* 8, 1914: The President desired me to go to church with him, but I compromised by having Loulie go. Mr. Bryan had just arrived from the West and I felt it

[1] Probably neither Wilson nor House took such suspicions very seriously; the investigation proved them to be without basis.

necessary to see him. I wanted to find out what his views were regarding the army. I found him in violent opposition to any kind of increase by the reserve plan. He did not believe there was the slightest danger to this country from foreign invasion, even if the Germans were successful. He thought *after war was declared* there would be plenty of time to make any preparations necessary. He talked as innocently as my little grandchild, Jane Tucker. He spoke with great feeling, and I fear he may give trouble. . . .

'*November* 25, 1914 [conversation with Wilson]: We spoke of the ever-present topic of the war. I have gotten from good authority that Italy would now be with the Allies if she had been prepared. She found her equipment was not sufficient to be effective, but she is putting herself in shape to get into the war just as soon as she is ready and can make her forces worth while. I thought Roumania would also join the Allies. He expressed pleasure at this, and hoped these two countries would not delay too long.

'I again insisted that Germany would never forgive us for the attitude we have taken in the war and, if she is successful, she will hold us to account. . . .

'I spoke again of our unpreparedness and how impractical Mr. Bryan was. I urged the need of our having a large reserve force, and he replied, "Yes, but not a large army," an amendment which I accepted. I particularly emphasized the necessity for greater artillery plants and more artillery.'

The arguments of House produced no immediate effect upon the President, who in his annual message to Congress refused to approve plans for a large reserve force and the principle of compulsory training; Wilson insisted that any revolution in our established military policy (if policy it might be called) would indicate that we had been 'thrown off our balance by a war with which we have nothing to do, whose causes cannot touch us.' Left thus without guidance, except of a negative sort, public opinion was slow to perceive the need of military efficiency, and in some quarters, as the following letter indicates, Wilson's attitude received the most enthusiastic approval.

Mr. George Foster Peabody to Colonel House

NEW YORK, *December* 16, 1914

DEAR COLONEL HOUSE:

As I am writing to you at the White House, I shall venture to say to you that I think General Leonard Wood's address to the Merchants' Association and others respecting unpreparedness of our army most unsuitable and also reflecting upon the President's magnificent presentation of the whole situation in his address to Congress.

I hope that he may be promptly called down.

I cannot tell you how profoundly I was stirred by the President's address and by the deep and widespread impression it made. I should have liked to write to him to gratify my enthusiasm, but I have the impression that in the press of such vitally important state problems he has not had the time to see the later letters I wrote. I should not want to burden him, much less intrude....

Very truly yours

GEORGE FOSTER PEABODY

Colonel House himself was not blind to the high cost of military preparation, in the moral as well as in the material sense, nor was he unaware of the evils which its extravagance had brought upon Europe. Lord Grey, in his memoirs, says: 'Every country [in Europe] had been piling up armaments and perfecting preparations for war. The object in each case had been security. The effect had been precisely the contrary of what was intended and desired. Instead of a sense of security there had been produced a sense of fear, which was yearly increasing.... Such was the general condition of

Europe; preparations for war had produced fear, and fear predisposes to violence and catastrophe.'[1] All this House appreciated, and he sympathized with Wilson's dread that military preparation in the United States might destroy the calm spirit necessary to the rescue of the world from a spell of madness.

But although to this degree, and because of his horror at the idea of mass slaughter, House regarded himself as a pacifist, he could not avoid the fact that international pacifism becomes mere anæmia unless organized to include in its influence all the great Powers. In the greatest crisis of history the United States was helpless to play any rôle except that of passivity. To protect our rights effectively, to aid the world to escape from the nightmare in which it was caught, there was need of a positive organization of our potential strength. This House, as we shall see, did not fail to urge upon the President.

Twelve months afterwards, in the autumn of 1915, Wilson yielded to the logic of events and did not lack the courage to confess that he had changed his mind; in a series of magnificent speeches he demanded vigorous military preparation and he led through Congress the largest naval bill of our history. But a precious year had been lost and the President encountered a pacifistic opposition which he himself had originally done something to foster. He paid a heavy price, for without the material force necessary to the support of his diplomacy, Wilson was destined later to miss the opportunity, if not of ending, at least of shortening, the war.

IV

Wilson's sense of aloofness from Europe and the war was quickly shattered by the march of circumstances, and he was soon to learn that the war could touch us very closely.

[1] Grey, *Twenty-Five Years* (Frederick A. Stokes Company), II, 279.

Ironically enough, in view of later developments, it was a dispute with the British over their control of trade which first awakened a general sense of our national proximity to the fighting front. British supervision of war-time neutral trade has always been strict, and its interpretation of the meaning of 'contraband' broad. From the British point of view it would have been flying in the face of Providence to surrender the opportunities offered by the mastery of the sea. The Entente Allies were naturally interested in preventing the arrival in Germany, directly or indirectly, of any articles that might help the enemy to prolong the war, for in a modern war almost any article of common necessity, such as cotton, oil, copper, or foodstuffs, may be of as much military value as what was formerly declared contraband of war. It was inevitable that the Allies, under British leadership because of the strength of the British navy, should seize and search neutral vessels which might carry contraband; it was equally certain that they would extend the definition of contraband.

On the other hand, as the largest of the neutral Powers the United States was vitally concerned in preserving open routes to the neutral countries of Europe and an open market in Europe for non-contraband goods.

The situation contained dynamite, and it is not pleasant to reflect that under existing international usages it is one which the United States must confront whenever Great Britain is at war with a Continental Power.

'*September* 30, 1914 [conference between Wilson and House]: When we were discussing the seizure of vessels by Great Britain, he read a page from his "History of the American People," telling how during Madison's Administration the War of 1812 was started in exactly the same way as this controversy is opening up. The passage said that Madison was compelled to go to war despite the fact that he was a peace-loving man and desired to do everything in his power to prevent it, but popular feeling made it impossible.

'The President said: "Madison and I are the only two Princeton men that have become President. The circumstances of the War of 1812 and now run parallel. I sincerely hope they will not go further."

'I told the British Ambassador about this conversation. He was greatly impressed, and said that in his cablegram to Sir Edward Grey he would call attention not only to the passage in the President's book, but to his comment to me upon it.'

In view of the strong sympathy for the Entente cause in the United States, the danger of an actual break was remote. Both Wilson and Grey were convinced that the future welfare of the world depended upon Anglo-American friendship, and each was anxious to yield as much to the other as might be necessary to assure it. But unless care were taken, a point might be reached beyond which neither could yield.

Ambassador Page in London had fortunately won the respect and affection of the British, and negotiations were always facilitated by the cordiality of the relations he maintained with the Foreign Office. On the other hand, he suffered from the defects of his virtues, placing such value upon Anglo-American friendship that he was not inclined to present American protests with the emphasis desired at Washington. Both Wilson and the State Department were convinced that the avoidance of future trouble could best be secured by letting the British understand clearly at the very beginning that we regarded British Admiralty policy as infringing our neutral rights and material interests.

Mr. Page looked at the problem in a different light. He was willing to make allowance for the British restrictions on trade, and he evidently felt that in comparison with the defeat of Germany and the maintenance of good feeling between Great Britain and America, the losses and inconveniences of neutrals did not count. 'Everything is going well here, I think,' he wrote to House, September 15, 1914. 'The British Government is most considerate of us in all large ways. The smaller questions of ships and prizes, etc., are really in the hands of the Admiralty — really, tho' not nominally — and they are conducted on a war basis.'

It was with some irritation that the Ambassador discovered that in the United States British seizure of ships and prizes was not regarded as a 'smaller question,' and he did not conceal his lack of sympathy with the arguments drafted by the legal advisers to the State Department in protection of American rights on the seas.

Colonel House to the President

New York, *October* 21, 1914

Dear Governor:

I have received the following cablegram from Page, through his son Arthur.

'God deliver us, or can you deliver us, from library lawyers. They often lose chestnuts while they argue about burns. See our friend [President Wilson] and come here immediately if the case be not already settled.[1] Of utmost importance.' . . .

I hardly know to what he refers, but perhaps you do. It may be the Declaration of London matter.

I notice that Northcliffe, in his papers, and the London *Post* are demanding that the Government seize neutral vessels carrying reservists or contraband cargoes.

If you think I can be of any service, please wire me and I

[1] The British had refused the American demand that the Declaration of London be generally accepted. The Declaration of London (1909), which Great Britain had never ratified, left among other articles copper and rubber on the non-contraband list and would have permitted the importation of foodstuffs by Germany.

will come to Washington immediately. Page is evidently disturbed.

Affectionately yours

E. M. House

The President replied that if Page was disturbed by the attitude of the State Department, he, Wilson, was a little disturbed by that of the Ambassador. If Page were to represent the American Government, he must see the matters under discussion in the light in which they were seen in the United States. Wilson insisted that Page's advice was of great value, but he expressed the fear that Page's intense feeling for the British case might prove a danger. Wilson himself was sometimes disparaging in his remarks about professional diplomats, but he did not enjoy having the work of the State Department, which emphasized the American point of view, referred to as that of 'library lawyers.'

Colonel House shared Mr. Page's conviction that too much depended upon the friendship of Great Britain and the United States to permit a quarrel over anything that was not vital; but he appreciated, as the Ambassador did not, the irritation caused in the United States by the British methods of holding up American cargoes, and he also realized that unless the United States maintained her rights as a neutral with vigor in the case of the seizure of cargoes, she would not be able to protest effectively should more serious attacks follow.

On the other hand, he believed that through the exercise of care in the drafting of protests and by maintaining close personal relations with the British Ambassador in Washington, much friction could be avoided.

'*September* 27, 1914: I took the 12.08 train to Washington and was met at the station by McAdoo and Eleanor. They went to the White House with me and took dinner with us.

After dinner we talked for a while, until a large package of papers came from the State Department marked "urgent." This was the signal for . . . the family to leave, and the President and I immediately got down to work.

'X had written a long letter to Page, concerning the Declaration of London and its effect upon neutral shipping. X's letter of instruction to Page was exceedingly undiplomatic, and I urged the President not to permit it to be sent. . . .

'I then suggested that he permit me to have a conference with Sir Cecil Spring-Rice and get at the bottom of the controversy. He expressed warm approval of this plan. After this we went to bed, pretty tired and somewhat worried.

'*September* 28, 1914: I had Hoover [1] arrange with Billy Phillips [2] for the use of his home, and I asked Sir Cecil Spring-Rice over the telephone to meet me there at ten o'clock. The conference was a most interesting one.

'I showed the Ambassador the letter X had prepared to send Page. He was thoroughly alarmed over some of the diplomatic expressions. One paragraph in particular he thought amounted almost to a declaration of war. He said if that paper should get into the hands of the press, the headlines would indicate that war with Great Britain was inevitable, and he believed one of the greatest panics the country ever saw would ensue, for it was as bad or worse than the Venezuela incident. He said he did not know what I had accomplished in a busy life, but he felt sure I had never done as important a piece of work as in this instance. . . .

'We discussed the best ways and means of getting out of

[1] Chief usher at the White House.

[2] Mr. William Phillips was at this time Third Assistant Secretary of State; his ability and diplomatic qualifications enabled him to perform services as important as they were unheralded. He was on terms of close friendship with Sir Cecil and it was at his house that House usually met the British Ambassador. Phillips became First Assistant Secretary in 1915, and later Minister to Holland and Ambassador to Belgium.

the difficulty, which he said would never have arisen if the State Department had talked the matter over with him frankly in the beginning. His Government's attitude had been known at the State Department for a month, and yet not a word of objection had been raised. If he had known what the feeling of this country was, he would have taken it up with his Government and their attitude would have been modified. As it was, they had already published their intention of doing the things to which our Government objected, and it would be difficult to handle it now in a way to save the *amour-propre* of his Government.

'We outlined a despatch for this Government to send to Page, and then we outlined the despatch which we thought he should send Sir Edward Grey. We agreed to be absolutely frank with one another, letting each know just what was being done, so there could be no subterfuge or misunderstanding.'

It would be difficult to find in all history another instance of diplomacy so unconventional and so effective. Colonel House, a private citizen, spreads all the cards on the table and concerts with the Ambassador of a foreign Power the despatches to be sent the American Ambassador and the Foreign Minister of that Power. If there is criticism of the method, it is stifled by its success.

As a result of this intervention, the threatened crisis was tided over; and during the next five weeks it proved possible to approach the problem of neutral shipping with equanimity, although no fundamental solution was discovered. House himself said nothing of what he had done.

Colonel House to Ambassador W. H. Page

NEW YORK, *October* 29, 1914

DEAR PAGE:

When your cablegram came, I communicated with the President, but found that everything was in process of adjustment. I cannot see how there can be any serious trouble between England and America, with all of us feeling as we do; but of course we must needs be careful in the manner of doing things — for the American people, as you know, are exceedingly sensitive regarding certain questions, and it would not be advisable for the President, with all his power and popularity, to go counter to this sentiment. . . .

Faithfully yours

E. M. House

Ambassador W. H. Page to Colonel House

London, *November* 9, 1914

My dear House:

. . . I want to thank you for what I suppose you did when I telegraphed you thro' Arthur. I sent the telegram thro' Arthur so that your name and mine shd. not be on the same telegram and thereby possibly excite suspicion. The situation is safe, but it can at any time be made critical by a captious manner. I did not and do not mean to criticize Lansing or anybody else — only to make sure that things are seen in their proper perspective.

Sir Edward values American friendship more than anything else of that kind. He is not going to endanger it. To this day, he hasn't confiscated a single American cargo, tho' there are many that he might have confiscated within his rights. Our continued good relations[hip] is the only thing that now holds the world together. That's the big fact. A cargo of copper, I grant you, may be important; but it can't be as important as our friendship. It's the big and lasting things that count now. I think of the unborn generations of men to whom the close friendship of the Kingdom and of our Republic will be the most important political fact in the world. — Have stiff controversies? Yes; I'm for them whole-heartedly, when we have a good reason. But there's no reason now; and, if there were, this is the time to be patient. There'll be plenty of time left to quarrel when this dire period is past. . . .

It's no time, then, to quarrel or to be bumptious about a cargo of oil or of copper, or to deal with these Gov'ts as if things were normal. Thank God, you are 3000 miles from it. I wish I were 30,000. . . .

Yours heartily

W. H. P.

Unfortunately, the oil and the copper exporters in the United States felt differently and protests poured in upon the State Department in Washington. For Mr. Page, who was in vital sympathy with the Allied cause, the situation was worse than trying. His nerves became taut. As usual, the minor questions were the more vexatious. What was dangerous was that, in his misunderstanding and irritation with the State Department, he should lose sight of the Washington point of view, which he was sent to London to represent. It was the more difficult to warn Mr. Page to be careful not to display pro-Ally feeling in that he looked upon himself as falling over backward in his neutrality, and was not in a frame of mind to receive criticism philosophically.

Ambassador W. H. Page to Colonel House

LONDON, *December* 12, 1914

MY DEAR HOUSE:

. . . I am trying my best, God knows, to keep the way as smooth as possible; but neither Government helps me. Our Government merely sends the shippers' *ex-parte* statement. This Government uses the Navy's excuse.

Oh, well, praise God it goes as well as it does. I get my facts as best I can — from other neutrals, from ship-captains, etc. — and I do the best I can, getting thanks for nothing, getting lectures for — nothing. I happened a little while ago to telegraph that I 'conferred' with the neutral Ministers, meaning, of course, that I talked with them and found out what facts I could. It was *their* ships that were stopped, with American cargoes. I got back a despatch from Washington saying I had no authority to be making shipping and trade agreements with neutral Powers — they did that themselves at Washington! Now what damfool in the State Department supposed that I was making agreements with any Govt. or that I was doing anything but trying day and night to get an American cargo released and to prevent more from being stopped — I don't know, nor care to know; and I haven't a trace of a shade of a dream of feeling about it. Anybody's at liberty to think anything about me he pleases; I've long since ceased to care a fig. A man in a difficult public place must turn heaven and earth to do his very uttermost duty — must try doubly and trebly hard at any cost and must absolutely exhaust every possible effort and resource and satisfy his most exacting conscience. He will be blamed then. He will be misunderstood. He will be misjudged. He must accept that and go on without paying the least heed to it. I can do that easily. I don't care a fig. I'm incapable of resenting any misunderstanding. *But* — BUT, you can't help doubting the *intelligence* of a man (whoever he is) that breaks loose with a sermon about my making 'agreements with other governments'; and you don't know just how much dependence to put in the next telegram about something else, that comes from the same source....

Everybody here, so far as I have heard (and I shd hear, you may be sure), regards us all as neutral of course, and so treats us — English, Germans, Austrians, French, and neutrals. Of the neutral members of the diplomatic corps I see much (in spite of my inability to make 'agreements with other countries'); and I can't tell you to save my life what the leanings are of any of them! I have felt no suspicion from any quarter but Washington. Suspicion, I have noticed, generally sleeps in the bed with Ignorance. . . .

Heartily yours

WALTER H. PAGE

Colonel House to Ambassador W. H. Page

NEW YORK, *December* 4, 1914

DEAR PAGE:

I have just returned from Washington. . . .

The President wishes me to ask you please to be careful not to express any unneutral feeling, either by word of mouth, or by letter, and not even to the State Department. He said that both Mr. Bryan and Mr. Lansing had remarked upon your leaning in that direction, and he thought it would materially lessen your influence.

He feels very strongly about this, and I am sending the same message to Gerard.

Faithfully yours

E. M. HOUSE

Ambassador W. H. Page to Colonel House

LONDON, *December* 15, 1914

DEAR HOUSE:

I'll tell you a story: Within a week two Americans who have lately come here have criticized me and the Embassy for being pro-German, and I often hear such remarks that come from the English.

And I'll ask you a question:

Is an Ambassador a man sent to keep another Government friendly and in good humor with your Government so that you can get and give all sorts of friendly services and make the world better?

Or is his business to snap and snarl and play 'smart' and keep 'em irritated — damn 'em! — and get and give nothing?

These I send you by Mrs. Page as my Xmas greeting.

W. H. P.

If the State Department had difficulties in impressing its point of view upon the American Ambassador in London, there was also cause for some anxiety because of petty misunderstandings with the British Ambassador in Washington. Sir Cecil Spring-Rice was a diplomatist of distinction and a scholar of charm. During the early weeks of the war, his relations with our Government were of the most cordial sort. House kept in close touch with him, and the following letter indicates the tone of their intercourse:

Ambassador Spring-Rice to Colonel House

BRITISH EMBASSY
WASHINGTON, *November* 5, 1914

MY DEAR COLONEL:

I hear you have come. How are you? . . .

We hope that the exports will continue as at present. But the evident intentions of the Germans are to get some fast cruisers out of the North Sea and effect a junction with those in the Atlantic, and so control for a short time the trade routes. We suspect the ships in United States ports of an intention to run out and get converted into commerce destroyers, which would be awkward. For this reason I am asking that ships in New York harbour should be periodically inspected and not allowed to leave unless their cargoes are innocent.

Do you gather that an attack will be made on the Administration in Congress for remissness about contraband matters? As a matter of fact, no American exporter has suffered any loss and all the protests of the Administration have been successful. But owing to changed conditions of modern war it is evident that the definition of contraband must be changed — i.e., for instance, it must include petroleum and copper (which in Germany is entirely used for cartridges, bombs, etc.); and the American doctrine of 'continuous voyage,' or that the character of the goods is determined by its ultimate destination, and not the port where it is landed, is evidently applicable to certain ports like Genoa, Rotterdam, and Copenhagen which are the back doors of Germany. A *just* cause of complaint would be the seizure of goods really destined for neutrals and we are making arrangements by which such goods will be hall-marked by the sender here if he wishes it. I hope by December these arrangements will be in working order and no further inconvenience suffered. I am telegraphing about this now and a man is arranging with the copper men here for an amicable understanding. A protest, reserving all rights, could be made at once in cases of unreasonable or prolonged detention.

Yours sincerely

CECIL SPRING-RICE

Unfortunately, Sir Cecil was in wretched health, and his nerves, even more than those of Page, were prone to become frazzled as unpleasant incidents arose. The following excerpts from House's memoranda indicate the delicacy of the situation as well as the extraordinary activity of the Colonel, for those were the days in which he was negotiating with the South American Ambassadors the first draft of the Pan-American Pact.

'*December* 29, 1914: I went from Naon to the home of Billy Phillips to meet the British Ambassador. I found him nervous and excited because of the premature publication and a garbled account of the protest made by the President to the British Government concerning the holding-up of neutral vessels. He did not mind the note, for he and I had already threshed that out and settled it long before it was sent. He had even received a reply from Sir Edward Grey indicating that the President's request would be granted. The note was merely a formal matter of routine after the real issue had been met, but what he objected to was the way in which it had been given publicity and the manner in which our press had treated it....

I tried to explain to Spring-Rice how badly the President felt. He accepted that part, but blamed the State Department most unreservedly and said it was impossible to conduct diplomatic negotiations of a delicate nature through the newspapers. He claimed that it was not the first time and that he hesitated to take up further matters with them; in fact, he intended to absent himself from the Department in future. He had no doubt we would all be pro-Germans within six months, that the Germans were strong and had a thorough organization, and they would finally break down any anti-German sentiment which now existed....

'He talked so many different ways, in almost the same sentence, that I concluded he was too upset for me to have any profitable discussion with him, and I therefore took my leave.'

As it turned out, the State Department was quite guiltless of any indiscretion, but then, as generally, it was made the scapegoat for the sins of others.

'*December* 30, 1914: I called up Phillips at the State Department [recorded House] and told him I was sorry Mr. Bryan was out of town, because I desired to suggest to him that he soothe the ruffled feelings of the British Ambassador. I asked Phillips to take part in this laudable endeavor. I said my trip to Washington had been largely nullified by the premature publication of the President's protest to the British Government and I hoped they would get the Ambassador in a normal frame of mind before I returned, for he blamed the State Department for the leak. Phillips said they had found exactly where the leak was, that it was not in the State Department, and indicated as nearly as he could over the telephone that it was ——, a fact which I already knew as well as I could know anything that had not happened under my own eyes. . . .

'*December* 31, 1914: I received the accompanying letter from Spring-Rice a few minutes ago. He is evidently in good humor again. I am exceedingly glad. . . .'

Ambassador Spring-Rice to Colonel House [1]

I have just received copy of the note that is the telegram to Page and it seems to me a very fair just courteous and firm presentment of the case to which no objection whatever could be raised on the ground of its form. I am sure it will create a very lasting impression and will remain on the records as an honourable effort to solve in an amicable manner the question at issue.

Such crises, flaring up and flickering down, wearied the President beyond anything else, and were not conducive to prompt settlement of the points at issue. When House brought to Mr. Wilson the gist of his various interviews, the President's face, he recorded, 'became grey.' The Ambassadors might have been recalled, but there were strong arguments against such a step. However unfortunate Mr. Page's relations with the State Department, it would have been impossible to find any one more capable of holding close personal relations with Sir Edward Grey. Nor would it have been easy to suggest to the British that they recall Spring-Rice. Wilson's solution was to send House to England to explain personally the American case on the holding-up of cargoes. He sympathized with the British, and at the same time realized the force of the view taken by the State Depart-

[1] Sir Cecil's letters to Colonel House were frequently unsigned and, as in this case, without any superscription. When they carried a superscription he generally addressed Colonel House as 'Mr. Beverly.' His manner, both personal and epistolary, was sometimes apt to suggest the mysterious.

ment. He was on terms of intimacy with Sir Edward Grey and Sir William Tyrrell.

Wilson's decision was hastened by another factor which assumed the first importance at the close of the year. All through the autumn Colonel House had engaged in frequent conferences with the German and British Ambassadors concerning the possibility of American mediation. The question asked by the President was whether this possibility might be changed to a probability, and he saw no means of answering it except through the European mission which House agreed to undertake.

CHAPTER XI

PLANS OF MEDIATION

The most serious difficulty . . . is the deep-rooted distrust England has for German diplomacy and promises. Something of this is also felt by the Germans for England.

House to Wilson, September 22, 1914

I

COLONEL HOUSE was not one of the multitude which, so long as the war lasted, believed the crippling of Germany as a great economic and political Power to be an essential element of future peace. On the contrary, he was convinced that a strong, albeit demilitarized, Germany was necessary to the economic stability of Europe and the welfare of the world. He consistently opposed the political disintegration of Germany which was openly or secretly advocated by her Continental enemies. In the opening week of the war House foresaw Germany's defeat, and he feared the consequences if this defeat should prove overwhelming. To his mind the greatest menace to civilization lay in the possibility of the domination of Europe by Tsarist Russia.

'*August* 6, 1914: It looks to me as if Germany was riding for a fall [he wrote], and it also seems to me that, if this should happen, France and Russia will want to rend her in twain. It is clearly to the interest of England, America, and civilization to have her integrity preserved, shorn, however, of her military and naval power.

'I expect to see the British Ambassador and outline this to him.'

Ten days later, in a message to Ambassador Gerard, House suggested the possibility of stopping the war before passions became so inflamed that neither side would consider laying down arms. It was no more than a suggestion, and House himself did not believe that it would lead to practical results. But the message is significant, for it sketched what was, four years later, to be the American plan for lasting peace and in it, as in the Pan-American Pact, is the principle of the League of Nations Covenant — an organization to guarantee territorial integrity and to provide for disarmament.

Colonel House to Ambassador Gerard

PRIDE'S CROSSING, MASSACHUSETTS
August 17, 1914

DEAR JUDGE:

... The Kaiser has stood for peace all these years, and it would not be inconsistent with his past life and services to be willing now to consider such overtures. If peace could come at this hour, it should be upon the general proposition that every nation at war should be guaranteed its territorial integrity of to-day. Then a general plan of disarmament should be brought about, for there would be no need under such an arrangement for larger armies than were necessary for police purposes.

Of course, this matter would have to be handled very delicately; otherwise sensibilities might be offended.

As far as I am concerned, I would view with alarm and genuine regret any vital disaster to the German people. The only feeling in America that has been manifested against Germany has not been directed against her as a nation, but merely against her as the embodiment of militarism. Our people have never admitted that excessive armaments were guaranties of peace, but they have felt, on the contrary, that in the end they meant just such conditions as exist to-day. When neighboring nations with racial differences and prejudices vie with one another in excessive armaments, it brings about a feeling of distrust which engenders a purpose to strike first and to strike hard.

With Europe disarmed and with treaties guaranteeing one another's territorial integrity, she might go forward with every assurance of industrial expansion and permanent peace.

Faithfully yours

E. M. House

The difficulty was that the victorious advance of the German armies through Belgium and northern France, during the month of August, prevented any consideration of peace in Berlin; on the other hand, the treatment they meted out to the invaded regions inflamed the French, Belgians, and British and crystallized their determination never to cease fighting until the damage had been repaired and Teutonic war methods punished. On the eastern front there was the same situation with reversed rôles. The Russians advanced triumphantly, while their devastation of East Prussia convinced the Germans that the menace of the barbarous Slav must be ended once for all.

But in September the Russians, while they were able to continue the invasion of Galicia, were driven out of East Prussia by Hindenburg, who immediately proceeded to threaten an attack upon Russian Poland. In the west the Germans were defeated on the Marne, and although they maintained themselves on the line of the Aisne it became obvious that the immediate and overwhelming defeat of France, which their military leaders had promised, was likely to remain an unfulfilled dream. As the autumn drew on, a condition of deadlock seemed to have been reached.

German war plans had been based upon the assumption of a short campaign, and the prospect of facing a vast coalition through a long-drawn-out struggle was one that appalled the army leaders; some of them have since confessed that with the battle of the Marne, and the beginning of the deadlock on the western front, they regarded the war as lost. Colonel

House was of the same opinion, and argued that if the Germans were wise they would accept what terms they might, before the ultimate consequences of defeat became apparent. At the very moment of the decision on the Marne, he had written to Zimmermann, suggesting that the time was approaching when President Wilson's offer of mediation might be taken in other than an academic sense.

Colonel House to the President

PRIDE'S CROSSING, MASSACHUSETTS
September 5, 1914

DEAR GOVERNOR:

I am enclosing you a letter to Herr Zimmermann. If you approve, will you not have it properly sealed and sent to the German Embassy for transmission?

Please criticize it frankly and return it to me for correction if you think best.

I have a feeling that Germany will soon be glad to entertain suggestions of mediation and that the outlook is more hopeful in that direction than elsewhere.

Affectionately yours

E. M. HOUSE

Colonel House to Herr Zimmermann [1]

WASHINGTON, D.C., *September* 5, 1914

DEAR HERR ZIMMERMANN:

Thank you for your letter of August 1. I gave it to the President to read and he again expressed his deep regret that the efforts to bring about a better understanding between the Great Powers of Europe had so signally miscarried.

He looks upon the present war with ever-increasing sorrow, and his offer of mediation was not an empty one, for he would count it a great honor to be able to initiate a movement for peace.

[1] The letter was approved by Wilson and sent to Zimmermann.

Now that His Majesty has so brilliantly shown the power of his army, would it not be consistent with his lifelong endeavor to maintain peace, to consent to overtures being made in that direction? [1]

If I could serve in any way as a medium, it would be a great source of happiness to me; and I stand ready to act immediately upon any suggestion that Your Excellency may convey or have conveyed confidentially to me.

With assurances of my high esteem, I am, my dear Herr Zimmermann,

Sincerely yours

EDWARD M. HOUSE

At the same time, House renewed his personal contacts with the Austro-Hungarian Ambassador, of whom he had seen much the previous summer on the North Shore.

'*September* 5, 1914: I am dining out to-night [he wrote] to meet Ambassador Dumba. I am laying plans to make myself *persona grata* to all the nations involved in this European war, so that my services may be utilized to advantage and without objection in the event a proper opportunity arrives. I have been assiduously working to this end ever since the war broke loose. I do not believe in leaving things to chance, and then attribute failure to lack of luck or opportunity. I am trying to think out in advance the problems that the war will entail and the obligations which will fall upon this country, which I hope the President will properly meet.'

[1] House's rather florid tribute to the pacific tendencies of the Kaiser must be read in connection with Zimmermann's letter of August 1 (above, p. 279). The implication of House's phrase is, 'If the Kaiser really loves peace as much as you say, now is the time to show it.'

Colonel House to the President

PRIDE'S CROSSING, MASSACHUSETTS
September 6, 1914

DEAR GOVERNOR:

Last night I had a conference with the Austrian Ambassador. He talked very indiscreetly and, if one will sit still, he will tell all he knows. I sat very still.

I learned that the Germans were making a mighty effort to gain a decisive victory in France and that, when that was accomplished, they would be ready to consider overtures for peace.

I also learned that their great fear was starvation. Austria is fairly self-sustaining and, because of her close proximity to Roumania, she would not unduly suffer; but Germany faces famine if the war continues.

England, it seems, lets no ship pass into neutral ports without first ascertaining whether or not it contains foodstuffs; and when it does, she exercises her right to purchase it.

What Dumba particularly wants, is for the American ships to defy England and feed Germany. . . .

He spoke of England's enormous power and said Germany's military power was not to be compared with that which England exercised over the entire world because of her navy. He forgot to add that England is not exercising her power in an objectionable way, for it is controlled by a democracy.

He strongly deprecated the war and said if he had been Foreign Minister in Austria it would never have occurred. He intimated that Germany and Austria felt that Russia would have been prepared in 1915, and therefore it was necessary to anticipate her. . . .

He deprecated the use of bombs.

Your very affectionate

E. M. HOUSE

II

Colonel House was under no illusion as to the difficulty of beginning parleys. He had observed the pathetic failure of the attempt of Mr. Oscar Straus, who had engaged in peace discussions with Count Bernstorff and hoped to pass a German offer to the Allies through Mr. Wilson; some one talked, and all hope of success immediately evaporated. The fiasco did not enhance House's respect for the discretion of the German Ambassador, nor would it tend to facilitate other attempts. Furthermore, although House argued that were he in the shoes of the German leaders he would make every concession for peace, he did not place great confidence in their political good sense. On September 10 he wrote: 'England will not stand for peace unless it also means permanent peace, and that, I think, Germany is not yet ready to concede.'

Nevertheless, when Bernstorff asked for an interview, the Colonel agreed to discuss the matter, for he did not want to leave any possible opening untried. If the German Government would actually authorize Bernstorff to make a reasonable offer, it would be good sense for the Allies to consider it carefully. In House's mind at this time a 'reasonable offer' seems to have meant evacuation of invaded territory and full compensation to Belgium.

Colonel House to the President

New York, *September* 18, 1914

Dear Governor:

Bernstorff came to see me this afternoon. I suggested that he meet Sir Cecil Spring-Rice at dinner. He is willing.

I am writing Sir Cecil, asking if it would be convenient for him to come to New York within the next day or two, but making no mention of my conferences with Bernstorff. If we can get these two together, we can at least make a start.

For the moment, England dominates her allies. Later, she may not. She would probably be content now with an agreement for general disarmament and an indemnity for Belgium. Germany, I think, would be glad to get such terms. Shall I go on, or shall I give Sir Cecil some satisfactory reason for wanting to see him?

Now that I am in touch with Bernstorff, I hope to persuade him to close his mouth for a while. He promises that no human being shall know of these negotiations.

The world expects you to play the big part in this tragedy —and so indeed you will, for God has given you the power to see things as they are.

Your faithful and affectionate

E. M. House

'I found Bernstorff [Colonel House recorded in a separate memorandum] in a different attitude from when I last saw him, which was in the spring. He was then *débonnaire* and cock-sure of himself and of his country. After telling him something of my visit to Germany and of my purpose in making it, and after speaking of the charming manner in which the Kaiser received me at Potsdam, I began to talk of the peace negotiations. I asked if he had met Sir Cecil Spring-Rice since hostilities began. He said he had not, that it was against diplomatic usage to do so. I thought the best thing that could be done now was for the two of them to meet, and I asked if he was willing to do so provided I could bring it about. He hesitated for a moment and then said he would be willing to do so provided it was known only to the three of us. I agreed that the President would be the only one informed. If anything developed from the conference, I promised permission from our Government for him to use code messages direct to his Government, which of course up to now he has not been able to do. He said if nothing came from the conference, he would not mention it to his Government or to any one else.'

Fortunately House was, even as early as this, on the most intimate terms with the British Ambassador. The two had already gone over important despatches to Page and Grey, together working for the elimination of undiplomatic phrases. Spring-Rice wrote to House in a private code, and the latter felt free to call on him at any time when the importance of the business in hand warranted. From him the Colonel had already gathered that the Allies would not consider a makeshift peace. 'You will understand that no peace is any good which simply means an armed truce with another war at the end of it.' Thus wrote the Ambassador to House on September 12. 'We want not only the end of a war but the end of all wars: and unfortunately no *treaty* has now the slightest importance. We have suffered too severely by trusting in treaties, and if we were to allow Belgium to suffer what she has suffered without compensation, we should be pretty mean quitters. It is an awful prospect for the world and I see no immediate remedy.'

None the less, House felt it worth while to attempt to arrange a meeting between Bernstorff and Spring-Rice — a highly unconventional proceeding, but House recked little of conventions; and when Spring-Rice telephoned that he could not leave Washington at the moment, House insisted that he must come at once. 'I will take the midnight train,' answered the Ambassador. It is hard to repress a smile at the thought of the diplomatists taking orders from the quietly persuasive Colonel.

'*September* 20, 1914: I met Sir Cecil [recorded House] at seven-thirty at the Pennsylvania. I did not get out of the car for fear of being seen.[1] We immediately took up the subject

[1] Spring-Rice had a horror of spies. Evidently he preferred that his interview with House should not be generally known, for House noted: 'Around eleven o'clock Sir Cecil went to the Majestic Hotel to see Sir Courtenay Bennett, the British Consul-General. He merely did this to give an excuse for his trip to New York in the event it became known.'

in hand. I found him unwilling to confer with Bernstorff, whom he considers thoroughly unreliable. He says he has a bad reputation not only in England but in Germany, and that he was sent to America because it was thought he could do no harm here....

'I explained to Sir Cecil the situation as I saw it. First, that at this time Great Britain dominated the Allies, which perhaps she would not do later. Second, that Great Britain could probably obtain from Germany, for the Allies, a disarmament agreement with compensation for Belgium. This was what Great Britain wanted and not the dismemberment of Germany, which would surely follow even over her protests, provided the Allies were signally victorious.

'He agreed to all this, but said the Germans were so unreliable, that their political philosophy was so selfish and so unmoral that he hesitated to open up negotiations with them. He was also afraid the time was not ripe for peace proposals.

'He said it would be necessary for all the Allies to be approached simultaneously, for it would not do for Great Britain to begin secret negotiations, even if they were willing, because Germany would not play fair and would later denounce Great Britain as being treacherous to her allies. Then there was difficulty with France's and Russia's representatives here. Jusserand, he said, had an extremely bad case of nerves at present, and the Russian Ambassador was a reactionary of the worst type and was little less than mad.

'He told me of despatches that had passed between Sir Edward and himself, and we discussed at great length what was best to do in the circumstances and what was best to tell Bernstorff.... He is frank and honest, and is a high-minded scholarly gentleman.

'He thinks the best thing for the present is for the President to keep constantly in touch with the situation and to give repeated assurances to the different Governments that he stands ready to act whenever they feel the moment has arrived. He believes it would not do for the President to make any proposals as to terms, but merely to hold himself in an absolutely neutral position. . . .

'I was successful in making Sir Cecil see that it was not wise for Great Britain to take any big gamble in this conflict. If she could get disarmament and compensation for Belgium, she had better accept it and not risk the stupendous consequences of defeat. I also made him see that if the Allies won and Germany was thoroughly crushed, there would be no holding Russia back and the future situation would hardly be less promising than the past.'

The cable which Spring-Rice sent to Sir Edward Grey as the result of this conversation, embodying the American point of view, was as follows:

Ambassador Spring-Rice to Sir Edward Grey

B[ernstorff] was willing that he should enter into communication with S.-R. direct. S.-R. answered that as three Powers were bound to make peace simultaneously, he could not receive a communication.

I think B. was not acting without instructions or knowledge of his Government. Conversations here are likely to be difficult.

But following considerations seem to force themselves on the attention of the world:

If war continues, either G[ermany] becomes supreme or R[ussia]. Both alternatives would be fatal to the equilibrium of Europe. Consequently the present moment is more propitious to an agreement favorable to the principles of equilibrium.

President may therefore (from this point of view) be anxious to facilitate negotiations now. The basis for these might well be Sir E. G.'s two principles: (1) End of militarism and permanent peace. (2) Compensation to Belgium.

If other Powers are willing to make suggestions in order to effect an agreement on the basis of these two principles, then negotiations could begin. If they have other proposals to make, it would be as well that they should be made known as soon as possible for reasons given above, and the P[resident] would be perfectly willing to facilitate exchange of ideas as friendly intermediary, without expression of opinion.

G[ermany] is doing her best to put E[ngland] in the wrong by causing a belief that E[ngland] is rejecting G[ermany]'s friendly overtures.

It would be dangerous for E[ngland] to persist in *non possumus* attitude. Although it is fully understood that she cannot negotiate without knowledge of other two, it would be to advantage of all three that G[ermany] should be forced to show her hand.

E. G.'s two principles would have sympathy of world.

Colonel House to the President

NEW YORK, *September* 22, 1914

DEAR GOVERNOR:

Bernstorff came to see me again yesterday in order to hear the outcome of Spring-Rice's visit.

I told him that Sir Cecil hesitated to go into a conference without the consent of his Government and without the knowledge of their allies. Bernstorff thought this reasonable. He justified his own action by saying that he thought the instructions from his Government warranted him in taking up negotiations of this sort. . . .

Bernstorff thought it was not too early to begin conversations, for the reason that they could hardly bring results in any event for some months.

Sir Cecil and I agreed that the Kaiser would probably be willing to accept such terms as England would be glad to concede, provided the German war party would permit him. The most serious difficulty that will be encountered during negotiations is the deep-rooted distrust England has for German diplomacy and promises. Something of this is also felt by the Germans towards England.

Another difficulty was expressed by Bernstorff, to the effect that neither side wished to be placed in the position of initiating peace proposals. This can be avoided, however, in some such way as is being done now, for they will soon find themselves talking about it and will not be so sensitive. . . .

Your faithful and affectionate

E. M. House

New York, *October* 6, 1914

Dear Governor:

Dumba came to see me and handed me the enclosed article, which he has written for publication in the *World's Work* for November. He wanted you to see it in advance.

He hardly tried to disguise his eagerness for peace measures to begin. I told him I did not think the Allies would want to commence conversations of this sort as long as the German forces occupied their territory. He replied, 'Perhaps, then, a German defeat at this time might not be an unmixed evil.'

I told him how anxious you were to be of service, but that you felt you had gone as far as it was wise to go without some encouragement.

Affectionately yours

E. M. House

Whatever the private protestations of Bernstorff and Dumba, the public announcements of the German and Austrian Governments were in a directly opposed sense and did not facilitate the beginning of peace negotiations. Public opinion in the Central Empires had been encouraged to expect a smashing victory and their official spokesmen continued to promise it. The Allied leaders echoed such sentiments on their side with a shade of increased intensity. The

British felt, and not without some justification, that it was hard to reconcile Bernstorff's suggestions of peace with the campaign of hate against England which Berlin was whipping up.

Ambassador Spring-Rice to Colonel House

WASHINGTON, D.C., *September* 24, 1914

MY DEAR COLONEL:

. . . The message went to its destination and is being considered by the big bugs there. In the meanwhile I note that the assurance made to you and others by your friend [Bernstorff] has been publicly and officially repudiated by his employers, so that he cannot be regarded as either authorized or responsible. Any suggestions from this quarter that one member of the firm [the Triple Entente] alone should discuss conditions with him, can obviously only be made with a view to sowing distrust among them. Any one who wants the terms of an arrangement to be discussed, must approach all the members of the firm simultaneously. . . .

I notice that our own selves are at the present moment the object of the most virulent attacks from the person who talked to you [Bernstorff] and from his friends and associates. There is no sign whatever of any peaceful intention and everything is done to envenom the situation, especially and very particularly as far as we are concerned.

I enjoyed our talk most of any I have had for a long time and I hope we shall have another one. . . .

Yours ever

C S R

Mr. H. C. Wallace's memorandum of a conversation with Ambassador von Bernstorff

September 25, 1914

I was lunching alone at the Ritz Carlton to-day and he came up and asked to sit with me.

He was anxious to know whether there were any subsequent developments, and I said I thought the difficulty was the necessity of talking with the partners [France and Russia].

During the conversation I asked whether he believed the time was propitious for negotiations to begin; and he answered there was not the slightest doubt, provided an opening wedge could be started on the Island [England]. In his opinion, a full coöperation could be counted on in his country, but he told me this was in strictest confidence. He said if negotiations could start on the Island and could be kept absolutely secret, that he could arrange for a favorable reception and visit to his country. His principal apprehension was public opinion on Island and partners — hence necessity of secrecy.

He also believed that unless something was done soon, the affair would be long-drawn-out, as nothing really decisive could occur for at least six months and probably a year; and, further, that if something occurs which makes either side particularly happy, public opinion would harass, if not defeat, plans short of subjugation. He also told me in confidence that his people had refrained from doing a number of very disagreeable things to avoid inflaming that nation.

If Winston [Churchill] voices the feeling of Government, it is useless to make effort; but I told him G[rey] had different views, and he replied that if that were true, great accomplishment might be made by sending some one from the P[resident] to the Island first and then across the Channel.

'*September* 29, 1914 [Spring-Rice and House in conference]: He said the cablegram to Sir Edward Grey, which we composed together, September 20, was being considered by his Government and they were discussing it with the Allies. When I pushed him, he admitted that perhaps it would be some time before we heard from it. I gathered that they intend doing nothing until what they consider a propitious time, and then they will use it as a means of beginning peace conversations. I could see that Sir Cecil was thoroughly of the opinion that Germany should be badly punished before peace was made. There was something of resentment and almost vindictiveness in his attitude. He said to forgive Germany now and to make peace, was similar to forgiving a bully and making peace with him after he had knocked you down and trampled upon you pretty much to his satisfaction.'

III

From the American Ambassadors in London and Berlin, House received confirmation of the fact that both sides were determined to carry the conflict to a finish. Mr. Page sympathized entirely with the popular point of view in England, which at that time saw no way of ending German militarism without annihilating Germany in the political sense. House did not agree, but maintained then and always that German militarism had failed at the battle of the Marne and that the only sure way to resuscitate it was to threaten the German people with political destruction and force them to accept a military dictatorship.

Mr. Page's letters displayed at times a prescience and, again, a surprising misreading of the future.

Ambassador W. H. Page to Colonel House

LONDON, *September* 15, 1914

DEAR HOUSE:

... You needn't fool yourself; they are going to knock Germany out, and nothing will be allowed to stand in their way. And unless the German navy comes out and gets smashed pretty soon, it will be a longer war than most persons have thought. It'll be fought to a finish, too. Pray God, don't let ... the Peace Old-Women get the notion afloat that we can or ought to stop it before the Kaiser is put out of business. That would be playing directly into Bernstorff's hands. Civilization must be rescued. Well, there's no chance for it till German militarism is dead....

Yours heartily

W. H. P.

LONDON, *September* 22, 1914

MY DEAR HOUSE:

... 'The war will begin next spring' — so said Kitchener yesterday. And probably that's true. The French will do all they can till cold weather comes, and the Russians will smash Austria. Then in the spring the English will go in with a million and a half fresh men and get the fox's tail. That's what Wellington did at Waterloo. That's the English way. — Look at their diplomatic management. Of course the war is really between Germany and England; but England made sure that Russia and France were both in before she went in. Germany has only Austria to help her. Italy failed, and Austria is already whipped. — Grey and Kitchener are too much for them.[1]

In fact the blindest great force in this world to-day is the Prussian war party — blind and stupid. Well, the most weary man in London just this hour is

Your humble servant

W. H. P.

but he'll be all right in the morning.

LONDON, *November* 9, 1914

MY DEAR HOUSE:

... Peace? I fear not for a very long time. The Germans feel as the woman feels whose letter I enclose. Their Gov't *can't* stop so long as the people feel so and so long as it has

[1] These statements do not do justice to the Ambassador's historical knowledge or his prophetic instincts.

food and powder and men. The English can't stop till the Germans are willing to reinstate Belgium and to pay for its awful rape. — Yet, I pray Heaven, I am mistaken; for the sheer awfulness of this thing passes belief. We say to one another, Rockefeller is worth 400 or 500 or 1000 millions of dollars. That means nothing: it is too big. If a man be worth $100,000, or half-a-million, or a million, or even ten millions, we can comprehend it. So, when I say that perhaps 3,000,000 men have been killed — that means nothing. We have no experience to measure it by. Hence this unbelievable courage goes on. . . . We have lost our common human bearings, and all the old measurements of things are thrown away, and we have no new measurements; we are simply dazed. . . .

Yours heartily

W. H. P.

The Ambassador's estimate of the killed was exaggerated, but his conclusion is of poignant interest, for it suggests the soul of the tragedy, Europe helpless to prevent the war in the first place, equally helpless to stop it: 'simply dazed.'

In Germany as in England, the only feeling was that of the necessity of endurance. The German people, like all the belligerents, regarded the war as one of self-defence. 'Their principal concern,' so ran a letter written from Leipzig by an American correspondent in August, 'is that America shall understand that they resisted war as long as they could do so with honor. My association with all kinds of Germans bears out their assertion that war was undesired. The general belief among them that they were forced into it by Russia, is perfectly sincere.'

With this consciousness, it was hopeless to expect from them a willingness to make sacrifices in order to secure peace. Even in the midst of their suffering, the Germans were buoyed up by the feeling that they fought for a sacred cause.

Countess von Moltke to Colonel House

CREISAU (SCHLESIEN), *October* 7, 1914

DEAR MR. HOUSE,

I have so often thought of your remark to me in Berlin in May: 'Europe is in a dangerous state.' How dangerous I never realized; I wonder if you did? The present state of affairs seems like a bad dream; one can hardly realize that this embittered struggle is a fact. . . .

Only one great value has this war brought with it to us in Germany at least — all that was best and noblest in the nation has risen to the surface; materialism, luxury and selfishness have slipped from us, and each one of us feels that we are better men and women than before. But it is a hard price to pay.

My husband is away fighting like every one else. The spirit among the troops is very sober but most confident. Every one, even the Social Democrats, feels that Germany did not want war, that therefore they are absolutely right in defending their country, and they all have unbounded confidence in those in command, in their ability and trustworthiness. . . .

Our only consolation is that we in Germany are making the best possible use of its lessons and growing morally in an astonishing way. Germany is being new-born, but the travail is heart-breaking. . . .

Yours very sincerely

DOROTHY MOLTKE

Ambassador Gerard to Colonel House

BERLIN, *November*, 1914

MY DEAR COLONEL:

. . . I had a long talk with the Chancellor to-day, who sent for me as he was here a few days from the Front. He says he sees no chance of peace now. Germany is much worked up over Americans selling munitions of war to France and England. Also over the condition of German prisoners in other countries, particularly Russia. The hate here against England is phenomenal — actual odes of *hate* are recited in the music halls. The people are still determined, and seem to be beating the Russians in spite of reports from the Allied press. On the French Front there is nothing to report. The Reichstag voted another large credit and then adjourned. Only Liebknecht objected, and since then his own party has reproved him. Life seems perfectly normal here and provisions are only slightly higher. Women send their only sons of fifteen to fight, and no mourning is worn and it is etiquette to congratulate a family who has lost a son on the battle-field.

The losses to date here alone are 4500 officers and 83,000 men killed — about 280,000 wounded and about 100,000 prisoners. Not great, by any means, out of a possible twelve millions. The finances are in perfect order and the country can continue the war indefinitely — a war which is taken quite coolly by the people at large.

We still have lots of work. I have been especially engaged in getting cotton in and chemicals and dyestuffs out. We have to have cyanide to keep our mines going and dyestuffs to keep endless industries, and the Germans know this and want to use this as a club to force us to send cotton and wool in. So they only let us have about a month's supply at a time. Also they fear lest we should re-sell to the English. . . .

My job is made harder by these sales of munitions by U.S.A. to France and England and by the articles and caricatures in American papers; but I still seem O.K. with the Government, and the Kaiser has intimated he wants me to visit him at the Front. . . .

Yours ever

J. W. Gerard

House realized acutely that it would not do to press the Allies unduly for a categoric response to the suggestion of parleys which he had sent to Grey through Spring-Rice. Such pressure might easily be construed as a move to save Germany from the defeat which many optimists believed would be inflicted upon her in the spring. The Colonel himself wanted to see Germany sufficiently beaten so that the issue of militarism would be settled for all time to come.

But he felt strongly that unless some beginning were made toward peace in the early winter, the most favorable opportunity would be lost. For the moment, military movements had reached a deadlock. In the spring each side would see the chance of victory and would refuse conversations until they had tried out their new armies. The end of the autumn was necessarily the psychological moment for negotiations.

There was at least one German who, in his belief that his country was headed toward destruction and could be saved only by an early peace, labored incessantly to begin negotiations. This was Count von Bernstorff. The distrust which his early career had awakened in the British was perhaps not entirely unmerited; yet the record of the following months was to prove the complete sincerity of his efforts for peace and for the preservation of friendly relations between Germany and the United States. House had been prejudiced against him and was never able to negotiate with him on the basis of complete frankness he used with the British. But he ended by admitting both the ability and the essential honesty of the German Ambassador.

IV

It may have been diplomatic wiles, it may have been self-deception; at all events, Bernstorff reiterated the willingness of Berlin to make terms that would satisfy the British. Perhaps his Government was willing to let Bernstorff make promises, and repudiate him at their convenience. Certainly a letter which House received from Zimmermann in December did not indicate clearly any change of the official German heart, although there was a hint that, if the other side made advances, Germany might not be unreasonable.

Herr Zimmermann to Colonel House

BERLIN, *December* 3, 1914

MY DEAR COLONEL:

Please pardon me for allowing so much time to elapse before answering your letter of September 5th which was besides long delayed in reaching me. I read what you wrote with great interest, but it seems to me that considering the turn events have taken so far and the apparently unabated zeal of our opponents, the question of mediation has not yet reached the stage for action.

When I say 'unabated zeal of our opponents' I have in mind such utterances as appeared for instance in the London correspondences of the New York *Sun* of October 9th and the New York *Tribune* of October 16, announcing that 'to no voice of the kind (i.e., mediation) will England, France or Russia now listen.'

On the other hand, you are fully aware of the fact that we have greatly appreciated the President's and your own good offices. You may be perfectly sure that the President's offer of mediation was received exactly in the spirit in which it was meant and that it was not for a moment considered an empty one.

Germany has always desired to maintain peace, as she proves by a record of more than forty years. The war has been forced upon us by our enemies and they are carrying it on by summoning all the forces at their disposal, including Japanese and other colored races. This makes it impossible for us to take the first step towards making peace. The situation might be different if such overtures came from the other side.

I do not know whether your efforts have been extended in that direction and whether they have found a willing ear.

But as long as you kindly offer your services in a most unselfish way, agreeing to act upon any suggestion that I convey to you, so it seems to me worth while trying to see where the land lies in the other camp.

Needless to say, your communications will always be welcome and considered confidential. . . .

Sincerely yours

ZIMMERMANN

Bernstorff insisted that if House would come to Germany, he would find the Berlin Government entirely reasonable. The two had lunch together in Washington in mid-December.

'*December* 17, 1914: We took up the question of European peace proposals [recorded House]. I informed him of the President's decision to leave the matter to me; that is, as to the proper time and as to the question of procedure. He said there would be no objections from his Government; that it would not be necessary to go to Germany first; that if I could get the Allies to consent to parleys, I would find the Germans willing. I replied that there was no use taking it up with the Allies excepting upon a basis of evacuation and indemnity of Belgium and drastic disarmament which might ensure permanent peace. He thought there would be no obstacle in that direction.

'I congratulated him upon this position, and thought it would have a fine effect and would show it was not Germany's fault if peace parleys were not started. I asked him to confirm this by cabling to his Government. He has maintained that he has no means of communication with his Government excepting through our State Department; but I said, "Of course I know that you can communicate with your Government when you desire, for any intelligent man can see that it would be impossible, under modern conditions, to prevent this." He then admitted that he could reach them.

'I regard my conversation with Bernstorff as satisfactory, although should actual parleys commence I may have difficulty in holding him to any verbal agreements they may make. However, I kept this misgiving well under cover.'

Three days later, House received the message from the British for which he had waited so long. It was not entirely unequivocal, but it indicated at least that there might be some chance of British consideration of a German offer.

'*December* 20, 1914: At 9.45, Phillips of the State Department telephoned to say the British Ambassador desired to see me in the morning about a matter of importance. I told Phillips I was leaving for New York to-night and to ask the Ambassador to come immediately to his house, and I would be over within five minutes. I excused myself to the President and went to Phillips' and met Spring-Rice. He had word from Sir Edward Grey concerning our peace proposals, and thought it would not be a good thing for the Allies to stand out against a proposal which embraced indemnity to Belgium and a satisfactory plan for disarmament. Sir Edward wished me to know that this was his personal attitude.

'I returned to the White House. The President . . . was much elated and wanted to know whether I could go to Europe as early as the coming Saturday. I stated that I could go at any time. He . . . thought before I left we could button-up our South American matters so as to leave me free. . . .

'*December* 23, 1914: When I met Spring-Rice, he said he had received another cablegram from Sir Edward Grey and, while he was personally agreeable to the suggestion made, he had not yet taken it up with his own Cabinet, much less with the Allies. He felt there would be difficulties with France and Russia, and great difficulty in effecting a plan by which a permanent settlement might be brought about. Sir Cecil wanted to go into a discussion of what such a settlement would entail. It seemed to me footless to undertake such a discussion at this time, for it would probably cover a period of weeks, if not months, even after the Powers had begun parleys. I told him it was not my idea that they should stop fighting, even after conversations began, and that an armistice need not be brought about until at least a tentative understanding as to what would constitute a permanent settlement was well within sight.

'He thought France would probably desire the French part of Lorraine, and he thought Russia would like Constantinople. He wondered if Germany would accede to the former request. I thought that was something to be threshed out later, and that the conversations should begin upon the broad lines of an evacuation and indemnity for Belgium and an arrangement for a permanent settlement of European difficulties, including a reduction of armaments.

'I was surprised to hear him say that the indemnity to Belgium could be arranged, for all the Powers might be willing to share the damages done that brave little nation. I was also surprised to hear him say that he saw signs of what he called "a general funk among the European nations," and he thought perhaps "most of them feared revolutions." . . .

'He could not understand why Germany would consent to peace parleys now when they seemingly were so successful, and he did not believe the German military party or the German people as a whole would permit such conversations being brought to satisfactory conclusions. That was also my opinion, as far as those two elements were concerned; but I thought the Kaiser, the Chancellor, the Foreign Secretary, and their *entourage* knew that the war was already a failure and did not dare take the risk involved, provided they could get out of it whole now. . . .

'Sir Cecil said he would cable Sir Edward Grey to-night and tell him of our conversation, and ask him to feel out the

Allies and let us know as soon as possible whether it was advisable for me to come to London.

'I asked him to explain that we had no disposition to force the issue, but it would be inadvisable to let the Germans have the advantage of having expressed a willingness to begin parleys upon such terms, and then have the Allies refuse. . . .

'Returning to the White House, I found the President anxiously awaiting me. After telling what had passed, we discussed what was best to do regarding Bernstorff, and we came to the conclusion that it would be well to leave him alone until I had heard something direct from the Allies; and then we could put the question squarely up to Bernstorff by telling him I was ready to go to London, but he must not let me go only to find Germany repudiating what he had said.'

V

Until December, Wilson had displayed more enthusiasm than House for the proposed mission to be attempted by the Colonel. House understood the British distrust of German sincerity and partly shared it. He realized more keenly than the President the difficulties involved in persuading war-blinded belligerents that compromise was better than the risk of annihilation. And he sympathized too thoroughly with the Allied point of view to desire a compromise peace, if it meant the continued life of German militarism.

But the crisis in our relations with the British that threatened to result from the dispute over restrictions on neutral trade, added a new factor. If the friendly understanding with the British were broken, there would be no possibility of American mediation. Furthermore, German opinion, which during the early weeks of the war had been friendly, was becoming hostile because of the export of American munitions to the Allied countries. Obviously no further progress toward mediation could be made through the Ambassadors in Washington. If he went abroad, more positive results might be secured from the chiefs of government; and House could at least help to appease the anti-American sentiment that was becoming apparent in all the belligerent nations. He was confirmed in this feeling by messages from Gerard and Sir Edward Grey.

Ambassador Gerard to Colonel House

BERLIN, *December* 29, 1914

MY DEAR COLONEL:

... Thanks for the 'tip' about the German ladies (American-born) who write home about this Embassy.[1] One is doubtless a Frau von ——, who threatened me (and in *writing*) that she would complain to the President because we would not accept her invitation to dinner or invite her here. As a matter of fact, we declined her invitations because we were tired, and would have invited her here in time were it not for her extraordinary outburst; and now, of course, we cannot be sand-bagged or black-jacked or blackmailed into inviting any one — and, anyway, the 'hand of Douglas is his own.' ...

Prospects of peace seem very dim. But in about three months more, the plain people in every land are going to be very sick of the business and then, unless one side has some startling success (which *all* hope for in the spring), Peace will come, grudgingly, slowly; and we hope to see you here in the rôle of the Angel thereof.

The Germans are a little irritated just now at our sale of munitions to the Allies. Also because of an extraordinary order that 'American Ambassador shall not inspect or visit prisons, camps, etc.,' issued by State Department; and they naturally feel that we cannot protect their interests in

[1] House had warned Gerard, as he had Page, to be careful not to express unneutral feeling. Complaints had come to Washington that the American Embassy in Berlin was anti-German. It is interesting to compare Gerard's placid reception of the warning with Mr. Page's reaction as related in the preceding chapter.

France, England, and Russia without such inspection. Also, they are quite 'sore' because Chandler Anderson from our Embassy in London was allowed to come here and inspect places where English were confined, but when we (and this was an express condition of allowing Anderson here) sought to send some one from here to look at English camps, we were met by this order (see my long cable to Department). Have been working hard getting cotton in and dyestuffs out.

The Emperor has been sick for a few days, but neither I nor any one else saw him. They say he is quite angry at Americans over the sale of arms, but I don't think he would shut up Krupps' factory if we were at war with Japan, and during the Spanish War many munitions from Germany found their way to Spain. There is no doubt, however, that a real neutrality would stop the sale, but would our people 'stand' for such a curtailment of American industry? . . .

Sincerely yours

J. W. G.

BERLIN, *January* 20, 1915

MY DEAR COLONEL:

Hope you can read my writing; but, as most of my stenographers are doubtless in the pay of the Foreign Office, it is safer than typewriting. . . .

Great talk in the newspapers and many anonymous letters, etc., coming here about sale of arms by U.S.A. to Allies. But you never could satisfy the Germans unless we joined them in war, gave them all our money and our clothes and the U.S.A. into the bargain. Besides, it would be unneutral to change the rules after the game had commenced, and, anyway, the German Government has not protested. Germany sold arms to Spain in 1898 and to Russia in the Russo-Japanese War, and to Huerta when we were having trouble with him; and, in any event, as I have said, we cannot satisfy the Germans. They write many articles accusing the President of being against Germany and say that Secretary Bryan is unneutral because his son-in-law is a British officer. . . .

In the meantime, however, I seem to be getting through most of the matters I have in hand, in spite of the unpopularity of Americans. Why was an order sent me from the State Department telling me not to visit or inspect the camps of British prisoners here? [1] That is the only way I can get good treatment for the prisoners. Is it because Page in London doesn't want to visit the camps in England? The Spanish Ambassador visits the camps of the French and Russian prisoners, and it is considered an essential part of the duty of an Ambassador who takes over the interests of another country to inspect personally or by members of the Embassy. Hundreds of poor devils have died already from neglect, which I might have prevented. Germany makes no pretense of keeping the Hague Convention about the treatment of prisoners. I buy clothes (with funds from English Government) for these prisoners — many of whom, captured in August, have only summer clothes, no change of underwear, and are alive with vermin. The food given is not sufficient and the officers are subjected to petty annoyances to make them revolt and get in fights with officers of their allies. In some camps the commanders are gentlemen as well as officers, and these annoyances do not occur.

If business lets up a little, I shall try to see the Emperor soon at the front and report how he feels. Every one here still confident, and the organization is so wonderful I don't see how they can lose. They will soon undoubtedly try to blockade England with submarines and attack the ports with Zeppelins as soon as the weather is more favorable. Zimmermann is still in charge of Foreign Office, as von

[1] The order was rescinded and Ambassador Gerard was permitted to inspect the prison camps.

Jagow is at the front. I get on very well with Zimmermann. . . .

Best wishes to Mrs. House from us both.

Ever yours

James W. Gerard

German antagonism toward the United States, combined with confidence in military victory, would not facilitate a plan for American mediation. Still more disheartening was a message from Sir Edward Grey passed on to House by the British Ambassador in Washington. Grey stated frankly that the British were disappointed by the attitude of the United States Government and were inclined to be suspicious of the motives that actuated President Wilson.

Sir Edward Grey to Ambassador Spring-Rice

January 22, 1915

Your message received.

It will give me great pleasure to see him [House] and talk to him freely. Of course, he understands that all that can be promised here is that if Germany seriously and sincerely desires peace, I will consult our friends as to what terms of peace are acceptable.

Before, however, setting out on his journey, it is as well that he should be informed as to the state of public opinion here. I fear it is becoming unfavorably and deeply impressed by the trend of action taken by the United States Government and by its attitude towards Great Britain. What is felt here is that while Germany deliberately planned a war of pure aggression, has occupied and devastated large districts in Russia, Belgium, and France, inflicting great misery and wrong on innocent populations, the only act on record on the part of the United States is a protest singling out Great Britain as the only Power whose conduct is worthy of reproach. . . .

At the beginning of the war there was, no doubt, a distinct and purely American sentiment which was stirred by the wrong done to Belgium and which approved of our action in going into war. This feeling was no doubt genuine and widespread and founded rather on ideals of conduct than on race, history, or language. But we feel that the Germans regard themselves as partisans, that they work actively in America as everywhere else by all means in their power, for the success in Europe of the German arms, and that they aim one way or another at making their influence felt in the press, in business, and in every branch of the Government. Upon their action and upon the success which has attended it so far, Germany founds hopes that the attitude of the United States Government will be increasingly disadvantageous to the Allies and, it may be added, more especially to Great Britain. . . .

I can hardly believe that such a policy is deliberately desired by any but the German-Americans in the United States. There is, however, an impression in Europe that there is a danger of the United States Government insensibly drifting into such a policy. If this apprehension is realized, then there can be no hope of a speedy conclusion of the war. Germany will not relax her hold on Belgium; and as for Great Britain, not to speak of the Allies, she cannot give up the restoration of Belgium unless and until she has exhausted all her resources and has herself shared Belgium's fate.

This is what people here are beginning to feel, and I should like him [House] to know it. The feeling has not yet found widespread public expression, but it is there and it is growing. In the struggle for existence in which this country is at stake, much store is set in England on the good will of the United States; and people cannot believe that the United States desires to paralyze the advantage which we derive from our sea power, while leaving intact to Germany those military and scientific advantages which are special to her.

I think it is only fair that he should be warned that should people in England come to believe that the dominant influence in United States politics is German, it would tend to create an untoward state of public opinion which we should greatly regret.

The above is purely personal and must be so regarded; but I think it is my duty under the circumstances to give this personal and friendly warning as to the probable trend of public sentiment.

E. Grey

British opinion, as expressed by Grey, of the official attitude assumed by the United States, was to a large degree unjustified and rested more upon emotion than upon fact. If the only protests raised by America had been directed against the British, this was because the only flagrant interference with American neutral rights, thus far, proceeded from the application of the British Orders in Council. British fear of German intrigues that might influence the policy of the United States was without foundation. If it was true that the German-Americans were agitating for an embargo upon munitions of war, it was equally true that the Government steadfastly refused to permit the embargo; thus the United States had not merely asserted their neutral rights of export as against the demands of Germany and German-Americans, and incidentally incurred German ill will, but at the same time supplied what Grey himself termed the 'need of the Allies.'

These facts were evidently not clearly appreciated by the British Government or people. There was all the more reason for sending to England some one capable of emphasizing them and explaining the American point of view.

Early in January, House decided to make the venture.

VI

'*January* 12, 1915: I took the 12.08 for Washington. I found Samuel Huston Thompson of the Department of Justice, and H. C. Wallace on the train. At Baltimore, Davies and Harris, Director of the Census, met me; so, altogether, I had no rest.

'McAdoo and Grayson were at the station to meet me. After I had dressed for dinner, I went into the President's study; and in a few minutes he came in. We had exactly twelve minutes' conversation before dinner, and during those twelve minutes it was decided that I should go to Europe on January 30. I had practically decided before I came to Washington that this was necessary, and I was certain, when I gave my thoughts to the President, he would agree with me it was the best thing to do.

'I thought we had done all we could do with the Ambassadors at Washington, and that we were now travelling in a circle. It was time to deal directly with the principals. I had a feeling we were losing ground and were not in as close touch with the Allies as we had been, and that it was essential to take the matter up directly with London and afterward with Berlin.

'There were no visitors for dinner. After dinner the President read from A. G. Gardiner's sketches of prominent men until half-past eight, when Senator La Follette came. When he left, the President resumed his reading. I was surprised that he preferred to do this rather than discuss the matters of importance we had between us. He evidently had confidence in my doing the work I came to Washington for, without his help.[1] . . .

'*January* 13, 1915: After breakfast this morning the President and I strolled from the elevator to his study, in which

[1] The primary reason for this trip to Washington was to confer with Naon, da Gama, and Suarez upon the Pan-American Pact, for House was at this time carrying on a three-ring circus of negotiations.

time I told him of my plans for the day; that is, I should see the South American Ambassadors, the British Ambassador, and Mr. Bryan. I considered it important for us to decide what reason to give Spring-Rice for my going over. I thought it was best to tell him I wanted to try out the Germans, and the President said, "Of course, if you stop over in London and see the British Government in the meantime, that would be expected and could not offend the sensibilities of the British Ambassador."

'I met Spring-Rice at Phillips' at 10.45. I found him in rather a sulky mood. He began to talk about this country's attitude toward the Allies, and indicated that the Allies would not receive the good offices of the President cordially. I soon got him in a good humor by telling him what a wonderful thing it would be to have the United States throw its great moral strength in behalf of a permanent settlement, and it was my purpose not to discuss terms with Germany so much as to discuss a plan which would ensure permanent peace.

'He thought this fine, and said I had hit the nail on the head. I told him how strongly the President felt upon obtaining a permanent settlement, and that it was not his intention to suggest any cessation of fighting until this condition had been agreed to by all the belligerents. He approved this programme, and thought if I explained it to Sir Edward Grey when I went to London, he would cordially approve. He wanted me to talk to the Russian and French Ambassadors and tell them of my purpose, as they might take offence at not being called into conference. My judgment was, not to see them; but I yielded to his advice. We agreed that we should all meet at Phillips' at four o'clock. . . .

'I was the first to arrive, then came Spring-Rice and, later, Jusserand and Bakhmetieff [the French and Russian Ambassadors]. I had asked Sir Cecil to inform the other two Ambassadors of our conversation in the morning and to get them into a receptive frame of mind. He evidently had not done so, and he was not particularly nice in helping me out. It was rather awkward at first. Both Jusserand and Bakhmetieff were violent in their denunciation of the Germans and evinced a total lack of belief in their sincerity. They thought my mission would be entirely fruitless.

'Later, I brought them around to the view that at least it would be well worth while to find how utterly unreliable and treacherous the Germans were, by exposing their false pretenses of peace to the world. That suited them better, and it was not a great while before we were all making merry and they were offering me every facility to meet the heads of their Governments. I found them somewhat sensitive about my going to London and Berlin; each thought Petrograd and Paris should also be visited. I agreed to this, but made a mental reservation that it would be late in the spring before I could get as far as Russia. . . .

'I gave Mr. Bryan a summary of my day's work with the European Ambassadors and of what the President desired me to do. He was distinctly disappointed when he heard I was to go to Europe as the peace emissary. He said he had planned to do this himself. . . .

'I replied that the President thought it would be unwise for any one to do this officially, and that his going would attract a great deal of attention and people would wonder why he was there. . . .

'He was generous enough to say that, if he did not go in an official way, I was the one best fitted to go in an unofficial way. . . .

'The President and I got down to work. We agreed upon a code to be used between us in sending cable messages while I am abroad. I thought he should write me a letter of instructions — something that I need not let go out of my hands, but which I might show in the event it was necessary for me to go to countries where I was not well known.

'Together we outlined what this letter should contain, and he is to send me a draft of it in a day or two for me to look over and make suggestions which seem pertinent. He said he would write it himself on his little typewriter, so that not even his confidential stenographer would know of it. . . .

'*January* 14, 1915: Count von Bernstorff called at 2.30. We had an interesting and satisfactory talk, and he expressed pleasure that I was going to Europe so soon and said he would notify his Government at once. I told him frankly of my meeting with the Allied Ambassadors yesterday, and that none of them thought the Germans were sincere in their desire for peace. . . .

'I suggested he advise his Government not to make useless and sensational raids upon England by Zeppelins or otherwise, for they could do nothing effective from a military standpoint and would merely destroy non-combatants, and that such raids would have a very bad effect upon my endeavors. . . .

'*January* 20, 1915: I asked the German Ambassador to come to see me this morning at twelve. . . .

'I asked him again, for the love of Heaven, to stop his people from killing non-combatants in England by dropping bombs. The attempt yesterday upon Sandringham, had it been successful, would have made impossible any discussion of peace. He promised to send this view to his Government, although he could not promise definite results, for the reason that the military and not the civil authorities dominated. He is to inform his Government of my expectation to be in Berlin soon after the middle of next month.'

VII

House returned to New York for his final preparations. He had many affairs to wind up, for besides the negotiations he had been conducting with the European diplomats regarding the possibility of mediation, and with the South

Americans regarding the Pan-American Pact, he had also on his hands many details of local politics which, with his continued residence in New York, were gently steered in his direction. He did not expect to remain long in Europe. As matters turned out, he stayed there for nearly six months.

Nothing illustrates so exactly the President's purpose in sending him abroad as the letter of credentials which House was to carry. In this letter Wilson emphasizes the fact that House was representing not an official attempt at mediation, but merely the desire of the President to serve as a channel for confidential communication through which the belligerent nations might exchange views with regard to terms upon which the present conflict might be ended and future conflicts rendered less likely. He disclaimed himself any desire to indicate terms or to play the part of judge, but merely that of the disinterested friend who had nothing at stake except interest in the peace of the world.

European despatches which at the last moment the President forwarded to House, gave cause for both hope and anxiety. The temper of the Germans was not reassuring. The British were likely to be reasonable, but they must always reckon with the territorial ambitions of France and Russia, which would prove a stumbling-block to a peace based on the *status quo ante.*

Ambassador W. H. Page to Secretary Bryan

London, *January* 15, 1915

I lunched to-day with General French [1] who came here secretly for a council of war. He talked, of course, in profound confidence.

He says the military situation is a stalemate. The Germans cannot get to Paris or to Calais. On the other hand, it will take the Allies a year, perhaps two years, and an incal-

[1] Commander-in-Chief of the B.E.F.

culable loss of men, to drive the Germans through Belgium. It would take perhaps four years and an unlimited number of men to invade Germany. He has little confidence in the ability of Russian aid in conquest of Germany. Russia has whipped Austria and will whip Turkey, but he hopes for little more from her.

Speaking only for himself and in the profoundest confidence, he told me of a peace proposal which he said the President, at Germany's request, has submitted to England. He tells me that this proposal is to end the war on condition that Germany gives up Belgium and pays for its restoration. French's personal opinion is that England would have to accept such an offer if it should be accompanied with additional offers to satisfy the other allies, such, for example, as the restoration to France of Alsace-Lorraine and the agreement that Russia shall have Constantinople. . . .

American Ambassador, London

Ambassador Gerard to the President

BERLIN, *January* 24, 1915

I do not think that the people in America realize how excited the Germans have become on the question of selling munitions of war by Americans to the Allies. A veritable campaign of hate has been commenced against America and Americans. . . .

Zimmermann showed me a long list, evidently obtained by an effective spy system, of orders placed with American concerns by the Allies. He said that perhaps it was as well to have the whole world against Germany, and that in case of trouble there were five hundred thousand trained Germans in America who would join the Irish and start a revolution. I thought at first he was joking, but he was actually serious. The fact that our six army observers are still here in Germany and not sent to the front is a noteworthy indication. Zimmermann's talk was largely ridiculous, and, impossible as it seems to us, it would not surprise me to see this maddened nation-in-arms go to lengths however extreme.

GERARD

VIII

Before sailing, House spent another twenty-four hours in Washington, partly to make final arrangements, chiefly to have the pleasure of personal farewell with the President, who at no time in his career showed himself more appreciative of the Colonel's efforts.

'*January* 24, 1915: I left to-day on the 12.08 for Washington. There was no one I knew on the train and I had a quiet and restful trip. Dr. Grayson met me in a White House car. The President was waiting for me and we immediately began to work and remained at it continuously for more than an hour, delaying dinner ten or fifteen minutes, which is a most unusual thing for the President to do....

'He insisted upon arranging for my expenses abroad and for those of my secretary, Miss Denton. I let him know how trustworthy she was, so he would not think me indiscreet in writing through her about matters of an important and confidential nature. He asked me to tell Sir Edward Grey his entire mind, so he would know what his intentions were about everything.... He said, "Let him know that while you are abroad, I expect to act directly through you and to eliminate all intermediaries."

'He approved all I had in mind to say to Sir Edward and to the Germans. He said, "There is not much for us to talk over, for the reason we are both of the same mind and it is not necessary to go into details with you."

'I asked if it would be possible for him to come over to Europe in the event a peace conference could be arranged and in the event he was invited to preside over the conference. He thought it would be well to do this and that the American people would desire it.[1] . . .

'*January* 25, 1915: I went to Phillips' at ten o'clock to meet the British Ambassador. He seemed pleased that I was holding to my intention to leave on Saturday. I again requested that he arrange with Sir Edward Grey, by cable, an engagement immediately upon my arrival. He said Sir Edward left Saturday afternoons and did not return until Monday morning, but, if I thought best, he knew Sir Edward would remain in town. I did not consider this necessary, for my boat would probably get in Saturday and I would not be in London until Sunday; therefore Monday would be time enough. He is cabling Sir Edward to ask me for lunch on Monday.

'Spring-Rice talked optimistically one minute, and pessimistically the next, absolutely contradicting himself. . . . He warned me that I should probably encounter sentiment in England hostile to my mission, based upon the belief that it was possibly actuated by a desire to help Germany. He said there was a party there which would seize upon any excuse for an early peace, and that they resembled the "Copperheads" of the North during our Civil War. I replied that he need not worry about my giving them comfort. . . .

'Phillips explained the arrangements he had made concerning money for my expenses. I dislike taking money even for them. I have never been paid by either a state or national Government for my services, and, while I am not being paid for them now, I have heretofore paid my expenses. I do not feel able to meet the expenses of such a trip as this, and it lifts a load from me to have the Government pay them. It was agreed that $4000 should be placed to my credit at once. I have a feeling this will last for six months. . . .

'It then came time to say good-bye. The President's eyes

[1] As events developed, when it came to the actual decision in the autumn of 1918 Colonel House did not favor Wilson's going to Europe.

were moist when he said his last words of farewell. He said: "Your unselfish and intelligent friendship has meant much to me," and he expressed his gratitude again and again, calling me his "most trusted friend." He declared I was the only one in all the world to whom he could open his entire mind.

'I asked if he remembered the first day we met, some three and a half years ago. He replied, "Yes, but we had known one another always, and merely came in touch then, for our purposes and thoughts were as one." I told him how much he had been to me; how I had tried all my life to find some one with whom I could work out the things I had so deeply at heart, and I had begun to despair, believing my life would be more or less a failure, when he came into it, giving me the opportunity for which I had been longing.

'He insisted upon going to the station with me. He got out of the car and walked through the station and to the ticket office, and then to the train itself, refusing to leave until I entered the car. It is a joy to work for such an appreciative friend.'

CHAPTER XII

A QUEST FOR PEACE

If every belligerent nation had a Sir Edward Grey at the head of its affairs, there would be no war....

Extract from Diary of Colonel House, February 7, 1915

I

On January 30, 1915, Colonel House sailed from New York upon the *Lusitania*. It was one of the last of her voyages. For House it was one of the first of the adventurous missions in which he attempted to translate into fact his doctrine that a new code of international ethics must be impressed upon the nations by demanding from Governments the same standard of morals as that which applies to individuals. This doctrine had proved the soul of his first mission of the year before, the Great Adventure, when he tried to bring about an understanding between the European states which would prevent the war he foresaw. He kept it constantly in mind as he approached the war zone in this attempt to discover some means by which a path to peace could be blazed and bases of permanent peace be laid.

House left with no trace of overconfidence. The emotions aroused in Europe were of such intensity that no well-informed person could be hopeful of finding a pacific opening; and the Colonel was extremely well-informed. The complexities were such that the least *gaucherie* would produce an 'incident' that might not merely ruin the influence of the United States, but even endanger her friendly relations with a belligerent Power. For this reason, if for no other, the mission must be unofficial. Mr. Bryan had told the Colonel that he was the one best fitted for the task. 'I hope he may be right,' wrote House, 'for I am leaving with much trepidation. The undertaking is so great, and the difficulties are so many, that to do it alone and practically without consultation or help from any one, is as much of a task as even I, with all my willingness to assume responsibility, desire.'

However difficult and delicate, Colonel House regarded the attempt as necessary. No matter how slight the chance of peace, that chance should be pursued upon every occasion. Europe was caught in a horror from which she could not rescue herself; if an outsider could help, the duty was imperative. Furthermore, as the war proceeded, feeling in the belligerent countries turned against the neutrals and especially the greatest neutral, the United States. 'He that is not with me is against me.' No one was better fitted than House to explain the motives of the United States Government, for he was the closest friend of the President.

Whatever the Colonel's trepidation, and a brave man always confesses nervousness, he must have been heartened by the confidence of a man who had watched him in the political crises of Texas for thirty years, the captain of Rangers, Bill McDonald.

Captain W. J. McDonald to Colonel House

DALLAS, TEXAS, *February* 6, 1915

MY DEAR ED:

... If I could have seen you before you left for Europe, I would have tried my utmost to persuade you not to take this trip on account of the waters being mined as well as other dangerous conditions in that Country. Don't suppose it would have done any good, though, after you decided to go, as you and I are very much alike when we make up our minds to go against anything. I am not certain of your mission there, but am sure you will make a success as you generally do when you take hold.

Wishing you a pleasant time and a safe return to Texas, I am

As ever yours

W. J. MCDONALD

In view of the tragic fate of the *Lusitania* three months later, the voyage of House in February holds some sentimental interest.

'*February* 5, 1915: Our voyage has about come to a close. The first two days we had summer seas, but just after passing the Banks a gale came shrieking down from Labrador and it looked as if we might perish. I have never witnessed so great a storm at sea. It lasted for twenty-four hours, and the *Lusitania*, big as she is, tossed about like a cork in the rapids.

'This afternoon, as we approached the Irish coast, the American flag was raised. It created much excitement, and comment and speculation ranged in every direction. . . .

'*February* 6, 1915: I found from Mr. Beresford, Lord Decies' brother, who crossed with us, that Captain Dow had been greatly alarmed the night before and had asked him, Beresford, to remain with him on the bridge all night. He expected to be torpedoed, and that was the reason for raising the American flag. I can see many possible complications arising from this incident. Every newspaper in London has asked me about it, but, fortunately, I was not an eye-witness to it and have been able to say that I only knew it from hearsay.

'The alarm of the Captain for the safety of his boat caused him to map out a complete programme for the saving of passengers, the launching of lifeboats, etc., etc. He told Beresford if the boilers were not struck by the torpedoes, the boat could remain afloat for at least an hour, and in that time he would endeavor to save the passengers.

'Ambassador Page met us upon our arrival. So also did the representatives of nearly every New York paper. They wished to know when they might have a talk with me. I told them they could do so then, for I would tell them as much as I would later — which would be nothing at all.'

Colonel House had all the advantage of being already upon intimate terms with the British statesmen, so that he need not waste time in preliminaries. Characteristically, however, he waited until he learned the essentials of the European situation as the British saw them, before he suggested the possibility of peace negotiations. And always he gave the impression of one who came to discover methods rather than as a meddler with an *idée fixe.*

Colonel House to the President

London, *February* 9, 1915

Dear Governor:

We arrived here Saturday afternoon, and I immediately arranged a private conference with Grey for eleven o'clock Sunday morning. We talked steadily for two hours and then he insisted upon my remaining for lunch, so I did not leave until two-thirty.

We discussed the situation as frankly as you and I would have done in Washington, and, as far as I could judge, there was no reservation. He said several times, 'I am thinking aloud, so do not take what I say as final, but merely as a means of reasoning the whole subject out with you.'

I gave him your book, which pleased him, and he regretted that the only thing he could give you in return was a book he had written on angling.

We went into every phase of the situation, he telling me frankly the position the Allies were in, their difficulties, their resources, and their expectations. That part of it is not as encouraging as I had hoped, particularly in regard to Italy and Rumania. There is no danger of their going with Germany, but there is considerable doubt whether they will go with the Allies. Germany's success has made them timid and there is also difficulty in regard to Bulgaria. Up to now it has been impossible to harmonize the differences between Bulgaria and Serbia. Germany is making tremendous efforts at present to impress Italy and Rumania to keep them from participating. If the differences between Bulgaria and Serbia could be adjusted, Rumania would come in at once and so probably would Greece; but they are afraid to do so as long as Bulgaria is not satisfied.

The difficulty with Russia is not one of men, but of transportation. They have not adequately provided for this, while Germany has to the smallest detail. It prevents them from putting at the front and maintaining more than one and one half million to two million men.

The most interesting part of the discussion was what the final terms of settlement might be and how the difficult question of armaments could be adjusted. . . .

He went into the discussion of what Russia and France would demand. I told him if France insisted upon Alsace-Lorraine, I would suggest that a counter-proposition should be made to neutralize them in some such way as Luxembourg now is. This would prevent the two [France and Germany] from touching anywhere and they could only get at one another by sea.[1] He thought that Russia might be satisfied with Constantinople, and we discussed that in some detail.

I let him know that your only interest was in bringing them together and that you had no desire to suggest terms, and that what I was saying was merely my personal view, expressed to him in confidence and as between friends.

There was one thing Grey was fairly insistent upon, and that was that we should come into some general guaranty for world-wide peace. I evaded this by suggesting that a separate convention should be participated in by all neutrals as well as the present belligerents, which should lay down the principles upon which civilized warfare should in the future be conducted. In other words, it would merely be the assembling at The Hague and the adopting of rules governing

[1] Compare the demilitarized zone finally arranged in 1925.

the game. He did not accept this as our full duty, but we passed on to other things. . . .

I am making a point to influence opinion over here favorably to you and to America. There has been considerable criticism of us, and I was told that at a public meeting the other day, when the name of the United States was mentioned, there was some hissing. I find, though, that intelligent people over here are wholly satisfied with your course. I took tea yesterday with one of the editorial writers of the *Times* and dined with the Managing Editor last night. To-night I dine with our friend, A. G. Gardiner. I shall write you about that later.

Affectionately yours

E. M. House

In a separate memorandum, Colonel House noted:

'When we had finished talking, Sir Edward smiled and said, "Here I am helping to direct the affairs of a nation at war, and yet I have been talking for three and a half hours like a neutral." . . .

'I put questions to him with great rapidity, so as to find what difficulties were necessary to overcome. He answered with the utmost candor, telling me the whole story as he would to a member of his own Government. It was an extraordinary conversation, and I feel complimented beyond measure that he has such confidence in my discretion and integrity.

'I have many times expressed my high regard for the character of Sir Edward Grey, but I wish to reiterate it here. If every belligerent nation had a Sir Edward Grey at the head of its affairs, there would be no war; and if there were war, it would soon be ended upon lines broad enough to satisfy any excepting the prejudiced and selfish.'

The conversation is significant, not merely because it indicates the embarrassment which the territorial aspirations of France and Russia then and always caused the British, but also because of Grey's suggestion that the United States should coöperate at the end of the war in a general organization designed to guarantee peace. Even more significant was the reiteration by House of his earlier plan, providing for a scheme of limiting armaments and a guaranty of territorial integrity.

The two men who sat discussing these questions before and after lunch, were destined to play a large part in the creation of the League of Nations. Grey from the very beginning of the war insisted that it might have been prevented if the conference he had proposed had been accepted by Germany; he never wavered in his conviction that until some international mechanism were established capable of providing a permanent international conference, the world would not be safe from the menace of war. Through Colonel House the conviction was ultimately impressed upon President Wilson and was finally translated into the Covenant of the League. And in the drafting of that Covenant the ideas and the diplomacy of Colonel House became of the utmost importance.

II

Colonel House arrived in England at the moment that Germany embarked upon a momentous course, which still more envenomed the feeling between the belligerents and intensified the difficulties of his mission. The military events of the autumn had disarranged German plans, for the surprising speed of the Russian mobilization, the success of the Russian invasion of Austrian Galicia, and the incursion into East Prussia compelled Germany to make a counter-attack in the East at the moment when the Germans had hoped to concentrate their main force upon the defeat of France. Hindenburg triumphantly drove the Russians out of East

Prussia, but his attack on Russian Poland failed. In order to rob the Russians of further offensive power, it seemed necessary to carry through the conquest of Poland and to liberate Galicia. This attack upon the Russian armies was the more important in that negotiations for an Austro-Italian settlement were not proceeding smoothly and there appeared imminent danger that Italy might join the Allies. To meet this new enemy, Austria must be freed from the threat of Russian attacks.

If Germany mobilized her main strength in the East, she would be unable to push a vigorous offensive against the French and British in the West. But here she possessed one great advantage, a superiority of munitions, and upon this she counted. It was vital that Great Britain, slow in the production of her own munitions, should not be permitted to import them from America, which always refused to lay an embargo. Hence Germany's determination to utilize the submarine.

Taking as a pretext the British restrictions upon the entrance of foodstuffs into Germany, a new departure which the Germans regarded as worthy of retaliation, they proclaimed a 'war zone' around the British Isles to take effect upon February 18, 1915. After that date, they threatened, German submarines would destroy any enemy merchant ship in this zone, without regard for the safety of the passengers or crews of the vessels attacked. They warned neutral shipping of the peril that would attend entrance into the war zone, since mistakes might occur, especially if belligerent ships continued the practice of raising neutral flags.

The response of the American Government was prompt and definite. It warned Great Britain of the peril inherent in the unauthorized use of the American flag. In more solemn phrases it warned Germany that if submarines should 'destroy on the high seas an American vessel or the lives of American citizens, it would be difficult for the Government of the United States to view the act in any other light than as an indefensible violation of neutral rights. . . . The Government of the United States would be constrained to hold the Imperial German Government to a strict accountability for such acts of their naval authorities and to take any steps it might be necessary to take to safeguard American lives and property and to secure to American citizens the full enjoyment of their acknowledged rights on the high seas.'

These new developments complicated House's mission, but did not alter his underlying purpose, which was to proceed to Berlin after his conversations with the British, provided he received a direct intimation that the Germans would receive him. The Colonel refused to go to Germany unless invited. At Washington, Bernstorff kept insisting that his Government wanted House and through him would express their desire for a 'reasonable' peace. On February 13, Wilson cabled House that he was stimulating German interest in peace through Bernstorff, who was confident that a letter of invitation was on the way.

House spent long hours almost daily with the officials of the Foreign Office, for he realized that a complete understanding was necessary both as regards trade disputes and the possibility of peace discussions. His proposed trip to Germany would be fruitless unless the British approved. He was anxious also to discuss the bases upon which a permanent world peace could be founded, something beyond the ending of the war and a settlement of the territorial aspirations of the warring states.

'*February* 10, 1915: I lunched with our Ambassador [the Colonel recorded] to meet Sir Edward Grey and Sir William Tyrrell. I wish I could give in detail every word of the conversation, for it was freighted with importance. We discussed at length the question of whether Germany was in earnest about beginning peace parleys. I maintained that she was, and that she was sparring for advantage; that she desired me to come on Bernstorff's invitation, unsolicited by the Government, in order that they might say, in the event negotiations failed, that they had never been a party to them.

'Sir Edward thought the Germans were not ready for parleys, but were fencing for the purpose of getting the Allies at a disadvantage so that they might say to Ferdinand of Bulgaria and others that the Allies were making overtures for peace. I took the view that, while it was doubtful whether the military party was yet ready for peace, I felt certain the Kaiser and his *entourage* were.

'Sir Edward said he had told Delcassé, French Minister for Foreign Affairs, of my visit and of our conversations of Sunday. Delcassé thought that the Allies had not yet achieved sufficient military success to begin negotiations, and he believes with Sir Edward that the Germans are insincere.

'Among other things, Grey told me that the British Ambassador [Sir Francis Bertie] at Paris had sent him a despatch advising him of my presence in London and suggesting that he get in touch with me. This amused us all very much.

'Grey and I did practically all the talking, Page and Tyrrell joining in every now and then. We went over some of the ground we had covered Sunday, regarding a permanent settlement, and Sir Edward reverted to his view that our Government should be a party to the making of peace. Much to my surprise, Page thought this would be possible and advisable. I told Sir Edward more directly than I did on Sunday that we could not do so; that it was not only the unwritten law of our country but also our fixed policy, not to become involved in European affairs.[1]

[1] House was evidently uncertain of Wilson's willingness to become entangled in European politics and realized the national prejudice against such entanglements. The covenant he proposed would not involve the United States in any purely European problems. Our participation in the war, naturally, altered his opinion as to the necessity of participating in a peace conference.

Photograph from Underwood & Underwood

SIR WILLIAM TYRRELL

'Tyrrell said we had not always followed this policy, reciting the Algeciras incident. Page also cited the Perry and Morocco Pirates incident. I held, nevertheless, that it would be impossible and that all we could do would be to join the neutrals and belligerents in a separate convention after the peace covenant was drawn up and signed by the belligerents. I told Grey that it would be impossible for our Government to take part in such questions as what should become of Alsace-Lorraine and Constantinople, and that we could not be a party to the making of the actual terms of peace, which this first convention must necessarily cover. I felt sure, though, that our Government would be willing to join all nations in setting forth clearly the rights of belligerents in the future and agreeing upon rules of warfare that would take away much of the horror of war.

'I suggested that this covenant should forbid the killing of non-combatants by aircraft, the violation of neutral territory, and the setting forth of certain lanes of safety at sea in order that shipping of all countries, both belligerent and neutral, would not be subject to attack when they were in those lanes.

'Sir Edward amended this latter suggestion by saying he thought Great Britain would be willing to agree that all merchant shipping of whatever nature, belligerent or neutral, would be immune. I accepted the amendment and was pleased to know that Great Britain stood ready to go so far.

'*February* 11, 1915: I lunched with Sir William Tyrrell today and we had a most interesting conversation. He spoke with entire frankness. . . .

'Tyrrell believed that in the convention I suggested yesterday, if an agreement should be made between all the Powers, neutral and belligerent, to establish rules governing future warfare, Great Britain would consent to the absolute freedom of merchantmen of all nations to sail the seas in time of war unmolested. This was brought out in our conference yesterday, but Tyrrell developed in his conversation to-day that Great Britain recognized that the submarine had changed the status of maritime warfare and in the future Great Britain would be better protected by such a policy than she has been in the past by maintaining an overwhelming navy.'[1]

The conversations were significant, for this is the germ of the idea soon to be developed by House, which he later termed the 'Freedom of the Seas.' As Grey and Tyrrell realized, the practical application of the idea would be of immense value to Great Britain, an island depending for its life upon the continuity of its merchant trade. But House saw that the Germans, blockaded as they were and also largely dependent upon overseas trade, would be attracted by it. It might serve as the beginning of negotiations.

The fact which must touch the sense of humor of the historian is that the 'Freedom of the Seas,' later so bitterly opposed by the British and regarded generally as a German trick, was first suggested by the British Foreign Office as a means of furthering British interests.

III

On February 12, House received the invitation from the Germans for which he had been waiting. It was not entirely satisfactory, for Zimmermann demurred at the suggestion of an indemnity for Belgium, but it gave the opening if the Colonel thought best to use it.

Herr Zimmermann to Colonel House

BERLIN, *February* 4, 1915

MY DEAR COLONEL:

. . . I read with interest what you were good enough to write with reference to the desired interchange of opinion.

[1] Grey had already advocated this policy in his instructions to the British Delegation to the Second Hague Conference, 1907.

While we are quite ready, as I wrote you before, to do our share to bring about the desired termination of the war, at the same time there are certain limits which we are unable to overstep.

What you suggest concerning the paying of an indemnity to Belgium seems hardly feasible to me. Our campaign in that country has cost the German nation such infinite sacrifices of human lives that anything in the form of such a decided yielding to the wishes of our opponents would cause the most bitter feeling among our people.

I heard that you are on your way to England at this moment and that a trip to Germany is in view. I shall be most happy to see you, should you carry out your intention, and shall hope for a personal interview more satisfactory than is possible through correspondence by letter.

With kindest regards, I am

My dear Colonel

Sincerely yours

Zimmermann

'*February* 13, 1915: I lunched alone with Sir Edward Grey [recorded House] at 33 Eccleston Square, which, by the way, he leases from Winston Churchill. We had a very simple lunch and I made it a point not to talk business while we were at the table. We talked of nature, solitude, Wordsworth.... He told of Roosevelt's visit with him in the New Forest and how it occurred. Roosevelt sent him word he would like very much to hear the song-birds of England, and Sir Edward undertook to gratify this wish. He said they heard forty-one distinct voices, no one of which Roosevelt recognized excepting the golden-crested wren, which I believe we also have in America.

'In speaking of Wordsworth, I asked if he went often to the English lake district. He replied that he had never been, that his country home was so much more attractive to him than any other place on earth that when he had time he always went there. He is the least travelled man of prominence I have ever known.

'When we went to the library, I showed him Zimmermann's letter and we discussed it long and carefully. I thought it was up to him and to me to decide when to begin negotiations for peace. As far as I was concerned, I did not want them to begin one moment before the time was ripe for a peace that would justify the sacrifices of the brave who had already given their lives, for it was even better for others to die if the right settlement could be brought about in no other way. On the other hand, neither of us would want to sacrifice one single life uselessly; and if we could accomplish now the desired result, we should do it.

'We went over the entire ground and discussed it in this spirit. I had a feeling that the sooner I went, the better — for our relations with Germany were growing worse, and soon I might not be welcome. I was afraid some foolish or wanton outrage, either by air or sea, might be committed which would so set opinion against Germany as to make it impossible for his Government to begin any discussion.

'We sat by the fire in his library, facing one another, discussing every phase of the situation with a single mind and purpose. He had information that Germany was starting an enveloping movement upon the Russian front with a view of impressing the Balkan States and, if she was successful in this, it might be that Bulgaria would come into the war — not, perhaps, against Great Britain or Russia, but against Serbia, which would be much the same thing.

'He told me of the plan to convey English troops to Salonika and to take them that way into Serbia. He thought if as many as 200,000 British troops could be safely taken there, Greece would gladly join the Allies. He did not think it fair to Greece to let her come into the war without some protection. The difficulty, he explained, was the maintenance of the troops after they were there, since only a single-track railway ran into Serbia.

'He said they had never tried to influence Holland to come into the war, for they had not been able to send sufficient troops there to protect her from an invasion in the event she declared war on Germany. He thought if Germany succeeded in the present enveloping movement [in the East], she would then turn to the West and again try to break through the lines and reach Paris.

'In conclusion, he did not think it wise for me to undertake a peace mission to Germany until after this enveloping movement had either succeeded or failed, for he did not believe the civil Government would be able to do anything in the direction of peace until von Hindenburg and the other military men had tried out their different campaigns.

'It was finally agreed that we should defer a decision until after I had lunched with the Prime Minister on Wednesday. He had told none of the Cabinet about our conversations, but he had made notes and it was his purpose to discuss them with the Prime Minister and no one else at present. . . .

'*February* 14, 1915: Sir Edward Grey told me yesterday that when this war was over, he intended to retire for a year and rest. I advised retiring permanently, for he would probably have taken so great a part in this European conflict, that to do anything else afterward would be like a great artist going out in his back yard and painting the fence. He . . . looked at me wide-eyed and serious.'

Colonel House to the President

LONDON, *February* 15, 1915

DEAR GOVERNOR:

. . . I am still undecided as to what to do about Berlin. The difficulties are these: This Government [the British] has to be extremely careful about giving us any encouragement whatever. They do not dare say what they actually feel, not only because it might make England's position misunderstood in Germany, but also because it would meet with a storm of disapproval here, for the reason that no one believes that anything like the kind of terms that England will demand will be met now.

As a matter of fact, there is no feeling whatever, excepting among a very small circle, for anything out of the war excepting a permanent settlement, evacuation, and indemnity to Belgium; but no one believes that Germany is ready for such terms.

Germany, on the other hand, is now controlled almost wholly by the militarists. There is a peace party there as there is here, and both, strangely enough, are conducting the civil Governments. Those here are much more powerful to act than those in Germany, where I believe they have but little power. As long as the military forces of Germany are successful as now, the militarists will not permit any suggestion of peace. . . .

I am formulating in my own mind, and am unravelling it from time to time to Grey and others in authority, to see how far it is feasible, a plan for a general convention of all neutral and belligerent nations of the world, at which you will be called upon to preside and which should be called upon your invitation.

It could meet concurrently with the peace conference, or, if peace is not in sight by August, it could then be called and it might be used as a medium of bringing about peace between the belligerents. This second convention, of course, would not deal with any of the controversies between the belligerents, but it would go into the rules of future warfare and the rights of neutrals.

It would be of far-reaching consequence — more far-reaching, in fact, than the peace conference itself. . . .

Affectionately yours

E. M. House

As a result of his conference with Grey and Asquith, House decided that the trip to Germany should be postponed, at least for a few weeks. The Colonel would reply to Zimmermann in such a way that, if Berlin were really serious, the door could be kept open. A message from Gerard, urging immediate action, did not change this decision, since it was plain that the Germans thought they were winning the war and Gerard himself found it difficult not to agree with them. So long as they were in this frame of mind, negotiations would be fruitless, for the Germans would merely utilize conversations for diplomatic purposes, without any real intention of making peace.

Colonel House to Herr Zimmermann

LONDON, *February* 17, 1915

MY DEAR HERR ZIMMERMANN:

Thank you for your kind letter of February fourth.

I thought I should be able to go to Berlin early next week, but it now seems best to remain here until I can have another word from you.

All of our conversations with the Ambassadors in Washington representing the belligerent nations were based upon the supposition that Germany would consent to evacuate and indemnify Belgium and would be willing to make a settlement looking towards permanent peace.

I can readily understand the difficulty which your Government would encounter in regard to an indemnity; therefore, if that question might for the moment be waived, may we assume that your Government would let the other two points mark the beginning of conversations?

If we could be placed in so fortunate a position, I feel confident that parleys could at least be commenced.

I need not tell you, Sir, what great moral advantage this position would give Germany, and how expectantly the neutral nations would look towards the Allies that they would meet so fair an attitude.

Your favorable reply to this will, I believe, mark the beginning of the end of this unhappy conflict.

I am, my dear Herr Zimmermann

Sincerely yours

E. M. HOUSE

Ambassador Gerard to Colonel House

BERLIN, *February* 15, 1915

MY DEAR COLONEL:

I received your letter from London. I saw Zimmermann also. He told me he had written you saying they would be glad to see you, etc., which is, of course, all they can do.

It is felt here that we are partial to England.

They are serious here about this submarine blockade, but are willing to withdraw it if food and raw materials are allowed to enter — in other words, if England will adopt either the Declaration of London or of Paris — but they say they will not stand having their civil population starved.

Make no mistake, they will win on land and probably get a separate peace from Russia, then get the same from France or overwhelm it, and put a large force in Egypt, and perhaps completely blockade England.

Germany will make no peace proposals, but I am sure if a reasonable peace is proposed *now* (a matter of days, even hours), it would be accepted. (This on *my* authority.)

The Allies should send a peace proposal or an offer to talk peace, to me *verbally and secretly here.* If it is accepted, all right; if not, no harm done, or publicity for the proposal — for I would only make it *in case I learned it would be accepted.* But Germany will pay no indemnity to Belgium or any one else. But, as I told you, this peace matter is a question almost of hours. The submarine blockade once begun, a feeling will come about which may make it impossible until after another phase of the war. If you can get such an intimation from the Allies and then come here, it will go, to the best of my belief. I do not think the Kaiser ever actually wanted the war.

The feeling, as I said, just now is very tense against America. The sale of arms is at the bottom, and the fact that we stand things from England that we would not from Germany (according to the Germans) is the cause. But it is very real and makes us all very uncomfortable.

Hope to see you soon.

Yours ever

James W. Gerard

P.S. I am sure of acceptance of proposal.

Colonel House to Ambassador Gerard

London, *March* 1, 1915

My dear Judge:

. . . These are slow-moving people [the British], and when I undertook to tell them of your opinion that quick action was necessary and it was a question of hours rather than days, I saw that it was hopeless. Of course, though, this is inevitable no matter how fast they wished to move, for the reason that they cannot act alone; and it takes an incredible time to get any satisfactory communication with the Allies, especially with Russia.

I see no insuperable obstacle in the way of peace and I feel if the belligerents would begin to talk, they might soon come to an agreement.

The army and navy machine here is now under a tremendous momentum and your prediction as to the final outcome is not shared by any one here, from the highest to the lowest. If this war lasts six months longer, England will have a navy that will be more than equal to the combined navies of the world. That is something for us Americans to think of; in fact, it is something for everybody to think of. . . .

Faithfully yours

E. M. House

Colonel House to the President

LONDON, *February* 18, 1915

DEAR GOVERNOR:

. . . I had a conference with Sir Edward Grey last Tuesday evening, and again yesterday at which the Prime Minister and Page were present.

Both Asquith and Grey thought it would be footless for me to go to Berlin until the present German enveloping movement in the east is determined. It looks, for the moment, bad for the Russians; and they do not want me to be in Berlin at such a time. If this movement fails and things get again deadlocked, they think I should take that opportunity to go there. . . .

I put the matter plainly to both Asquith and Sir Edward, asking their advice as to what to do, telling them we were all interested alike in bringing about the desired result, and it was a question of how best to do it. They accepted this position and Sir Edward thought, at the moment, I should write to Zimmermann along the lines that I did.

The idea was that unless they at least conceded these two points,[1] the matter had as well be dropped until they were willing to do so.

Sir Edward said that England would continue the war indefinitely unless these cardinal points were agreed to. . . .

I told them at yesterday's conference that it would not do to close the door too tightly, for we must leave it ajar so it could be widely opened if Germany really desired peace. Asquith smiled and said, 'You will be a very clever man if you can do that successfully.'

The situation grows hourly worse because of the German manifesto in regard to merchantmen [2] and the sowing of

[1] Evacuation of invaded territory and guaranties for permanent peace.

[2] On the day on which this letter was written, the German threat of February 4 was to come into effect: that every enemy merchant ship found in the war zone would be destroyed 'without its being always possible to avert the dangers threatening the crews and passengers.'

mines. I tried hard to get Sir Edward, and afterwards Asquith, to meet this situation before to-day; but with the usual British slowness, they put it off until Thursday or perhaps next Tuesday.

The psychological time to have ended this war was around the end of November or the first of December, when everything looked as if it had gotten into a permanent deadlock. You will remember we tried to impress this upon Sir Cecil and tried to get quicker action, but without success. . . .

Affectionately yours

E. M. House

'*February* 18, 1915: I went to 33 Eccleston Square at 7.30 to see Sir Edward Grey and was with him a half-hour. I handed him Gerard's letter and also one from Penfield. . . .

'Sir Edward talked as frankly as usual and said the terms Gerard proposed would only be entertained by Great Britain in the event all the things he predicted would happen, had already happened; that is, that Russia and France were completely beaten and Egypt and other British territory occupied by the enemy.

'I again urged upon him better coördination between the eastern and western fronts. He did not think this possible, because of the Russian governmental system. It seems to me perfect folly not to work more in harmony; that is, when the Germans are attacking in the east, they should be severely pressed in the west, and *vice versa*. . . .

'*February* 20, 1915: I called on Sir Edward Grey at 33 Eccleston Square at 7.15. Lord Kitchener was with him when I arrived, but he left within a few minutes.

'Sir Edward said that the Allies intended forcing the Dardanelles and that perhaps it would take them three or four weeks.[1] This is not only a spectacular movement, but, if suc-

[1] 'It is interesting to note how far afield this prophecy was.' [Note by E. M. H.]

cessful, will have far-reaching effect upon the Eastern situation, besides giving Russia an outlet and inlet. He also told me that Kitchener said his reports from Russia were that the Germans had not captured more than one division, and the situation in the East was nothing like as bad as represented. Sir Edward qualified this, however, by saying that Russian news was never quite reliable. He thought after matters had quieted down upon the Eastern front and a deadlock had once more been arrived at, and the Dardanelles had been forced, it would be well for me to go to Germany.'

Colonel House to the President

London, *February* 23, 1915

Dear Governor:

In reply to your cablegram of the 20th, indicating that you thought there was danger of my yielding too far to the wishes of this Government in deferring my visit to Berlin, I tried to give you some explanation in my reply which I sent yesterday.

Up to now, all we know is that Germany refuses to indemnify Belgium and refuses to make any proposition herself. She may or may not be willing to evacuate Belgium and consider proposals looking to permanent peace. But even if she concedes these two cardinal points, it is well to remember that neither Russia nor France is willing now to make peace on any such terms.

When the Russian Minister of Finance and the French Minister for Foreign Affairs were here, Sir Edward told them of your letter and of my presence. He also told them what I thought might be accomplished now and he asked them whether or not they would like to have a conference with me. They both preferred not doing so, stating that the time was not opportune for peace proposals, for the reason that it was certain that Germany, being so far successful, would not acquiesce in such terms as their Governments would demand.

The British public and a majority of the Cabinet would not look with any greater favor upon the only terms that Germany would now concede, than would France and Russia.

Since the war has begun and since they consider that Germany was the aggressor and is the exponent of militarism, they are determined not to cease fighting until there is no hope of victory, or until Germany is ready to concede what they consider a fair and permanent settlement.

It is almost as important to us to have the settlement laid upon the right foundations as it is to the nations of Europe. If this war does not end militarism, then the future is full of trouble for us.

If there was any reason to believe that Germany was ready to make such terms as the Allies are ready to accept, then it would be well to go immediately; but all our information is to the contrary and the result of my visit there now would be to lose the sympathetic interest which England, and through her the Allies, now feel in your endeavors and without accomplishing any good in Germany.

You may put it down as a certainty that Germany will only use you in the event it suits her purposes to do so; and she will not be deterred from this if at any time she sees that it is to her advantage to accept your good offices.

Asquith told Page yesterday that he sincerely hoped that I would not make the mistake of going just now. That simply means, if I do go they will probably cease to consider you as a medium.

If Zimmermann replies to my letter, then I shall go to Berlin and have a conference with him; but it will accomplish nothing for the moment, for he will not now go further; and the Allies will not be willing to begin parleys upon such a basis.

Sir Edward is extremely anxious for England to take the highest possible grounds and not ask for anything excepting the evacuation and indemnifying of Belgium and a settlement that will ensure permanent peace. But, there again, he comes in conflict with colonial opinion. The South African colonies have no notion of giving up German Africa which they have taken, as they say it will be a constant menace to them to have so powerful and warlike a neighbor.

The same applies to . . . the Caroline Islands, Samoa, etc., which the Australians have taken.

Sir Edward is trying assiduously to work up an opinion upon broader lines, and he may or may not be successful; but he is not now in a position to say that his wishes will prevail. . . .

Germany may be successful. If France or Russia gives way, she will soon dominate the Continent; and it is not altogether written that one or the other will not give way. Even if the Allies hold together, there is a possibility that the war may continue another year. . . .

I try very hard not to think of it any more than I did at home, and I try to talk of it as little as possible, so that my mind may be clear to look at the situation dispassionately.

The one sane, big figure here is Sir Edward Grey; and the chances are all in favor of his being the dominant personality when the final settlement comes, and I believe it is the part of wisdom to continue to keep in as close and sympathetic touch with him as now. . . .

I note now with interest that occasionally Sir Edward speaks of 'that second convention which the President may call.' He has come to look upon it as one of the hopes for the future and, if we accomplish nothing else, you will be able to do the most important world's work within sight.

I have reason to believe that this Government will be ready to make great concessions in that convention in regard to the future of shipping, commerce, etc., during periods of war.[1] It is my purpose to keep this 'up my sleeve' and, when

[1] Another reference to the plan of the 'Freedom of the Seas.'

I go to Germany, use it to bring favorable opinion to you by intimating that I believe when the end comes you will insist upon this being done; in other words, that with your initiative and with Germany's coöperation, Great Britain can be induced to make these terms. This, I think, will please the Germans and may go a long way towards placating their feelings toward us. . . . .

Affectionately yours

E. M. House

IV

As one might expect, Colonel House took care to come into contact with every one who might give information or assistance in his mission of good will: politicians of all parties and shades of opinion, men of business, journalists.

'*February* 14, 1915: I lunched with Lady Paget, and in the afternoon Sidney Brooks took tea with me. He said there was much curiosity in London as to the purpose of my visit, and he had explained that my trousers had worn out earlier this year than usual and I had come to have Poole renew them. He asked me seriously if I desired anything said of my visit or whether I wished the *Times* to comment at all upon Anglo-American relations. I asked him to please say nothing for the moment. He said the *Times* was at my disposal whenever I wished to use it for the purpose of my mission, whatever that mission was. . . .

'*February* 20, 1915: I went to the Embassy and found Hoover discussing with Page the difficulties he is encountering from day to day in his Belgian relief work. He is a resourceful fellow and needs to be, for he has a most complex situation to contend with, having the German, the Belgian, and British Governments at cross-purposes. . . .

'*February* 25, 1915: I lunched with Lord Bryce to-day at

his apartment at No. 3 Buckingham Gate. We had a most delightful time. He arranged for us to be entirely alone, not even Lady Bryce being there.

'He inquired after the President, and I told of the President's having read me Gardiner's sketch of him in "Pillars of Society," the opening sentence of which I remember was: "If one were asked to name the greatest living Englishman I think it would be necessary to admit, regretfully, that he is a Scotsman born in Ireland."

'Bryce smiled and said he had not read it, and was afraid to do so for fear his head might be turned; at the same time, I noticed he asked me again the title of the book.

'We gradually drifted into a discussion of the war and of the problems for its solution. It seemed to me a good opportunity to test the wisdom of my views upon so clear and subtle a political mind; and I told him forthwith, though in strict confidence, pretty much what I had planned. This embraced, of course, the proposition regarding the cessation of the manufacture of armaments for a period of years, the calling of the second convention by the President, and its scope and character.

'Bryce was visibly interested. I told him, too, what I had tried to do toward preventing the war, at least between the Western Powers. He was as interested in this as in the other, and agreed that it might have been possible if war had been deferred a short while longer. He had also heard that Great Britain and Germany were on the eve of a settlement concerning the Bagdad Railroad and a division of the sphere of influence in Africa. This convention was yet to be signed when the war burst forth. . . .'

Colonel House to the President

LONDON, *March* 1, 1915

DEAR GOVERNOR:

The King's Private Secretary, the Lord Stamfordham, called yesterday to bring an invitation to me from the King to call at eleven o'clock for a private audience. I was curious to know what he wanted.

I was with him for nearly an hour. He is the most bellicose Englishman that I have so far met. I had hopes that he might want to talk concerning peace plans, but he evidently wanted to impress me with the fact that this was no time to talk peace. His idea seemed to be that the best way to obtain permanent peace was to knock all the fight out of the Germans, and stamp on them for a while until they wanted peace and more of it than any other nation.

He spoke kindly of the Germans as a whole, but for his dear cousin and his military *entourage*, he denounced them in good sailor-like terms. He is the most pugnacious monarch that is loose in these parts.

He told me a good deal about the navy and its operations and also of what they hoped to do on land. He seemed more certain than any one I have met that France and Russia would stick to the last man. He said what would happen to Germany when the French got in there, if they ever did, would be a plenty; and he said his cousin, the Czar, had written him that Russia was aflame from one end to the other and was determined to win if they had to put in the field twenty million men.

As for England, he said she was sending the flower of the nation to the front and that the world would be forced to acknowledge, before the spring and summer were over, that her army was equal to her best tradition.

He spoke of our relations and expressed the greatest gratification that we were on such good terms. He said the hope of the world lay in their continuance.

He asked me to convey to you his most respectful compliments and assurances of distinguished consideration.

Some one had evidently given him a glimpse of your character, for he voiced almost all I said of you before I could say it myself. . . .

Affectionately yours

E. M. HOUSE

Colonel House asked the King why he did not take occasion to speak to the British public in the forceful manner in which he had talked to him regarding the war and war measures. He replied, House recorded, 'that he did not do so for the reason that his distinguished cousin, the Kaiser, had talked so much and had made such a fool of himself that he had a distaste for that kind of publicity. Then, too, he added, this was a different sort of monarchy and he did not desire to intrude himself in such matters.'

Colonel House to Mr. Gordon Auchincloss

LONDON, *March* 2, 1915

DEAR GORDON:

. . . I am lunching and dining with some one of importance every day. On Tuesday I go into the Conservative camp further than I have yet done, by dining to meet Balfour, Lord Curzon, and several others. . . .

4 U's [1] and I keep in constant communication by cable; but so far as I can see, my main object now must be to mark time and not offend by overdoing. . . .

Unless one has undertaken such a job himself — and there has been none like it up to now — he cannot possibly imagine the pitfalls that lurk on every hand. It keeps one sidestepping every moment; and if I succeed in doing nothing more than keeping out of trouble, I shall consider I have been fortunate.

[1] An obvious representation of W. W.

I have succeeded in keeping my name absolutely out of the European press, which is a good beginning, and I remain in as much obscurity as is possible for one having such work in hand. No one, of course, not even Page, knows when I see the different Ministers or personages of importance; and my comings and goings are as unchronicled as if I were a crossing-sweeper.

Paternally yours

E. M. House

'*March* 4, 1915 [conference between House and A. J. Balfour]: We got along famously together, I doing most of the talking, although at times he would become enthusiastic and would get up and stand by the fire and declaim to me just as earnestly as I had to him. I took a liking to him at once, and have a sincere desire that it should be reciprocated. I like the quality of his mind. It is not possible to allow one's wits to lag when one is in active discussion with him. In that respect, he reminds me somewhat of the President. I am inclined to rank him along with the President and Mr. Asquith in intellectuality, and this, to my mind, places him at the summit.'

Colonel House to Mr. Gordon Auchincloss

London, *March* 5, 1915

Dear Gordon:

... I have seen almost every Liberal of importance in the Kingdom, and for the past week I have devoted myself to the Conservatives, as it will be very helpful, not only to the Government, but to me individually in the final negotiations.

Balfour was very complimentary in regard to the suggestions I have made, and said they were unique and practicable as far as he could see at the moment.

I have seen for a long while that the limiting of armaments was the insuperable obstacle in the way of a permanent settlement, and I have not been able to think of a way that was satisfactory to me until I was on the *Lusitania* with my mind free to devote to the subject. It then occurred to me that if all the important nations, belligerents and neutrals, should agree to cease the manufacture of munitions of war for a period of ten years or more, the question then of how large an army Germany should have, or France should retain, or the size of Germany's or Great Britain's navy, need not be discussed.[1]

The armies and the navies would remain as they are at the end of the war; but without the manufacture of any further battleships or munitions of war, everything would automatically become obsolete in a few years. What we need to do is to play for time. Time will make Germany democratic and there will be no more danger in that direction than from the United States, England, or France. Russia is another problem, which may or may not have to be dealt with in the future.

This plan would involve the shutting-down of Krupps' and of Armstrong's and other manufacturers, and it would leave the world at the end of ten years on a peace footing. The money that it would save to each nation every year would be sufficient to pay the interest on the great war debts that they are piling up.

All this, of course, is not to be mentioned except to Sidney and Martin,[2] from whom I keep nothing. . . .

Paternally yours

E. M. House

'*March* 5, 1915: Sidney Brooks called in the afternoon. He was on his way to the Foreign Office to offer his services in an effort to present the British side of questions arising be-

[1] The proposal is obviously based upon the assumption of a military stalemate, which at that time seemed probable to House.

[2] Dr. Sidney Mezes, and Mr. E. S. Martin, editor of *Life*.

tween the United States and Great Britain. He hopes to be able to do better work than has been done. He said up to now the Foreign Office had done it as badly as human ingenuity could suggest. He asked if I thought they could have done it worse. I thought not, and Brooks seemed pleased at this tribute to their efforts. . . .

'Chalmers Roberts and I took supper at Scot's. Afterward I went to the Ambassador's, as he wished to show me Colonel George O. Squier's diary, which he said I must keep in the deepest confidence. It embarrassed me to have to tell him that I had had a copy of the diary for more than two weeks.

'We talked of home, of the President, McAdoo, and conditions, and we had a genuinely good time. I like Page. He is direct and without guile. . . .

'*March* 8, 1915: I dined with Lord Loreburn. John Burns was the only other guest. They are both sane, reasonable, able men, and we talked of the war and of the jingoes and of the difficulties of peace. I told them of the demands of France and of those of South Africa concerning the German African colonies. Burns thought the latter could be met, but considered those of France more serious. . . .

'*March* 9, 1915: We dined with Lady Paget. She had a notable gathering. The other guests were Lord Curzon, Mr. A. J. Balfour, Sir John Cowan, Mr. Cust (who will be Lord Brownley), Lord and Lady Desborough (Lady-in-waiting to the Queen), Duchess of Marlborough, Mrs. John Astor, and Mrs. George Keppel.

'Curzon and I had considerable talk together when coffee was served, and I found him the worst jingo I have met. He wants to make peace in Berlin no matter how long it takes to get there. He is an able man, expressing himself forcefully and well. We got along agreeably, for he seemed to want to be as pleasant as possible. With that type I seldom or never argue, because our views are too far apart to ever harmonize.

'Balfour has a much more charming personality. I talked to Cust and succeeded in changing his point of view as to the United States. . . .'

Colonel House to the President

LONDON, *March* 8, 1915

DEAR GOVERNOR:

. . . Since I last wrote, I have seen something of the peace party, headed by such men as the recent Lord Chancellor, Lord Loreburn, Mr. Hirst of the *Economist*, and others.

Northcliffe is of the ultra set on the other side. He remarked to one or two friends of mine that if you had sent me over here to discuss peace, I should be run out of England. . . . I mention this to show the extreme difficulties of the situation. Sidney Brooks told me, however, that he had found no one with whom I had talked now antagonistic to our purposes.

I shall find this anti-peace feeling much stronger in Germany among the military party; but if I can get directly at the Kaiser, I hope to be able to make some impression. The great question is, who really controls in Germany? This is something I am afraid I shall have to find out for myself. . . .

Affectionately yours

E. M. HOUSE

V

In the meantime, Grey and House had decided that the moment had arrived for the Colonel to go to Berlin. Messages had come from von Jagow through Washington that the Germans awaited him; and although letters from Zimmermann and Gerard contained no intimation of Germany's willingness to make concessions, it seemed worth while to discover the real situation in Berlin.

Herr Zimmermann to Colonel House

BERLIN, *March* 2, 1915

MY DEAR COLONEL:

Many thanks for your letter of February 17th. I regret to see that you consider giving up your trip to Berlin which I had counted on as offering a much more satisfactory opportunity for an interchange of ideas than has been possible up to now.

I read with interest what you believe to be a possible beginning to the desired end. It seems to me, however, that you are taking as a basis a more or less defeated Germany or one nearly at the end of her resources. It is hardly necessary for me to show in how far this is not the case. Although I can assure you that Germany has the welfare of Belgium very much at heart, still she is not able to forget what a terrific cost was paid for the resistance our men encountered there.

You may be sure, as I said before, that Germany's wish for a permanent peace is as sincere as your own. If England would consent to give up her claim to a monopoly on the seas together with her two-to-one power standard, I think it might be a good beginning.

I remain, my dear Colonel

Sincerely yours

ZIMMERMANN

Ambassador Gerard to Colonel House

BERLIN, *March* 6, 1915

MY DEAR COLONEL:

I hope you are coming here soon. Von Jagow said he hoped you were coming, and while I see no prospect of peace now, you could acquaint yourself with the general situation and be in a better position to talk in the other capitals. . . .

The feeling against America is in abeyance, waiting to see what happens with relation to the latest English declaration about the blockade of Germany. I have as yet no official information.

The Chancellor is not *boss* now. Von Tirpitz and Falkenhayn (Chief of Staff) have more influence, especially as the Chancellor bores the Emperor, and there are great intrigues going on among all these conflicting authorities. The people who were in favor of accepting a reasonable peace proposal were, strange to say, the military general staff end, and it was von Tirpitz who did not want our last proposals accepted.[1] . . .

I hate to write in these spy times and do most earnestly hope you are coming soon, or, if you are going to Italy, I will run down and report to you there if you want. . . .

Ever yours

JAMES W. GERARD

'*March* 7, 1915 [conference with Grey]: We both think the time has come for me to go to Germany. I have decided to go *via* France, and I asked his opinion as to whether I should see Delcassé. At first he thought not. He said Delcassé was decidedly of the opinion, when he was here, that it was no time for peace parleys, and he did not believe he had changed this point of view. I was afraid he would consider it a discourtesy if I did not see him. Looking at it from that viewpoint, Grey thought I was right and it would be best to see him, though he cautioned me to be guarded in what I said. I assured him he need have no fear of my being indiscreet.

'Grey thought France would insist upon Alsace-Lorraine. The French believe the Allies will win and that they can impose terms of peace upon Germany; later, perhaps, they would find that to impose peace conditions upon Germany would necessitate continuing the war for a number of

[1] The United States proposed that Germany should give up the submarine war zone around Great Britain, provided the British relinquished the food blockade.

years and, when that was realized, they might be willing to make concessions.

'He did not know the mind of Russia, but he believed by giving them Constantinople and the Straits, they would be willing to acquiesce in almost any other terms that might be agreed upon....

'The difficulty I expect to find here in the final negotiations is, there is no man who dominates the situation.... In Germany I shall find the situation even more uncertain. If there were a Palmerston or a Chatham here, and a Bismarck in Germany, it would be easier.'

The Quest for Peace had thus far revealed nothing but the unwillingness of any of the belligerents to yield an iota of their aspirations. Yet the mission had not been wasted. House had established relations with the British which not merely helped to tide over the difficulties of the present, but which must prove invaluable in preventing misunderstanding for the future. The memoirs of the British Foreign Secretary indicate how thoroughly the Colonel had succeeded in establishing a sympathetic understanding. 'It was not necessary,' writes Grey, 'to spend much time in putting our case to him. He had a way of saying, "I know it" in a tone and manner that carried conviction both of his sympathy with, and understanding of, what was said to him.' And again: 'Our conversations became almost at once not only friendly but intimate. I found combined in him in a rare degree the qualities of wisdom and sympathy. In the stress of war it was at once a relief, a delight, and an advantage to be able to talk with him freely. His criticism or comment was valuable, his suggestions were fertile, and these were all conveyed with a sympathy that made it pleasant to listen to them. After a day that began about seven in the morning I broke off work by seven in the evening and took things easily at my house for an hour before dinner. It was arranged that in this hour House should come whenever he wanted to have a talk.' [1]

The Colonel's mission would have been worth while if only because of this close personal understanding with the Foreign Secretary, and it was one of the imponderables that weighed heavily in the diplomatic history of the following years.

Appreciative of Grey's honesty and moderation, fearful of the demands of France, suspicious of German sincerity, yet determined if possible to find a thread to throw across the chasm: such were the feelings of House when on March 11 he left England for Paris and Berlin.

[1] Grey, *Twenty-Five Years* (Frederick A. Stokes Company), II, 124.

CHAPTER XIII

THE FREEDOM OF THE SEAS

If peace parleys were begun now upon any terms that would have any chance of acceptance, it would mean the overthrow of this Government and the Kaiser.

Zimmermann to House, March 21, 1915

I

Colonel House to the President

PARIS, *March* 14, 1915

DEAR GOVERNOR:

We arrived here Thursday night. A destroyer accompanied our boat a good part of the way, and we passed one floating mine about one hundred yards away. Otherwise the trip was without incident. . . .

I have just returned from my interview with Delcassè.[1] The interpreter was the Assistant Secretary for Foreign Affairs.[2] I let him read your letter and told him I came to present your compliments, but that you did not desire to intrude yourself upon them or to hurt their sensibilities in any way by making an immature suggestion of peace.

I said this before he had a chance to say anything, for I knew quite well what was in his mind. He was visibly pleased when this suggestion was made, and it placed us on a good footing.

I then told him that you had foreseen for a year or more that, unless something was done to prevent it, some spark

[1] Minister for Foreign Affairs. Théophile Delcassé had been a prime mover in the Entente with Great Britain, and largely responsible for the energetic foreign policy of France from 1904 on. He was the *bête noire* of the Germans, who regarded him as the collaborator of Edward VII and Grey in the attempt to 'encircle' Germany.

[2] Jaquin de Margerie, at that time Director of Political Affairs of the Foreign Office; in the post-war period appointed French Ambassador to Germany.

might cause the present conflagration, and you had sent me to Europe last May for the purpose of seeing what could be done to bring about a better understanding; that I had gone to Germany and had come to France, but they were changing Government at the time and it was impossible to talk to them.

I wanted to let him know that you had had the threads in your hands from the beginning and that you understood the situation thoroughly. . . .

In reply he said that France greatly appreciated your keen interest and noble desire to bring about peace, and he was glad I had come to Paris and would look forward with interest to seeing me when I returned from Germany. He said he would then tell me in the frankest way what France had in mind and was willing to do. I did not press him to tell me this then, because I happened to know what they have in mind and I did not want to go into a footless and discouraging discussion.

I had accomplished more than I anticipated, for it was not certain that I would be received cordially. Even Sir Edward was a little worried. The main thing accomplished was that France has at least tentatively accepted you as mediator; and that, I think, is much. . . .

Gerard tells me, through Winslow, that he does not believe the Germans would hesitate a moment to go to war with us. On the other hand, Winslow says that when you sent them the note to Germany which was almost an ultimatum,[1] he saw a distinct change for the better at the German Foreign Office the very next day. They had been insolent before, but were all right afterwards.

They all seem to think that the Germans have literally gone crazy. I am not so sure of it myself. I can see gleams of sanity in much they are doing.

[1] A reference to Wilson's note of February 10, warning the German Government that in case of the destruction of an American vessel or American lives it would be held to a 'strict accountability.'

I shall be exceedingly careful about cabling you or even writing from Berlin, for it is dangerous to the last degree. Winslow tells me that their system of espionage is something beyond belief and that one can never be sure that papers have not been tampered with.

I find that the ruling class in France do not desire peace, but that a large part of the people and the men in the trenches would welcome it. This, I think, is also true of Germany. . . .

Affectionately yours

E. M. House

P.S. Gerard also sent word that he thought the Kaiser would be deposed in the event Germany was not successful in this contest.

'*March* 14, 1915: Willard Straight called this morning. He is a great friend of Casenave [1] and also of Margerie, and Margerie is a friend of Casenave and Delcassé, so the circle is fairly complete. I told Straight some things I wished told to Delcassé through Casenave and Margerie. This Straight promised to undertake. I wish Delcassé to know that in my opinion France is taking a big gamble in demanding peace terms that Germany will never accept unless the Allies reach Berlin. I am sorry I am not on such terms with Delcassé to tell him these things myself, for I do not like using third parties.

'Straight is to convey the thought that it will be of advantage to the Allies to have the good will of the President, and that the best way to get it is through me. Another idea I wished conveyed was that the really essential thing and the big thing was to strive for a permanent settlement and not for any small territorial advantage, which in itself would leave wounds which in time would lead to further trouble.'

[1] In charge of the Press Bureau at the Foreign Office.

Colonel House to the President

PARIS, *March* 15, 1915

DEAR GOVERNOR:

De Casenave came to see me to-day. He is at the head of the Press Bureau and his principal duties are to see that the French papers contain the proper kind of reading matter in regard to England, America, and other nations. . . .

I asked him to be very frank and to tell me of French opinion. He said the French people at large thought that America had nothing in mind further than a dollar. He said a few Frenchmen had gone to America, had stayed there some weeks, not knowing the language, had visited such places as the pork packeries of Chicago, and had come away to write books concerning the avarice of our people. He said this had been done to such an extent that the opinion was fixed in France that we were guided entirely by mercenary motives.

He said when he gave to the French papers directions as to what to say in regard to America, they smiled and shrugged their shoulders. . . .

I am trying to make a friend of de Margerie of the Foreign Office. He has lived in America, speaks English well, and is said to be almost as much of a force in the Foreign Office as Delcassé, besides being in Delcassé's confidence. I have some mutual friends on this job and I will remain here long enough upon my return to try and clinch it.

I shall attempt the same thing in Germany, probably using Zimmermann as a medium. If I can establish such relations, the situation can scarcely get away from us. . . .

Affectionately yours

E. M. HOUSE

II

All his conversations in Paris merely confirmed the forebodings which House had experienced in England. The aspirations of the French for territorial annexations put out of court immediately the bases for peace which he had discussed with Grey. A message from Gerard indicated that the Germans were equally determined upon wide annexations. 'He was sure,' House noted after receiving the message, 'that they were not in a frame of mind to consider such peace terms as the Allies would think of offering.... The French not only want Alsace and Lorraine, but so much more that the two countries are not within sight of peace. If it is brought about, it will be through the sanity and justice of Sir Edward Grey and British opinion.'

House might have given up his proposed trip to Germany then and there. But he saw the chance of placing German-American relations on a better footing, through personal conversations, and did not wish to lose the opportunity of indicating to the Germans some basis of future compromise with the British. He determined, however, that it would be worse than useless to raise the question of immediate peace parleys in Berlin.

Colonel House to Mr. Gordon Auchincloss

BERLIN, *March* 21, 1915

DEAR GORDON:

We left Paris at eight o'clock Wednesday morning. We went close to the firing line, somewhere between ten and twelve miles. Soldiers boarded the train as we passed through this territory and pulled down all shades and stationed themselves in the corridors so we could not look out. We were within hearing of the guns.

The different Governments are always notified of our coming, before we reach the borders, and every facility has been extended to us. If this were not done, travelling would be practically impossible — that is, where we have gone.

At Basle I had a conference with Minister Stovall from

Berne and Consul-General Wilbur from Zurich, and at Frankfort with Consul-General Harrison.

We arrived in Berlin yesterday morning in a snowstorm. Gerard met us and brought us to his house. I have had a conference with Zimmermann and he was exceedingly cordial and delightful. I have always liked him and I am glad we have resumed our friendly relations.

I cannot write you very fully, excepting to say that there is nothing that even looks like peace within sight. However, I am accomplishing many things that I have in mind and I hope I am doing some good. It looks as if there would have to be a decisive victory on one side or the other before parleys can begin.

If I succeed in establishing cordial relations at the different belligerent capitals, I will have done all that I expected at this time. . . .

Paternally yours

E. M. House

Colonel House to the President

Berlin, *March* 20, 1915

Dear Governor:

. . . We arrived in Berlin this morning and Gerard immediately arranged a private conference for me with Zimmermann. I let him read your letter, which impressed him favorably as it does every one. I told him frankly what I had done in England, whom I had met there, in what way, and my conclusions.

He was surprised to hear of the lack of bitterness in England towards Germany and was equally surprised when I told him that the difficulty was with France. They have evidently tried to cultivate good relations with both France and Russia, for the purpose of making separate terms with them. I think I convinced him that England did not desire Germany crushed and that, in the final analysis, terms would have to be agreed upon between these two countries. This is so patent that I wonder they do not recognize it. It is fortunate it is true, for the difference between the two is not great and they could get together now if it were not for the fact that the people in both Germany and England have been led to expect much more than is possible of realization. Neither Government can fulfil these expectations. If they attempted to make peace upon a different basis from that which the people have been led to believe will ultimately come about, there is a possibility that the Governments would be overthrown. That is the real trouble now. Just how it can be overcome, is the question.

I am trying to get every one to soften down through the press and create a better feeling. Zimmermann tells me that the main thing Germany wants is a settlement which will guarantee permanent peace. It is the same cry in each of the belligerent states.

I showed Zimmermann the different points where our interests and theirs touched, and expressed a desire that we work together to accomplish our purposes. I brought up the second convention [for organizing permanent peace] in this connection, and he received it most cordially. I told him in particular that we as well as Germany desired that some guaranty should be had in the future as to the protection and uninterruption of our commerce, either as neutral or as belligerent. I told him that we recognized England had a perfect right to have a navy sufficient to prevent invasion, but further than that she should not go.

He was exceedingly sympathetic with this thought, and I think it will have a tendency to put us on a good footing here.

The Chancellor is out of town for a few days, but Zimmermann is to arrange a meeting as soon as he returns. He also suggested that the Emperor might want to see me. Gerard says this is impossible, that he has not seen him for months because of his intense feeling against us on account of our shipment of munitions of war to the Allies. It is not important now whether I see him or not, and I shall leave it to Zimmermann's judgment....

I am somewhat at a loss as to what to do next, for it is plain at the moment that some serious reverse will have to be encountered by one or other of the belligerents before any Government will dare propose parleys. I can foresee troublous times ahead, and it will be the wonder of the ages if all the Governments come out of it intact.

The world has been strained as never before in its history, and something is sure to crack somewhere before a great while.

It looks as if our best move just now is to wait until the fissure appears.

Affectionately yours

E. M. House

Berlin, *March* 21, 1915

Dear Governor:

I am gradually getting at the bottom of things here and, while I cannot write with perfect freedom, I can tell enough to give you a fair idea of it.

I am seeing a great many people, just as I did in England, and I hope to have soon a composite picture that may be of value.

I met last night an able and sane man by the name of Dr. Rathenau.[1] I am told he is a great power in commercial Germany. He has such a clear vision of the situation and such a prophetic forecast as to the future that I wonder how many there are in Germany that think like him. It saddened

[1] The dominating figure of the early *post-bellum* German Republic. Foreign Secretary from January 31, 1922, to June 24, 1922; Germany's representative at the Genoa Conference, 1922; assassinated by reactionaries, June 24, 1922.

me to hear him say that as far as he knew, he stood alone. He said he had begun to wonder whether all the rest were really mad, or whether the madness lay within himself. . . .

It was almost pathetic to hear him urge us not to cease in our efforts to bring about peace. He said it was the noblest mission that was ever given to man and that he would pray that we would not become discouraged. I hear this note struck in all the countries. Mothers and wives, fathers and brothers, have spoken in the same strain and have seemed to feel that the only hope lies in our endeavors.

Affectionately yours

E. M. House

'It is a sad commentary,' added House, 'that the Governments of each of the belligerents would probably welcome peace negotiations, and yet none of them are able safely to make a beginning.' For each Government, in order to evoke the belligerent enthusiasm necessary to a prosecution of the war, had created a Frankenstein monster which emphatically vetoed any whisper of peace. Zimmermann stated, wrote House on March 24, 'that if peace parleys were begun now upon any terms that would have any chance of acceptance, it would mean the overthrow of this Government and the Kaiser.'

Colonel House to the President

Berlin, *March* 26, 1915

Dear Governor:

While I feel I have accomplished much of value here, I leave sadly disappointed that we were misled into believing that peace parleys might be begun upon a basis of evacuation of France and Belgium.

I have been cordially received and have added many new friendships to the old. I find the civil Government here as sensible and fair-minded as their counterparts in England, but they are for the moment impotent.

It is a dangerous thing to inflame a people and give them an exaggerated idea of success. This is what has happened and is happening in almost every country that is at war. . . .

If those that are in charge of the civil Government now hold their power when peace comes, there will be no doubt of their coöperation — provided, of course, our relations grow no worse, and without actual war they could not be worse.

This is almost wholly due to our selling munitions of war to the Allies. The bitterness of their resentment towards us for this is almost beyond belief. It seems that every German that is being killed or wounded is being killed or wounded by an American rifle, bullet, or shell. I never dreamed before of the extraordinary excellence of our guns and ammunition. They are the only ones that explode or are so manufactured that their results are deadly.

I have pointed out the danger of such agitation against us and have tried to show how much it would lessen our influence in helping Germany when our help is needed. I have indicated where our interests touched at various points and how valuable it would be to both nations to work in harmony rather than at cross-purposes. . . .

There is a general insistence here, as elsewhere, that when a settlement is made it must be an enduring one; but ideas as to how this may be brought about are as divergent as the poles. . . .

Gerard has been exceedingly helpful here. He has not interfered in the slightest and has insisted upon my seeing the different Cabinet Ministers and influential Germans alone. He is very courageous, and is different from some of our representatives, inasmuch as his point of view is wholly American.

Affectionately yours

E. M. House

As in London, House made a point of meeting varied

types, although he sought out especially those who represented the moderate point of view. He had long talks with Rathenau and von Gwinner,[1] with Solf, the Minister for the Colonies who later played a major rôle in the final armistice negotiations, with Helfferich — 'a young man,' House noted, 'who is considered one of the rising powers in Germany,' — with the Foreign Minister, von Jagow, and with the Chancellor.

III

Apart from his desire to obtain information and create an atmosphere friendly to the United States, House wished to try out on the Germans the plan which he believed might serve as the basis for a future compromise between Germany and Great Britain. It was the plan which came to be called the 'Freedom of the Seas.'

The problem presented itself in the following aspects to Colonel House. Existing maritime regulations permitted the capture of private property of neutrals on the high seas, if it came within the category of contraband, and it was inevitable under conditions of modern warfare that the definition of contraband should be progressively extended to include practically all materials and articles of industrial life. In any war between Great Britain and a Continental Power, the first thought of the British was naturally to use their control of the sea so as to interrupt the direct and indirect imports of the Continental enemy. A quarrel between Great Britain and the United States, the largest exporting neutral, must necessarily follow, for British restrictions meant the destruction of American trade. The events of 1914 and 1915, as well as those that led to the War of 1812, offered a practical example of this ever-recurring factor of discord, the sole factor that seriously threatened the cordial relations of the two countries.

[1] Banker, and promoter of the Bagdad Railway.

Apart from the peril of complications with America, there were other elements in the situation which did not seem to favor Great Britain. The British, living on an island, dependent for their lives upon trade with the outside world and especially with their colonies, were in a position of real danger that was not clearly recognized. They had believed that so long as their fleet remained supreme, they were perfectly safe. But the introduction of the submarine raised the question whether Great Britain's ocean-going trade, carried as it was by British ships, could not be destroyed and the nation be deprived of the foodstuffs and raw materials which entered her ports, even though her surface fleet remained intact. Such a threat to the security of national life became very lively in 1917.

Germany was dependent, although not to the same degree, upon overseas trade. In their struggle with England, the Germans counted upon the neutral ports of Holland, Denmark, Norway, and Sweden. But the British, in control of the sea, could confiscate or seriously harass trade bound for these ports, and thus threaten the starvation of Germany. So much the Germans themselves, in their protests against the British food blockade, admitted.

What House proposed was that the contraband list should be restricted so as to include only actual implements of warfare; everything else should be placed upon the free list. The trade of merchant vessels, whether belligerent or neutral, should be allowed to proceed freely outside territorial waters so long as they carried no contraband. They might even enter any belligerent port without hindrance, unless that port were actually and effectively blockaded by the enemy's fleet. Such a blockade in the case of England would be practically impossible, because of the multitude of available harbors and the strength of the British fleet. An effective blockade was equally impossible in the case of Germany, as the events of the war demonstrated.

For what, then, could a fleet be used, one will ask. Simply for purposes of defence, Colonel House replied; to prevent the landing of a hostile military force and to keep essential ports open.

The proposal was less revolutionary than many thought, and it had behind it the force of both British and American traditions. Sir Edward Grey had instructed the British delegation to the Second Hague Conference in 1907 to work for a restriction of the contraband list, and it was at his inspiration that the delegation carried the idea to its logical limit and expressed a willingness to abandon the principle of contraband of war entirely.[1] In their talks with House in February, Grey and Tyrrell had approved also the principle of the immunity of belligerent merchant shipping in time of war; in fact, it was that approval which lay at the bottom of House's present suggestion.

What is equally striking is that in 1907 Elihu Root, then Secretary of State, in his instructions to the United States delegates to the Hague Conference, advocated almost precisely what House now suggested, the exemption from capture of belligerent private property, although he said nothing about the restriction of contraband.

'The private property of all private citizens or subjects of signatory Powers [so ran his instructions], with the exception of contraband of war, shall be exempt from capture or seizure on the high seas or elsewhere by the armed vessels or by the military forces of any of the said signatory Powers, but nothing herein contained shall extend exemption from seizure of vessels or their cargoes which may attempt to

[1] The following declaration was made on the part of Great Britain: 'In order to diminish the difficulties encountered by neutral commerce in time of war the Government of H.B.M. is prepared to abandon the principle of contraband in case of war between the Powers which may sign a convention to that effect. The right of visit would be exercised only in order to ascertain the neutral character of the merchantmen.'

enter a port blockaded by the naval forces of any of the said Powers.'

This was in entire consonance with the Final Act of the First Hague Conference, which gave preference to 'inviolability of private property in naval warfare.'

It was only the use of the term 'Freedom of the Seas' as applied to this suggestion which was new; and this, it appears, was originated by Colonel House. Grotius in 1609 used the term *mare liberum*, and the eighteenth and nineteenth centuries became accustomed to such slogans as 'a free sea or war,'[1] 'free ships, free goods,' 'free flag, free goods.' The phrase 'freedom of the seas' was itself used in 1798 by the French Revolutionary leader, Barère, in his famous summary of French foreign policy: 'Freedom of the seas, peace to the world, equal rights to all nations.' But it remained for Colonel House to utilize the phrase as applicable to what Choate had called, in 1907, 'immunity of private property at sea,' and to include the proposal of a rigid restriction of contraband of war.

House's plan for the Freedom of the Seas was thus based upon the approval of both British and American authorities. It carried with it immediate and ultimate advantages which in the case of the United States would eliminate practically all factors of complication with European belligerents. If contraband were restricted, the trade of the United States might proceed with almost as much freedom in time of war as in that of peace. The advantages to the world at large were still more obvious, since the rôle of a navy would become chiefly defensive and naval disarmament might proceed apace.

Germany would undoubtedly gain much by the Freedom of the Seas. An enemy possessing a strong fleet, like Great Britain, would still be free to blockade German ports if it

[1] In England, on the eve of the War of Jenkins' Ear.

could reach them, but could not cut off the foodstuffs and raw materials which the Germans received through neutral ports and contiguous countries. Great Britain would thus lose an offensive weapon of doubtful legality. But as compensation, how greatly British defensive strength would be enhanced! The disadvantages of her island position would largely disappear, her food supply would be secure, and her commerce with the far-flung portions of the Empire would be assured without the protection of a costly fleet. Submarines would not be able to prey upon merchant shipping. Under the principle of the Freedom of the Seas, the Power with the most colonies and the widest overseas trade stood to gain most.

So much was plain to Colonel House, although he was careful not to whisper in Berlin that he believed the British would win the lion's share of advantage. To him the great irony of the war was that his proposal was so eagerly swallowed by the Germans, so scornfully refused by British opinion.

The weak point in House's plan lay in the danger that an unscrupulous nation, after accepting its principle, would proceed to disregard its engagements. The British could not escape the fear that Germany, which had broken its promises in the Belgian treaty, was quite capable of agreeing to the Freedom of the Seas and, after securing the partial disarmament of Great Britain thereby, might embark upon a wholesale destruction of British merchant shipping. To meet this danger, House was insistent upon an association of nations bound to unite forcibly against any nation that violated its international promises.

The Colonel believed that the acceptance of the Freedom of the Seas, as a principle of international law, was essential to stability of relations between the United States and European Powers. He also believed that the idea could be used as a means to start peace negotiations between the belligerents. If the British would agree to his proposal, with all its ultimate advantages for them, he planned to present this fact to the Germans as a diplomatic victory for Germany that would justify peace parleys and satisfy German public opinion.

Colonel House to the President

BERLIN, *March* 27, 1915

DEAR GOVERNOR:

Some way has to be thought out to let the Governments down easy with their people. That is almost, if not quite, our hardest problem.

It occurred to me to-day to suggest to the Chancellor that, through the good offices of the United States, England might be brought to concede at the final settlement the Freedom of the Seas, and to the extent I have indicated to you. I told him that the United States would be justified in bringing pressure upon England in this direction, for our people had a common interest with Germany in that question.

He, like the others I have talked to, was surprised when I told him the idea was to go far beyond the Declaration of Paris or the proposed Declaration of London. I said that some one would have to throw across the chasm the first thread, so that the bridge might have its beginning, and that I knew of no suggestion that was better fitted for that purpose than this; that if England would consent, this Government [the German] could say to the people that Belgium was no longer needed as a base for German naval activity, since England was being brought to terms.

I have sown this thought of the Freedom of the Seas very widely since I have been here, and already I can see the results. . . . I think I can show England that, in the long run and looking at the matter broadly, it is as much to her interest as it is to the other nations of the earth.

The Chancellor seems to think, and so does Zimmermann, that I have offered in this suggestion the best idea as a peace beginning. . . .

I have told them frankly and with emphasis that they could not expect us to lay an embargo on the exportation of munitions of war, and that they must soften their press and people on this point. They have promised to do this. I have told them I would help them in the big thing later and that they must be content with our efforts in that direction.

I leave here fairly satisfied with the situation, as we now have something definite to work on and as the warring nations have tentatively accepted you as their mediator. . . .

Affectionately yours

E. M. House

Unfortunately, the Germans did not possess either the discretion or the tact necessary to the development of House's plan for the Freedom of the Seas. He hoped to win British approval, for he knew of Grey's sympathy. All he wished from Germany, for the moment, was an acquiescent silence. But the Germans lost no time in advertising the idea as their own and thereby immediately ruined all chance of success. In the United States, Herr Dernburg, in charge of German propaganda, announced that if England granted the Freedom of the Seas, Germany would retire from Belgium; if England refused, Germany would establish a permanent fortified base on the English Channel. Englishmen were entirely ignorant as to what the Freedom of the Seas meant, or whether it would be advantageous or not to refuse it; but coming in this fashion as a threat, public opinion immediately decided that it was something made in Germany and that every true Britisher would spill the last drop of his blood before considering it. From that moment began the unreasoning prejudice against the idea, which ultimately became invincible.

IV

In the meantime House had left Germany, passing back to Paris through Nice and Biarritz, where he engaged in conferences with the American Ambassadors to Italy and to Spain.

'*April* 2, 1915 [Nice]: Page [1] and I have continued our talks. He has given the Italian situation in detail, going into the intricacies of Italian politics, especially as to the rivalry between the present Premier, Salandra, and the late Premier, Giolitti.

'Page thinks Italy is acting in a wholly selfish way and that it matters little with her whether she supports the Allies or the Dual Alliance, provided she is on the winning side. The aristocracy are favorable to Germany and the people to the Entente. Nowhere throughout Italy is the feeling against Germany anything like as bitter as it is against their old-time enemy, Austria.

'Page does not believe Italy would last long in the conflict, and that if she had entered at the beginning of the war she would probably have been easily defeated and disarmed. He believes she will finally enter the war on the side of the Allies when she can see the end of the struggle within a few months.

'He thinks England has made something of a mistake in not giving her some assurance as to her aspirations for new territory, or, we might say, old territory which she seeks to recover. This would include a portion of Austria, around what the Italians term the Gulf of Venice, the twelve islands which she has long coveted, and a sphere of influence in Asia Minor. . . . [2]

[1] Thomas Nelson Page.

[2] At that moment, negotiations were being carried on which ended with the Treaty of London, a guaranty by the Entente that Italy should receive the territories she claimed

'*April* 8, 1915 [Biarritz]: Ambassador Willard came from Madrid to-day, arriving at 2.30.... He says the King dominates Spain and at heart he is an advanced Liberal. He is well informed and is altogether an intelligent and up-to-date ruler. His Ministers are not nearly so progressive, and hold him back to a considerable degree.

'The King desires to figure in peace overtures, but is willing to allow the President to take the lead and will coöperate with him in a secondary capacity. I told Willard I did not see how he could figure in it jointly, since it would have to be done by one or the other and, unless the situation changed it would doubtless be the President. However, the situation could change to the disadvantage of the President, for, if all the belligerents become dissatisfied and embittered with our neutral policy, they might conceive the idea that any one would be preferable to the President as a mediator. I explained to Willard that I was appealing to the self-interests of both sides, and that in itself would probably induce them to accept Wilson.

'Willard said the King was pro-French, but not especially pro-British; that he was anti-German, but pro-Austrian. His reason for not being strongly pro-British, even though his wife is English, is because he feels that he has not been very courteously treated by the British upon his several visits to England. Then, too, there is always Gibraltar to sting Spanish pride....'

Colonel House to the President

PARIS, *April* 11, 1915

DEAR GOVERNOR:

This is the first time I have had an opportunity to write you freely since I left here. My visit in Berlin was exceedingly trying and disagreeable in many ways. I met there no one of either high or low degree who did not immediately corner me, and begin to discuss our shipment of munitions to the Allies, and sometimes their manner was almost offensive.

Upon the streets one hesitated to speak in English, for fear of being insulted....

I feel, however, that with the Government and with the influential people with whom I talked, a better understanding of our purposes was brought about; and I hope this feeling will sooner or later reach the people at large....

The trouble with Germany is that it is antiquated in some of its ideas. They started upon the rule of force at a time when the most advanced nations were going in the opposite direction.

I endeavored to make it clear to the German Government that their best interests could be served by working along harmoniously with us. If we can keep this view before them, they will probably want you as mediator, for they are narrowly selfish in their purposes and have no broad outlook as to the general good of mankind.

I found a lack of harmony in governmental circles which augurs ill for the future. The civil Government are divided amongst themselves.... The military and civil forces are not working in harmony.

The Emperor is still in absolute authority, although he is criticized pretty generally by both the civil and military branches of the Government. Falkenhayn and von Tirpitz seem to have more influence with him than any one, but Falkenhayn is not popular with the army in general.

The Crown Prince seems to be left out of all important councils and is generally ignored by both the civil and military Governments, though he seems to be more popular with the people than his father because he is said to be without egotism and more democratic in his manner.

Hindenburg is the popular hero and is the only one that dares to assert himself against the Emperor. I believe there are troublous times ahead for the Kaiser and that one dénouement of the war may be a more democratic Germany. . . .

Affectionately yours

E. M. House

At Paris Colonel House did not raise the question of peace, for there was less chance of it than ever. In the East, the Germans were driving the Russians out of Poland. In the West, the French were planning a great drive in the Champagne regions. The British were developing the attack upon the Dardanelles. Italy was on the point of joining the Allies. Both sides were trying to win over Bulgaria. Every one hoped for victory. House confined himself to securing information and solidifying his personal relationships, especially with Delcassé and Poincaré. House met Poincaré for the first time on this occasion. An American diplomat warned him not to be disappointed by the coldness of manner characteristic of the French President. 'I replied,' wrote House, 'that his coldness and silence would not embarrass me if it did not embarrass him, and I could be as quiet, and for as long, as anybody.'

Colonel House to the President

[Telegram]

Paris, *April* 13, 1915

In a private conference with Delcassé, he was good enough to express his satisfaction at the way negotiations have been carried on up to now. He said that I had given Berlin a correct idea of France's attitude and he approved what I had said and done there. . . .

He wished me to convey to you the appreciation of France for the fairness with which you have maintained our relations with the belligerents. I shall see Poincaré before I leave.

E. M. House

Colonel House to the President

PARIS, *April* 17, 1915

DEAR GOVERNOR:

I have just cabled you of my interview with Poincaré. I had been told that he was austere in his manner and I was quite unprepared for the warmth with which he welcomed me.

He seemed to understand my relation to you and he expressed his appreciation of your having sent me to France.

When I wrote the cable to you on Thursday, I made a request that you send some message that could be repeated to him and to Delcassé. I afterwards struck this out, for fear lest it might give you too much trouble. When I received your cablegram yesterday, sending messages to them both, it seemed like a case of telepathy.

Poincaré was visibly pleased. I have not seen Delcassé since, but will do so in a day or two in order to discuss with him the second convention. There is nothing you could do that would promote better feeling than occasionally to send some word that I may repeat to those in authority in the country in which I happen to be. We are all susceptible to these little attentions.

I find your purposes badly misunderstood in France. They believe the American public largely sympathetic to the Allies; but there is a feeling, which I am sorry to say is almost universal throughout France, that you personally are pro-German. It is the most illogical conclusion that one could imagine, and I can scarcely keep within the bounds of politeness when I discuss it. . . .

Affectionately yours

E. M. HOUSE

Colonel House to Secretary Bryan

PARIS, *April* 15, 1915

DEAR MR. BRYAN:

. . . Everybody seems to want peace, but nobody is willing to concede enough to get it. They all also say that they desire a permanent settlement so that no such disaster may occur hereafter, but, again, there is such a divergence of ideas as to how this should be brought about that for the moment it is impossible to harmonize the differences.

Germany is not willing to evacuate Belgium at all, nor even France, without an indemnity, and Count von Bernstorff's suggestion that this could be arranged was wide afield. The Allies, of course, will not consent to anything less; and there the situation rests.

With warm regards and good wishes for Mrs. Bryan and you, I am

Faithfully yours

E. M. HOUSE

'*April* 16, 1915: I can see from my interviews [wrote House], not only with Delcassé and Poincaré but with others, that I would have made a mistake if I had attempted to talk peace at this time. France as a whole has an idea that the President is not altogether in sympathy with the Allies and that he is inclined to be pro-German, and that it is for that reason he has tried to push peace measures and in order to save Germany's face. It is very discouraging to have to talk to intelligent people and argue with them about such a matter, but that is what I have to do.

'Another impression they have here is that the President is catering to the pro-German vote. I explain to them that a man of the President's intelligence would hardly cater to fifteen per cent of the American vote in order to lose eighty-five per cent of it. This they had never thought of. In fact, it seems to me they do not think much at all.

'The ignorance of Europe concerning itself, to say nothing of America, is appalling.

'France, to-day, does not understand England, her purposes, or her forces in the war. They have an idea that they, themselves, are doing it all and that England is idling. Only a few Frenchmen who have been in England understand the momentum gathering force there, and the indomitable energy and tenacity which in the end will probably turn the scales in favor of the Allies.'

Colonel House to President S. E. Mezes

PARIS, *April* 18, 1915

DEAR SIDNEY:

... We lead a busy and interesting life and do not get time to thoroughly enjoy the bombs that drop before and after us. We just missed them in Paris and also missed them as they were dropped on the stations and railway sheds along our journey. Now that the weather is milder, we have a better sporting chance, as all the belligerents promise that an acceleration of their activities in this direction will soon commence.

Martin is evidently looking forward with interest to a bomb catching me somewhere on the Allies' territory — as he believes that would bring about war with Germany, which he considers would be worth dying for. On the other hand, the St. Louis *Globe-Democrat* writing editorially hopes I may be spared, for the reason that, desirable as my taking off would be, the price of a war with Germany would be too great to pay....

Fraternally yours

E. M. HOUSE

'*April* 19, 1915: Last night Ambassador and Mrs. Sharp gave a dinner. The guests besides ourselves were, the Infanta Eulalia of Spain, the Spanish Ambassador and his wife, Ambassador Willard, Robert Bliss, Mrs. Crosby, and Mr. and Mrs. Tuck. I sat by the Infanta and immediately caught her attention by complimenting her recent article in an American magazine, on the Kaiser. I thought she had written charmingly of him, and any one who knew him would recognize how truthful it was. She said she was fond of the Kaiser, and had tried to make the French people understand that he was not the ogre they imagined. We had a spirited talk about the war and its outcome. She knew the situation in Italy thoroughly and of the dangerous position in which the King was. She also knew that the King and aristocracy were for Germany, but the people were in favor of the Allies. . . .

'She spoke of the petty jealousies and differences among Royalty, and laughingly said that when the family silver spoons were to be divided, it was always a question as to who should have this spoon and who should have the other. In talking of the Kaiser, I thought he had not surrounded himself with an efficient Cabinet. She said that was one of his faults, for he wanted to do everything himself and did not desire any dominant figure on the boards excepting himself; consequently he had been badly served.'

Colonel House to the President

PARIS, *April* 20, 1915

DEAR GOVERNOR:

. . . The Spanish Ambassador told me that the King of Spain wished him to meet me and ask me to come to Madrid. He confirmed what Willard had said, and that is, the King would like to take some part in peace negotiations and is willing to follow your lead.

I told the Ambassador that you did not desire me, at the moment, to visit the neutral countries and that I was confining myself to the belligerents, and that we were not making any peace overtures, but were simply studying conditions.

I told him, however, that after visiting Russia I might go to San Sebastian and meet the King. This makes it indefinite and many things may happen to prevent my going. . . .

Evidence still comes to me each day of the misunderstanding which the French people at large have of our position. They are very much afraid that peace will be made overnight and that the Germans will not receive the punishment for their misdeeds which they feel they so richly deserve.

In the course of the next two or three months, the conviction will break in upon them that the wonderful things they expect the army to do, have not happened; and they will then become more reasonable in their attitude.

I notice that Dernburg has taken the cue from Berlin and is saying that Belgium must be retained unless the 'Freedom of the Seas' is established. Yesterday I noticed that a prominent Hamburger said the same thing, and it looks as if the German Government had accepted my suggestion that this was the best way to save their faces before the people.

I took lunch to-day with Joseph Reinach. He is a German-French Jew whose people have lived in France some sixty years. He is said to be thoroughly patriotic and is a man of influence.

He writes for the *Figaro*, and I outlined some things I thought it would be well for him to incorporate in his next article. I drew his attention to the fact that it was more to France's interest to have the United States come in at the final settlement and exercise its moral influence than it was to ours.

I also made him the same talk I have made to others concerning you and your purposes. . . .

Reinach gets German papers from friends in Switzerland, and he said he saw a great change within the last two weeks in their attitude towards England. I am wondering whether what I said to them in Berlin has begun to bear fruit and they see the wisdom of modifying their hate campaign in that direction.

Your affectionate

E. M. HOUSE

House left Paris for London on April 28. His visit to France had been without result so far as hastening the chance of peace was concerned, but he had solidified the personal relations which were later to be of immense diplomatic value. In England he at once renewed his intimacy with British friends and created new contacts of interest and importance.

'*May* 5, 1915: I lunched with Lord Northcliffe. The only other guest was L. J. Maxse, of the *National Review*.

'Northcliffe spoke freely about the war and criticized the Government without stint. He thought Kitchener too old for the job and that he did not understand the sort of warfare he was now engaged in. He did not think the British appreciated the magnitude of the task before them, or that they were meeting the situation with anything like the determination and ability the occasion required. Neither Northcliffe nor Maxse thought there was a big man connected with either the Government or army. He told of the number of men they had in France at this time and the number in every place. It was most indiscreet to tell these facts, if, indeed, they are facts. I do not wonder the Germans get so much information, for I hear the most profound secrets of the army and navy repeated in a way that makes me shiver. . . .

'*May* 6, 1915: I dined with General Sir Arthur and Lady Paget. The others present were Mrs. McGuire, daughter of the late Lord Peel, Lady Fingall, Arthur Balfour, and Sir Horace Plunkett.

'During dinner the conversation drifted upon the subject of whether Great Britain was doing her full duty, and was performing as important a part in the war as her resources and position demanded. I allowed the talk to run along for a few minutes, and then I broke in by saying that of all the belligerents Great Britain had performed her part best. Germany was considered the dominant military nation of the world and Great Britain the dominant naval power. Germany had failed to maintain her dominance on land, while Great Britain had asserted her supremacy at sea and was the undisputed master of it within a week after hostilities began. In addition to this, she had raised an enormous army, something it was thought would not be required of her, and she was the only belligerent with a world-wide vision of the war and its consequences — differing from France, Germany, and even Russia, who looked upon it from local points of view and as to its effects upon them.

'When Great Britain entered the war, every neutral country felt that Germany was doomed to defeat, and I was sure Germany herself had the fear of God in her heart. I was interrupted from time to time by the English "hear, hear," and when I had finished Balfour said, "That is the most eloquent speech I have ever heard." This, of course, was polite. . . .

'When the ladies left the table, Sir Arthur told us of his recent visit to Russia, Bulgaria, Rumania, Serbia, and Greece, from which countries he has just returned. He was with the Grand Duke for ten days, and he gave a better idea of his ability and character than I have yet had. He spoke glowingly of the Russian army, and regretfully of Russian corruption which prevented the Grand Duke from equipping his army properly. He said the Grand Duke was displeased at the manner of Joffre's insistence that he change his plan of campaign and attack Prussia, at a time when the Grand Duke thought he should merely fortify himself against the Prussians and direct his entire energies against Austria. This change of policy he claims has caused Russia to lose innumerable men and treasure.

'*May* 7, 1915: I went to Sir Edward Grey's at ten o'clock. I handed him the King's invitation to call at 11.30. . . . I decided, however, to go with Grey to Kew and get a glimpse of it. Before we started, I showed him some telegrams and letters — one from Ambassador Willard bearing on the Spanish situation, one from Thomas Nelson Page on the Italian situation, and, most important of all, the President's cable concerning the retention of American cargoes. . . .

'The gates of Kew Gardens were not open when we arrived, but we got through by the porter's lodge. I have never seen the gardens so beautiful; it is to me one of the superlatively beautiful spots in England. Grey showed me the different trees and told something of them. The blackbirds were singing, and we talked of how different they were to those in far-away Texas.

'Grey's eyesight is failing, the doctors having warned him that unless he stops reading he will lose his sight to the extent of not being able to read again. He said he supposed this was the sacrifice he had to make for his country and he was going on in that spirit, knowing well what lay before him.'

V

In the meantime House had taken up again with Sir Edward the question of the Freedom of the Seas, concerning which the two had corresponded while House was still in Paris, and which, as House wrote Wilson, he hoped to use as a means of starting negotiations between the belligerents. Grey was suspicious of the Germans, perhaps not without justification, and he wished to make sure that if England accepted the Freedom of the Seas, Germany would agree to general military disarmament.

Colonel House to Sir Edward Grey

PARIS, *April* 12, 1915

DEAR SIR EDWARD:

. . . I did not find conditions in Berlin favorable for any discussion looking towards peace; consequently I did not remain long or say much. The visit, however, had great value and I feel that I now know the true conditions there, making a more intelligent line of action possible.

I found but few points where our interest and theirs touched strongly enough for me to create a sympathetic feeling, but one of these was what we might term the Freedom of the Seas. It was upon that subject alone that I awoke sufficient enthusiasm to warrant the hope that in it lies the way to peace.

Looking at the matter from a narrowly selfish standpoint, they could not believe that England would concede enough in this direction for Germany to consent to those things without which no peace can ever be possible. But from my conversations with you, I knew that you saw a future more secure and splendid for England in this new direction than in the old. I gave no sign of this, but left them thinking what concessions they might make in order to reach so promising an end.

While I am eager to discuss this and other matters with you, still I feel that it is well to move leisurely and to assume a certain indifference as to time. . . .

Your very sincere

E. M. HOUSE

Colonel House to the President

PARIS, *April* 12, 1915

DEAR GOVERNOR:

. . . What I want to do, is to get Sir Edward's consent to what might be termed a paper campaign. If he agrees to this I will write to him, even though in London, and have him reply. Copies of this correspondence will be sent either to the German Chancellor direct, or to him and Zimmermann through Gerard.

This will necessitate replies, and we may have them talking to one another before they realize it. . . .

Your affectionate

E. M. House

Sir Edward Grey to Colonel House

33 Eccleston Square, London
April 24, 1915

Dear Colonel House:

. . . Your news from Berlin is not encouraging; it reduces Bernstorff's peace talk at Washington to 'Fudge.'

What you hear from Berlin and found there is confirmed to me from another source — neutral but not American.

As to 'freedom of the seas,' if Germany means that her commerce is to go free upon the sea in time of war, while she remains free to make war upon other nations at will, it is not a fair proposition.

If, on the other hand, Germany would enter after this war some League of Nations where she would give and accept the same security that other nations gave and accepted against war breaking out between them, their expenditures on armament might be reduced and new rules to secure 'freedom of the seas' made. The sea is free in times of peace anyhow.[1]

Yours sincerely

E. Grey

[1] A curious irrelevancy, in view of the fact that war-time trade was the subject under discussion. Perhaps Grey had in mind an argument, which Wilson later accepted, that with a league of nations to prevent war the question of war-time trade became academic.

Colonel House to the President

LONDON, *April* 30, 1915

DEAR GOVERNOR:

I arrived here Wednesday night. I have already had two conferences with Sir Edward Grey, and I am to have the first formal one with him, by appointment through Page, this afternoon at five o'clock.

Of course no one but you is to know of the other two conferences.

I have outlined to him the full plan of the Freedom of the Seas and how best it can be brought to Berlin's attention and what concessions they must give in return. I shall not let them know how receptive he is to the idea, but shall try to impress upon them how hard we are working to accomplish the desired end and give them little driblets of hope from time to time. The thing thus is held within our hands.

Sir Edward tells me that public opinion here will have to be educated in this direction, particularly the Conservatives, and I shall endeavor to do this. . . .

We will have to keep this programme absolutely confidential between yourself, Sir Edward, and myself; and even the men I shall discuss these things with, will not know our full purposes. . . .

I told Sir Edward I felt sure that the Berlin Government wanted peace and that they were deterred mainly by German public opinion, which will have to be educated to the making of concessions. . . .

Your affectionate

E. M. HOUSE

Even as early as this, the historian will observe, House had begun to make plans for the Peace Conference, for he believed in being prepared. A note which he made after this conversation with Grey throws light on what the Colonel wanted to have accomplished by the Paris Conference in 1918 and 1919.

'*April* 30, 1915: I told Grey . . . how I planned to organize this convention by getting the material that was to come before it thoroughly prepared and digested, in order that nothing should be left to chance. I would try to get the commissioners from each of the neutral States, and from as many of the belligerent States as possible, in accord with us before they came to the convention.

'I explained my methods of organization in political conventions in the past; that while they were seemingly spontaneous, as a matter of fact nothing was left to chance. While measures were apparently drawn by different delegations, in the end it was found they fitted into the platform like a mosaic.[1] I could see Grey was intensely interested in this programme. I showed why no opposition could withstand such thorough organization. . . . We would be actuated by unselfish motives and would not propose anything that was merely to the advantage of Great Britain or the United States, but would advocate only such things as would redound to the good of the entire world. If we held to this principle, with thorough preparation and organization we would be able to do great and lasting good — good which would be limited only by the extent of our ability to conceive and execute it.

'In order to get the proper material and to prepare for an

[1] The illness which laid Colonel House low just before the meeting of the Paris Peace Conference prevented him from carrying through the organization he planned. Henry Wickham Steed, foreign editor of the *Times*, says in this connection: 'One serious misfortune — which proved to be a disaster — befell the Conference through the illness of Colonel House. A severe attack of influenza incapacitated him for any work during this critical formative period. Consequently his guiding influence was absent when it was most sorely needed; and, before he could resume his activities, things had gone too far for him to mend.' — *Through Thirty Years*, II, 266.

intelligent discussion of the questions which might come before the peace conference, I desired to see some of the best minds in England as to particular subjects. I mentioned Lord Loreburn as being one with whom to advise on Admiralty questions. Grey approved Loreburn, but suggested, in addition, Lord Mersey, and said Balfour could also be of service.

'Grey makes the point clear that whatever guaranty of good faith the Allies would wish from Germany, Germany would receive a like guaranty from the Allies. His mind and mine run nearly parallel, and we seldom disagree. I know in advance, just as I know with the President, what his views will be on almost any subject. I often come in contact with very able men whose minds run in an opposite direction from mine, and I find it difficult to agree with them upon any question. It is therefore my good fortune that Fate has given me two such friends as Woodrow Wilson and Edward Grey.

'Grey came to Page's at five. I took the precaution to remain downstairs in order to meet him when he first came in and to walk up to the drawing-room with him. In this way there was no embarrassment nor any pretense of not having met before.

'He stayed for a half-hour and the conversation was unimportant, as we had covered most of it before. I merely filled in the gaps by telling something further of my recent travels. I told Page that one of the General Staff in Berlin had said that Sir Edward's ambition was to be a George Washington, a Lincoln, a Bismarck, and a Napoleon. Page thought this very amusing, but Sir Edward . . . took it seriously and argued upon the peculiar bent of the German mind that could compare Washington and Lincoln with Bismarck and Napoleon.'

Colonel House to the President

London, *May* 3, 1915

Dear Governor:

. . . I saw Lord Loreburn this morning. He is not only a man that can be thoroughly trusted, but I believe he is my friend. He told me that he thought if we could bring about the Freedom of the Seas, it would be the greatest act of statesmanship that had been accomplished in centuries. He thought it would be of 100 per cent value to other nations and 120 per cent to England, though we would have great difficulty in getting the English mind to see this.

He spoke of Balfour as having great ability, but thought his mind was too feminine to grasp the significance of such a measure. He advised, just as Sir Edward did, that I see Bonar Law, who he said had an inferior mind, but who was practical and could probably be convinced sooner on that account.

He said if we could incorporate this idea into the peace convention, it would not only be a great act of statesmanship, but it would be perhaps the greatest jest that was ever perpetrated upon an unsuspecting nation — having, of course, Germany in mind.

I told him I shivered in Berlin when I proposed it to the Chancellor and the Foreign Office, for fear they would see that it was more to England's advantage than their own and would therefore not be willing to make concessions because of it. . . .

Lord Loreburn is one of the warmest admirers you have in Great Britain, which is naturally a great bond of sympathy between us.

Your affectionate

E. M. House

Colonel House to Herr Zimmermann

LONDON, *May* 1, 1915

MY DEAR HERR ZIMMERMANN:

Since I saw you in Berlin, I have been to Switzerland and France and came here a day or two ago. I have carried out my plans as expressed to the Chancellor and you and have seen many of our representatives at the different European capitals, who came by appointment to meet me, and I have discussed with them the questions I had in mind.

I have seen Sir Edward Grey and have mentioned to him the interest which the United States and Germany had in the Freedom of the Seas, and I am pleased to tell you that he was at least willing to listen to the suggestion.

He explained to me, however, that if he himself could be brought to the idea, it would only be upon an agreement that would guarantee the making of aggressive warfare on land as impossible as it was intended to make it upon the sea. In other words, if the commerce of the world, even in time of war and even between belligerents, was to go free and to have access to its own ports and to neutral ports without molestation, the land should be as free of menace as the sea.

He did not undertake to commit himself to the suggestion, and he particularly wanted me to know that he was speaking for himself and not for the Government or for the people.

He has promised to discuss the matter with his colleagues, and I shall undertake to get some estimate of the general sentiment in regard to such a proposal.

Of course, you understand that the conversation was predicated upon the evacuation of Belgium and France and upon the consent of all the Allies.

If the belligerents really desire to make an honorable peace that will be of far-reaching good, not only to themselves but to the entire world, I think the opportunity will soon be here.

If you will give me some assurance that you consider these questions at least debatable, it will go a long way to aid us in our endeavors. I shall understand that no commitments are made, either directly or indirectly, and that everything is unofficial; but this seems to me to be the most promising starting-point.

It will take a long while to make a successful campaign in England in regard to the Freedom of the Seas; but we will undertake it with both pleasure and enthusiasm, provided our efforts are cordially seconded by the other nations at interest.

Please present my very warm regards to their Excellencies, the Chancellor and the Secretary of State for Foreign Affairs, and believe me, my dear Herr Zimmermann,

Very sincerely yours

E. M. House

VI

The chief difficulty that obstructed the development of House's plan was obviously the inability of the British to comprehend the advantages they would derive from the Freedom of the Seas. This lack of comprehension rested in part upon a false sense of security and a failure to realize the extent of the danger threatened by the German submarine. It was also based upon a natural emotion, aroused by the war, which compelled the average citizen to believe that anything acceptable to Germany must *ipso facto* be inacceptable to Great Britain. Any intensification of the bitter feeling between the two countries would inevitably spell failure for House's hopes.

Precisely at this moment, the German navy committed the outrage upon humanity which a modern Talleyrand must certainly have pronounced 'worse than a crime, a blunder,' and which immediately rendered hopeless any attempt to reconcile the belligerents.

It was not entirely unforeseen by House, who on May 5 received a cable from Wilson asking him for advice in view of the attack upon an American oil boat.[1] House warned him that the German threat of using submarines recklessly might have to be taken at its face value.

Colonel House to the President

[Telegram]

LONDON, *May* 5, 1915

I believe that a sharp note indicating your determination to demand full reparation, would be sufficient in this instance.

I am afraid a more serious breach may at any time occur, for they seem to have no regard for consequences.

EDWARD HOUSE

On the morning of May 7, House and Grey drove out to Kew. 'We spoke of the probability of an ocean liner being sunk,' recorded House, 'and I told him if this were done, a flame of indignation would sweep across America, which would in itself probably carry us into the war.' An hour later, House was with King George in Buckingham Palace. 'We fell to talking, strangely enough,' the Colonel wrote that night, 'of the probability of Germany sinking a trans-Atlantic liner.... He said, "Suppose they should sink the *Lusitania* with American passengers on board...."'

That evening House dined at the American Embassy. A despatch came in, stating that at two in the afternoon a German submarine had torpedoed and sunk the *Lusitania* off the southern coast of Ireland. Many lives had been lost.

Thus did Germany interpret the Freedom of the Seas.

[1] The *Gulflight*, torpedoed by a German submarine on May 1, but not sunk. The master died of heart failure the next morning, and two sailors were drowned.

CHAPTER XIV
SUBMARINE VERSUS BLOCKADE

I think we shall find ourselves drifting into war with Germany. . . .
House to Wilson, June 16, 1915

I

The sinking of the *Lusitania* destroyed all hope of beginning negotiations between Germany and Great Britain. It was now, rather, a question as to whether the United States itself could remain out of the war. Ambassador Page regarded immediate intervention as inevitable, and cabled Wilson to that effect. 'Page strongly urges the President,' House recorded, 'to bring us into the struggle upon the side of the Allies, stating that he does not believe we can retain the good opinion of any one if we fail to do so.'

Colonel House himself believed that the United States could not long stand aside, in view of Germany's reckless course. 'It seems clear to me,' he wrote on May 9, 'that the *Lusitania* is merely the first incident of the kind and that more will follow, and that Germany will not give any assurance she will discontinue her policy of sinking passenger-ships filled with Americans and non-combatants.' That the United States must receive such an assurance or enter the war to enforce it, he believed then and always. On May 9 he sent the President a carefully pondered cable. It is historic, for Mr. Wilson read it to his Cabinet at the same time that he read them his note of protest to Germany.

Colonel House to the President

[Telegram]

London, *May* 9, 1915

It is now certain that a large number of American lives were lost when the *Lusitania* was sunk.

I believe an immediate demand should be made upon Germany for assurance that this shall not occur again. If she fails to give such assurance, I should inform her that our Government expected to take such measures as were necessary to ensure the safety of American citizens.

If war follows, it will not be a new war, but an endeavor to end more speedily an old one. Our intervention will save, rather than increase, the loss of life.

America has come to the parting of the ways, when she must determine whether she stands for civilized or uncivilized warfare. We can no longer remain neutral spectators. Our action in this crisis will determine the part we will play when peace is made, and how far we may influence a settlement for the lasting good of humanity. We are being weighed in the balance, and our position amongst nations is being assessed by mankind.

EDWARD HOUSE

LONDON, *May* 11, 1915

DEAR GOVERNOR:

. . . I cannot see any way out unless Germany promises to cease her policy of making war upon non-combatants. If you do not call her to account over the loss of American lives caused by the sinking of the *Lusitania*, her next act will probably be the sinking of an American liner, giving as an excuse that she carried munitions of war and that we had been warned not to send ships into the danger zone.

The question must be determined either now or later, and it seems to me that you would lose prestige by deferring it.

Germany has one of two things in mind. She may believe that we will not go to war under any provocation; or that we will be impotent if we do and she desires us to enter. The first is more understandable than the second, although she probably thinks if we became involved we would stop the shipment of munitions in order to equip ourselves.

She may also think that in the peace conference we would be likely to use our influence to settle upon broader and easier terms for Germany.

Or she may think that being able to torpedo our ships would contribute to the isolation of England.

If, unhappily, it is necessary to go to war, I hope you will give the world an exhibition of American efficiency that will be a lesson for a century or more. It is generally believed throughout Europe that we are so unprepared and that it would take so long to put our resources into action, that our entering would make but little difference.

In the event of war, we should accelerate the manufacture of munitions to such an extent that we could supply not only ourselves but the Allies, and so quickly that the world would be astounded.

You can never know how deeply I regret the turn affairs have taken, but it may be for the ultimate good. My heart goes out to you at this time as never before, and I think of you every hour of the day and wish that I was by your side. My consolation is that I may be of greater service here.

Your affectionate

E. M. House

Colonel House's conversations in London make it clear that both he and his British friends believed that Germany had embarked upon a course which would inevitably bring the United States into the war. The Colonel discussed with Kitchener the value of American intervention to the Allies.

'*May* 12, 1915: Lord Kitchener has asked to meet me and invited me to come to the War Office or to York House as I preferred. I seldom go to any of the offices, so I met him at York House at six o'clock. . . .

'He was very cordial. When I put the question as to whether it would be of benefit to the Allies for the United

States to come in on their side, he said, "Nobody but a damn fool could think it would not be of benefit to us, and I am surprised that any Englishman could question it." This was apropos of the editorial I showed him from the *St. James Gazette*, and of conversations I had had with some of his countrymen.

'He said, "God forbid that any nation should come into such a war," and he asked me to say to the President that he did not want him to think that Great Britain either made the request or had a desire for us to enter, but if we considered it necessary to do so, in his opinion it would greatly shorten the war and would save innumerable lives, not only of the Allies, but of the Germans as well.

'He said the war was one of attrition and the moment we entered, the Germans, unless they were totally mad, would know that the end was a certainty and would endeavor to make the best terms they could. It was a case of a mad dog turned loose, and every one trying to do his share toward stopping him. If we entered, and I would let him know, he would at once put his mind upon the problem and would aid us not only as to organization but in any other way we desired. He paid a magnificent tribute to American valor and said: "With American troops joined with the British, we will not need French troops on the West Front, but can keep them as a reserve."

'He has 2,200,000 men under arms, and of these 500,000 are now in France and 650,000 are ready to go the moment they are needed. In addition, there are 120,000 in the Dardanelles. He spoke of the army and the war as if it were his army and his war, and very much as a monarch would speak.

'We talked for the best part of an hour, although I tried to leave repeatedly because I knew how busy he must be and how valuable his time was to his country. When I got up to leave, he arose, but continued to walk up and down the room and talk. He repeated time and again that the war would be shortened enormously if the United States entered, and that it would be helpful to an extent which no one but a man of his experience could estimate. He said the coming in of Italy was as nothing compared to that of the United States, even though she had a large trained army....

'He was greatly interested when I gave it as my opinion that the Germans did not have a man of the "first class" in official life. He was also interested in von Tirpitz and Falkenhayn. The latter, I thought, was a much abler man than von Tirpitz and an abler man than von Moltke, whom he superseded. Kitchener spoke several times of their method of warfare, and said he did not dream that a nation claiming to be civilized would stoop to the things they had done. He was especially bitter concerning asphyxiating gases and said the only thing he could do was to reply in kind.

'This is the first time I have met Kitchener, and he seemed to me to be forceful and able, though, perhaps, without the spark of genius — unless, indeed, his great power of organization might be termed that.[1] I was impressed by his fairness and the impartial way he discussed our possible entry into the war. While it was the clever way to talk to me, he did not do it for that reason, for how could he know what would or would not influence me? He doubtless realizes, as the King does, that my advice to the President will be a potent influence in this crisis, but there was nothing of eagerness or urging in his remarks. He took no pains to hide his opinion that our entry would be decisive, and yet he said no word to

[1] Kitchener's organizing ability, however, was better fitted to the crises of his earlier career than to that which he faced as Secretary of War in 1915. The value of Kitchener's name was inestimable and he built up a great army, but he was used to a situation that could be handled by himself as dictator and he never understood the need of an able General Staff at the War Office. 'His conception of work,' wrote Grey, 'was that it must be a one-man job. He shouldered the responsibility and did the work of a Titan; but he did not realize that general responsibility must be shared with the Cabinet, and strategic responsibility with the most independent and expert military brains, organized in a General Staff and working with him.' — *Twenty-Five Years*, II, 246.

hasten that decision. Kitchener is not the greatest intellect with which I have come in touch, but he has a manner indicating great reserve force, and if I were going tiger hunting I would gladly have him for a companion.

'*May* 13, 1915: I lunched with Arthur Balfour. We had a most interesting talk. I told of my interview with Kitchener and of my advice to the President regarding the *Lusitania* incident and read him my cablegram, which he complimented warmly. I talk to Balfour with more freedom than any man in Great Britain with the exception of Grey, for I trust him implicitly. Grey and Balfour are two great gentlemen, and I feel sure of their discretion.

'Balfour criticized the Government for depending so much upon America for munitions of war. He thought at the very outset they should have accelerated the manufacture of munitions to such an extent that by now they would have needed no outside aid. . . .'

During the six days that followed the sinking of the *Lusitania,* Colonel House received no intimation of the action that President Wilson planned. He did not seriously suspect him of an inclination to avoid the issue which Germany had raised, but he did confess some anxiety as a result of a speech which was generally interpreted as proof of Wilson's invincible pacifism. On May 11 he recorded:

'Page and all of us are distressed by the President's speech at Philadelphia, in which he is reported to have said, "There is such a thing as being too proud to fight." Page sent him a long cablegram, which he submitted to me for criticism.'

Mr. Wilson faced a choice of two alternatives: to break diplomatic relations forthwith, on the ground that the sinking of the *Lusitania* and her thousand passengers was a crime against civilization, or to demand an official disavowal and the assurance that inhuman acts of such a kind would not be repeated. To break relations without giving Germany any chance to alter her submarine methods was contrary to the President's instincts, and it is unlikely that the nation would have supported him with the degree of unity which such a decided step demanded.

He chose the second alternative, and on May 13 he sent to Germany a note conceived and expressed with vigor, but avoiding both the form and tone of an ultimatum. Rehearsing the earlier attacks made by submarines that had resulted in the loss of American lives, 'a series of events which the Government of the United States has observed with growing concern,' he demanded that the Germans should

'disavow the acts of which the Government of the United States complains, that they will make reparation so far as reparation is possible for injuries which are without measure, and that they will take immediate steps to prevent the recurrence of anything so obviously subversive of the principles of warfare. . . . Expressions of regret and offers of reparation in case of the destruction of neutral ships sunk by mistake, while they may satisfy international obligations, if no loss of life results, cannot justify or excuse a practice, the natural and necessary effect of which is to subject neutral nations and neutral persons to new and unmeasurable risks.'

The note did not satisfy the bellicose insistence of Mr. Roosevelt for an immediate break with Germany. Another ex-President, however, William Howard Taft, described it as 'admirable in tone . . . dignified in the level the writer takes with respect to international obligations . . . it may well call for our earnest concurrence and confirmation.' Mr. Page himself expressed satisfaction and telegraphed to the President, 'May I be allowed to express my personal congratulations on the note.' And he added that most of the members of the British Government, as well as Lansdowne, Balfour, and Bonar Law of the Opposition, gave 'private expressions of praise.'[1]

Articulate opinion, indeed, with rare exceptions both at home and abroad, commended the note; it was only later, after many months of German diplomatic evasions, that critics with the advantage of hindsight complained that Wilson should have issued an ultimatum and set down for Germany a time-limit — a course which might or might not have led her to give up the submarine campaign immediately. Sidney Brooks, writing in *The English Review*, insisted that 'this note ranks with the greatest diplomatic literature. It seems as if one could see the President wrestling with the Wilhelmstrasse for the soul of Germany.' *The Times* declared that 'nothing less than the conscience of humanity makes itself audible in his [Wilson's] measured and incisive sentences.' From France, it is true, Whitney Warren wrote to House that there was a growing inclination to believe that 'the President has been influenced in the past and is still influenced by German tradition and inspiration.' And the depatriatized Americans of Paris, always hostile to Wilson, attacked him bitterly for truckling to Germany. But official opinion both there and in England agreed that the President had acted not merely wisely but adequately.

Ambassador Sharp to Colonel House

Paris, *June* 2, 1915

My dear Mr. House:

. . . While practically everybody over here has endorsed the President's note to Germany, following the sinking of the *Lusitania*, yet it makes a loyal American rather 'hot under the collar,' as we say, to read little squibs like those I have marked. . . . However, those in authority in the French Government fully understand and appreciate the attitude of

[1] *Life and Letters of Walter H. Page*, III, 245.

President Wilson and have great confidence in the integrity of his purpose.

Sir Francis Bertie, the British Ambassador, told me the other day that he was very much in hopes that we would not go to war with Germany, as we could be of very much more assistance to the Allies out of the war than actively in it. . . .[1]

Very truly yours

WILLIAM G. SHARP

Mr. J. St. Loe Strachey[2] *to Colonel House*

LONDON, *June* 1, 1915

MY DEAR COLONEL HOUSE,

. . . As I was walking home here just now I was thinking to myself — 'We don't want America to come in.' The thought of dragging our own kith and kin into this hideous struggle is *odious,* but I do wish that the Americans could tell the Germans, 'if you dare to destroy Westminster Abbey, America will never forgive you. It is *ours* as well as *theirs.*'

And yet with these lunatics that might after all be the worst way of protecting it. I suppose it is childish, but I would rather see half London smashed than the Abbey and Westminster Hall destroyed. Except for that, Zeppelins will never give me a bad night.

Yours very sincerely

J. ST. LOE STRACHEY

II

Colonel House evidently did not believe that Germany would alter her methods of naval warfare unless some more potent factor than the protests of the United States could be brought to bear. On May 18 he wrote to Secretary McAdoo: 'The German mind seems not to understand anything ex-

[1] In his private papers the British Ambassador expressed quite the contrary opinion.

[2] Editor of *The Spectator.*

cepting hard knocks and they have a curious idea that we will not fight under any circumstances. As a matter of fact, this idea is prevalent throughout Europe and will sooner or later involve us in war.' A fortnight later, after another submarine attack, he recorded: 'I have concluded that war is inevitable.'

Both House and Page agreed that unless Germany yielded to the demands set forth in Wilson's note and ceased the torpedoing of ships without warning, the United States could not avoid intervention.

Unlike Page, however, House shared the sentiment of President Wilson that war with Germany could not be justified unless every possible means to secure a peaceful settlement were first attempted; and he worked assiduously to discover a plan by which Germany might be induced to give up the cruel and illegal submarine warfare. He had the coöperation of Sir Edward Grey, who, with a singular largeness of view rare amid the passions of war, was ready to consider any reasonable compromise.

Colonel House to the President

London, *May* 14, 1915

Dear Governor:

I took lunch with Sir Edward Grey to-day. The principal topic of our conversation was the *Lusitania* disaster and the action you might take.

Grey told me he did not see how you could do differently from what you have done, and he intimated that if we had done less we would have placed ourselves in much the same position in which England would have been placed if she had not defended Belgian neutrality. In other words, he thought that we would have been totally without friends or influence in the concert of nations, either now or hereafter. I am sure that this is true.

If we had failed to take action in a determined way it

would have meant that we would have lost the friendship of the Allies on the one hand, and would not have mitigated any of the hate which Germany feels for us. Sooner or later we would have had to reckon with Germany unless she is completely crushed, and we would not have had a sympathetic friend among the great nations.

Grey asked me what I thought Germany's reply would be. I told him that if I were writing Germany's reply I would say that if England would lift the embargo on foodstuffs, Germany would consent to discontinue her submarine policy of sinking merchantmen. Grey replied that if Germany would consent not only to discontinue that mode of warfare, but would also agree to discontinue the use of asphyxiating gases and the ruthless killing of non-combatants, England would be willing to lift the embargo on foodstuffs.

I am rushing a cablegram to you, outlining this. It distresses me that I cannot have you, Grey, and Berlin within talking distance. If that could happen, so much could be accomplished that is impossible under present conditions.

I am writing this hastily, in order to catch to-night's mail. It may interest you to know that Italy has signed an agreement with the Allies to come into the war before the 26th.[1] This agreement will be carried out unless the Italian Parliament refuses to sanction it. I have had this information for ten days or more, but have not written it because there seemed so many slips between the agreement and its completion....

Your affectionate

E. M. House

[1] The Treaty of London, signed April 26, 1915, one of the 'secret treaties.' It did not set a date for Italy's entrance into the war, providing merely that she should use all her resources in making war with the Allies upon all their enemies. On May 23, Italy declared war against Austria, but did not declare war on Germany until August 27, 1916. On April 30, 1917, Mr. Balfour explained the details of the treaty to President Wilson.

The conversation with Grey suggested the possibility of an arrangement which might go far towards settling the dispute with England over the holding-up of cargoes and also might avert the livelier danger of an open break with Germany, over the submarine. The European War, as it touched the United States, had now become a struggle between German submarine and British blockade. Both weapons infringed American neutral rights. If the belligerents could be induced to give up their use, much of our difficulties would disappear. And to many the compromise seemed fair, for if the British food blockade threatened to starve Germany out, the German submarine threatened to destroy British commerce.

The suggestion was not new. In February, President Wilson, following a hint of Ambassador Bernstorff, had made a similar proposal to the British. Since the Germans averred that the submarine war zone was merely retaliation for the British attempt to starve non-combatants, Wilson argued that, if the British would permit foodstuffs to pass, Germany ought to give up her illegal submarine warfare. Grey had approved the proposal. Talking to House on February 27, he pointed out that with an agreement of this kind the British could carry on the war indefinitely. British public opinion, however, did not appreciate how dangerous a weapon the submarine might become, and felt that Great Britain would be sacrificing too much by lifting the embargo upon food. Ambassador Page himself held this opinion and, regarding the President's suggestion as something made in Germany, did not push it vigorously.

'I went to the Embassy to see the Ambassador [wrote House]. He did not return from his week-end with the Prime Minister until 12.15. . . . Page told of the two unhappy days he had spent in the country. One of the perquisites of the Prime Minister is the use of an old castle near Dover, and in it Page was lodged for two cold, wet, miserable nights. There were no fires excepting one here and there, and, though Page is a vegetarian, there seemed nothing to eat excepting meats of many varieties....

'Page was inclined not to make a personal appeal to Grey in behalf of the acceptance of the President's proposal concerning a compromise with Germany on the question of the embargo. I called his attention to the President's cable to me requesting me to say to Page that he desired the matter presented with all the emphasis in his power. He then said he would make an appointment with Grey and do so, though one could see he had no stomach for it. He did not consider the suggestion a wise one, nor did he consider its acceptance favorable to the British Government. I argued to the contrary, and tried to convince him that the good opinion gained from the neutrals would be compensation enough for any concessions this Government might make, and that the concessions were not really more than those made by Germany.'

Evidently the British Cabinet, with the exception of Grey, shared Page's belief that it was preferable to retain the offensive weapon of the food blockade against Germany, even if it meant braving the threat of the submarine, the danger of which then and even later they did not fully realize. On March 15, they refused the compromise.

The crisis of May was so much more acute than that of February, that House seized eagerly upon the chance of renewing the proposal that Germany give up the submarine warfare provided that Great Britain would relax the food blockade. He was sincere in his belief that the British would gain both a moral and a material advantage thereby, and he was convinced that it offered the sole means of preventing American intervention, which otherwise would be inevitable as the result of German submarine attacks.

'Grey was very fine about it [recorded Colonel House].

He said of course it would be to the advantage of Great Britain for the United States to enter the war, and if he agreed to do what we requested it would mean that the United States would remain neutral. Nevertheless, he wanted to do what we considered to be for our best interests and what, indeed, he thought was in the long run for Great Britain's best interests.

'We discussed this feature at length, I maintaining that Great Britain was taking long chances upon being isolated by German submarine warfare, and if her commerce could be free from this menace, she could carry on the war indefinitely without fear of ultimate defeat.'

President Wilson immediately cabled to House expressing deep interest in the suggestion. He looked upon it, not merely as a means of ending the crisis in German-American relations, but also as affording a possible solution of the quarrel with England over the blockade. For the sake of diplomatic consistency, he asserted, he would soon have to address a note to Great Britain regarding the interruption of American trade with neutral ports. It would be a great stroke on England's part, said the President, if she would of her own accord relieve the situation and put Germany wholly in the wrong, a small price to pay for the ending of submarine outrages.

Colonel House to the President

London, *May* 20, 1915

Dear Governor:

When your cable of the 16th came, I asked Page to make an engagement with Grey in order that we might protest against the holding-up of cargoes and find definitely whether England would agree to lift the embargo on foodstuffs, providing Germany would discontinue her submarine policy. Page promised to make the appointment. He did not do so, and finally told me that he had concluded it was useless because, in his opinion, the British Government would not consider for a moment the proposal to lift the embargo.

It was then I sent you the discouraging cable. However, when your second cable of Tuesday came, I went to see Sir Edward without further consultation with Page.

I found Grey was even more receptive of the suggestion than when I saw him last, and he promised to use all his influence in favor of such a proposal, provided one was made by Germany. He added, however, that the discontinuance of asphyxiating or poisonous gases must also be included in any agreement made.

He explained that the Cabinet was in dissolution and that he could only speak for himself and that he did not want me to consider that he spoke for the Government. I expressed a willingness to accept his personal assurance in regard to his own endeavors, with the understanding that it committed no one but himself. He said that in ordinary times if the Cabinet refused to acquiesce in his view, he would resign; but that he did not feel justified in doing this in time of war. I took occasion to express your high regard for him and to assure him that we would consider his resignation a calamity.

He dictated, while I wrote, the understanding between us, which was literally this:

1st. Permitting staple foodstuffs to go to neutral ports without question.

2d. All foodstuffs now detained to be brought before the prize court as quickly as possible.

3d. Claims for cotton cargoes now detained to be made as soon as shippers certify as to each cargo, that they are the real owners to whom payment should be made.

Should England agree to the first proposition, Germany was to cease submarine warfare on merchant vessels and discontinue the use of asphyxiating or poisonous gases.

Propositions two and three are matters between this Government and ours and have no reference to Germany and will be carried out at once.

I told Grey that I would immediately cable Gerard, asking Germany to withhold her answer to your note until I could communicate with him further. I also told him I would suggest to the German authorities, through Gerard, that they answer the note by making the proposal in question. . . .

I assumed the entire responsibility, so if things go wrong you and Sir Edward can disclaim any connection with it.

If Germany refuses to consider this proposal, it will place you in the position of having done everything possible to avert war between the United States and Germany.

Sir Edward took a copy of the memorandum I made, so that there might be no misunderstanding between us. Of course there would be none, anyway, for he remembers well what he says and never recedes from his word. . . .

It is unfortunate that the Cabinet is to be re-formed, for I am confident with the present members the plan would go through, provided Germany makes the proposal. The new element to go in is less apt to favor the proposal than those already there. Affectionately yours

E. M. HOUSE

Colonel House to Ambassador Gerard

[Telegram *via* Copenhagen]

LONDON, *May* 19, 1915

. . . Can you not induce the German Government to answer our note by proposing that if England will permit foodstuffs in the future to go to neutral ports without question, Germany will discontinue her submarine warfare on merchant vessels and will also discontinue the use of poisonous gas? Such a proposal from Germany at this time will give her great advantage, and in my opinion she will make a grave mistake if she does not seize it.

EDWARD HOUSE

'*May* 19, 1915: Page thought I was making a mistake in doing anything [wrote House], and that it would result in bad feeling between England and the United States provided Germany assented and Sir Edward Grey could not get his Government to agree. I answered that this was a matter I could not control; that my purpose was to place the United States and the President clearly in the right, so if trouble came between Germany and ourselves the President would have done everything within his power to prevent war, and could maintain his position taken in the note with a clear conscience and with the certain approval of the American people.

'I took dinner with Lord Haldane. By common consent we dined alone, so as to discuss matters freely.... He showed me the diary he kept during his memorable visit to Berlin on February 9 and 10, 1912. He was sent over, as the world knows, as the representative of the King and British Government, to try to bring about a better understanding with Germany and to draw up a tentative treaty to that effect....

'I took it as an indication of his confidence that he let me read this. He explained, however, that he felt I should know everything that had passed between the German and British Governments, in regard to Asia Minor, the African Colonies, and the larger relations concerning the Triple Entente, and what Great Britain might do in the event either Germany or England should become involved with nations other than themselves.

'Grey had spoken to Haldane about my proposal concerning the lifting of the embargo on foodstuffs and the discontinuance of the submarine campaign. He said his own influence would be in favor of the proposal, but he did not know what action the new Ministry would take.

'He spoke of himself and of his years of service to his country, and his voice saddened when he told of how he had been maligned and misunderstood since the war with Germany began.[1] He gave me two of his books, and we talked at length of Germany, her future, and the German people. I mentioned my proposal as to the Freedom of the Seas. He thought it splendid, and I understood that I could count upon his influence in behalf of that measure when the proper time came. . . .

'*May* 21, 1915: I lunched with Grey and read him the President's despatch. . . . He has seen nearly all the present Ministry and enough of the Opposition who would probably be in the Cabinet, to be able to say that in his opinion, if Germany made the proposal I had suggested it would be considered by his Government.

'He is always cautious in his statements, and I conclude that what he says means that the British Government will accept the proposal. It will be a great diplomatic triumph for the President if brought about, and it will settle our contentions with both Governments. . . .'

Whatever the ultimate decision of the British Cabinet might have been, the German Government put an end to any chance of a compromise settlement by a brusque refusal to consider House's suggestion. In public the plaintiveness of German protests against the cruel starvation of women and children by the British was not diminished, but in private the German leaders were evidently unwilling to pay the price necessary to raise the blockade. They were determined to make full use of the submarine, and they were the less inclined to heed American warnings in that they were not con-

[1] Haldane, as Minister of War in the Asquith Cabinet, had created the territorial organization and made possible the immediate despatch of an efficient Expeditionary Force. 'But for his work,' wrote Grey to Asquith, 'this Force would not have been available at a moment's notice. . . . That Haldane of all people should have been . . . accused of lack of patriotism or public spirit is an intolerable instance of gross ignorance, or malice, or of madness.' (Grey, *Twenty-Five Years*, II, 244.) But the Conservatives made Haldane's exclusion from the new coalition Cabinet a condition of their own participation.

vinced the United States would support such warnings by other than verbal factors. Two messages from Ambassador Gerard to Colonel House carried the news of the failure of the proposed compromise and indicated the cause.

Colonel House to the President

[Telegram]

London, *May* 24, 1915

Gerard cables me as follows: 'Zimmermann told me yesterday that Dumba, Austrian Ambassador, had cabled him that Bryan told him that America was not in earnest about *Lusitania* matter.' Of course Mr. Bryan did not say that, but I think you should know what Zimmermann told Gerard. . . .

Edward House

Ambassador Gerard learned of the cable from Dumba in a curious fashion. Zimmermann had come to lunch with him and after his customary two quarts of Moselle was talking freely to an American lady, wife of a German. He assured her that there would be no break with the United States over the *Lusitania*, since Wilson was not serious in his protest. The Ambassador, as soon as he learned the gist of the conversation, called upon Zimmermann and demanded the source of his information. Zimmermann at once pulled out the cable from Dumba and laid it before him. Mr. Gerard faced a problem. It was essential that he inform Wilson, and he could hardly do so through the State Department, since his cable would go straight to Mr. Bryan. Thus he turned it over to House, knowing that he would at once inform the President. Dumba's message carried disastrous effects, since it convinced the Germans that they could carry on their submarine campaign with impunity. Hence their refusal of the compromise that House suggested.

Colonel House to the President

[Telegram]

LONDON, *May* 25, 1915

I have following cable from Gerard:

'I gave your suggestion to von Jagow this morning. This proposition of permitting the passage of food in return for the cessation of submarine methods has already been made and declined.

'If raw materials are added, the matter can perhaps be arranged. Germany is in no need of food.'

Of course the conditions they make are impossible. This does away with their contention that the starving of Germany justifies their submarine policy. I think this strengthens your already unassailable position.

EDWARD HOUSE

Colonel House to Ambassador Gerard

[Telegram]

LONDON, *May* 25, 1915

The Allies would never agree to allow raw materials to go through; therefore I can do nothing further and there is no need for Germany further to delay acting on our note.

I am terribly sorry, because the consequences may be very grave.

EDWARD HOUSE

'*May* 26, 1915: I lunched with Sir Edward Grey again to-day. I read him all the telegrams that had passed between the President, Gerard, and myself since we last met. We first discussed Gerard's cable saying Berlin had refused to accept my suggestion. Grey thought it had at least placed Great Britain in a more advantageous position, and he expressed himself as being glad it had been sent, for *it settled the German contention that they were compelled to wage their submarine policy against Great Britain because she was endeavoring to starve sixty-five million German non-combatants.*

'In talking to other members of the Government, he said some of them had thought in the event Germany accepted the proposal it would mean that she was actually running short of food and it would not be well for England to relax. Grey, however, argued that there were too many advantages on the other side to let that one prevail. He said, too, he was anxious for us to know that England was doing what she could to keep us from war with Germany, and not trying to push us in. My admiration and affection for him grows.'

Thus ended the most favorable opportunity for settling the controversy that later was to exercise momentous effect upon the course of the war and the fate of Germany. Had Berlin accepted the compromise, not merely would Germany have obtained the food of which, as she complained, her starving civilian population was deprived by an illegal blockade, but she might have avoided the quarrel with the United States that brought America into the war. 'Whom the Gods would destroy —'

III

Germany's refusal to seize the opportunity that had thus been offered her convinced Colonel House that further stay in Europe was useless. The chance of beginning peace negotiations between the belligerents, if it had ever existed, had completely disappeared. On both sides emotion was so thoroughly envenomed that any suggestion of a pacific arrangement was regarded as criminal. House was also convinced that German policy meant American intervention and he wished to be near the President so as to urge him to wage war with vigor.

'I have concluded that war with Germany is inevitable [he

wrote on May 30] and this afternoon at six o'clock I decided to go home on the S.S. *St. Paul* on Saturday. I sent a cable to the President to this effect.

'I discussed the matter with Wallace, who will go with us, and I also discussed it with Page, who advised our going if we cared to get home within the year. Page is always a candid adviser. . . .

'*June* 1, 1915: I told Plunkett I was leaving for America and my reasons for doing so. I said it was my purpose to persuade the President not to conduct a milk-and-water war, but to put all the strength, all the virility, and all the energy of our nation into it, so that Europe might remember for a century what it meant to provoke a peaceful nation into war.

'I intended to suggest a commission, with perhaps a member of the Cabinet as chairman, to facilitate the manufacture of munitions of war and war materials. Plunkett wanted me to see some of the British Cabinet and talk with them before I left. He arranged for me to meet Lloyd George at six o'clock. . . .'

A letter from the American Ambassador in Berlin indicated that Germany had embarked upon the new course with confidence, and strengthened House's conviction that war could not be avoided.

Ambassador Gerard to Colonel House

BERLIN, *June* 1, 1915

MY DEAR COLONEL:

I am afraid that we are in for grave consequences. This country, I fear, will not give up the torpedoing without notice of merchant and passenger steamers; and their recent victories over the Russians have given them great confidence here. They seem also to be holding their lines in the Dardanelles and their lines in France and Belgium with ease, and probably Italy will be defeated.

The only thing that can gain the war for the Allies is universal service in England and the throwing into the balance of at least two million new English troops. If the English knew what the Germans have in store for England in case of success, the very dead in the graveyards would volunteer for the war.

It is the German hope to keep the *Lusitania* matter 'jollied along' until the American people get excited about baseball or a new scandal and forget. Meantime the hate of America grows daily.

As to food and even raw materials, the Germans have enough for war purposes. They need raw materials for the trades, but have everything needed for the manufacture of munitions; and as they are spending all the money for war supplies in their own country their financial situation is good for the present. They expect some other country to pay the cost of the war.

In governmental circles there is no talk of giving up Belgium. They want to keep it and exact great indemnities from other countries.

They are building new and great submarines (2800 tons), and are putting so many in the water that I think they will soon become a serious menace to England. That is why a great land army is necessary. . . .

Will cable if anything comes up. Best wishes to Mrs. House.

Yours as ever

James W. Gerard

If, contrary to expectations, Germany agreed to abandon or modify the submarine warfare or if the crisis should be tided over, House was equally desirous of being in the United States and near the President, for in that case the dispute with Great Britain over the holding-up of American cargoes would certainly become acute. The difference was serious enough at best, and mutual misunderstanding threatened to make it worse. Colonel House was anxious that President Wilson should comprehend the difficulties which Sir Edward Grey faced, how hard he was pressed by British opinion and the Admiralty, and how important it was that the United States remain on friendly terms with the Allies. Whatever the irritation caused by the restriction of American trade, House never wavered in his conviction that our welfare was bound up in German defeat. All this Ambassador Page had urged in many long letters. But the very number and length of the letters, touched as they were by pro-Ally emotion, lessened the influence of the Ambassador, who, in Washington, seemed more like the spokesman of Allied interests than the representative of the American Government. As House realized acutely, a purely objective summary of the situation with emphasis upon American interests would carry more weight.

'*March* 4, 1915: Yesterday [wrote House], when Page was drawing up his despatch to the President asking that he do nothing for the moment concerning the proposed blockade of Germany, he had a lot of things in it which I advised eliminating. It was the strongest sort of pro-British argument, and I knew it would weaken his influence both with the State Department and with the President. He reluctantly cut it down to a short statement....'

Colonel House to the President

London, *May* 25, 1915

Dear Governor:

... There is nothing new to report here, and it looks as if things might be settling down for a long war.... I want very much to see you and to go over the situation in person. There are so many things that cannot be written, and I think it would be well worth while for me to make the trip even if it is necessary to return within a short time.

There is no doubt that the position you have taken with both Germany and Great Britain is correct; but I feel that our position with the Allies is somewhat different, for we are bound up more or less in their success, and I do not think we should do anything that can possibly be avoided to alienate the good feeling that they now have for us. If we lose their good will, we will not be able to figure at all in peace negotiations, and we will be sacrificing too much in order to maintain all our commercial rights.

The situation, I know, is most trying and difficult, and you have acted with extraordinary patience and good judgment.

Affectionately yours

E. M. House

Colonel House had constantly impressed upon his British friends the importance of recognizing the irritation and loss caused in the United States by the holding-up of American cargoes and mails. From the moment of his arrival in February, 1915, he emphasized the fact that, even though this was the only serious cause of friction between the two countries, it was nevertheless one that would lead to grave results unless eclipsed by the dispute with Germany. The latter infringed the rights of humanity, whereas the controversy with Great Britain was of a far less vital sort. But it touched the pockets and the sensibilities of many Americans.

Furthermore, it was impossible for the President to protest with vigor against German infractions of the law of nations, so long as the Germans had some ground for complaint that he permitted the British to alter maritime regulations at will. Letters from the President and Cabinet members gave House a clear picture of the difficulties which they faced in Washington. The friendly tone of the President's message goes far to answer the criticism that the *gaucherie* of American protests tended unnecessarily to embitter Anglo-American relations.

He reiterated his emphasis upon the change that was coming over American opinion because of British interference with neutral trade and expressed the fear that it might be impossible to prevent the passage by Congress of an embargo upon shipments of arms. Wilson intimated that he would try to prevent it, but he wished Grey to realize the danger. He conveyed the warning through House rather than Page because he wished it to be absolutely unofficial and spoken merely in personal friendship. Secretary Lane expressed similar sentiments.

Secretary Lane to Colonel House

WASHINGTON, *May* 5, 1915

MY DEAR COLONEL:

I am glad to receive your note. There is little that I can say as to conditions here. The President is bearing the burden well. Notwithstanding all the insults of Germany, he is determined to endure to the limit, to turn the left cheek and then the back, if necessary; but of course, he cannot suffer insult after insult to the point of humiliation, for the country would rise in rebellion. We are a sensitive people, as our English friends discovered a hundred years ago.

And the English are not behaving very well. They are holding up our ships; they have made new international law. We have been very meek and mild under their use of the ocean as a toll road. Of course, the sympathy of the greater part of the country is with the English, but it would not have been as strongly with them, not nearly so strongly, if it had not been for the persistent short-sightedness of our German friends. I cannot see what England means by her policy of delay and embarrassment and hampering. Her success manifestly depends upon the continuance of the strictest neutrality on our part, and yet she is not willing to let us have the rights of a neutral.

You would be interested, I think, in hearing some of the

discussion around the Cabinet table. There isn't a man in the Cabinet who has a drop of German blood in his veins, I guess. Two of us were born under the British flag. I have two cousins in the British army, and Mrs. Lane has three. The most of us are Scotch in our ancestry, and yet each day that we meet we boil over somewhat, at the foolish manner in which England acts. Can it be that she is trying to take advantage of the war to hamper our trade?...

If Congress were in session, we would be actively debating an embargo resolution to-day....

After all, our one great asset is the confidence of the people in the President. They do not love him, because he appears to them as a man of the cloister. But they respect him as a wise, sane leader who will keep them out of trouble, and whatever fool things are done they are willing to blame on Bryan, which is gravely unjust. I am growing more and more in my admiration for Bryan each day. He is too good a Christian to run a naughty world and he doesn't hate hard enough, but he certainly is a noble and high-minded man, and loyal to the President to the last hair....

As always yours

F. K. L.

Even in England there were a number of thoughtful persons who felt that interference with neutral cargoes bound for neutral ports, even though the goods were ultimately destined for Germany, was not worth the difficulties it would provoke. Such opinion, although held by a minority, was not entirely confined to pacifist circles.

'*March* 3, 1915: Both Brooks and Pollen [1] [wrote Colonel House] agreed with me that Great Britain was entering into a dangerous phase of warfare in undertaking to establish a paper blockade against Germany, an actual blockade being

[1] A. H. Pollen, journalist and naval authority.

seemingly impossible. I argued the point very earnestly, for I wanted their influence and that of their papers in the trouble I can see looming up between our two countries.

'*March* 4, 1915: Francis W. Hirst, editor of *The Economist*, called this morning for the second time. I missed him yesterday when he was here. I found in him an entirely new type of Englishman.... He is antagonistic to the Government, though a Liberal. He criticized Grey and Asquith severely, though Asquith is a near relative.... He is against the war, and claims he is far from being alone, for he believes the war unpopular in England, and if public opinion could find expression it would be shown to be. He desires me to meet Lord Morley and the former Lord Chancellor, Lord Loreburn. He says both of them are against the war and they believe peace should be brought about now.

'Hirst thinks the President should take an active stand against the proposed blockade, believing if he would prohibit all exports to all the belligerents, he could force this Government to do practically what he desired. He wished the President to lay down a new international code of laws and insist upon every nation living up to it. I tried to point out some of the difficulties of such a procedure.

'He said that his predecessor on *The Economist*, Richard Bagehot, whom the President admires so much, declared that England should have done this in 1870....

'*March* 9, 1915: Mr. Robert Donald, editor of *The Daily Chronicle*, took tea with me. He is an able and reasonable Scotchman. We talked of the embargo, and of war and everything relating thereto. He is a great friend of Lloyd George and thinks he is the greatest man in the Kingdom. He thought it a mistake for Great Britain to declare a blockade against Germany, and believed if it is enforced our Government would be justified in placing an embargo on munitions of war. He is to touch upon this matter cautiously in his paper, and will try to influence the Government in the direction we desire. . . .'

IV

Colonel House to the President

LONDON, *May* 7, 1915

DEAR GOVERNOR:

Your cablegram concerning the delaying of cargoes came to me yesterday. I already had an engagement with Sir Edward Grey this morning, so I did not make an earlier appointment.

I read him your message and told him that in my opinion the situation was critical and that it would not do to temporize with the matter; that the Germans were doing everything possible to embarrass you and to force you to place an embargo upon arms.

He said he understood the situation perfectly. He took a memorandum, which he read to me afterwards and which was to be sent to each member of the Cabinet in the form of a communication. He put it strongly and urgently, and he told me he would do all that was possible.

He said he had to contend with public sentiment here that demanded a complete blockade of Germany. I think, too, he has opposition in the Cabinet with Kitchener and Winston Churchill. . . .

Sir Edward wants to do everything that is possible, and he desired me to let you know that he had great difficulties here to contend with. . . .

I have seen a great many people since I last wrote you, among them the Russian Ambassador. I found him a very able man, but as ignorant of your purposes as the people of France. . . .

When I came over here it was practically the universal opinion in France and England and, I find now, in Russia also, that you were inclined to be pro-German even though the American people as a whole were otherwise. I have a feeling that Sir Cecil [1] has fostered this sentiment, because what I have heard here sounds very much like what he said to me on several occasions. He told Norman Hapgood that the Administration was pro-German, and he has told others the same thing.

I took occasion to tell Sir Edward that Sir Cecil was very nervous and was constantly seeing spooks and that he had told me that we would all be pro-German before the end of the war. I did this because I was sure he had written the same thing to Sir Edward. . . .

Your affectionate

E. M. HOUSE

LONDON, *May* 27, 1915

DEAR GOVERNOR:

I saw Sir Edward Grey yesterday and discussed the holding-up of cargoes.

As to cotton, he said this Government, following precedent, had a right to make it contraband of war just as our Government did during our Civil War. But out of consideration for our wishes they had not done so, and therefore he hoped we would be lenient.

He also said they were doing everything that was possible now to avoid friction with us and that orders had gone out to pass upon all questions speedily, so they could no longer be charged with delay.

He told me some things of interest concerning the Balkan States. One was that Rumania had agreed to come in, provided the Allies would give her certain Hungarian territory.[2] Sir Edward refused to consider such terms, for the

[1] Sir Cecil Spring-Rice, British Ambassador in Washington.

[2] The Banat of Temesvar and the Transylvanian forelands. Serbia's claim to the southwestern portion of the Banat was insistent. The Peace Conference in 1919 recognized much of Serbia's claim, dividing the Banat between that Power and Rumania.

reason that what she wanted would be unfair to Serbia. His reply was that since Great Britain went into this war to defend the rights of one small nation, it would not transgress upon the rights of another, even though great advantage to the Allied cause might accrue.

If it were not for Ferdinand, Bulgaria would probably come in with the Allies, and, if she did, then Greece would also. They all fear lest some one of the Balkan States will remain out and be in a condition to take advantage of the exhaustion that may occur....

I am glad Balfour is in the new Cabinet. He is a man of the Grey type, and I feel sure that there will be less trouble with the holding-up of cargoes now than when the Admiralty was administered by Churchill.[1]

Sir Edward leaves Monday to be gone a month, and Lord Crewe will probably act for him during his absence. He is to arrange with Crewe for me to see him at any time I desire, and at his home. He lives close by. I never go to the Foreign Office or any of the other Government Offices on account of the publicity. They all understand my reasons for this....

Your affectionate

E. M. House

Before leaving for the United States, Colonel House entered many long conferences with members of the new Cabinet and with others of influence, in order that no misunderstanding should mar Anglo-American relations. In most of these conversations he laid strong emphasis upon the blockade problem, for he regarded it as vital that the British should appreciate the American point of view.

'*May* 22, 1915: Lord Bryce called at ten o'clock. I told

[1] An unfulfilled prophecy, despite the calm good sense of Mr. Balfour and his friendly feeling toward the United States.

of some of the troubles between Great Britain and the United States, regarding the holding-up of cargoes. He expressed a willingness to use his influence with the Foreign Office, but I asked him to do nothing for the moment, for I am sure he cannot do more than I have already done with Grey.

'We agreed that it was not the Foreign Office at fault, but the War and Admiralty Departments. I talked to him about the Freedom of the Seas, and he asked if it had to do with "capture and search at sea." He did not seem in favor of it, saying he had heard that Dernburg very much desired it. I replied that I was the instigator of it in Germany, and the Germans were merely echoing the thought I had given them. He laughed and said he felt better, for, if we were doing it, he was quite sure it was not a bad thing, and that in the future he would look at it with more friendly eyes.

'*June* 2, 1915: I met Lloyd George at ten, as previously arranged. I was surprised at the freedom with which he criticized the War Department. He said Great Britain should now have all the shells they could use, since they were the largest engineering country excepting the United States, and had all sorts of factories that could be made to turn out explosives. He showed me a list of shrapnel and explosive shells that were used by the British in recent battles. In one battle, 50,000 shrapnel were fired and only 1600 high explosives, while it should be the reverse.

'He said he had found soldiers to be self-opinionated and unsatisfactory, but he indicated his intention of putting an impetus on munition production that would revolutionize the situation. He had a list of firms and corporations from whom they were getting munitions in the United States. While important, it was not as large as I had thought....

'He stated that it would be a serious menace to the Allied cause if we should stop the shipment of munitions of war at this time....

'This was, I believe, George's first day as Minister of

Munitions in his new Whitehall quarters. There was no furniture in the room except a table and one chair. He insisted upon my taking the chair, which I declined to do, declaring that a seat on the table was more suitable for me than for a Cabinet official.

'He spoke again and again of "military red-tape," which he declared he would cut out as speedily as possible. He was full of energy and enthusiasm, and I feel certain something will soon happen in his department. He reminds me more of the virile, aggressive type of American politician than any member of the Cabinet. . . . He has something dynamic within him which his colleagues have not and which is badly needed in this great hour. . . .

'After lunch I went to keep an appointment with the new Chancellor of the Exchequer, Reginald McKenna. . . . I took occasion to tell him that Germany had saved England from a good raking over the coals because of her embargo policy, which was entirely illegal and to which we submitted merely because Germany was so prodigal in greater infractions. I urged him to use his influence at Cabinet meetings to modify their actions in this direction. If they did not, and we composed our differences with Germany, I assured him we would hold his Government to a stricter accountability. It was not a question of what the President thought of the controversy between the belligerents, but what he had to do in justice to a large portion of the American people, who were insisting that their rights were being infringed.

'He entirely agreed with this and hoped the differences could be ironed out satisfactorily. It was also agreed that in the event we came into the war on the side of the Allies, he would communicate with me unofficially, in order that I might help in facilitating the solution of financial questions arising between the two Governments. . . .

'At half-past five, I went to Lansdowne House to call on the Marquis of Lansdowne. . . . I spoke strongly of his

Government's policy in holding-up neutral cargoes, and let him know that, if Germany was not acting so much worse, they would be called to an accounting. I did not believe Great Britain, under similar circumstances, would permit it for a moment, and the President had bent almost to the breaking point in order to avoid a disagreeable controversy with them.

'I gave a sketch of the President in which I depicted him as a Scotchman with all the tenacity of purpose of that race, and bade him remember that while the President at heart sympathized with the Allies and their purposes, yet he was President of the United States, and our people did not differentiate between those violating international law, and he had of necessity to maintain an equitable attitude.

'*June* 3, 1915: Lord Crewe and I lunched alone, in order to have a farewell talk about matters which could not be discussed before a third party. . . .

'I read him the President's despatches to me regarding the shipping controversy, and urged him to impress upon his colleagues the necessity of straightening this out, provided we did not immediately drift into war with Germany. I told him the President was being criticized for writing one kind of note to Germany and demanding an immediate answer, and writing another kind to Great Britian and having no reply for months. I considered it necessary for them to prepare an answer at once to the note sent in February concerning the stoppage of cargoes, and to hold it in readiness for delivery in the event it was asked for. On the other hand, I would advise the President not to ask for it until the German submarine controversy was settled one way or the other; and if it was settled by war, there would be no need for an answer. But if our differences with Germany were settled, then an immediate answer should be forthcoming. I spoke of how pressed the President was in this matter, and that it would not do to act in the future as they had acted in the past.

'*June* 4, 1915: I read the King one or two cables I had

sent the President, principally about the interference with our shipping. I wish all official England to understand our Government's attitude upon this question, in order that there may be no misunderstanding should it be necessary to act with vigor later.

'His Majesty talked of the recent Zeppelin raid and thought a very much more serious one would occur soon, believing they would attempt to burn London. I showed him the last cartoon in *Life* which Martin sent in advance of publication, which depicts his distinguished cousin Wilhelm hanged at the end of a yardarm. I was not sure of the wisdom of showing this, but he seemed to enjoy it thoroughly. The more I see of the King, the better I like him; he is a good fellow and deserves a better fate than being a king. . . .

'I lunched with Mr. Balfour. The only other guest was Sir Horace Plunkett, who has our confidence. Balfour said he intended to have the *St. Paul* convoyed as effectively as the British navy could do it. . . .

'There is a distinct feeling of depression in England at present, largely due to the lack of high explosives, and also to the fact of Russia's continued defeat because she, too, lacks munitions of war.

'He said that what the navy needed most now was torpedo-boat destroyers, and he was contracting for a large number of other small fast boats of this type. They have plenty of battleships. He spoke of how fortunate they had been with their transports, saying they had not lost one. He reached over, like any good American, and knocked on wood.

'I went into our shipping troubles as I have with other members of the Government, and I think I made him understand just what difficulties our Government was laboring under.'

V

House sailed on the *St. Paul*, June 5. Arriving in the United States a week later, he summarized for the President his impressions of European affairs and emphasized the gravity of the crisis which the American Government must face.

Colonel House to the President

ROSLYN, LONG ISLAND
June 16, 1915

DEAR GOVERNOR:

The situation, as far as the Allies go, is not encouraging. Much to their disappointment and to the surprise of the Germans, they have not been able to make the progress which they thought the spring and summer weather would bring about. They have made two cardinal errors. One was the attempt to force the Dardanelles by sea only. They found this was impossible and, before they could send a land force to coöperate with the fleet, the Turks under the direction of German officers had time to make the Straits almost impregnable. They will finally get through, but at a terrible cost.[1]

The second mistake was in not accelerating during the winter months the manufacture of high explosives. When the spring campaign opened and they attempted to storm the German trenches, they found that they not only had insufficient ammunition, but what they had was of the wrong kind. This mistake was more largely made by the English than by the French.

The Germans, through their espionage system, evidently knew the weakness of the Allies; consequently their great concern regarding the munitions of war coming from America. When I was in Berlin in March, it seemed to me that they were talking nonsense when they said that if we would stop the shipment of munitions the war would end within a short time.

[1] The prophecy was not fulfilled, for, although the cost was paid, the Allied expedition withdrew from Gallipoli in the following winter.

THE PRESIDENT AND COLONEL HOUSE OFF DUTY

The English have been unable to do more than hold their ground, and the Russians have been utterly unable to withstand the German onslaught, for the reason that they have neither sufficient arms nor ammunition. It has resolved itself into a war of munitions rather than one of men.

Germany was much more willing for peace in the autumn than she has been since. I am enclosing you a letter from Gerard bearing upon this phase.

There was the greatest possible concern in England when I left, although they are confident of ultimate victory if the Allies hold together; but it will be delayed longer than anticipated, and perhaps it would not come at all if their American supplies were for any reason shut off.

I need not tell you that if the Allies fail to win, it must necessarily mean a reversal of our entire policy.

The sinking of the *Lusitania*, the use of poisonous gases, and other breaches of international laws, made it impossible for me to continue the discussion in England of the Freedom of the Seas or the tentative formation of a peace covenant. If these things had not happened, I could have gone along and by midsummer we would have had the belligerents discussing, through you, the peace terms.

The difficulty is not with the German civil authorities, but with the military and naval as represented by the Kaiser, von Tirpitz, and Falkenhayn. The feeling is not good between the Foreign Office and von Tirpitz, for their differences are irreconcilable. In my opinion, von Tirpitz will continue his submarine policy, leaving the Foreign Office to make explanations for any 'unfortunate incidents' as best they may.

I think we shall find ourselves drifting into war with Germany, for there is a large element in the German naval and military factions that consider it would be a good, rather than a bad, thing for Germany.

Regrettable as this would be, there would be compensations. The war would be more speedily ended, and we would be in a strong position to aid the other great democracies in turning the world into the right paths. It is something that we have to face with fortitude, being consoled by the thought that no matter what sacrifices we make, the end will justify them.

Affectionately yours

E. M. House

The mission of Colonel House had not accomplished the miracle of peace, which in 1915 was a practical impossibility. But he had accomplished what few persons guessed — a thorough understanding with those who guided the fortunes of the Allies. Henceforth, whatever the disputes of State Department and Foreign Office, the personal relations he had created would preserve an underlying cordiality. He had been given a private code that would permit him to communicate speedily and informally with Sir Edward Grey, and the British Foreign Secretary promised to write him frankly and frequently. House had obviously won the confidence of the British Government at a moment when public opinion in England was turning against America. He had made a host of friends abroad who would send him constant and reliable information. And President Wilson, supposed to be ill-informed and isolated, was through Colonel House kept in close touch with the inner currents of European politics.

Sir Horace Plunkett to the President

The Plunkett House, Dublin
June 4, 1915

Dear Mr. President:

... Colonel House, in his own quiet, tactful, and marvellously persuasive way, has, to my certain knowledge, rendered an inestimable service to the Government of this country by his counsel and advice in regard to its attitude to the United States in this crisis. What similar service he may have rendered to you, and to his people, in other European countries you will know. He sails to-morrow, and I can well believe that, as he cannot be in Europe and America at the same time, it may be better that he should now be at your side. As I have had the privilege of introducing him to some people he wished to meet over here, and of explaining to them some aspects of American public life which it was necessary for them to know in order to appreciate the value of Colonel House's help, I have offered to be of any assistance in my power, should misunderstandings arise in his absence which informed unofficial intervention may be best qualified to remove. I have also offered to keep him advised of any events or movements of opinion, which, from the possession of his confidence, I feel he ought to know. I merely wish to assure you, Mr. President, that something will be done to minimize the loss to us over here which must be set against the gain to you and to the United States in having Colonel House at Washington.

I am, with deep respect

Yours sincerely

HORACE PLUNKETT

It was, therefore, with his eyes fully opened to all aspects of the European situation, that President Wilson faced the long-drawn-out crisis in our relations with Germany which followed the sinking of the *Lusitania*.

END OF VOLUME I